THE MEXICAN ECONOMY, 1870–1930

SOCIAL SCIENCE HISTORY

Edited by Stephen Haber and David Brady

The purpose of the Stanford Series in Social Science History is to promote deeper and more enduring foundations for historical social science by publishing a broad range of interdisciplinary research. Toward that end, the works in this series integrate the theoretical and statistical tools of economics, sociology, and political science, with their emphasis on logical consistency and careful hypothesis testing, with the study of institutions and the close attention to gathering data and assessing its quality that has traditionally been the province of historians.

They also cover topics from across the spectrum of the social science and humanities disciplines: economic history and development, political science, sociology, and classics. The goal is to produce works that, individually, shed new light on their specific topic, and, taken as a whole, demonstrate the value of history as cornerstone of the social sciences and the power of social scientific analysis for understanding the past.

THE MEXICAN ECONOMY, 1870–1930

Essays on the Economic History of Institutions, Revolution, and Growth

Edited by

JEFFREY L. BORTZ

AND STEPHEN HABER

STANFORD UNIVERSITY PRESS

Stanford, California

Library of Congress Cataloging-in-Publication Data

The Mexican economy, 1870–1930 : essays on the
economic history of institutions, revolution, and
growth / edited by Jeffrey Bortz and Stephen Haber.
    p. cm.—(Social science history)
    Includes index.
    ISBN 0-8047-4207-3 (alk. paper)—
    ISBN 0-8047-4208-1 (pbk. : alk. paper)
    1. Mexico—Economic conditions—19th century.
2. Mexico—Economic conditions—20th century.
I. Bortz, Jeff. II. Haber, Stephen H. III. Series.

HC135 .M525518 2002
330.972—dc21   2001049259

Typeset by G&S Typesetters in 10.5/13 Bembo

Original Printing 2002

Last figure below indicates year of this printing:
11   10   09   08   07   06   05   04   03   02

CONTENTS

TABLES

FIGURES

CONTRIBUTORS

Edward Beatty is Assistant Professor of History at the University of Notre Dame and a Fellow at the Kellogg Institute for International Studies.

Jeffrey L. Bortz is Professor of History at Appalachian State University.

Aurora Gómez-Galvarriato is Professor of Economics at the Centro de Investigación y Docencia Económicas.

Stephen Haber is Professor of History and Political Science at Stanford University and the Peter and Helen Bing Senior Fellow at the Hoover Institution. He is also Director of the Social Science History Institute and a Senior Fellow at the Stanford Institute for Economic Policy Research.

Sandra Kuntz Ficker is Professor and Researcher at the Universidad Autónoma Metropolitana-Xochimilco, México.

Carlos Marichal is Professor of Latin American History at the Centro de Estudios Históricos, El Colegio de México.

Noel Maurer is Assistant Professor of Economics at the Centro de Investigación Económica at the Instituto Tecnológico Autónomo de México.

Paolo Riguzzi is a Researcher at El Colegio Mexiquense, Zinacantepec, Estado de México.

There has been, in recent years, a quiet revolution taking place in Latin American economic history. The source of this revolution has been a convergence of the disciplines of economics and history.

Historians, Latin Americanists among them, have long believed that institutions—humanly devised rules, regulations, norms, and cultural values—exert a powerful effect on economic outcomes. They have not, however, had a set of methods that allowed them to measure the impact of institutions on those outcomes. Indeed, at the same time that the field of Latin American history was deeply concerned with economic questions, Latin American historians tended to eschew the analytic techniques of economics. This meant that while historians could study the evolution of laws, policies, and social norms, they had no way of determining whether those institutional changes had positive or negative effects on growth and distribution.

Economists, of course, have long had a well-developed set of methods to study the impact of institutional change on economic performance. The problem was that they did not, for the most part, believe that institutions mattered. In the zero transactions cost world of neoclassical economics, economic agents can easily contract around any institution designed to constrain their activities. Institutions in this world are simply the legal expression of what takes place in the market, and the institutions that exist in a particular society are, by logical extension, economically efficient. In this view, then, the study of institutional change is the study of epiphenomena.

In the past decade this strong neoclassical interpretation of institutions has come under heavy assault. Economists are now increasingly convinced that institutions matter—and matter a great deal—for a wide variety of economic and political outcomes. They have therefore turned their attention to the study of institutional change. In so doing, the discipline has tended to become increasingly historical. The reason is not hard to divine: the historical record is the only natural laboratory that economists have to study the causes and consequences of institutional change.

Not surprisingly, the Latin American field has been strongly influenced by the convergence of history and economics. The reasons are obvious. First, the field of Latin American history has, since its inception as a scholarly discipline, been focused on the political, social, and economic ramifications of poverty and inequality. It is simply not possible to write about Latin American history in a coherent manner and not confront the causes and consequences of underdevelopment. Thus, all modern Latin American historians have had to be, in one form or another, economic historians. The movement of Latin American historians to the New Institutional Economics was therefore an easy jump. Second, from the point of view of economists, Latin American history provides an ideal laboratory for the study of institutional change. The reason is that institutions change dramatically in Latin America, and markets, generally speaking, have not been developed enough to anticipate these changes in institutions. Moreover, Latin American history also provides cases in which changes in institutions actually worked *against* growth. It is therefore possible in the Latin American context to test hypotheses drawn from the New Institutional Economics in ways that are simply not possible if researchers confine their analysis to the developed economies of the North Atlantic. In short, there is perhaps no more ideal a laboratory for the New Institutionalism than Latin America's economic history.

This volume brings together a group of scholars who have been working on the new institutional economic history of Mexico during the Porfiriato (1876–1911), the revolution (1911–17), and the immediate postrevolutionary period (1917–30). This fifty-five-year period witnessed two dramatic institutional reforms, the first of which took place during the Porfiriato, and the second of which took place during the revolution and its aftermath.

This volume began with a planning conference that took place at the Universidad de las Américas-Puebla in early 1998. Participating in that planning conference were Edward Beatty, Jeffrey L. Bortz, Enrique Cárdenas Sánchez, Sandra Kuntz Ficker, Aurora Gómez-Galvarriato, Stephen Haber, Moramay Lopez Alonso, Carlos Marichal, Noel Maurer, and Paolo Riguzzi. We wish to thank the Universidad de las Américas, and particularly its rector, Enrique Cárdenas Sánchez, for organizing that conference.

The papers commissioned at the planning conference were then presented at a conference held at Stanford University's Social Science History Institute in 1998. We were fortunate in that conference to be able to draw on a group of discussants from the community of political scientists and economists who work in the fields of political economy, international economics, and U.S. and European economic history. That is, the discussants were drawn from outside the narrow confines of Latin American area studies. We wish to thank all of the participants in that conference—paper presenters and discussants alike—who generated three intense days of discussion and debate. The participants included Edward Beatty, Jeffrey L. Bortz, Gonzalo Castañeda, Lance Davis, Sandra Kuntz Ficker, Judith Goldstein, Avner Greif, Phillip Hoffman, Moramay Lopez Alonso, Carlos Marichal, Noel Maurer, Ronald McKinnon, Robert Packenham, Paolo Riguzzi, Jean-Laurent Rosenthal, Kenneth Sokoloff, Barry Weingast, Gavin Wright, and Mary Yeager.

No undertaking of this type is possible without considerable institutional support. We wish to express our gratitude to Ms. Marie Toney, Ms. Gloria Spitzer, and Mr. Scott Wilson, Administrator, Former Administrator, and Associate Director, respectively, of the Social Science History Institute, for all of their efforts in bringing this project to fruition—from the planning conference through the preparation of the final manuscript. We also wish to express our deepest thanks to the William and Flora Hewlett Foundation, and to its Program Officer for the U.S.-Latin American Relations Program, Dr. David Lorey, for the Foundation's support of this project from its inception to its completion.

J.L.B.
S.H.

THE MEXICAN ECONOMY, 1870–1930

Chapter 1

The New Institutional Economics
and Latin American Economic History

JEFFREY L. BORTZ AND STEPHEN HABER

Since its inception as a scholarly discipline in the 1940s, the field of modern Latin American history has fundamentally been about the causes and consequences of widespread poverty and inequality. Whether or not they self-identified as economic historians, virtually all scholars of the region have had to address the question of underdevelopment and its ramifications. Indeed, without a discussion of underlying economic conditions, Latin American historians have found that it is simply not possible to present coherent narratives about social movements or political conflicts.

Curiously, even though the field of Latin American history has long been focused on economic questions, it has tended to eschew the application of analytic tools and quantitative techniques from modern economics. The lack of a formal theory (a set of hierarchically organized and logically consistent if-then statements) and a corpus of methods to operationalize the theory in a systematic manner has meant that rich and detailed empirical work in Latin American economic history has often been guided by ad hoc theoretical statements and the haphazard presentation of evidence.[1] This has, until recently, tended to hamstring the development of a coherent discipline of Latin American economic history. It has also meant that the work of Latin American historians has tended not to resonate outside of the narrow confines of their home discipline.

In recent years, the disjuncture between the interests of Latin American historians in economic questions and their simultaneous rejection of theo-

1

ries and methods from economics has been on the decline. In part, this shift in methods has occurred because of the gradual debilitation of dependency theory, which dominated the work of Latin American historians in the 1970s and 1980s.[2] Briefly stated, scholars came to the realization that propositions that emanate from dependency theory could be neither proven nor disproven because the theory offered no concept of relative autonomy or dependence.[3] The lack of a coherent theoretical framework, coupled with dependency's rejection of systematic empirical methods, meant that the dependency research program could not answer the basic (and important) questions it originally posed about the origins of Latin American underdevelopment.[4] As the limits to the approach became obvious, historians gradually abandoned it as the central organizing concept of their scholarly work, and in so doing they began to employ the quantitative techniques that had been employed for quite some time by economic historians of the United States and Western Europe.[5]

In equal part, the erosion of the division between history and economics has occurred because economists have started to relax many of the strong assumptions of neoclassical economics. Briefly stated, economists have increasingly come to the conclusion that institutions—the humanly devised constraints that both permit and bound all types of social interactions—are not mere epiphenomena. They play a crucial role in all kinds of economic and political outcomes. This has made the work of mainstream economists more consistent with empirical reality. It has also provided a theoretical framework, alternately called the New Institutional Economics or Positive Political Economy, that can serve to motivate and guide the work of historians. It should therefore not come as a surprise that much of the recent work in Latin American economic history has been strongly informed by insights from the NIE.

That "institutions matter" is not, of course, a controversial (or new) proposition in Latin American history. Most historians, Latin Americanists among them, firmly hold to the notion that human beings devise all kinds of social constructs that affect their behavior in empirically verifiable ways. Although historians may firmly believe that "institutions matter," they have, however, lacked the analytic and quantitative tools to explain *which* institutions mattered, *how* they mattered, and the *extent to which* they mattered.

What the NIE has offered to historians are two sets of tools. The first is that the NIE is a formalized theory that permits the specification of testable hypotheses. Second, because its roots are in formal political science and economics, fields that have long traditions of statistical hypothesis testing against systematically gathered data, the NIE is easily linked to the methods of econometric history that Latin American historians have been employing with some success over the past decade.[6] The combination of new methods and a new theoretical framework have, in turn, produced a growing corpus of work that is bringing about a substantive revision of the economic history of Latin America. In particular, scholars have begun to look at how the particular organization of political systems gave rise to particular economic policies or regulations, and how those policies or regulations, in turn, exerted an empirically demonstrable impact on the rate of growth, the structure of economies, and the distribution of income and wealth.[7]

The New Institutional Economics

Before proceeding to discuss the empirical contributions offered by this volume to this growing body of literature, a few words about the core concepts of the NIE are in order. The NIE argues that economic growth is caused by productivity increases that are brought about by the more efficient allocation of factors of production through more smoothly functioning firms and markets. Smoothly functioning firms and markets, in turn, are the product of changes in institutions—the laws, rules, and informal agreements within societies that both permit and bound economic or other types of social behavior. Institutions in this context are understood not as the organizations that societies are composed of (the banks, churches, factories, governments), but as the sets of rules that govern how those organizations work.[8] An institution is a set of rules or procedures that an individual or corporate body is prescribed to follow when interacting with others in a particular situation. Institutions limit the universe of actions that an individual can take, and therefore function as societal constraints that guide and coordinate social interaction. Ultimately, the function of institutions is to provide a set of rules— established patterns of admissible behavior—to regulate and reduce uncertainty about those interactions.[9] All things being equal, according to the NIE, societies that create institutions that clearly specify and enforce property rights, ease the formulation and enforcement of contracts, limit the ability of governments to intervene in the economy for their own short-term advantage, and generally support the operation of efficient markets will generate more rapid rates of economic growth than those that do not.

The NIE relaxes many of the strong assumptions of traditional economics with respect to the motivations of, and the information available to, individual decision makers. Neoclassical economics had assumed that the rules of social interaction are given, in the form of the rules of an efficient market economy, and that people do not deviate from the equilibrium path indicated by those rules. One of the basic assumptions of neoclassical economics was that economic agents had perfect information and zero transactions costs. In this world of perfect information and zero transactions costs, institutions were not consequential: any attempt to constrain the activities of economic agents could be easily mitigated by contracting around whatever rules or regulations governments created. The problem is, of course, that we do not live in a world of perfect information and zero transactions costs. In the real world of asymmetric information, bounded rationality, and non-zero transactions costs, the specific content of policies, regulations, and formal rules matters—and matters a great deal—in the ability of individuals, firms, and markets to respond to economic opportunities. Institutions are not epiphenomena; they are crucial in determining the rate and structure of economic growth.

This has resulted in three insights. First, there is a whole range of economic activity that may not take place because the costs of transacting are too high. The outcome is slower economic growth. Second, formal rules may be designed in such a way as to permit particular groups of economic agents to engage in a particular activity while constraining everyone else from doing so. The outcome is a stream of rents that can only be earned by that particular group, with negative distributional and efficiency consequences for the rest of society. Third, economic agents may choose not to obey the rules of social interaction. Instead, they may devote resources to changing the inherited set of rules, often with the goal of redefining the rules so as to generate rents for themselves.[10]

This is not to say, however, that economic institutions are created in a random fashion. One of the insights of the NIE is that the political determination of economic institutions is the result both of interest group demands *and* the specific features of decision making in the political system—which are themselves governed by institutions. In fact, the political system *is* a set of institutions designed to aggregate individual preferences. On the one hand, these political institutions include the rules about *who* has the authority to legislate and enforce the regulations that govern economic activity and *what* the legitimate extensions of that authority are. On the other hand, these political institutions also specify the way in which a polity might change the rules about who has the authority to regulate and the legitimate extent of regulation. Thus, the study of the origins and consequences of economic institutions requires also the study of the institutions that structure political decision making.

One can think of institutional environments as sets of nested institutions. There is a political system—a set of institutions—that generates sets of laws, regulations, and enforcement mechanisms that serve to both permit and bound economic activity. These laws range from those that affect nearly all economic agents (laws regarding the specification of property rights, for example) to those that are specific to particular industries, firms, or classes of workers. Examples would include tariffs on specific products, laws that regulate entry into particular lines of economic activity (the regulations that govern the chartering of banks, for example), or laws that regulate wages and hours for particular occupations. These laws, in turn, have a direct impact on the structure and efficiency of firms and markets.

There are, of course, a broad range of rules and regulations that both permit and impinge upon the activities of economic agents. Most of them, however, can be grouped into two broad categories: those that specify and enforce property rights, and those that specify and enforce the rents obtained from those property rights. There are institutions that define the rules regarding the possession, use, and transfer of property. It is these rights to property that governments abrogate by, for example, nationalizing them or transferring them to another private party. There are also, however, a whole range of institutions, which take the form of government policies or regulations, that affect the ability of those who hold property rights to earn rents from that property. From the point of view of economic agents, these are equally important because an asset that provides no rent is, by definition, valueless—even if the right to the property has not been abrogated or diminished. In fact, from the point of view of governments, it may make sense to support and enforce property rights precisely so that they can create a stream of rents that can be taxed.

Permit us a discussion of the impact of import tariffs to make the distinction between property rights and the rents from property clear. Imagine a situation in which a particular industry has grown under a protective tariff. Industrialists own the factories and the related assets (buildings, land, and the like) and they earn a stream of rents from those assets. Now imagine that the government eliminates the tariff, pushing product prices down below the level where industrialists can earn a positive rate of return on their assets. The property rights of industrialists have not been abrogated—they still own the factories. Their rents, however, have been reduced, and this, in turn, reduces the value of the factories. Changes in tax regimes, labor laws, monetary policies, exchange rates, and a whole host of other regulations can exert similar effects on rents. As we shall see, both classes of institutions—those that specify and enforce property rights and those that specify and enforce the rents earned from property rights—are equally crucial to the process of economic growth.

There is thus a complex interaction between the institutions that govern the polity and the institutions that govern the economy. Working backward, we can specify the relationship in the following way. Economic institutions (sets of rules and regulations that specify property rights, regulate entry, create and administer taxes, encourage the formation of human capital, and the like) directly affect the performance and structure of markets, industries, and firms. Some of these institutions develop outside of the political system, through an evolutionary process of private contracting. Ultimately, however, these institutions become subject to the influence of the political system, because they require third-party enforcement. More often than not, however, economic institutions are the direct product of the political system. Indeed, economic institutions are often formulated in order to accomplish political ends, such as the distribution of rewards or benefits to a legislator's constituents. The reform of economic institutions through the political process may also come about because of a perceived failure of the existing economic structure. The political determination of economic institutions means, therefore, that they may, or may not, be designed in order to improve social welfare or increase per capita income.

Political decision making is, in turn, governed by its own set of institutions that determine the governance structure of a society (rules about who has the authority to enact and enforce economic legislation) and the specific features of decision making within each branch of the government. On the one hand, these institutions serve to delineate a division of labor to perform government tasks. On the other hand, these institutions structure the process by which the constituent branches of the government go about drafting, debating, and enacting particular pieces of legislation. As a practical matter, the specific features of this division of labor within the government exert a powerful effect on the actual substance of economic regulation. The political institutions that delineate a division of labor within the government are themselves bounded by yet another set of institutions—those that structure the way that the political system can decide to change the rules about decision making. This type of political institution (rules about the rules, so to speak) includes constitutions and constitutional amendments, as well as the judicial review of proposed policies and laws. Changes in any of these sets of political institutions (as well as changes in economic institutions) are themselves bounded by sets of informal institutions (socially and culturally embedded norms and values). These informal institutions provide legitimacy to the formal institutions of the society and at the same time set limits on the degree to which changes in those formal institutions will be viewed as legitimate. In short, economic activity and economic change take place within a complex and interdependent web of political and social institutions, some of which are formal (legally codified) and some of which are informal (culturally embedded).

There are essentially three variants in the literature on institutions and economic growth. One variant focuses on the institutions that govern the operation of markets. This strand of the literature focuses on how changes in institutions make credible commitments possible, property rights more secure, and contracts enforceable, thereby lowering transactions costs and increasing the range of exchanges that are mediated through the market. This, it is argued, increases allocative efficiency and encourages entrepreneurs to adopt longer time horizons, thereby increasing investments in physical and human capital.[11] A second, and related, variant of the NIE focuses on the institutions that limit governments. This body of literature argues that economic growth will be enhanced if governments are constrained in their ability to reduce the property rights or increase the tax burdens faced by economic agents. The focus here is on the mechanisms that constrain governments from using their authority to engage in opportunistic behavior in order to satisfy their short-term financial needs at the expense of long-term economic growth.[12] A third variant of the literature focuses on the institutions that affect contracts within firms. Changes in the rules and norms that bound or limit the types and nature of intra-firm contracts, it is argued, have an impact on the ability of firms to engage in organizational or technological innovations that increase productivity.[13]

Latin American History and the New Institutional Economics

In recent years, the NIE has begun to make its impact felt in the field of Latin American economic history. The reason is not hard to divine: the NIE offers a theory relevant to understanding the causes of Latin American underdevelopment. It therefore offers a set of theoretical insights that can be employed in crafting narratives about the interaction of political and economic phenomena over time.

At the same time that Latin American historians have been influenced by the NIE, the NIE has found Latin American history to be fertile ground for empirical research. The reason is that Latin American history provides precisely the kind of natural laboratory for testing hypotheses about the distributional and efficiency consequences of institutional change that is necessary for revising and elaborating the new theory. In fact, many of the case studies selected for empirical analysis in the NIE literature to date are weak and partial tests of the theory. Scholars have typically chosen cases for analysis in which putatively more efficient institutions produced faster economic growth.[14] Yet, if positive institutional innovations (more secure property rights, credible commitments by governments to not expropriate private assets, and the like) exert a positive influence on economic growth, then it should also follow that negative institutional changes (such as revolutions that make property rights less secure, the rise of predatory states, or government regulations that distort markets) should produce slow or negative rates of economic growth. Latin American history provides exactly these kinds of institutional environments.[15]

Latin American history also provides a natural laboratory for the NIE in another crucial sense: most of the empirical literature to date in the NIE has looked at economies in which institutional change proceeded gradually. The incremental nature of institutional change in these economies, coupled with the fact that there are often multiple institutions undergoing such incremental changes at any one time, means that it is difficult, if not impossible, to pinpoint particular institutional reforms that have been crucial for economic growth. This problem is accentuated by an additional factor: most of the work done to date has focused on economies that have had long histories of well-developed markets. In these economies, the market has anticipated institutional changes, meaning that it is extremely difficult to demonstrate the effects of any particular institutional reform.[16] Indeed, in economies in which there are well-developed markets, there is an endogeneity that may exist between the market and institutional development; markets as they become more efficient may affect the process of institutional development, which, in turn, feeds back into markets, and so on. Latin American history provides precisely the opposite kinds of cases. Institutions in Latin America have often changed in a dramatic fashion. Moreover, these changes have often worked to reduce property rights or divert the stream of rents from property away from the owners of property. Finally, markets in Latin America—in particular during the nineteenth and early twentieth centuries—could not anticipate institutional changes because markets were poorly developed.

Empirical Research Results

This volume focuses on Mexico's economic history during the late nineteenth and early twentieth centuries. The essays employ theoretical insights from the NIE, econometric hypothesis testing, and traditional archival methods in order address a series of interrelated questions about the political economy of growth during the Porfiriato (1876–1911), the revolution (1910–17), and the immediate post-revolutionary period (1917–30). We focus on Mexico during this period for both practical and theoretical reasons. Until the last decades of the nineteenth century, Mexico faced the twin problems of chronic political instability and slow economic growth. At the end of the century, and particularly during the period of the Porfirio Díaz dictatorship (1876–1911), a series of institutional reforms reignited growth, and, in so doing, created rents that could be used to end political instability, either by giving the Díaz government the ability to credibly threaten its opponents with military force or by giving it the ability to buy them off. These institutional reforms came out of distinctly political processes—indeed, they often had to be brokered among multiple groups of economic elites and regional political bosses. They therefore were often structured so as to encourage investment by specifying property rights or creating streams of rents for particular groups of entrepreneurs. In short, there was nothing laissez-faire about Porfirian Mexico. It is therefore an excellent natural laboratory to understand how institutional changes can foment economic growth. It is also an excellent case with which to understand the way that the specific features of political institutions give rise to specific economic institutions, and to understand how those economic institutions may have both positive and negative effects on growth and distribution. In fact, the distributional consequences of Díaz's institutional reforms gave rise to the Mexican Revolution of 1910–17, and the revolution, itself, produced a further round of dramatic change in Mexico's political institutions. These changes, in turn, dramatically restructured the institutions that governed property rights and the institutions that determined the allocation of rents generated by property rights.

Our interest, therefore, is both the identification of Mexico's institutions and the measurement of their economic effects. We have organized the essays in this volume into three sections: the institutional reforms of the financial system during the Porfiriato; the institutional reforms of Mexican foreign trade during the Porfiriato; and the institutional reforms affecting labor relations during the Porfiriato and the revolution. We realize, of course, that the process of institutional reform both during the Porfiriato and the revolution was not constrained to these three areas. There was a broad range of institutional change relating to subsoil rights, intellectual property rights, rights in landed property, and rights to rents created by investments in new industries that are not discussed here. We concentrate on these three issues, however, because there is a critical mass of scholarship that addresses them.

We start our analysis with the financial system, the network of banks and securities markets that facilitate the valuation and exchange of assets in the real economy. We begin with finance for two reasons. First, because financial systems provide credit intermediation and a payments system, the performance of banks and securities markets has a direct impact on the performance of other sectors. A robust and efficient financial system can enhance economic growth; an inefficient financial sector can retard it. Second, financial systems are notoriously sensitive to the specific features of government policies and regulations because the functioning of financial systems relies heavily on legal contracts and legal definitions. Financial systems allow claims on real—and often relatively immobile and illiquid—resources to be represented by relatively liquid contracts. Rules laid down by the government determine the security of these claims, and how easily they may be traded or transferred. Thus, politically created institutions have a special role in the formation and evolution of financial systems. Moreover, governments often have strong incentives to structure institutions so as to maximize their own ability to borrow from the financial system.

In the case of Porfirian Mexico, the government's financial needs were decisive in shaping the banking system. The result was a set of institutions that on the one hand allowed for the development of a financial system dominated by modern financial intermediaries, and on the other hand that limited Mexico's long-run growth opportunities. As Maurer and Haber describe in Chapter 2, "Institutional Change and Economic Growth: Banks, Financial Markets, and Mexican Industrialization, 1878–1913," there had essentially been a deal struck between the bankers and the government in which the former agreed to provide credit for the latter, in exchange for which the latter restricted entry into the banking system. This was good for government finance, and it was good for the existing banks. What impact did this have, however, on the rest of the economy? Maurer and Haber employ panel regression techniques and detailed data from censuses of the Mexican textile industry, along with insights from the economics of information, to estimate the consequences of Mexico's peculiar banking structure on the size, structure, and efficiency of Mexican manufacturing. They find that only those entrepreneurs with personal ties to the banks, which is to say those manufacturers who were also bankers, were able to obtain bank credit. These bank-related firms were larger than their competitors, and they grew faster. Maurer and Haber also find, however, that bank-related firms were no more productive than their competitors. That is to say, Mexico's banks picked insiders, not winners. Had the regulatory environment permitted the entry of more banks, more entrepreneurs would have had access to the credit markets.

Mexico would have had a larger, less concentrated, and more efficient textile industry. That is, there was a deadweight loss to Mexico of restricting entry into banking.

The efficiency of the banking system is further analyzed by Maurer in Chapter 3, "The Internal Consequences of External Credibility: Banking Regulation and Banking Performance in Porfirian Mexico." Here the focus is not on the linkages of the banking system to the rest of the economy, but on the impact of Mexico's regulatory system on the behavior of the banks. Through an analysis of bank rates of return, estimates of Tobin's q, and a model of bank liquidity preferences, Maurer finds that laws that provided special privileges to particular banks adversely affected the efficiency of the banking system and strengthened the monopoly power of the nation's two largest banks. Maurer also demonstrates that the supposed benefits of vesting one bank, the Banco Nacional de México (Banamex), with special rights and privileges did not produce the benefits to the banking system that its proponents claimed. Banamex did not, in fact, act like a quasi-central bank, stabilizing the rest of the banking system. In short, both chapters illustrate the power of political systems to shift rents while limiting economic growth.

Why did the Mexican government create such a concentrated banking system? This question is addressed by Carlos Marichal in Chapter 4, "The Construction of Credibility: Financial Market Reform and the Renegotiation of Mexico's External Debt in the 1880s." Marichal traces the emergence of Banamex to a pivotal moment in the transition from a weak to a strong state in Mexico. This private bank permitted the government to confront, for the first time, its chronic external debt problem. The monopoly structures that limited and concentrated economic growth, discussed in Chapters 2 and 3, were a crucial part of restoring the government's credibility in international financial markets.

Chapter 5, by Paolo Riguzzi, "The Legal System, Institutional Change, and Financial Regulation in Mexico, 1870–1910: Mortgage Contracts and Long-Term Credit," completes the study of the origins of Mexico's financial system by looking at the emergence and evolution of mortgage banking in Porfirian Mexico. Riguzzi argues that the institutional innovation of mortgage credit would have had a huge impact on Mexican economic growth, since most of the labor force was employed in agriculture and most of the GNP was generated in agriculture. The development of modern mortgage banking was blocked, however, by two sets of institutional problems. The first was that the government granted a monopoly on long-term lending to a single bank, thereby limiting the supply of mortgage credit. Even once this monopoly ended, however, a second institutional problem prevented mortgage lending. Mortgage banks, as well as private lenders who might want to make mortgage loans, were discouraged from lending because of the poor specification of property titles in rural Mexico. Without clearly drawn titles, and without a legal system that would allow the repossession of property in the event of nonpayment, there was little incentive to lend on agricultural property.

Just as Mexico's economic institutions protected the country's bankers from competition, so too did its economic institutions protect its manufacturers. The second section of this volume turns to the study of institutions that governed Mexico's external commerce. Chapter 6, "Institutional Change and Foreign Trade in Mexico, 1870–1911," by Sandra Kuntz Ficker, argues that Mexico had been protectionist throughout the nineteenth century. Mexico's industrial growth after 1885 was not, therefore, a function of protectionism on a global scale, but was the product of a specific set of institutional reforms that both reformed the tariff and simplified customs regulations. The combined policy was more effective because it targeted specific industries. By streamlining customs regulations and by decreasing the tariff on most imports, the Mexican government was able to facilitate imports, thereby speeding the growth of those sectors of the economy that were import dependent. By separating and measuring nominal levels of protection and dutiable imports, Kuntz Ficker demonstrates that the Mexican government, freed from complete fiscal dependence on customs duties, continued to protect some industries within the framework of a more liberal and more effective commercial policy. She also estimates the reduction in costs to importers from the simplification of customs regulations. The result of state policy was a significant increase in per capita imports between 1891 and 1910.

Edward Beatty, in Chapter 7, "Commercial Policy in Porfirian Mexico: The Structure of Protection," continues the analysis of the institutions that governed Mexico's foreign trade. Beatty argues that tariff-based protection was substantial from the 1880s to 1910, that tariff reforms increasingly sought developmental rather than fiscal objectives, and that tariff policy favored import-substitution industrialization. To demonstrate this, he measures Mexico's nominal and effective rates of protection, finding that nominal protection levels remained consistent with import-substituting industrialization objectives. He also finds effective rates even higher, their cascading structure further supporting industrialization objectives.

How can it be that the Porfiriato was characterized both by declining tariffs (à la Kuntz Ficker) and protectionism (à la Beatty)? The answer is that governments can reduce *average* tariffs at the same time that they raise the tariffs on a *select group* of targeted goods. In fact, the growth of domestic industry in Mexico required *both* narrowly focused tariff protection and a more open economy. The former was necessary because the manufacturers of final goods, like beer, cigarettes, and cotton cloth, could not have survived without trade barriers. The latter was necessary because manufacturers needed access to low-cost capital and intermediate goods. Had Mexico had the same tariff rates on capital and intermediate goods imports as it had on final products, the rate of effective protection might well have approached zero. Whatever benefit that might have been conferred by the tariff on the final goods would have been reduced by the higher cost of inputs created by tariffs on those products. In fact, effective rates of protection can actually be negative if the tariff on imported inputs is substantially higher than the tariff on the final goods produced.[17] In short, there was nothing inconsistent about Mexico's tariff policy. The evidence, in fact, indicates that it conformed to what economists call a cascading tariff structure: high tariffs on final goods, lower tariffs on intermediate inputs, and very low tariffs on capital goods.

For bankers and manufacturers, Porfirian Mexico was a world in which formal institutions mattered a great deal. Bankers were protected from interstate competition and from the threat of new entrants into their regional markets. Manufacturers were protected from foreign competitors at the same time that the reforms outlined by Kuntz Ficker allowed them (and other producers) to more easily obtain the foreign-produced goods they required to grow their enterprises. Mexico's workers, however, were not protected by formal institutions. There were, in fact, no laws that governed labor contracts, save the laws of supply and demand. This all changed, however, with the Revolution of 1910. What, exactly, was the nature of these institutional changes, what effects did they have on the division of rents between factory owners and factory workers, and what were their long-run economic implications?

The third section of this volume therefore turns to the study of the institutions that governed labor relations before, during, and after the Mexican Revolution. In the first of the two chapters that comprise this section, Jeffrey Bortz argues that textile workers violently assaulted the old labor regime in the factories during the revolution. His "The Legal and Contractual Limits to Private Property Rights in Mexican Industry During the Revolution" (Chapter 8) argues that this labor revolution changed the socially expected organization of the labor process in such a way as to fundamentally alter private property rights. These changes in informal institutions—the changes in the norms that governed labor relations on the factory floor—were soon codified into formal institutions, first by state governors who had to obtain the support of their militant labor constituencies and later by the Constitution of 1917 and ensuing federal legislation. Bortz argues that property rights in industry have two meanings—the appropriation of product, but also the right of the owners to control the labor process. In order to deal with the new-found strength and violence of textile workers, the new state constructed a wholly new legal system of work. The new set of laws, rules, and informal agreements of Mexican factories effectively limited the right of owners to run the mills as they wished, therefore constraining private property rights in new ways. The owners of factories lost the rights to hire, fire, discipline, and set work rules. In the cotton textile industry, property alone no longer controlled workers or the work process.

This line of analysis is further pursued in Chapter 9 by Aurora Gómez-Galvarriato in "Measuring the Impact of Institutional Change in Capital-Labor Relations in the Mexican Textile Industry, 1900–1930." Gómez-Galvarriato utilizes data from the Orizaba textile mills, among the largest and most important in the country, to construct time series of real wages and productivity in the cotton textile industry from 1900 to 1930. Her data demonstrates that the institutional changes in the country's labor regime, discussed in Bortz's chapter, indeed strengthened workers at the expense of owners, diverting rents from the latter to the former. After the revolution, real wages for cotton textile workers increased significantly, while productivity growth slowed as a result of the owners' loss of control over the work process. She suggests that the institutional solution to rising wages without rising productivity was an alliance among factory owners, labor leaders, and the government to once again use high tariffs. Mexico's industrialists may therefore have faced an inhospitable labor regime, but they were able to pass along the costs implied by the labor relations system to the rest of society via high levels of trade protection. The long-run outcome of this arrangement was an industry that would become progressively more sclerotic and would therefore require continually higher levels of protection.

Conclusion and Implications

Taken as a group, what implications do the essays in this volume have for Mexican economic history? This question is taken up at length by Stephen Haber in the concluding chapter of this volume. A few words foreshadowing Haber's conclusions, however, seem appropriate at this juncture.

One of the striking things about the Mexican economy is that it has grown significantly since the last decades of the nineteenth century, but it has never succeeded in growing fast enough to catch up with the advanced industrial countries. There is a long literature that has grappled with the causes and consequences of Mexico's persistent backwardness. That literature has operated, however, without a clearly specified underlying theory. This has meant that although the literature has described the phenomenon of growth alongside persistent backwardness, it has not offered an explanation.[18] The NIE offers a body of theory that explains how you can get institutional change that permits economic growth, but does so by creating rents for particular economic or political groups. The very nature of the political and economic bargain that allows for sustained growth simultaneously prevents the development of an economy characterized by either internal or external competitiveness.

Porfirian Mexico is perhaps a canonical case of an economy in which growth was created via the specification of institutions that created rents for select groups of economic agents. There was nothing laissez-faire about Porfirian Mexico, even though the government espoused the precepts of nineteenth-century liberalism. Porfirio Díaz faced the twin threats of political disorder and economic stagnation when he seized power in 1876. Díaz, like his predecessors, had a limited set of instruments to cope with both problems simultaneously. The government could either try to preserve its stay in power and restore stability or provide a favorable environment for economic activity. If it concentrated on the problem of disorder, it would need to borrow heavily from the private sector, given the lack of an administrative structure that could effectively tax the country's slim economic base. With a long history of predatory governments, the private sector (both domestic and foreign) was not willing to lend sufficient funds to the government, leaving governments with two options: predation (forced loans, arbitrary exactions, and confiscations of property) or collapse. If, instead, the government wanted to promote economic activity by making commitments to respect property rights (by, for example, honoring previous debts), then it would have no resources to fight its political opponents and restore political stability.

Díaz and the political elite surrounding him understood that solving this dilemma was crucial to their own political survival. If they could reform Mexico's internal institutions, it would be possible to secure foreign loans for the government, attract foreign direct investment, and entice domestic investors into lucrative and productive economic activities. This would foment economic growth and enlarge the tax base, which would simultaneously create rents for elites who supported the government and provide the government the resources (through tax revenues and loans) to defeat its opponents. Unlike previous regimes, Díaz faced an external environment in which such a strategy had a very high likelihood of success. The world economy in the last quarter of the nineteenth century was characterized by falling international transport costs, increased capital mobility, and open markets. Thus, the rents from integrating Mexico with the rest of the world through a reform of Mexico's domestic institutions were enormous.

Beginning the process of institutional change necessary to set off this virtuous cycle of economic growth and political order meant, however, that in the first iteration the government was going to have to create sets of institutions that would create rents for important members of Mexico's domestic private sector—particularly a significant group of nascent bankers and manufacturers. This would allow these groups to prosper, and they, in turn, would provide financial and political support to the Díaz dictatorship. This strategy actually worked: the Mexican economy grew, international investors funneled nearly $2 billion into Mexico, and the Díaz government defeated or bought off its potential rivals. Mexico thus obtained political stability and economic growth, but at the cost of the creation and diversion of economic rents to the groups that supported Díaz.

In the medium term, this produced impressive rates of economic growth. The Mexican economy had scarcely grown since independence. Under Díaz, it grew by 2.1 percent per year in real per capita terms. In the longer term, however, Díaz faced a problem. The integration of groups of economic and political elites into policy making, who in turn earned substantial rents from their relationship to the dictatorship, meant that Díaz's ability to rapidly integrate other groups into the political system was constrained—existing groups would not easily give up their sources of rent. The problem was that Mexico's rapid economic growth was quickly creating other such groups, particularly in the northern border states. The result was that these other groups eventually challenged Díaz's control of the political system. Once that happened, non-elite groups, including Mexico's growing working class, could not only press their demands for the reform of the institutions that governed their activities, but could also press their demands for a revision of the institutions that governed the political system. In short, the distributional consequences of the institutional reforms of the Porfiriato resulted in the Mexican Revolution.

For a brief time, as both the Bortz and Gómez-Galvarriato chapters show, Mexico's political and economic institutions were very much up in the air. Very quickly, however, the political system converged on a structure similar to that of the Porfiriato, with political institutions once again centralizing power around the presidency. There was an important difference, however. In addition to the traditional groups—the bankers and the industrialists— that had used their access to power to generate economic rents, there was now an additional group: organized labor. The Mexican Revolution, therefore, did not undo Mexico's rent-seeking political economy. It did, however, increase the number of groups that could receive rents through the political system. The result, once again, was a political economy that could produce sustained growth, but also persistent backwardness.

Notes

1. As one recent reviewer put it: while the field did not lack motive, it lacked method. See Maurer 1999: 14.

2. For a discussion of the rise and decline of dependency theory, see Packenham 1992; Haber 1997a.

3. Even scholars who were somewhat sympathetic to the intuitive appeal of dependency theory noted the lack of clear specification. As Thorp and Bertram put it: "For all the intuitive appeal of the dependency analysis, it embodies several areas of difficulty and imprecision. . . . This imprecision stems from a further and fundamental weakness: the lack of a developed economic model underlying the notion of 'relatively greater autonomy.'" Thorp and Bertram 1978: 13–14.

4. Some scholars, such as Paz and Sunkel, did try to provide a potentially falsifiable structure to dependency, but few followed their lead. See Sunkel and Paz 1970.

5. One indication of the decline of dependency theory is that it no longer serves as the dominant organizing theme of textbooks or synthetic monographs, as it did through the late 1980s. Victor Bulmer-Thomas, in his 1994 *The Economic History of Latin America Since Independence*, for example, dispenses with the dependency framework in two paragraphs (pp. 12–14). For a discussion of the earlier texts, see Eakin 1988.

6. For an introduction to the literature on the new economic history of Latin America see Haber 1997b; and Coatsworth and Taylor 1998.

7. For some recent examples see Summerhill 2000; Engerman, Haber, and Sokoloff 2000; and Maurer forthcoming.

8. This definition differs from the common view of institutions as entities such as schools, government agencies, and the like. Here, we follow North's distinction between institutions, which are simply the restrictions on acceptable behavior, and institutional entities or organizations. See North 1990: 4–5. Institutions can be both formal and informal. Formal institutions are often legally codified. Examples include labor laws, environmental laws, regulations governing the operation of banks and securities markets, laws governing the formation and dissolution of families, and other legally codified restrictions on the activities of individuals and corporate bodies. Informal institutions are not legally codified: they include the norms and values that are often culturally

embedded in societies. Examples include norms and values related to honesty, civic mindedness, group identity, and the like.

9. See Calvert 1995: 217.

10. For a discussion of the genesis of the NIE, see Clague 1997.

11. For an introduction to this literature see North 1990.

12. North and Weingast 1989; Clark 1996; Weingast 1997.

13. Coase 1988; Williamson 1993, 1985.

14. Rosenthal 1992; North and Weingast 1989. For a critique of North and Weingast, see Clark 1996.

15. For an exception, see Haber and Razo 1998.

16. Economic agents realize that there is about to be a reform of institutions, and so bid asset prices up or down accordingly before the reform actually takes place. See Clark 1996.

17. Permit us a heuristic example drawn from cotton textiles to illustrate the point. Imagine that the tariff on cotton cloth is 100 percent. Imagine now that the tariff on raw cotton, textile dyes, and textile machinery is 200 percent. The nominal rate of protection is very high. The effective rate of protection will, however, be negative. Any advantage provided by the 100 percent tariff will be swamped by the fact that all of the inputs would cost 200 percent more. A textile firm facing such a tariff structure would be highly unlikely to survive unless it could reduce labor costs to a small fraction of those prevailing in other countries.

18. To the degree that there is a theoretical framework underlying this literature it is implicit and draws from neoclassical economics. For excellent introductions to this literature see Reynolds 1970; and Solis 1971.

References

Calvert, Randall L. 1995. "The Rational Choice Theory of Social Institutions: Cooperation, Coordination, and Communication." In Jeffrey S. Banks and Eric A. Hanushek, eds., *Modern Political Economy*. Cambridge, England.

Clague, Christopher. 1997. "The New Institutional Economics and Economic Development." In Christopher Clague, ed., *Institutions and Economic Development: Growth and Governance in Developed and Post-Socialist Countries*, pp. 13–36. Baltimore.

Clark, Gregory. 1996. "The Political Foundations of Modern Economic Growth: England, 1540–1800." *Journal of Interdisciplinary History*, vol. 26, no. 4: 563–88.

Coase, Ronald. 1988. *The Firm, the Market, and the Law*. Chicago.

Coatsworth, John H., and Alan Taylor, eds. 1998. *Latin America and the World Economy Since 1800*. Cambridge, Mass.

Eakin, Marshall C. 1988. "Surveying the Past: Latin American History Text-
    books and Readers." *Latin American Research Review*, vol. 23, no. 3:
    248–57.
Engerman, Stanley L., Stephen Haber, and Kenneth L. Sokoloff. 2000. "In-
    equality, Institutions, and Economic Growth: A Comparative Study
    of New World Economies Since the Sixteenth Century." In Claude
    Menard, ed., *Institutions, Contracts, and Organizations: Perspectives from
    New Institutional Economics*. Northampton, Mass.
Haber, Stephen. 1997a. "Economic Growth and Latin American Economic
    Historiography." In Stephen Haber, ed., *How Latin America Fell Behind:
    Essays on the Economic Histories of Brazil and Mexico, 1800–1914*, pp. 1–
    33. Stanford.
————, ed. 1997b. *How Latin America Fell Behind: Essays on the Economic His-
    tories of Brazil and Mexico, 1800–1914*. Stanford.
Haber, Stephen, and Armando Razo. 1998. "Political Instability and Economic
    Performance: Evidence from Revolutionary Mexico." *World Politics*,
    vol. 51: 99–143.
Maurer, Noel. Forthcoming. *The Power and the Money: Credible Commitments, Po-
    litical Instability, and the Financial System in Mexico, 1876–1934*. Stanford.
————. 1999. "Progress Without Order: Mexican Economic History in the
    1990's." *Revista de Historia Económica*, vol. 17: 14.
North, Douglass C. 1990. *Institutions, Institutional Change, and Economic Perfor-
    mance*. Cambridge, England.
North, Douglass C., and Barry R. Weingast. 1989. "Constitutions and Com-
    mitment: The Evolution of Institutions Governing Public Choice in Sev-
    enteenth Century England." *Journal of Economic History*, vol. 44, no. 4:
    803–32.
Packenham, Robert A. 1992. *The Dependency Movement: Scholarship and Politics
    in Development Studies*. Cambridge, Mass.
Reynolds, Clark W. 1970. *The Mexican Economy: Twentieth Century Structure and
    Growth*. New Haven.
Rosenthal, Jean Laurent. 1992. *The Fruits of Revolution: Property Rights, Litiga-
    tion, and French Agriculture, 1700–1860*. Cambridge, England.
Solis, Leopoldo M. 1971. *La realidad económica mexicana: Retrovisión y perspecti-
    vas*. Mexico City.
Summerhill, William R. 2000. *Order Against Progress: Government, Foreign In-
    vestment, and Railroads in Brazil, 1854–1913*. Stanford.
Sunkel, Osvaldo, and Pedro Paz. 1970. *El subdesarrollo latinoamericano y la teoria
    del desarrollo*. Mexico City.
Thorp, Rosemary, and Geoffrey Bertram. 1978. *Peru 1890–1977: Growth and
    Policy in an Open Economy*. New York.
Weingast, Barry R. 1997. "The Political Foundations of Limited Government:
    Parliament and Sovereign Debt in Seventeenth- and Eighteenth-Century

England." In John N. Drobak and John V. C. Nye, eds., *The Frontiers of the New Institutional Economics*, pp. 213–46. San Diego.

Williamson, Oliver. 1993. *The Economic Analysis of Institutions and Organizations*. Paris.

———. 1985. *The Economic Institutions of Capitalism: Firms, Markets, and Relational Contracting*. New York.

Part I

Financial System Reforms During the Porfiriato

Chapter 2

Institutional Change and Economic Growth: Banks, Financial Markets, and Mexican Industrialization, 1878–1913

NOEL MAURER AND STEPHEN HABER

During the Porfiriato, the Mexican government reformed the laws governing banking and the chartering of joint stock corporations. What effects did these institutional reforms have on economic growth? Did these institutional reforms accelerate or impede the growth of the real economy?

To address these questions this chapter focuses on three interrelated questions. First, what impact did Porfirian law have on the structure of the banking industry? Second, what was the relationship between the structure of the banking industry and the extension of credit to the "real" economy? Third, did imperfections in credit extension have a measurable impact on the performance of the real economy?

To answer these questions, we employ firm-level census data and tax records covering Mexico's largest manufacturing industry, cotton textiles, over the period 1878 to 1913. Although we focus solely on textiles, it is reasonable to expect that the patterns displayed in this industry hold across the manufacturing sector. Using detailed evidence from bank annual reports, the financial press, and the minutes of bank boards of directors, we identify which firms were connected to chartered banks, which firms raised capital from the securities markets, and which firms relied solely on traditional merchant networks to finance investment.

Our argument runs in the following terms. Porfirian law limited the number of banks that could operate in any market. Prior to the development of

modern credit reporting, banks tended to lend on the basis of personal connections, something true in the antebellum United States as well as Porfirian
Mexico, and to an extent characterizing Mexican banking until the present
day. The upshot was that only a limited number of textile firms could get
access to bank capital. We find that textile firms with inside connections to
banks grew faster than firms that relied on traditional merchant networks.
These bank-connected firms, however, were not any more productive than
their competitors who did not receive bank financing.

We also argue that laws that permitted the formation of limited-liability
joint stock companies appear to have been important mostly because they
facilitated relationship banking. The evidence indicates that firms took advantage of the limited-liability laws to allow them to easily collateralize bank
loans. Banks held stock in these joint stock textile companies as a guarantee for the loans, allowing them to seize the firms' assets in the event of
default without the need for costly and prolonged litigation. In this sense,
reforms in general incorporation law allowed firms to find a way around a
poorly functioning legal system. Thus, joint stock companies were larger
than other firms, and grew faster, but like bank-connected firms were no
more productive.

The few joint stock companies that were openly traded on the stock market were massively larger than their competitors. However, it appears that
going to the stock market provided only a one-time gain. The few firms that
listed on the Bolsa received a large infusion of capital at the time of their listing that allowed them a one-time gain in size and productivity. That one-
time advantage, however, was whittled away over time.[1]

In short, we find that the political economy of Porfirian Mexico gave rise
to formal institutions that produced a concentrated banking system. Because of the high cost of obtaining information, these banks provided credit
only to those manufacturing firms that were owned by bank directors. This
produced allocation inefficiencies: banks connected to manufacturing firms
were no more productive than their competitors. Had Mexico had banking laws that made it easier to charter a bank, it would have industrialized
faster.

We organize the argument as follows. The first section briefly describes
the history of Mexican financial law and the growth of the banking system.
The second section describes how the resulting financial system was used to
finance textile manufacturing. The third section describes our data and the
methodology used to analyze it. Section four presents our results in graphi-
cal form. Section five formalizes the analysis presented in section four, using

multivariate statistical techniques to control for intervening variables and to determine the direction of causality. Section six concludes.

Banking Law in the Porfiriato

Mexico's first chartered bank, a branch of the British Bank of London, Mexico, and South America, began operations in 1863, but the origins of the Porfirian financial system date back only to 1875. In that year, starting with the establishment of the Banco de Santa Eulalia in the northern border state of Chihuahua, two banking clusters began to emerge, one in Chihuahua and the other in Mexico City. In 1884, in the wake of a serious financial crisis prompted by the federal government's overissuance of railroad subsidy promises, the federal authorities engineered the merger of the two largest Mexico City banks into the Banco Nacional de México, or Banamex. The explicit intention was to model Banamex on the early Bank of England, granting it a monopoly over the issuance of paper money in return for providing credit to the federal government and the rest of the banking system in times of trouble.

For better or for worse, Banamex never played the role intended for it. Political opposition to the proposed monopoly over paper money soon crystallized around the local branch of the Bank of London, Mexico, and South America, which enjoyed extensive connections with many prominent Porfirian financiers and politicians. The resulting legal and political battles lasted thirteen years, and the law giving Banamex its privileges never went into effect.

Between 1884 and 1897, Mexico possessed no general banking laws. Since Mexico's Spanish traditions essentially held that all economic activities undertaken without authorization from either a general law or a special concession were illegal, Mexico did not undergo a period of free banking. Rather, bank charters were granted at the whim of the secretary of finance. Under Manuel Dublán, who served between 1884 and 1893, bank charters were issued fairly liberally. His successor, José Yves Limantour, changed that policy, revoking many of the bank charters issued by Dublán and refusing to issue any new ones pending the promulgation of a general banking law.

The resulting law, the General Credit Institutions and Banking Act of 1897, was a compromise between three competing interests. First were the Mexico City financiers and political elite arrayed around Banamex and BLM, whose concessions granted them lower reserve requirements and the exclusive right to branch across state lines. Second were the smaller banks established under Dublán, which wanted to preserve their right to issue bank-notes and limit further competition as much as possible. Third were the local political and economic elites in the various states, which wanted to establish their own banks to finance their entrepreneurial activities.

The act of 1897 preserved most of Banamex's and BLM's privileges. They continued to enjoy the exclusive right to branch nationally and enjoyed a reserve requirement on their banknote issues of only 33 percent, compared to 50 percent for most of their competitors. In addition, Banamex enjoyed the exclusive privileges of providing financial services to the federal government: collecting tax receipts, making payments, holding federal deposits, and underwriting all foreign and domestic federal debt issues.

The existing banks were rewarded with very strict limits on competition. The law set a minimum capital requirement of 250,000 pesos (roughly U.S.$125,000), and was written in such a way as to allow only a single bank to be established in a state, although existing banks were grandfathered in under the law and several banks were granted the right to establish branches in adjoining states. These banks, along with new ones founded under the new law, were not permitted to branch outside their concession territory, issue new stock without the special permission of the secretary of finance, or establish branches or agencies within the Federal District. In addition, they were required to maintain a reserve requirement of at least 50 percent on their note issues. The law also allowed for the establishment of mortgage banks and *bancos refaccionarios*, which were denied the right to issue banknotes and were subject to various restrictions on the types of investment they could make. Without the right to issue notes, these banks could not compete, and Porfirian entrepreneurs took out few charters for them.

What this means is that Mexico had very few banks. In 1909, Mexico possessed forty-two formally incorporated financial institutions of various kinds.[2] For comparison, in the same year the United States enjoyed the services of 18,723 banks and trust companies.[3] Figure 2.1 presents estimates of the Herfindahl concentration index for the banking system, defining market share as the proportion of the total assets of the banking system belonging to an individual bank. As the figure makes clear, the passage of the 1897 act produced a one-time wave of entry, driving down the Herfindahl from around 0.45 to about 0.20, where it remained for the rest of the period. Nevertheless, with forty-two banks and banking companies in operation by 1910, the banking system remained about as concentrated as one with only five equally sized institutions.[4]

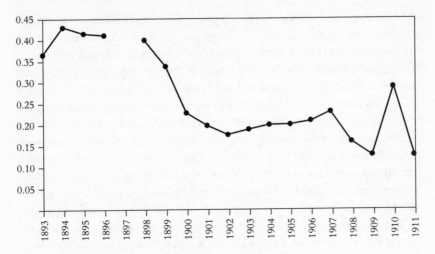

Figure 2.1. Herfindahl Index for Mexican Banking

SOURCE: *Economista Mexicano*, various issues.

Textile Finance in Porfirian Mexico

Banks made financing decisions based on the personal connections of their directors. Essentially, Porfirian banks worked as investment clubs. A group of entrepreneurs, after obtaining a bank charter, would pay in the required minimum capital and then immediately lend the proceeds among themselves. They would then sell shares in the bank on the Mexico City exchange or overseas, and in that way attract outside capital for their own particular entrepreneurial activities. Since the number of banks was highly limited, the implication is that far fewer potential entrepreneurs could receive credit than in countries like the United States.

Investors knew quite well when buying bank stock that they were actually investing in the diversified economic activities of the bank's directors, but they preferred bank stock over direct investments in industry for three reasons. First, the federal government tightly regulated the banks, requiring them to issue monthly balances and placing highly paid inspectors in their offices. Reporting requirements for non-bank companies were far looser and regularly flouted: few of the already few companies that listed directly on the stock exchange complied with the requirement that they publish annual balance sheets and profit-and-lost statements in the financial press. Bank balance sheets, however, had to be published regularly and bore closer relationship to the actual state of the enterprise than balances released by other companies.

Second, bank directors usually possessed specialized knowledge about the activities and regions in which they invested—more so than investors in Mexico City or overseas. In fact, these banks actually functioned as the heart of a "grupo" of enterprises owned or controlled by their directors: it would have been difficult for outsiders to replicate their knowledge of the market or industry. However, it was relatively easy to establish mechanisms designed to monitor the activities of the directors. In addition, since the directors and outside investors were playing a repeated game with each other, inasmuch as the directors would return to the stock and bond market for new capital, reputations were very important and very carefully guarded. In essence, these banks passed the problem of asymmetric information from one between bank directors and borrowers to one between shareholders and bank directors.[5]

The third reason is that by getting the banks to diversify for them, investors lowered the risks they faced. Bank directors had both the incentives and leverage to monitor firms owned by other directors because a default by one of these firms would damage the credibility of the entire group, hurting the ability of the other directors to raise capital for their own enterprises. Thus investing in banks served as a mechanism by which investors could monitor managers in firms over which they had no direct knowledge or control. Firms organized as joint stock companies in order to give bank directors more leverage over borrowing firms in the case of default. Loans would be made not to the firm, but to its owners personally, who pledged shares in the firm as collateral. The other directors in the bank could then simply seize the stock in the event of default. It should therefore not be surprising that very few joint stock textile firms were actually publicly traded.

Data and Methods

We draw on the textile data set and methods developed by Razo and Haber in their study of long-term productivity growth in the Mexican textile industry.[6] This study employs part of their larger data set, covering the following firm-level censuses: 1878, 1883, 1888, 1889, 1891, 1893, 1895, 1896, 1912, and 1913. We also include data from a sample of excise tax records for the years 1898, 1900, 1902, 1904, 1907, and 1909.

We transformed the raw data to create a uniform data set. First, we changed every relevant variable from its initial frequency to an equivalent annual value. Second, because some multi-mill companies reported some variables at the mill level and others at the company level, we consolidated mills into companies, and used the latter as our observational unit of analysis. Third, we employed the estimated price index developed by Razo and Haber for cotton textile goods for the period 1850–1933, which uses available Mexican cotton price data and in its absence, an algorithm derived from U.S. cotton sheeting and textile prices, the peso–dollar exchange rate, and the tariff on imports.

We proxied capital by the number of spindles because it was the only uniform and consistent definition of capital across censuses. We know, however, from detailed machinery reports in some of the censuses, that spindles constituted the most important capital input for the production of cotton textile goods.[7] This corresponds to the findings of work on the United States textile industry. In fact, the literature on the U.S. textile industry tends to use spindlage as the measure of capital or capacity.[8]

Total labor-hours were not available. We therefore followed Razo and Haber as well as the work of Atack and Sokoloff on productivity in the United States and of Bernard and Jones on international productivity comparisons, employing total workers as the measure of the labor input.[9]

We used multivariate regression techniques for a two-dimensional analysis of textile companies (our observational units) by both particular points in time as well as for extended periods of time. For any time *t*, we are able to estimate ordinary least-squares regressions of potential explanatory factors for each cross section of observational units. At the same time, we have constructed time series for individual observational units. These series enable us to follow the changes of certain variables over time. Putting the two together enabled us to construct a panel data set where we can check for both concurrent and long-term effects of the explanatory variables we propose in our models.

We used an unbalanced panel procedure to estimate basic pooled and fixed-effects specifications of regressions for the years 1878–1913 of the following type:

$$Y_{it} = \alpha + \beta \cdot X_{it} + u_{it}$$

where Y_{it} is the dependent variable of firm *i* at time *t*; α is the overall intercept term for all firms;[10] β is a vector of coefficients corresponding to the X_{it} vector of independent variables, and u_{it} is a stochastic term. We assumed usual normality and independence conditions to obtain least-squares estimates of β.

For our productivity regressions, we followed Razo and Haber and assumed a Cobb-Douglas production function of the form $Y = A \cdot K^{\gamma} \cdot L^{1-\gamma}$ with constant returns to scale where *K* and *L* represent the capital and labor inputs and A is a function that captures improvements in technology over time.[11] In order to use linear estimation procedures, we took natural logarithms of a normalized production function of the form $y = k^\alpha$ where $y = Y/L$ and $k = K/L$ and added explanatory variables to arrive at the following model:

$$\text{Ln } y = \alpha + \beta_1 \cdot \text{Ln } k + \beta_2 \cdot \text{Ln } L + \beta_3 \cdot \text{Time Trend} + \delta \cdot \text{Dummies} + \gamma \cdot \text{Interaction Terms}$$

Relationships between banks and textile firms were identified in three ways, the first two of which always coincided with the third. The first, applicable for limited-liability companies, was significant holdings of textile stock directly by a bank, such as Banamex's mammoth holdings in the Compañía Industrial Manufacturera (CIMSA). Another was the pledging of significant amounts of corporate stock as a guarantee for a personal start-up loan by the founders of a textile firm. As mentioned earlier, firms were usually financed by personal loans to the directors, who then pledged stock in the firm as collateral. This has been commonly considered the strongest indicator of a tight bank–firm relationship,[12] and appears from the available data to have been coterminous with our third measure, interlocking directorates between banks and textile firms. Since direct evidence from internal bank accounts is available only for five banks—Banamex, the Banco Oriental, the Banco de Zacatecas, the Banco de Jalisco, and the Banco Mercantil de Veracruz—our investigation focused on interlocking directorates as an indicator of a bank–firm relationship. This marker provides the additional advantage of identifying relationships between banks and firms not organized as limited-liability companies.

By comparing the listed owners of textile firms with those of the banks reported in their annual reports, we determined which textile firms enjoyed an inside relationship with a bank. Attachment was constant, and no firms connected with a bank changed hands to a nonconnected owner during the period. In the cases of limited-liability firms, we identified bank relationships for the four publicly traded firms whose boards of directors were known. For the others, relationships were identified from available bank records at the Archivo General de la Nación (AGN) or Archivo Histórico del Banco Nacional de México (AHBNM).

It should be noted here that textile firm directors were more likely to participate with other entrepreneurs in founding banks than banks were to lend money to unrelated firms and demand in return equity or a seat on the board. In fact, Banamex was the only bank we identified that followed the second strategy. A strong relationship holds in either case.

Table 2.1a

Average Value of Output per Firm, by Type of Firm

Year	Other	Bank-Connected, Not Joint Stock Co.	Joint Stock Co., Not Actively Traded	Actively Traded
1878	$113,495			
1883	$108,399	$130,865		
1888	$ 15,884	$184,455		
1889	$131,785	$110,564		
1891	$139,703	$236,278	$155,731	
1893	$145,222	$191,938	$205,018	$2,023,004
1895	$170,626	$257,054	$334,906	$2,025,356
1896	$225,567	$295,695	$501,619	$2,273,531
1898	$206,946	$296,865	$377,186	$2,083,160
1900	$238,660	$316,536	$426,522	$3,138,567
1902	$189,476	$267,478	$480,406	$3,912,760
1904	$295,389	$386,839	$397,625	$4,295,000
1905	$275,836	$330,400	$557,500	$4,090,000
1906	$290,957	$357,882	$496,200	$4,480,000
1909	$255,406	$316,625	$512,889	$4,180,000
1910	$267,444	$391,333	$454,947	$3,260,000
1911	$249,422	$439,125	$641,111	$3,660,000
1912	$240,875	$657,861	$362,765	$4,392,111
1913	$153,899	$366,385	$606,536	$2,775,649

NOTE: These data are presented graphically in Figure 2.3a.

Data Analysis

Tables 2.1a, 2.1b, and 2.2 provide descriptive statistics for three classes of mill, by year: those owned by a firm or individual connected directly to a bank; those owned by a limited-liability company; and those owned by one of the four limited-liability companies that actively traded their own stock on the Mexico City exchange.

Several patterns in the data become immediately apparent. First, most firms were organized as individual proprietorships or limited partnerships, even after the general incorporation laws of 1889. Joint stock companies never amounted to more than about a quarter of all cotton textile companies. Second, few of these joint stock companies actually traded on the stock

Table 2.1b
Average Output in Meters of Cloth per Firm, by Type of Firm

Year	Other	Bank-Connected, Not Joint Stock Co.	Joint Stock Co., Not Actively Traded	Actively Traded
1878	1,008,180			
1883	934,805	1,205,277		
1888	1,188,599	2,212,823	2,899,805	
1889	1,030,290	1,016,134	1,712,869	
1891	1,313,622	2,091,119	2,013,714	
1893	1,278,668	1,669,799	1,543,093	16,094,439
1895	1,332,623	2,476,966	4,283,923	17,527,616
1896	2,012,961	2,695,441	4,564,217	20,265,158
1912	1,480,837	4,441,733	2,883,424	12,366,361
1913	1,768,365	3,759,048	3,066,297	15,706,479

NOTE: These data are presented graphically in Figure 2.3b.

Table 2.2
Average Installed Spindlage per Firm, by Type of Firm

Year	Other	Bank-Connected, Non-Limited	Limited, Non-Traded	Actively Traded
1878	3,369			
1888	3,198	4,782	6,085	
1891	4,010	6,230	7,535	
1893	4,406	4,839	3,843	59,928
1895	3,595	5,616	9,199	36,524
1896	4,284	5,408	7,762	39,546
1912	3,147	5,932	10,814	38,721
1913	3,599	5,945	10,370	38,841

NOTE: These data are presented graphically in Figure 2.4.

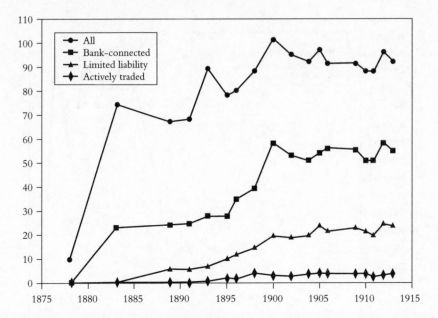

Figure 2.2. Number of Firms, by Type

exchange. Only four companies, which collectively owned sixteen mills, actively traded in Mexico City. Third, the vast majority of joint stock companies also enjoyed bank relationships; in fact, as we noted previously, part of the reason for establishing a joint stock company was to facilitate access to bank capital.

Figure 2.2 indicates the relative number of various types of firm: bank-connected firms, limited-liability firms, publicly traded joint stock companies, and other firms. The number of mills belonging to companies or individual owners with a bank relationship underwent two significant growth spurts: one in the early 1880s, after the emergence of organized banking under the early Commerce Code, and the other between 1896 and 1900, during the wave of bank start-ups engendered by the enactment of the General Banking Act of 1897.[13] The growth in limited-liability companies is smoother, but plateaus in 1900 along with the number of firms enjoying close bank relationships.

The data on average real output by value also show clear patterns. Traded firms start out hugely larger than their competitors, by an order of magnitude, and stay big. Limited-liability firms (all of which save one are either

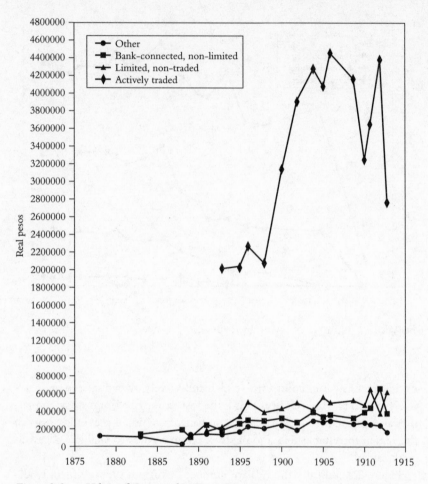

Figure 2.3a. Value of Output, by Firm Category

partly owned by a bank or have an interlocking directorate with one) and partnerships or proprietorships enjoying a bank relationship grow faster than other companies, from a similar starting point, and the limited-liability companies seem to have a slight advantage over firms organized in other ways (see Figure 2.3a).[14] Measuring output in meters shows similar results, although the output of the limited-liability companies appears to stagnate after 1896 (see Figure 2.3b).

Our capacity measure, installed spindlage, behaves similarly (see Figure 2.4). The four traded companies start out big and stay big. The size of

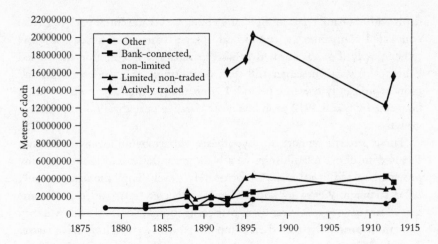

Figure 2.3b.   Output in Meters

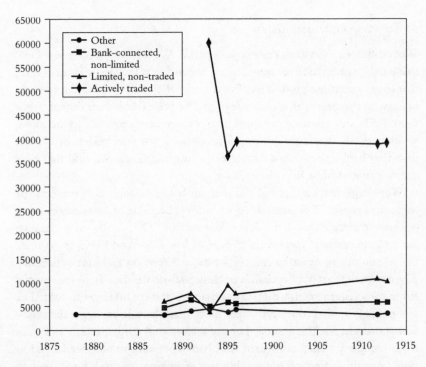

Figure 2.4.   Average Spindlage per Firm, by Firm Category

firms without bank relationships barely budges over the entire period. Bank-connected companies are significantly bigger than other firms, but grow rather slowly if at all. Limited-liability companies, discounting the traded behemoths, start out larger still than partnerships or proprietorships, and grow significantly over the period. Unfortunately, the lack of observations between 1896 and 1912 prohibits more detailed periodization of spindlage growth.

These patterns support our hypothesis, but are by no means conclusive. Firms with direct relationships to a bank grew faster, and limited liability provided an additional kick. Unfortunately, "eyeballing" the data can only tell us so much. We do not know if bank-connected firms gained a one-time size advantage or grew faster than their competitors. Nor do we know if they were more productive than their competitors, which could have driven faster growth. Therefore, we used panel data techniques to test whether bank-connected firms enjoyed higher productivity or grew faster.

Multivariate Regression Results

What difference did bank connections make? We test five hypotheses. First, that bank-connected firms were bigger. Second, that they grew faster. Third, that they were more productive. Fourth, that they employed different technology, to the degree that technology can be proxied by their capital/labor ratio. Fifth, that causality ran from firm characteristics to bank connections; in other words, that faster growing firms chose to associate with banks, rather than that bank connections caused firms to grow faster. We find that only the first two of these hypotheses hold.

Were bank firms larger and did they grow faster? Table 2.3a presents the regression results. The natural log of output, by value at 1900 prices using our textile price index, is the dependent variable. Our explanatory variables are time, geographic location, and type of firm. We used FGLS to estimate the regressions in order to control for autocorrelation and heteroskedasity. The results support our "eyeball" conclusions from the data. Bank-connected firms grew faster (roughly 50 percent faster), but were no larger to start. The few publicly traded companies were more than three times larger than their competitors at their founding, but grew no faster. Organization as a joint stock company (when combined with bank connection) produced an additional marginal effect on output, but our regression results did not allow us to determine whether this was a one-time-only or dynamic advantage.

These results hold when we measure growth in meters rather than by

Table 2.3a

Output Growth Regression Results

Dependent variable = value of output in 1900 pesos
Obs 1488
N 178

	Spec 1	Spec 2	Spec 3	Spec 4	Spec 5	Spec 6	Spec 7	Spec 8
Adj. R-square	0.10	0.14	0.32	0.32	0.32	0.32	0.32	0.32
Constant	10.71	10.41	10.48	10.56	10.50	10.48	10.56	10.58
t-stat	(111.1)	(80.96)	(91.89)	(86.53)	(90.84)	(91.64)	(92.16)	(92.46)
Time	0.05	0.05	0.04	0.03	0.04	0.04	0.03	0.03
t-stat	(20.36)	(20.19)	(15.94)	(10.49)	(14.48)	(15.75)	(12.34)	(11.96)
Border		0.05	0.00	0.00	−0.01	0.00	0.00	0.00
t-stat		(0.22)	(−0.02)	(−0.01)	(−0.04)	(−0.03)	(−0.01)	(0.01)
Central		0.55	0.53	0.53	0.53	0.53	0.53	0.53
t-stat		(3.80)	(4.19)	(4.20)	(4.17)	(4.19)	(4.20)	(4.17)
Bank			0.18	0.00	0.19	0.18		
t-stat			(3.23)	(−0.03)	(3.32)	(3.23)		
Bank*time				0.01			0.01	0.01
t-stat				(1.80)			(3.72)	(3.68)
Limited			0.27	0.25	0.05	0.27	0.25	
t-stat			(3.26)	(2.90)	(0.26)	(3.27)	(2.90)	
Limited*time					0.01			0.01
t-stat					(1.21)			(2.85)
Traded			1.77	1.76	1.76	1.56	1.76	1.77
t-stat			(9.86)	(9.83)	(9.83)	(3.22)	(9.83)	(9.98)
Traded*time						0.01		
t-stat						(0.47)		

Table 2.3b
Output Growth Regression Results

Dependent variable = meters of cloth
Obs 750
N 158

	Spec 1	Spec 2	Spec 3	Spec 4	Spec 5	Spec 6	Spec 7	Spec 8	Spec 9
Adj. R-square	0.06	0.17	0.24	0.25	0.24	0.25	0.26	0.26	0.26
Constant	13.20	12.71	12.78	12.89	12.77	12.76	12.83	12.84	12.84
t-stat	(129.4)	(89.14)	(96.36)	(95.27)	(96.03)	(96.00)	(97.09)	(97.22)	(97.37)
Time	0.02	0.02	0.02	0.01	0.02	0.02	0.01	0.01	0.01
t-stat	(9.20)	(8.98)	(5.60)	(2.33)	(5.42)	(5.89)	(3.03)	(2.98)	(3.06)
Border		0.14	0.07	0.05	0.07	0.07	0.05	0.05	0.07
t-stat		(0.54)	(0.28)	(0.19)	(0.29)	(0.28)	(0.20)	(0.21)	(0.28)
Central		0.95	0.92	0.91	0.92	0.92	0.91	0.91	0.90
t-stat		(5.54)	(5.80)	(5.79)	(5.81)	(5.80)	(5.79)	(5.77)	(5.75)
Bank			0.14	−0.19	0.14	0.14			
t-stat			(1.76)	(−1.54)	(1.73)	(1.75)			
Bank*time				0.02			0.01	0.01	0.01
t-stat				(3.46)			(3.83)	(3.83)	(4.28)
Limited			0.19	0.11	0.27	0.19	0.10		
t-stat			(1.46)	(0.86)	(1.05)	(1.50)	(0.78)		
Limited*time					0.00			0.00	
t-stat					(−0.38)			(0.59)	
Traded			0.91	0.81	0.93	2.64	2.78	2.86	2.85
t-stat			(3.94)	(3.50)	(3.92)	(3.92)	(4.16)	(4.30)	(4.30)
Traded*time						−0.06	−0.07	−0.07	−0.07
t-stat						(−2.74)	(−3.07)	(−3.14)	(−3.08)

Table 2.4

Spindlage Growth Regressions

Dependent variable = installed spindlage

Obs	640						
N	156						
Adj. R-square	0.08	0.15	0.28	0.28	0.29	0.28	0.28

	Spec 1	Spec 2	Spec 3	Spec 4	Spec 5	Spec 6	Spec 7
Constant	7.45	7.18	7.18	7.22	7.23	7.18	7.25
t-stat	(87.31)	(58.12)	(64.14)	(63.61)	(64.84)	(63.99)	(64.95)
Time	0.02	0.02	0.01	0.01	0.01	0.01	0.073
t-stat	(10.79)	(10.39)	(5.18)	(3.32)	(3.63)	(5.13)	(2.99)
Border		0.10	0.01	0.01	0.01	0.01	0.01
t-stat		(0.43)	(0.06)	(0.07)	(0.03)	(0.06)	(0.03)
Central		0.52	0.62	0.62	0.61	0.62	0.61
t-stat		(3.49)	(4.51)	(4.54)	(4.53)	(4.50)	(4.52)
Bank			0.17	0.03	0.20	0.17	
t-stat			(2.82)	(0.31)	(3.34)	(2.82)	
Bank*time				0.01			0.01
t-stat				(1.68)			(2.79)
Limited			0.35	0.33	−0.20	0.35	
t-stat			(3.95)	(3.76)	(−1.13)	(3.95)	
Limited*time					0.02		0.01
t-stat					(3.54)		(4.62)
Traded			0.52	0.49	0.42	0.44	0.41
t-stat			(3.33)	(3.10)	(2.70)	(1.01)	(2.62)
Traded*time						0.00	
t-stat						(0.19)	

value, presented in Table 2.3b. Bank-connected firms grew by approximately 2 percent per year, while independent firms remained stagnant. The large traded companies, as before, enjoyed a huge one-time advantage, but then *shrank* in size. We then reran the above regression using installed spindlage as the dependent variable, as a measure of capacity (see Table 2.4). Overall, the results paralleled our results in Tables 2.3a and 2.3b, save for one difference: when spindlage is used as the dependent variable, it becomes clear that organization as a joint stock company provided a marginal increase in the firm's growth rate, and not simply a one-time spurt. This advantage only applied to firms also connected to banks, and was not related to whether the

firm was publicly traded. In fact, the marginal effect on future growth from
being publicly traded was zero—the big conglomerates were simply born
bigger. It was organization as a joint stock company and connection to a
bank that provided a dynamic effect: these companies grew by more than 3
percent per year in terms of installed spindlage, three times as fast as their
competitors.

These results are entirely consistent with anecdotal evidence on bank behavior and our predictions about the advantages of limited liability and the
function of banks. The directors of partnerships and proprietorships received
personal loans from their bank to start their companies, giving them access
to a source of capital denied their independent competitors. These loans,
however, were secured only by the firm directors' personal reputation. If the
directors wanted to return to their "house bank" for more long-term capital—as opposed to short-term financing of stocks and inventories—they
needed to offer collateral, and the best way to do that, given the constraints
of an inefficient legal system and poor property registers, was to organize as
a joint stock company and pledge shares as collateral when new loans were
needed. This explains why the dynamic effect for these companies shows up
most strongly in installed spindlage.

Did these size and growth differences translate into differences in total
factor productivity (TFP)? We used generalized least squares to estimate the
coefficients. Table 2.5 shows various specifications of the relationship, using
the natural log of the value of output per worker as the dependent variable.
The results are clear: regardless of the specification we used, we could find
no significant difference in TFP between bank-connected and independent
firms. When meters of cloth is used instead of value as the output measure,
limited-liability companies show 20 percent *lower* TFP than their competitors (Specification 4 of Table 2.6). The four publicly traded firms enjoyed a
one-time productivity advantage at the time of their incorporation—a surprising result, since the coefficients indicate little or no economies of scale
in the industry—but that advantage was dissipated over time. The only significant effect is a regional one: firms located in and around Mexico City
were roughly 25 percent more productive.

Were there any technical differences between the different types of firms?
One would imagine that bank-connected firms would face a lower cost of
capital than their competitors, and therefore should have had a higher capi-
tal/labor ratio. Table 2.7 shows that there were no significant differences in
capital intensity between the various firm types. Firms located in central
Mexico or along the United States border generally employed more spindles

Table 2.5

Productivity Growth Regressions

Dependent variable = value of output in 1900 pesos

Obs	492					
N	139					
Adj. R-square	0.35	0.37	0.37	0.37	0.36	0.36

	Spec 1	*Spec 2*	*Spec 3*	*Spec 4*	*Spec 5*	*Spec 6*
Constant	3.82	3.93	4.06	3.91	4.12	4.14
t–stat	(11.38)	(11.99)	(11.89)	(11.30)	(11.91)	11.40
Ln(K/L ratio)	0.65	0.61	0.60	0.61	0.59	0.59
t–stat	(10.08)	(9.38)	(9.13)	(9.29)	(8.98)	8.84
Ln(Workers)	0.07	0.05	0.03	0.05	0.02	.02
t–stat	(1.59)	(1.18)	(0.64)	(1.17)	(0.52)	0.34
Time	0.03	0.03	0.03	0.03	0.03	0.03
t–stat	(9.71)	(9.63)	(8.83)	(9.41)	(9.52)	(8.91)
Border		−0.04	−0.06	−0.04	−0.04	−0.02
t–stat		(−0.29)	(−0.41)	(−0.25)	(−0.26)	(−0.13)
Central		0.24	0.25	0.24	0.24	0.23
t–stat		(2.46)	(2.55)	(2.41)	(2.44)	(2.28)
Bank			0.10			0.12
t–stat			(1.33)			(1.55)
Limited				−0.02		−0.14
t–stat				(−0.19)		(−1.25)
Traded					0.39	1.06
t–stat					(1.76)	(1.70)
Traded*time						−0.02
t–stat						(−1.80)

per worker, but this was unrelated to their type of organization or access to bank credit. In other words, there is no evidence for significant technological differences for bank-related firms during the period.

Which way did causality run? Did firms grow large because they were connected to banks, or did banks simply choose larger, faster growing firms to associate with? That is to say, did banks pick insiders or did banks pick winners? The historical evidence suggests the former. Most of the banks involved in the industry were created by textile entrepreneurs, Banamex being the only significant exception. The 1893 textile census provides the information to test this hypothesis more rigorously. The census contained data

Table 2.6
Productivity Growth Regressions

Dependent variable = meters of cloth produced

Obs	579				
N	145				
Adj. R-square	0.19	0.25	0.25	0.25	0.25

	Spec 1	Spec 2	Spec 3	Spec 4	Spec 5
Constant	7.19	7.29	7.25	7.10	7.33
t-stat	(23.79)	(24.38)	(0.31)	(22.79)	(23.68)
Ln(K/L ratio)	0.46	0.42	0.43	0.44	0.42
t-stat	(8.77)	(8.10)	(8.12)	(8.36)	(7.95)
Ln(Workers)	0.02	−0.01	−0.01	0.01	−0.02
t-stat	(0.44)	(−0.32)	(−0.13)	(0.31)	(−0.42)
Time	0.01	0.01	0.01	0.01	0.01
t-stat	(3.01)	(3.01)	(3.01)	(3.46)	(2.93)
Border		−0.07	−0.06	−0.02	−0.07
t-stat		(−0.45)	(−0.41)	(−0.11)	(−0.45)
Central		0.35	0.35	0.32	0.35
t-stat		(3.29)	(3.23)	(2.92)	(3.28)
Bank			−0.05		
t-stat			(−0.70)		
Limited				−0.21	
t-stat				(−2.13)	
Traded					0.08
t-stat					(0.45)

on the prices that firms faced for labor, fuel, and raw materials, as well as information on their output and inputs of labor and capital. Therefore, we ran a series of logit regressions to test whether bank association can be predicted by differences in technology, age, profitability (defined by the operating margin), or size.

The results are unambiguous (see Table 2.8). Bank-connected firms in 1893 did not earn higher profits, use more capital-intensive technology, or enjoy higher labor productivity than their competitors. Banks did not pick more profitable, faster growing firms to associate with. Rather, banks allocated credit to insiders, whose firms could then grow faster.

What was the causal mechanism that allowed bank-connected firms to grow faster? We hypothesize that firms not connected to banks could only grow as fast as they could plow back profits from previous production cycles.

Table 2.7

Capital Intensity Differences Between Firm Types

Dependent variable = spindles/worker
Obs   632
N   155

Adj. R-square	0.04	0.09	0.09	0.09	0.09
	Spec 1	*Spec 2*	*Spec 3*	*Spec 4*	*Spec 5*
Constant	2.84	2.64	2.64	2.64	2.65
t-stat	(48.65)	(32.82)	(32.80)	(32.89)	(32.73)
Time	0.004	0.003	0.004	0.00	0.00
t-stat	(2.25)	(1.86)	(2.03)	(1.49)	(1.58)
Border		0.26	0.27	0.25	0.26
t-stat		(1.86)	(1.91)	(1.74)	(1.86)
Central		0.35	0.35	0.35	0.34
t-stat		(3.62)	(3.59)	(3.67)	(3.57)
Bank			−0.05		
t-stat			(−0.85)		
Limited				0.06	
t-stat				(0.71)	
Traded					0.16
t-stat					(1.08)

Bank-connected firms did not face this constraint. We used the same detailed 1893 census data to test this hypothesis, by testing whether liquidity constraints—proxied as lower operating margins—directly affected firm growth for a cross section of sixty different enterprises.

We ran the following three specifications on cross-sectional data from the 1893 and 1895 censuses:

$$VALGROW = CONSTANT + B_1 MARGIN + B_2 BANK \cdot MARGIN$$
$$METGROW = CONSTANT + B_1 MARGIN + B_2 BANK \cdot MARGIN$$
$$SPINGROW = CONSTANT + B_1 MARGIN + B_2 BANK \cdot MARGIN$$

where VALGROW is the percentage growth between 1894 and 1895 of output in 1900 prices, METGROW the percentage growth of meters of output, and SPINGROW is the percentage increase in installed spindlage. MARGIN is the firm's operating margin (calculated as revenues − wages − fuel costs − raw cotton costs), BANK is a dummy variable for bank association, and BANK · MARGIN is a multiplicative interaction term between bank association and operating margins that we used to test if bank-associated firms

Table 2.8

Cross-Sectional Logit Specs, 1893

Dependent variable = 1 if bank-connected, 0 if otherwise

Obs.	69				
N	69				
R-square	0.051	0.075	0.079	0.059	0.087

	Spec 1	*Spec 2*	*Spec 3*	*Spec 4*	*Spec 5*
Constant	−0.929	−30.07	−29.90	−1.244	−34.01
t–stat	(0.3)	(−1.0)	(−1.0)	(0.1)	(−1.1)
Profit margin	0.854	0.835	0.847	−1.245	0.300
t–stat	(1.5)	(1.4)	(1.4)	(−1.4)	(0.4)
Date founded		0.016	0.016		0.018
t–stat		(1.0)	(1.0)		(1.1)
Ln(Spindles/worker)			−0.013	−0.023	−0.023
t–stat			(−0.4)	(−0.7)	(−0.7)
Ln(Output/worker)				0.001	0.001
t–stat				(1.0)	(1.1)

were less sensitive to their operating margins than other firms (1894 output and margins were calculated using data from the second half of 1893 and the first half of 1894 contained in the "1893" census).

The results in Table 2.9 indicate that bank relationships played a significant role in alleviating liquidity constraints. When output is measured in constant value, firms that broke even in 1893–94 grew by roughly 1 percent the subsequent year, as indicated by the constant term. The estimated coefficient of 1.03 on the MARGIN variable suggests that firms without bank relationships reinvested their entire profit margin in expansion, growing by almost exactly the amount of their margins. Bank-related firms, however, exhibited a much weaker connection between their operating margins and growth. The negative coefficient of −0.45 on the BANK · MARGIN variable indicates that bank firms reinvested only 55 percent of their operating profits in short-term expansion. The interpretation is that firms lacking bank associations were constrained in how fast they could grow. Had they not been, they would not have reinvested all their profits. Bank-related firms, however, were far less constrained, and paid out more than half their profits in dividends or loan repayments. The results for growth of output in meters parallel the results for growth in the value of output, although the statistical significance of the coefficients is substantially less. This, of course, should

Table 2.9

Liquidity Sensitivity Test Results

Dependent var:	GROWTH, 1894−95, IN		
	Value	*Meters*	*Spindlage*
Obs.	60	60	60
Adj. R–square	0.53	0.17	0.02
Constant	1.01	1.37	1.29
t–stat	(21.12)	(9.80)	(12.96)
Margin	1.03	1.45	−0.11
t–stat	(7.11)	(3.40)	(−0.38)
Bank*Margin	−0.45	−0.76	0.42
t–stat	(−2.30)	(−1.31)	(1.03)

not be surprising, given the limitations of using meters of cloth as a proxy for real output. Profits, after all, are measured in pesos, not meters of cloth.

The credit market, however, was not perfect. Had it been, one would have expected there to have been no relationship between margins and growth for bank-connected firms. In other words, the additional growth of the bank-related companies did not fully compensate for slower growth by the independent firms, leading to more concentrated industrial structure. In fact, one outcome of this financial system was a high and increasing level of concentration in the textile industry. As Table 2.10 shows, both the Herfindahl index and four-firm ratio for the industry increased as a result of the growth of the financial system.

Analysis and Conclusions

The data indicate that the advantage from bank relationships for a firm came entirely from the easing of capital constraints. It did not come from "entrepreneurial talent" being granted to the firms from the bank, better marketing, or different technology. Thus, the data also show that firms that were bank connected did not have higher total factor productivity.

Limited liability appears to have functioned as a way around ill-defined property rights and an inefficient legal system. Save a single outlier, all joint stock companies also possessed close bank relationships. These firms grew faster than other bank-connected firms, due to their ability to pledge their shares as collateral, but they were no larger at the time of incorporation,

Table 2.10

Textile Industry Market Concentration Measures

Year	Four-Firm Ratio	Herfindahl Index
1843	0.376	0.053
1850	0.449	0.069
1853	0.430	0.068
1862	0.319	0.049
1865	0.342	0.050
1878	0.160	0.021
1883	0.189	0.023
1888	0.217	0.025
1891	0.228	0.027
1893	0.284	0.036
1895	0.363	0.048
1896	0.371	0.051
1902	0.381	0.064
1906	0.338	0.049
1912	0.271	0.034

NOTE: These data are presented graphically in Figure 2.5.

which is what would have been expected had limited liability induced entrepreneurs to sink more capital into their ventures. In addition, despite a lack of legal or administrative constraints, only the four largest joint stock companies chose to list their shares on the Mexico City stock exchange, further weakening the argument that limited liability provided benefits other than the ability to borrow more from banks.[15]

Banks did not pick winners, nor were winners more likely to found banks. Relationship banking simply allowed those entrepreneurs lucky enough to obtain a bank concession to more easily finance their enterprises. Their firms grew more rapidly than their competitors. Because only some entrepreneurs could found banks, and in turn use them to finance their textile mills, Mexico had a more concentrated industrial structure than it would have had otherwise. In fact, as the data presented in Figure 2.5 show, Mexico's industrial structure became more concentrated just as the formal banking system began to develop.

One implication of our results is that Mexico would have industrialized faster with more liberal bank incorporation laws. There would have been more textile firms, since a larger number of entrepreneurs could have used

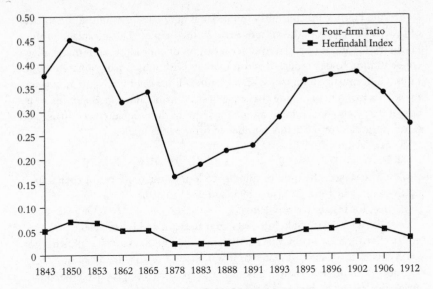

Figure 2.5.   Market Concentration Measures

the banking system to finance their expansion. In addition, bank credit would have been allocated more efficiently. Entrepreneurs with a comparative advantage in managing manufacturing concerns would have been able to obtain bank financing, rather than bank credit being constrained to those entrepreneurs who were politically well positioned so that they could obtain a bank charter. Mexico would have had a larger and less concentrated textile industry. It might also have had a more efficient textile industry.

Notes

1. It is not clear why more companies did not list their shares. The formal institutional barriers to doing so were extremely low. One hypothesis is that the firms that listed independently—as opposed to raising capital from the market by means of a chartered bank—were already large enough that the firms could "insure" themselves against idiosyncratic shocks and therefore invite the confidence of investors. In other words, listed firms were not big because they listed, they listed because they were already big, and the size advantages directly derived from the listing were smaller than they appear. See Maurer and Sharma 1999.

2. Maurer 1997: 1.

3. Binder and Brown 1991: 52.

4. The Herfindahl concentration index is defined as the sum of the squares of the market shares of the various firms in the market. The advantage of the Herfindahl index as opposed to other measures of concentration is that it allows concentration to be compared across markets with substantially different structures. Conceptually, a market with a Herfindahl index of 0.5 is just as concentrated as a market containing two equally sized firms, and a market with an index of 0.33 is as concentrated as one made up of three equally sized firms, and so on, regardless of the actual number of firms in the market.

5. See Maurer 1999.

6. Razo and Haber 1998.

7. For instance, the ratio of spindles to looms, the other major capital input, was 30:1 in 1857, 28:1 in 1893, and 28:1 in 1913.

8. See, for instance, Kane 1988.

9. See Atack 1985; Sokoloff 1984; and Bernard and Jones 1996.

10. For OLS estimates, this coefficient would be the same for all firms; for fixed effects, it was not estimated as it was allowed to vary freely among cross sections. Both models, the basic pooled and fixed effects, produced the same qualitative results with minor differences in the magnitude of the estimated coefficients. In some cases, as with the time trend, the estimates were nearly identical. Thus, to avoid repetition, we report only results from the basic pooled model.

11. We tested for both this production function and for Translog production functions but found the Cobb-Douglas production function to be a better model for our panel data set.

12. See Gerschenkron 1962; and Schumpeter 1939.

13. See Maurer 1997 for details on the timing of bank start-ups.

14. Output per firm for bank-connected firms of all types stagnates between 1905 and 1910. This is probably not coincidental. In 1905 the finance ministry actively moved to limit the further expansion of the non-national banks of issue, prohibiting further stock issues by all banks save Banamex and the Banco de Londres y México. These restrictions were eased after 1910, and several new banks (without the ability to issue banknotes, but with the right to create demand deposits) listed on the exchange in that year. Since these banks raised a great deal of their resources through equity issues, these prohibitions could not help but affect the growth of their associated firms.

15. For a more detailed explanation of investors' reluctance to purchase equity in any but the largest textile firms, see Maurer and Sharma 1999.

References

Atack, Jeremy. 1985. *Estimation of Economies of Scale in Nineteenth Century United States Manufacturing.* New York and London.

Bernard, A. B., and C. I. Jones. 1996. "Productivity Across Industries and Countries: Time Series Theory and Evidence." *The Review of Economics and Statistics*, vol. 78, no. 1: 135–46.

Binder, John, and David Brown. 1991. "Bank Rates of Return and Entry Restrictions, 1869–1914." *Journal of Economic History*, vol. 51, no. 1: 47–66.

Gerschenkron, Alexander. 1962. *Economic Backwardness in Historical Perspective.* Cambridge, Mass.

Haber, Stephen. 1997. "Financial Markets and Industrial Development: A Comparative Study of Governmental Regulation, Financial Innovation, and Industrial Structure in Brazil and Mexico, 1840–1930." In Stephen Haber, ed., *How Latin America Fell Behind: Essays on the Economic Histories of Brazil and Mexico, 1800–1914.* Stanford.

Kane, N. F. 1988. *Textiles in Transition: Technology, Wages, and Industry Relocation in the U.S. Textile Industry, 1880–1930.* Westport, Conn., and London.

Lamoreaux, Naomi. 1994. *Insider Lending: Banks, Personal Connections, and Economic Development in Industrial New England.* Cambridge, England.

Maurer, Noel. 1999. "Banks and Entrepreneurs in Porfirian Mexico: Inside Exploitation or Sound Business Strategy?" *Journal of Latin American Studies*, vol. 31: 331–61.

———. 1997. "Finance and Oligarchy: Banks, Politics, and Economic Growth in Mexico, 1876–1928." Unpublished Ph.D. dissertation, Stanford University.

Maurer, Noel, and Tridip Sharma. 1999. "Enforcing Property Rights Through Reputation: Groups in Mexico's Early Industrialization, 1878–1913." Unpublished working paper, Instituto Tecnológico Autónomo de México.

Razo, Armando, and Stephen Haber. 1998. "The Rate of Growth of Productivity in Mexico: Evidence from the Textile Industry, 1850–1933." *Journal of Latin American Studies*, vol. 30: 481–517.

Schumpeter, Joseph. 1939. *Business Cycles: A Theoretical, Historical, and Statistical Analysis of the Capitalist Process.* Vols. 1 and 2. New York.

Sokoloff, Kenneth. 1984. "Was the Transition from the Artisanal Shop to the Nonmechanized Factory Associated with Gains in Efficiency? Evidence from the U.S. Manufacturing Censuses of 1820 and 1850." *Explorations in Economic History*, vol. 21, no. 4: 351–82.

Chapter 3

The Internal Consequences of External Credibility: Banking Regulation and Banking Performance in Porfirian Mexico

NOEL MAURER

In recent years, economists have become increasingly interested in the relationship between politics and economics, producing an impressive body of theory known as the New Institutional Economics (NIE). This work, associated with Douglass North, Thráinn Eggertsson, and Oliver Williamson, has progressed to the point where we can begin to make a priori predictions about the economic effects of particular institutional arrangements. One of the tasks of economic history is to provide empirical evidence in order to test and refine the theory behind the NIE, since history is the only laboratory we have in order to test hypotheses about which institutions are vital for economic growth, and which are merely peripheral.

Banking is one excellent place to test institutional theory, because the financial industry is notoriously sensitive to regulation. Banking in Porfirian Mexico (1876–1911) provides a particularly interesting laboratory because its banking laws were written in such a way as to favor a select group of politically connected insiders associated with the Banco Nacional de México, or Banamex. Banamex towered above the nation's other banks, never controlling less than one-third of the total assets of the banking system, and enjoyed a number of special privileges ostensibly designed to encourage it to carry out the functions of a lender of last resort and act as primary creditor to the federal government. The smaller banks (forty-two by 1910) were tightly regulated by federal authorities in the name of preserving financial stability.

The previous chapter addressed the impact of this financial system on the real economy. This chapter addresses the impact of this financial system on the efficiency of the financial system itself. It poses the following question: did the privileges awarded Banamex produce an inefficient financial system that allowed Banamex to earn monopoly rents?

This chapter argues that Banamex carried out no discernible central banking functions in return for its privileges, despite contemporary claims. In addition, Banamex's owners benefited from their special position, to the detriment of the overall efficiency of the banking system. The cost, in foregone investment, was substantial for the Mexican economy. Inasmuch as Banamex's privileges were the result of the dictatorial nature of Porfirian politics, dictatorship was not good for economic growth. In short, Mexico's political economy gave rise to formal institutions that discouraged competition. Reduced levels of competition, in turn, resulted in an inefficient banking system and monopoly rents for the largest firms in the industry.

The first section briefly outlines the structure of Mexican banking regulation during the period and discusses contemporary perspectives on Banamex's role in the financial system, noting that the authors of Mexico's banking policies were well aware that they reduced competition, but justified that by claiming that Banamex (and the Banco de Londres) carried out central banking functions.[1] It then analyzes these claims, concluding that Banamex was not a central bank in the nineteenth-century conception. The second section briefly examines several measures of banking profits, demonstrating that Banamex earned far steadier returns and faced lower risks than its competitors, and the third section presents econometric evidence of monopolistic behavior by the bank. The chapter concludes with a brief counterfactual exercise that attempts to estimate the cost of Banamex and the banking regulation that supported it for Mexico's economy during the period.

Banamex and Mexican Bank Regulation

Banamex was born in 1884 in a federally sponsored merger of the Banco Nacional Mexicano and Banco Mercantil Mexicano. The merger was prompted by a financial crisis caused by a wave of uncertainty over whether the federal government would actually be able to pay all the railroad subsidy certificates it had issued over the previous four years. Banamex was created to rescue the Banco de Montepío, which had invested highly in subsidy certificates and illiquid mortgage loans. The new bank was to act as a source of emergency liquidity for the rest of the banking system from that time onward and provide a secure source of short-term credit for the federal government. In return, it would receive a monopoly over the issuance of banknotes and become the official banking agent and underwriter for the federal government. This meant that all federal receipts and payments would pass through its coffers, giving it a relatively secure source of liquidity. In short, this situation did not appear all that different from the agreements that birthed the Bank of England in 1694 or other European central banks in the eighteenth and nineteenth centuries.

Banamex never received the promised monopoly over note issue. Politically important elites associated with the Banco de Londres y México—including a future finance minister, José Yves Limantour—brought legal suit against Banamex. The resulting political compromises preserved many of Banamex's privileges, but also extended them to the Banco de Londres. Only these two national banks could branch across state lines or issue new stock on the Mexico City exchange without the express permission of the finance minister. Both banks also faced easier specie reserve requirements against their note issues and demand deposits (33 percent versus 50 percent for their competitors), and Banamex enjoyed the additional advantages associated with being the federal government's official banking agent. These laws took their final form in 1897, when the national banks' privileges were enshrined in law, and entry into banking was rigidly restricted. The General Banking Act of 1897 also imposed a prohibitive tax on the note issues of any banks to begin operations in a state after the establishment of a locally based bank of issue. Existing state-level banks were grandfathered in under the law and Secretary Limantour occasionally allowed the state-level banks to branch outside their charter territories. Nevertheless, the end result was a series of local oligopolies consisting of the state bank(s) and the branches of the two national banks.

The authors of the General Banking Act were well aware that the law would entrench a concentrated financial structure. Finance Secretary José Limantour wrote, "The new law will no doubt give birth, at least in the early years of its operation, to a sort of banking oligarchy."[2] He justified this, however, by claiming that Banamex and the Banco de Londres would come to fill an indispensable public role: "There can be no doubt that . . . [Banamex and the Banco de Londres] will develop into banks of rediscount, and, by that very fact, become the true protectors of the local banks, with which they neither should nor can come into conflict."[3] In other words, Banamex would reclaim the role as lender of last resort that had been originally foreseen for it in 1884.

These expectations were not entirely specious. Charles Goodhart has advanced the hypothesis that central banking institutions are not the exogenous creations of national governments, but are endogenous products of sufficiently sophisticated financial systems. One bank or similar institution, usually the largest in the system, will begin to play the role of a "banker's bank," providing financial services to other banks. If a single bank has a monopoly over banknote issue, this process will be expedited, as the other banks begin to use its notes as reserves, but Goodhart does not consider it central. Eventually, the other banks will become the quasi-central bank's primary clients, and in this way the nascent central bank will internalize the overall health and solvency of the banking system and begin to act as a classical nineteenth-century central bank in the Bagehotian tradition. The Bank of England, the Banque de France, Banca d'Italia, and Commonwealth Bank of Australia all began in such a fashion.[4] Work by Gary Gorton on the role of American clearinghouses before the Federal Reserve Act of 1913 supports Goodhart's hypothesis, even in a case where no single bank enjoyed a monopoly over note issue or the banking business of the central government.[5]

Therefore, modern economists have provided some support for Limantour's belief that the national banks would eventually become "banks of rediscount," playing an indispensable public role as lenders of last resort. In fact, Limantour later claimed that Banamex played exactly such a role. In the aftermath of the Crisis of 1907−8 he wrote that "under the present trying conditions [Banamex] has rendered vital service to the commercial and industrial interests of the nation . . . thus giving another proof of its great usefulness to the community."[6] Limantour was not alone in this assessment. Charles Conant, in a report to the U.S. National Monetary Commission, wrote that Banamex exercised "the functions of a central bank."[7]

Were contemporary claims correct? Did the Goodhart hypothesis apply to Porfirian Mexico? Did Banamex carry out central banking functions? The rest of this section addresses this question.

THE FUNCTIONS OF A CENTRAL BANK

In the late nineteenth century, a central bank operating under a specie standard served two basic functions. The first was to establish and maintain a uniform national currency. The second was to ensure a stable banking system and prevent financial panics.

Maintaining a uniform national currency, or, in the words of Porfirian officials, "amply and securely systematizing the fiduciary currency,"[8] appears to be an odd job under a specie standard. After all, the Mexican federal government specified that a peso was equal to a silver disk of a specific size, with a specific silver content and a specific design. That was Mexico's currency, and Mexicans accepted it in payment throughout the national territory. What then did "systematizing the fiduciary currency" mean?

Essentially, it meant ensuring that all the other instruments that functioned as money maintained a fixed value against the silver peso. The banknotes issued by Mexican banks during this period functioned as money inasmuch as they were exchanged in payment for goods and services, but they were not legal tender. Rather, they were instruments issued by banks and accepted voluntarily by the public, which the banks promised to redeem for legal tender upon demand. Since banknotes were only redeemable for silver at the branch of issue, they circulated at a discount outside the immediate area. The same problems applied to checks. In effect, Porfirian Mexico had several different currencies linked by a fluctuating exchange rate. A central bank, then, would have the responsibility of ensuring that all banknotes and checks denominated in pesos be exchangeable for silver at a 1:1 rate across Mexico.

A monopoly over note issue would obviously make this much easier, but it is possible under multiple banks of issue. For example, the Second Bank of the United States (BUS) created a national monetary union for a time by instituting policies that ensured that banknotes could circulate far from their place of origin without a discount. In fact, the creation of a "national currency" that would be everywhere exchangeable for specie at a fixed rate was one of the primary reasons why Congress chartered the BUS in 1816.[9]

This brings us to the second mission of a central bank: stabilizing the banking system. An imprudent or unlucky bank might at some point prove unable to redeem its banknotes or pay checks drawn upon it. The public could then easily mistake an isolated failure for a general problem and rush to withdraw its deposits and redeem its banknotes. Sufficiently large withdrawals and redemptions would cause even healthy banks to close their doors and bring the banking system to a standstill, with an immensely negative effect on the economy. However, if one large bank acts contrary to its own short-term interest and lends like mad, boldly supplying credit to the other, troubled banks, then the panic may end. "Once the mob sees that there is money to be had, it may cease to be a mob."[10]

A central bank, acting as a "lender of last resort," can prevent such general crises by making its own specie reserves available to the commercial banks by exchanging them for the commercial banks' illiquid assets. In effect, the commercial banks would sell some of their loans and discounts to the central bank at less than their face value in exchange for legal tender that could then be used to reassure or pay off depositors and note holders. A central bank could also aid the other banks by deliberately holding their banknotes in its vaults, not redeeming them until after the crisis is over, in effect making the other banks an interest-free loan for the duration.

In addition, central banks should contract their own note issues in good times in order to maintain their ability to control the rest of the banking system and ensure that the other banks follow prudent policies. Since the central bank's greatest tool in this respect is the ability to turn in large amounts of the banknotes of an imprudent bank, the central bank must work to maintain itself as a net creditor and limit its own note issues. Otherwise the offending bank could simply exchange central bank notes for its own notes and neutralize the central bank's attempts to police it.

BANAMEX AS A CENTRAL BANK

Banamex was certainly well placed to assume central banking functions. A large chunk of its liquid reserves was made up of federal government funds in transit, an extremely low risk liability. Balanced budgets after 1894 meant steady or growing government reserves, much of which went into Banamex's vaults. In addition, Banamex's ability to branch nationally meant that it could grow larger and better diversify its operations than any of its competitors (except the Banco de Londres) and that its notes would remain in circulation longer.

Banamex's minutes and reports indicate that its owners and managers believed themselves entrusted with ensuring the smooth operation of the financial system. For example, in 1901, Banamex directors stated that during the previous year, acting in the bank's "role as the premier credit institution in the Republic," they combined "prudent and liberal" measures to combat the "violent" growth of business activity, raising interest rates to 10 percent. But Banamex directors also wrote, contradictorily, that they closed none of their "*cajas de comercio*, rather amplifying their resources," and they granted "extensions [on loans] to those who have asked for them under good conditions."[11]

The next year Banamex directors wrote, "Our industries, and even trade in general, suffered the crisis in the last half of the year . . . the bad cereal harvest of 1900, whose effects were felt in 1901, aggravated the situation, prolonging the restriction of popular consumption, particularly of cotton textiles, to the point where many factories had to suspend operations. The situation was delicate for the Bank, *because it had to alleviate the crisis . . .*" (emphasis added). However, they went on to say: ". . . without abandoning the prudent rules that always govern its conduct. So it proceeded to keep the interest rate as low as possible, but procuring enough time to call in previously granted credits and assure those that have been renewed."[12] In other words, it kept rates low, but restricted credit to favored customers. This is credit rationing, a potentially sound policy for a commercial bank, but it does little to provide liquidity to a credit-starved market.

Another example of the bank's pretensions to the status of central bank can be found in the bank's 1908 report, after the Panic of 1907 in the United States caused tumult in Mexican money markets. It read,

> Even though [the situation] seemed to indicate that we strengthen our specie reserves and reduce our operations, we have not wanted to do this . . . for fear of aggravating the situation and producing a true crisis . . . we have continued making [credits]. . . . Thanks to the efforts we undertook . . . we can say today with satisfaction that the Yucatecan crisis has been overcome, that business in that important part of our national territory has returned to normal, and we hope that in the course of this year will continue in its accustomed development.[13]

Banamex's words simply do not provide enough information to judge the claim that it was a central bank. We must turn to its deeds. To properly judge them, we must define the proper role of a central bank under a specie standard and plurality of note issue. First, to have a credible claim to the central bank title, Banamex would have had to have encouraged the circulation of its notes at par far from their place of issue. Second, the bank should have attempted, as much as possible, to control the note issues of the local banks by holding more claims against the local banks than the local banks held against it and by using its holdings of banknotes to discipline the state banks. Third, Banamex should have acted to supply liquidity to the banking system in times of crisis, implying that its specie reserve ratios should have moved in reverse from the rest of the system.[14]

ENCOURAGING A NATIONAL CURRENCY

For the first decade of its existence, Banamex did nothing to encourage the circulation of its notes at par. For example, in 1891 the bank published a list of the discounts (see Table 3.1) the head office in Mexico City charged against the note issues of its branches.

This is in marked contrast to the policy followed by the Second Bank of the United States (BUS). From 1816 to 1836, the BUS guaranteed the acceptance of the notes of its branches at par throughout the United States.[15] Banamex, on the other hand, undertook no such policy until 1894, ten years after its creation, when the bank's board finally unified the exchange rate between its branches' various note issues. This was not, however, an ironclad guarantee: the bank reserved the right to suspend payments when "excessive amounts" were presented.[16] This right was indeed exercised: in 1905 merchants complained that the Mazatlán branch manager had refused to exchange Banamex notes for silver pesos. A letter from the manager to the head office explained that the public had presented huge quantities of notes

Table 3.1

Banamex Note Discounts

Chihuahua	0.75%
Durango	1.00%
Guadalajara	0.75%
Guanajuato	0.50%
Mazatlán	2.00%
Mérida	1.00%
Monterrey	0.75%
Oaxaca	2.00%
Puebla	0.25%
San Luis Potosí	0.50%
Veracruz	par
Zacatecas	0.50%

SOURCE: AHBNM 1891, *Actas de consejo*, vol. 4, December 1.

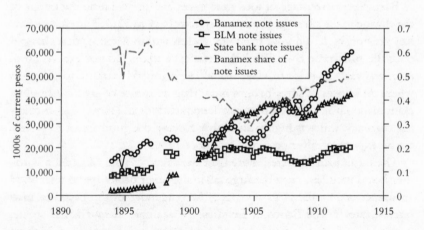

Figure 3.1. Banknote Circulation

for redemption, and he simply acted to defend his specie reserves. The head office replied to the complainants that the manager was required only to change notes issued at that branch, and had acted correctly.[17]

Despite this less-than-ironclad commitment to maintaining a national circulation at par, the percentage of total note circulation accounted for by Banamex notes rose after 1906, as shown in Figure 3.1. This was due to three factors that caused the local banks to basically cease issuing new notes after that year. The first was a change in the federal government's attitude. The second was the increasing use of checks. The third was the contraction prompted by a change in the silver/gold mint ratio to reflect the ratio in international markets.

The change in the federal government's attitude first became evident in 1905, when Congress banned the chartering of new banks of issue. Limantour then jawboned the local banks into restricting their circulation. In 1906 he further pressured them to limit their new issues to changes in their specie reserves.[18] When several banks requested permission to issue new stock, Limantour vituperatively denied their petitions, accusing them of seeking to defraud their current shareholders.[19]

Check clearing became much easier after 1899. By 1906, the volume of checks cleared through the Centro de Liquidaciones each *month* totaled roughly 20 percent of the total assets in the banking system. The annual turnover of checks reached 5 percent of GDP.[20] Mexican observers noted the rise and correctly predicted that banknotes would become increasingly less important.[21]

Banamex's percentage of total note issues also grew due to the effects of the change in the silver/gold mint ratio from 16:1 to 32:1.[22] Gresham's Law had previously driven gold from circulation within Mexico: that changed once the mint ratio rose. What the reform's authors did not expect, however, was that the price of silver would rise on world markets, to the point where 32 ounces of silver bought more than an ounce of gold. Since silver coins made up all of Mexico's small denominations and most of its circulating currency, this was highly disruptive, forcing the government to place a tax on exports of silver pesos in December 1906.[23]

The other banks suffered more than Banamex.[24] Pablo Macedo, a Banamex board member, cited the large fall in the other banks' specie reserves in an unsuccessful attempt to convince the remainder of the board to raise interest rates.[25] The Banco de Londres, for example, hemorrhaged specie, prompting a decline in its note circulation. Banamex's reserves, unlike those of the other banks, changed little. After the crisis passed, Banamex took advantage of the subsequent boom to increase its note issues, blatantly contravening a November 1905 agreement with the finance ministry to limit its note issues to the amount of specie in its vaults.[26] For this it received no sanctions.

Banamex, therefore, increased its share of national note circulation after 1906. But this says little about Banamex's pretensions to be a central bank, since a commercially oriented bank would have also expanded its note issues under the circumstances. Banamex expanded its issues during the boom from 1905 to 1907, at a time when federal policies limited the other banks from following suit, and again when recovery from the effects of the Panic of 1907 began in late 1909. During the crisis, from 1907 to 1909, its note issues were stagnant.

CONTROLLING THE STATE BANKS

Banamex's books record several credits made to the local banks, but contain no indication of loans made to it by other banks. Since Porfirian financial reporting standards did not require the banks to break out resources "due from other banks" or "due to other banks," there is no way to directly esti-mate Banamex's net position against the rest of the financial system. We can, however, use data published by the Secretaría de Hacienda to calculate a lower bound estimate of Banamex's net holdings of state banknotes. This can at least tell us whether Banamex attempted to keep up the ability to regu-late state bank issues through a policy like the one followed by the BUS un-der Nicholas Biddle: immediately redeeming local banknotes for specie in order to keep the value of the state banknotes close to par and increase the amount of BUS notes in circulation by issuing notes on the specie received.[27]

Banknotes never became more than a third of the state banks' total re-serves, as Figure 3.2 illustrates. This is because they could not be legally used to support deposits or the holding bank's own note issues. We cannot know how many of these notes were Banamex's, but a good lower bound estimate

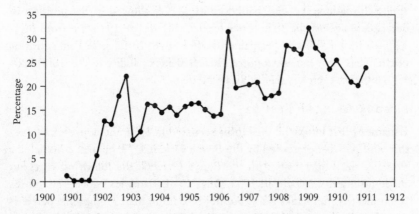

Figure 3.2.   Banknotes as a Percentage of All State Bank Liquid Reserves

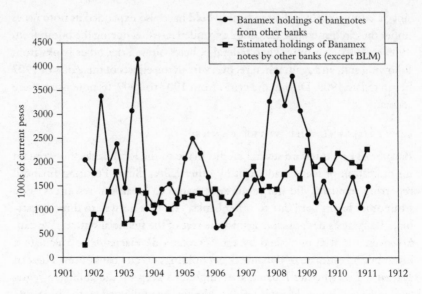

Figure 3.3.   Banknote Holdings

(presented in Figure 3.3) is that the percentage at least matched Banamex's share of total outstanding note issues. This estimate assumes, for example, that the Banco de Durango held Banco de Chiapas notes in proportion to the Banco de Chiapas's share of all note issues. This is highly improbable: Banamex notes were likely held disproportionately, especially considering that only they could be used to make federal tax payments.

Figure 3.3 provides no indication that Banamex attempted to maintain an ability to regulate the state banknote issues.[28] It allowed its net position to deteriorate against the state banks temporarily in late 1903 and from mid-1905 to mid-1907, and permanently after 1908. If the state banks disproportionately held Banamex notes, then Banamex's ability to control the local banks was even less than indicated here.

LENDER OF LAST RESORT?

Banamex's first interbank operation occurred in 1901 and consisted of a rediscount of paper presented by the Banco Oriental.[29] Banamex conducted a similarly sized operation with the Banco Oriental the following year, but made no interbank loans in 1903. After 1904, Banamex's advances and rediscounts to other banks grew, but never to more than a minuscule percentage of the bank's total portfolio, as Table 3.2 shows. Most of this business was commercial in nature, often conducted at interest rates higher than those

Table 3.2

Banamex Advances to Other Banks

Year	Bank	Amount	Loan Rate (%)	Market Rate (%)	Proportion of Port-folio (%)
1904	Banco Central	1,500,000	6.0	9.0	1.2
	International Banking Company	1,500,000	8.0	8.0	1.2
	Banco de Jalisco	400,000	8.0	8.0	0.3
	Descuento Español	400,000	8.0	8.0	0.3
	Descuento Español	200,000	7.0	8.0	0.2
	Cía. Bancaria Católica	250,000		8.0	0.2
1905	Banco Merc. de Yucatán	900,000	9.0	8.0	0.5
	Banco Yucateco	900,000	9.0	8.0	0.5
	Banco Oriental	500,000	7.0	8.0	0.3
	Banco Oriental	400,000	8.5	8.0	0.2
	Banco de Tamaulipas	300,000		8.0	0.2
	Banco de Tabasco	200,000		8.0	0.1
1906	Descuento Español	900,000	8.0	8.0	0.4
	Descuento Español	500,000		8.0	0.2
	Banco Americano[d]	400,000	8.0	8.0	0.2
	U.S. Banking Company	300,000		8.0	0.1
	Banco de Tamaulipas	200,000	8.5	8.0	0.1
	Monte de Piedad de Morelia	150,000		8.0	0.1
1907	BMCI	900,000	6.0	9.0	0.3
	Banco de Nuevo León	400,000		10.0	0.2
	Internat'l Banking Co.[b]	100,000	3.0	9.0	0.0
1908	Banco de Sonora[c]	50,000	10.0	10.0	0.0
	Banco de Michoacán[d]	370,000	0.0	10.0	0.3
	Banco de Campeche	117,000	0.0	10.0	0.1
1909	Descuento Español	950,000	6.0	9.0	0.7
	Banco Oriental	950,000	6.0	9.0	0.7
1910	None				

SOURCE: Loan dates and size from AHBNM, *Actas de consejo*. Market discount rates from *El Economista Mexicano*.

[a] AHBNM (1907), *Actas de consejo*, vol. 7, January 8. This was actually a deposit in an interest-bearing checking account.

(*continued*)

Table 3.2
(continued)

[b]This loan was part of a joint operation with the Banco de Londres and Banco Central, whereby the three banks loaned Mx $1.2 million to the Banco Americano for the purchase of a hacienda from one of Banamex's prominent shareholders, Juan Llamedo.

[c]AHBNM (1908), *Actas de consejo*, vol. 7, May 18. This loan was authorized by the bank's Mazatlán branch. Since Banamex authorized its branches to advance credits up to 50,000 pesos without the approval of the Mexico City HQ, other small advances by branches to the state banks may not be included in these figures. The Mazatlán loan only came to the head office's attention because the branch wished to increase it above the limit. The head office refused.

[d]Both this and the subsequent credit to the Banco de Campeche were not loans, per se. Rather, Banamex assumed responsibility for these troubled banks' existing note issues, in return for which they would be converted into *bancos refaccionarios*, and no new banks of issue would be permitted to take their place in those states.

prevailing in the market. It amounted to only a tiny proportion of Banamex's total lending and made up an even smaller percentage of all bank credit. Banamex extended more credit to the banks when times were good and money plentiful, before 1907, and less when times were tight. Only one operation could be said to have had a noncommercial aim: the June 1904 loan to the Banco Central at 6 percent, three points below the prevailing market rate, which provided the Banco Central with some much-needed liquidity.[30]

Banamex did not extend much credit to the rest of the banking system directly. It may, however, have rediscounted paper presented by other banks without booking them as advances to the presenting bank. Rediscounting would have caused Banamex's other assets to rise, since it would now have had the rediscounted paper on its balance sheet while causing the earning assets of the other banks to fall against their specie holdings. One would have then expected Banamex's reserve ratio—the ratio of specie plus banknotes to all other assets—to move against the rest of the banking system, and to fall during financial panics.

Banamex's specie reserve ratios, as Figure 3.4 demonstrates, did not move against the changes in the rest of the banking system. The well-documented financial crisis of 1907, caused by the failure of the Knickerbocker Trust Company in New York, is a perfect example. Banamex's specie reserves shot upward, as one would expect from a private bank during a financial crisis. The bank prohibited its branches from making loans for the entire third quarter of 1907; when they were again allowed to lend, it was at an elevated interest rate.[31] Banamex even called in most of its secured credit lines and did not reopen them until 1910.[32]

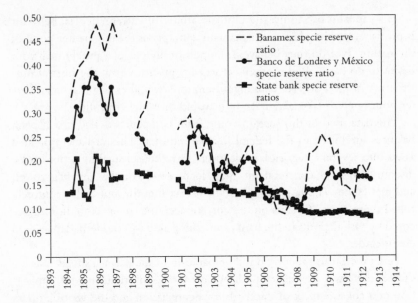

Figure 3.4. Specie Reserve Ratios

In June 1908, Banamex's board of directors debated whether the increase in the bank's cash holdings meant it should consider dropping interest rates: Hugo Scherer, a prominent board member, finally persuaded them to allow a small drop in its discount rate on commercial paper from 10 percent to 9 percent.[33] It dropped its rates again in August, to 8.5 percent,[34] and to 8 percent in November.[35] The reason for the cuts was that Banamex feared losing market share. Despite the rate cuts, its specie holdings remained elevated until mid-1910, and as Figure 3.1 shows, its note issues did not begin to rise until 1909. It was only in 1910, with the prospect of the receipts from a major foreign loan to the federal government filling its vaults, that Banamex finally began to reduce its specie reserves.[36]

In short, the claims by contemporaries that Banamex carried out central banking functions appear to have had little basis in fact. Rather, they were intended for political consumption, in order to justify the privileges Banamex enjoyed under Porfirian law.

Banking Profits

If Banamex was not a central bank, then how did its privileges affect its performance as a commercial institution? In other words, did Porfirian politics produce tangible benefits for Banamex's owners?

In a capitalist economy, the ultimate arbiter of entrepreneurial behavior is profit. Capitalists do not finance new enterprises for the greater good of the nation. Nor do they behave monopolistically out of a purely malicious desire to do harm. Rather, they act to earn profits. Given the institutional structure of the Porfirian banking system, one would expect that firms better positioned to take advantage of it would earn higher profits.

The data used in this section come from two sources. The first is bank balances submitted to the federal finance ministry. These balances divided assets into several categories: vault specie, banknotes issued by other banks, discounts, loans on collateral, mortgage loans, credits on the current account, and real estate. The law limited credits to six months, but banks routinely rolled them over. "Credits on the current account" refer to credit lines secured by cash deposits in the bank, something akin to a modern-day secured credit card.

Federal officials supervised the preparation of the balance sheets. Nevertheless, there was a tendency to delay debt write-offs, requiring the application of a consistent set of standards for depreciation and the writing down of bad debts. I added back investment amortization expenses and write-offs to derive the value of the banks' portfolios before they applied these charges. I then spread them out over the previous five years to smooth variations in bank returns.

Liability categories were paid-in capital, reserves, sight and term deposits, creditor accounts, bond issues, and banknotes in circulation.[37] There are no data on which paid interest and which did not. This did not directly affect the hypotheses tested here, but limited the questions that could be asked.

The second source of data is the end-of-month prices for the banks' outstanding securities and their dividend payments from the *Economista Mexicano* and the *Boletín Financiero y Minero*, Mexico's leading financial journals. Papers quoted both bid and ask prices for banking shares: these were averaged when the analysis required a single price for bank stock.

The first measure of profit I use is the net real return-on-assets (ROA). The net real ROA is defined as the change in a bank's real net worth plus dividend payments, over the value of all assets.[38] It regards profits as earned by firms, not individuals, and is an essentially backward-looking measure. That is to say, it is a simple measurement of how well a firm did over the course of the year. I adjusted for price level changes by revaluing assets, liabilities, and dividends in constant 1895 pesos.[39]

In certain years it was necessary to reconstruct the bank's profit-and-loss statements from information contained on the balance sheets. After operat-

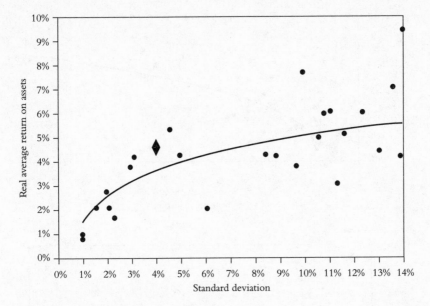

Figure 3.5. Average Return on Assets

ing and interest expenditures were deducted, profits had to be either distributed to shareholders or retained within the firm. Liability accounts on the balance sheet track both retained earnings (in various reserve funds) and dividend accounts slated for distribution to shareholders. In order to estimate income in those years when profit-and-loss statements were unavailable, changes in the reserve funds were added to dividend payments. Then the bank's depreciation expenses for office equipment and allowances for doubtful accounts were added back and the expenses from the standardized amortization and debt write-off schedules subtracted.

Figure 3.5 maps the average ROA for the banks over the 1901–10 period against the standard deviation of their returns. In other words, it compares the returns the banks earned on their asset portfolios against the ex-post risks they faced. Banamex's position is highlighted. Although Banamex appears to be on the efficient frontier, these figures indicate no particular advantage for the bank. The returns it earned on its asset portfolio roughly matched its risk.

Because banks are so highly leveraged, however, the real return-on-assets is not necessarily the correct profit measure. What interests shareholders is how much of the return-on-assets they can capture for themselves, instead of transferring them to depositors or bondholders. Therefore, a more appro-

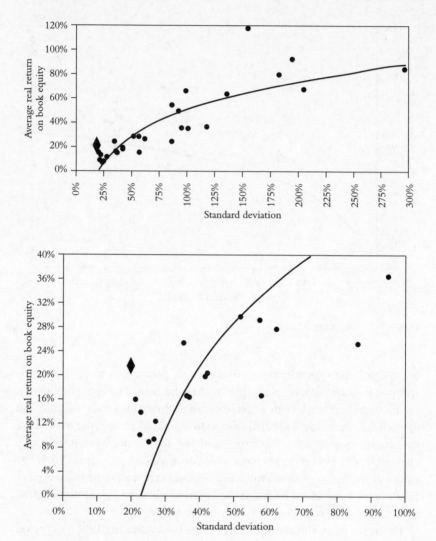

Figure 3.6. (above)   Average Return on Equity
Figure 3.7. (below)   Average Return on Equity (close-up)

priate measure is the real return-on-equity, or the change in a bank's real net worth plus dividend payments, valued in constant pesos, over the bank's real net worth at the beginning of the year.

When profits are measured in this way, Banamex clearly stands out from the pack. Figures 3.6 and 3.7 map the banks' average return on equity in the

1901–10 period against standard deviation. (Figure 3.7 is a close-up of the relevant region of Figure 3.6.) Compared to the risks it faced, Banamex earned far higher returns on its capital than any of its competitors. In fact, using the standard deviation of returns as a measure of risk, Banamex was the single least risky banking institution during the Porfiriato, yet it earned its investors higher returns than did at least eleven riskier institutions.

Nevertheless, real returns on equity are an ex-post measure of profit, and the standard deviation of the returns is an ex-post measure of risk. They tell us little about investor expectations. Did investors recognize Banamex's lower riskiness and higher profitability? One way to answer this question is to examine the yield on banking stock. The yield is the stock's dividend expressed as a percentage of its market value. What makes yields important is that they are affected by the returns on alternative investments. Arbitrage causes the yield rate to reflect the performance of all other assets into which investors could have placed their money. The stock of firms whose earnings per share tend to be consistently below average will fall until their yields match the market average. Conversely, the stock of firms whose performance is outstanding will rise.

Perceived risk and expectations about future performance will prevent yields from completely equilibrating. Persistently high yields, above those earned by relatively risk-free assets, such as government bonds, characterize stocks that investors perceived as particularly speculative. Low yields, on the other hand, reflect confidence in the stock's solidity and future performance. The difference between the yield and the return on risk-free assets indicates the risk premium demanded by investors in that firm, and not monopoly profits or economic rents, which are capitalized in the value of the firm's stock. In fact, secure monopolies should exhibit very low yields, since investors would see them as less risky than firms operating in more competitive environments.

Table 3.3 presents yields on a sample of bank stocks between 1900 and 1910. Banamex's average yield was 5.5 percent, the lowest in the sample.[40] Banamex's yield, in fact, was only 0.4 percentage points above the average returns obtained by holders of federal peso-denominated debt.[41]

Given Banamex's privileges, the low risk is not surprising. A more interesting question is whether Banamex succeeded in earning rents off its privileged position, that is, returns above those justified by the risks it faced. One way to get at an answer to this question is to estimate Tobin's q for the individual banks. Tobin's q is simply the ratio of the market value of a firm to the replacement cost of all the firm's assets.[42] Conceptually, this ratio represents the difference between the cost of capital faced by the firm and the re-

Table 3.3

Yields on Banking Common Stock (percentage)

	1901	1902	1903	1904	1905	1906	1907	1908	1909	1910	Avg.	SD
Banamex	5	5	7	5	5	5	5	5	5	4	5.5	0.7
Londres y México	7	6	6	6	5	5	6	6	5	5	5.8	0.6
Central	6	7	8	8	6	6	6	9	6	6	6.8	1.1
Internacional Hip.	8	7		8		9	5	4	6	6	6.7	1.7
Coahuila	11	9	10	9	10	8	9	9	8	7	8.9	1.1
Durango	8	8	8	8	8	7	7	7	8	8	7.6	0.6
Estado de México	8	7	7	9	7	7	7	6	6	6	6.9	0.8
Guanajuato	8	6	8	8	7	7	6	6	6	6	6.6	0.9
Hidalgo		12	8	8	9	7	7	4	6	5	7.4	2.2
Jalisco	8	9	8	9	7	7	7	7	5	6	7.5	1.4
Minero (BMC)	9	8	8	0	7	6	7	7	6	6	6.5	2.4
Monterrey	9	7	8	6	8	7	7	7	8	7	7.3	0.8

												Promedio	%
Veracruz (BMV)	9	8	7	7	8	7	7	7	7	7	6	7.4	0.9
Morelos			6	6	7	8	6	8	8	8	8	7.3	0.8
Nuevo León	10	10	9	9	8	7	7	7	7	8	7	8.3	1.2
Occidental	7	7	7	7	6	7	6	6	6	6	6	6.4	0.3
Oriental	7	7	8	8	6	6	7	7	6	6	6	6.8	0.8
Querétaro				14	11	7	7	7	11	7	7	8.8	3.2
Sonora	10	8	8	8	6	7	6	8	6	6	6	7.2	1.0
San Luis Potosí	11	12	7	10	9	8	8	8	8	7	6	8.8	1.9
Tabasco		18	8	8	10	7	8	8	5	8	8	9.7	3.8
Tamaulipas			12	16	9	8	8	8	6	7	8	9.1	3.3
Zacatecas	7	7	6	7	8	7	7	6	7	7		6.8	0.6
Michoacán			5	6	8	8	8	8	6	6		6.9	1.2
Comercial de Chihuahua								6	6	6		6.4	
Laguna				8	8	7	6	6	6	6	6	5.8	0.2

SOURCE: *Boletín Financiero y Minero.*

turns earned by the firm.[43] In theory, these two values should equilibrate, and q should be equal to one. The reason is that if q is greater than one, the firm is earning returns greater than its cost of capital. Other firms could profitably enter the market by duplicating the assets of incumbent firms, or incumbent firms could profitably expand their operations. Eventually q will fall to one. However, a firm that can bar entry through either legal provisions or the possession of a special fixed asset will earn rents in excess of its cost of capital.[44] The market value of a monopolistic firm, then, will represent the capitalized value of these rents and exceed the replacement value of its assets.

Firms operating in competitive industries can have a q ratio of greater than one if they have access to fixed assets that allow them to earn higher returns than their competitors. Three common forms of this type of special asset are geographic advantages, proprietary innovations and technology, and legal privileges. In theory, the value of these special assets should be captured in their replacement value, as listed on the firm's balance sheet. In practice, this is rarely the case. Therefore, while a value of q greater than unity indicates that a particular firm is earning some kind of rent, it does not prove that the industry is uncompetitive.[45]

Banks pose a special challenge to the use of q as a measure. Remember that q measures the difference between a firm's cost of capital and the returns to the firm from the assets it used that capital to purchase. Banks, however, have access to several sources of capital unavailable to other businesses: depositors and banknote holders. Their cost of capital, therefore, includes not only the yields demanded by stock- and bondholders, but the interest rates demanded by depositors and the discounts demanded by note holders. In essence, deposits and outstanding notes represent a form of ownership for a bank, and their value should be included in the numerator of a bank q-ratio.

Table 3.4 contains the q-ratios calculated for the banks traded on the Mexico City exchange. Most of them were very close to unity. A few possessed ratios well under one: these firms were "worth more dead than alive," since, in theory, shareholders could simply demand that the bank convert all its loans into cash, pay off all depositors and other creditors, and walk away with more money than their shares were worth.

Circumstances explain most of these cases. The Banco de Michoacán's and the Banco Campeche's q-ratios fell below one in 1909 and 1910. Both were extremely hard hit in the aftermath of the Panic of 1907 and were forced to permanently abandon their right to issue banknotes. The Banco de la Laguna (which was not allowed to issue banknotes) started up in 1908, an extremely bad year for Mexico. Its q-ratio subsequently increased. The Banco de Chiapas almost failed in 1908 and was purchased by the Banco Oriental. The only bank whose persistently low q-ratio is a mystery is the Banco Mexicano de Comercio e Industria (BMCI). The BMCI lacked the right to issue banknotes, which may explain the low valuation on its stock; what is unclear is why it stayed in business at all.

Conversely, Banamex, the Banco de Londres, and the Banco Central all enjoyed Tobin's q figures substantially greater than one, and much greater than their competitors'. Investors in these banks capitalized some kind of asset that did not appear on their balance sheets, and valued it highly. Moreover, these banks' ratios did not decrease with time.[46] Whatever the advantage was that these banks held over their competitors, it was not being eroded away. Banamex enjoyed a q-ratio that was, on average, 32 percent above that of the other banks.[47]

In short, Banamex's special privileges generated returns for its owners. The bank was not merely "first among equals": it was in a league of its own. The first section of this chapter demonstrated that Banamex served no public functions.[48] We can now see that it also earned supernormal returns. Banamex benefited directly from its special privileges, at least inasmuch as it enjoyed smoother profits, lower risks, and a stock valued above its net worth. This is not, however, sufficient to demonstrate that its privileges were bad for the efficiency of the banking system, or that they enabled Banamex to exercise market power. The next section addresses this issue.

Market Power and Bank Efficiency

A good definition of bank efficiency is the ability to smoothly transfer resources from savers to investors. Porfirian banks kept large shares of their assets tied up in their vaults, as gold and silver coins or banknotes. The amount of these nonproductive liquid assets, as a percentage of a bank's total assets, is known as the liquidity ratio. Banks with high liquidity ratios keep more of the resources available to them tied up in their vaults, where they could be thought to do little more good for the economy then cash stashed under a mattress. These banks might then be assumed to be rather inefficient. Unfortunately, this assumption would be incorrect.

There are all sorts of good reasons for banks to hold liquid assets. Sometimes banks experience gaps between inflows and outflows of funds. These gaps can arise because of unexpected withdrawals by depositors or debtors' failure to pay on time. Banks maintain liquid reserves to fill them. Banks may also want to hold liquid assets in order to stabilize the expected return on their asset portfolios: the riskier their credits, the more liquid, risk-free assets they will want to own. Therefore, in order to determine if banks are

Table 3.4

Tobin's q Estimates for Porfirian Banks

	1900	1901	1902	1903	1904	1905	1906	1907	1908	1909	1910	Avg.
Banamex	1.30	1.34	1.31	1.33	1.30	1.34	1.25	1.20	1.30	1.41	1.26	1.30
Londres y México	1.07	1.12	1.15	1.12	1.21	1.23	1.19	1.19	1.13	1.21	1.17	1.16
Banco Central	1.01	1.51	1.09	1.07	1.03	1.22	1.25	1.33	1.16	1.25	1.25	1.20
BMCI							0.61	0.61	0.55	0.43	0.49	0.54
Int. Hipotecario	1.04	0.96	1.00	1.00	0.97	1.12	1.14	1.24	1.15	1.17	1.15	1.08
BHCTM										1.07	1.06	1.06
Peninsular de Yucatán									0.94	0.99	0.94	0.96
Aguascalientes	0.78		1.07	0.96	0.98	0.98	1.03	1.04	1.04	1.00	1.00	1.01
Coahuila		0.99	1.03	1.02	1.01	1.03	1.06	1.04	1.00	1.03	1.03	1.00
Durango	0.59	0.62	1.05	1.06	1.03	1.06	1.08	1.07	1.05	0.99	1.02	0.96
México state	0.62	1.02	0.74	1.02	1.00	1.13	1.17	1.15	1.06	1.03	1.01	0.99
Guanajuato	0.71	1.03	1.02	1.01	1.01	1.10	1.17	1.16	1.10	1.06	1.02	1.03
Guerrero							1.06	0.76	1.06	0.97	0.95	0.96
Hidalgo	0.81	1.10	1.09	1.04	1.07	1.10	1.12	1.12	1.07	0.98	0.99	1.06
Jalisco		0.99	1.03	1.04	1.01	1.12	1.10	1.08	0.94	1.05	1.05	1.03
Minero (Chih.)	0.51		1.09	0.74	0.98	1.02	1.06	1.08	1.00	1.04	1.05	0.96

Monterrey (NL)	0.56	1.01	1.09	1.06	1.02	1.03	1.09	1.12	1.06	1.02	1.07	1.01
Veracruz	1.16	1.08	1.13	1.11	1.05	1.09	1.16	1.11	1.03	1.04	1.06	1.09
Morelos				0.87	0.99	1.04	1.07	1.08	1.01	0.98	0.98	1.00
Nuevo León	0.64	1.12	1.14	1.17	1.13	1.13	1.18	1.17	1.16	1.10	1.16	1.10
Oriental (Pue.)		1.02	1.04	1.04	1.04	1.03	1.02	1.04	1.04	1.00	0.94	1.02
Occidental	0.30	1.08	1.05	1.05	1.37	1.13	1.15	1.12	1.09	1.13	1.11	1.05
Querétaro				1.03	0.99	1.03	1.05	0.92	1.01	0.99	1.00	1.00
Sonora	0.81	1.08	1.10	1.03	1.01	1.06	1.14	1.14	1.10	1.08	1.08	1.06
SLP	0.87	1.08	1.06	1.07	1.06	1.06	1.07	1.07	1.04	1.05	1.06	1.04
Tabasco		0.62	0.90	1.23	1.12	1.09	1.10	1.05	1.06	1.00	1.00	1.02
Tamaulipas		0.67	0.67	0.99	1.01	1.05	1.07	1.09	1.08	1.03	1.02	1.00
Zacatecas	1.13	1.13	1.12	1.11	1.09	1.07	1.05	1.07	1.07	1.04	1.05	1.09
Michoacán		0.34	0.70	1.04	1.01	1.02	1.03	1.00	0.98	0.84	0.74	0.87
Comercial Refac.					1.02	0.98	1.06	0.98	1.02	1.02	1.02	1.01
Campeche									1.01	0.90	0.70	0.87
Chiapas									0.44			0.44
De la Laguna									0.69	0.97	0.99	0.89
Oaxaca									1.08			1.08

SOURCE: *Boletín Financiero y Minero.*

holding "inefficient" amounts of liquid assets, one must take into account the riskiness of their liabilities and other assets.

Why, however, would banks use their resources inefficiently? Remember, liquidity ratios are, by definition, the inverse of the loan/asset ratio. Low loan/asset ratios mean that the bank is not lending out as much of the resources available to it as it could. Monopolists, according to the simplest models of imperfect competition, restrict output in order to drive up the price of their products. Since a bank's "products" are loans and discounts, one would expect a monopolistic bank to restrict the amount of loans and discounts it makes relative to the resources available to it. In short, a monopolistic bank would be expected to take in deposits and then sit on a good slice of them, leaving them in the form of coins or banknotes gathering dust in a heavily armored vault. That way our hypothetical monopolist could drive up interest rates—the price of its "product"—and maximize its profits by restricting the supply of loanable funds. In that sense, what is inefficient from the point of view of the nation's financial system is efficient from the perspective of a bank enjoying some degree of market power.

Some economists, notably Joseph Stiglitz, have proposed that moral hazard may not lead banks to raise interest rates as much as they could, fearing that such rises would lead to a deterioration in the quality of their loan portfolio as good risks dropped out of the market. Instead, he proposes, banks may engage in credit rationing: keeping rates low enough to ensure a surfeit of applicants, and then rationing credit out to them. A bank enjoying market power in this respect, then, would not raise interest rates. This kind of behavior, if it occurred, is entirely compatible with the simple model of monopoly presented above. The bank enjoying market power would still lend less than its competitors and enjoy a less risky loan portfolio, resulting in higher net profits. (If it did not, then why would the bank engage in credit rationing to begin with?) Nor is the possibility that some banks were better than others at rationing credit a problem for the model. If one bank (say, Banamex) was more effective or better able to ration credit than its competitors, then that bank would be expected to hold lower liquid reserves than its competitors, since it would be facing lower portfolio risk. If that bank still held higher reserves, then the interpretation that it was attempting to exercise market power is only strengthened by the hypothetical differential use of credit rationing.

The following section presents a model of bank liquidity preferences in order to test the hypothesis that Porfirian entry restrictions for local banks and the special privileges granted the national banks permitted monopolistic behavior.[49]

THE MODEL

Picture a simplified version of a bank balance sheet:

A = assets   L = liabilities
R = liquid assets   D = total deposits
E = earning assets   C = capital funds available for portfolio selection

The demand for liquid assets to fill gaps between inflows and outflows of funds will lead a bank faced with variable deposits to hold a certain proportion of its assets, K_1, in liquid form. However, even if deposits were entirely stable, banks would choose to hold some percentage of liquid assets, K_2, in order to satisfy their demand for liquid risk-free assets in order to stabilize the expected return on their portfolios. In the real world, banks hold liquid assets for both reasons. Since liquid assets held for one purpose satisfy the other, K_1 and K_2 are not independent. The simplest rendering of this interaction effect is a multiplicative term, producing the following initial equation:

$$R = K_1L + K_2A + K_3LA$$

Plugging in the accounting identity $L = A$ and dividing through by A to put all our variables in ratio form produces

$$R/A = K_1 + K_2 + K_3A$$

K_1 depends upon the stability of the various items on the balance sheet. The ratio of equity to total liability is used as a measure of liability risk, since equity is the most stable source of funds a bank can have. Increases in the equity ratio, ceteris paribus, should result in decreases in R/A. Therefore, K_1 can be represented as a function of the equity ratio.

If economies of scale exist in banking, then one would expect the proportion of nonproductive liquid assets to decline with bank size. Thus, increases in the natural log of total assets, A, should be negatively correlated with the liquidity ratio, R/A.

The perceived riskiness of a bank's portfolio can be represented by the ratio between those assets the banks considered "safe" and those considered "risky." Safe assets were defined as securities holdings (primarily government bonds), secured credit lines, and mortgage loans. Risky assets were commercial discounts and collateralized loans.[50] Increases in the ratio of safe assets to risky assets should prompt decreases in R/A.

It might be argued that older and more experienced banks would be more conservative. There is, however, no a priori reason to assume so: older banks might be surer of their investment practices and hold fewer liquid assets than younger, newer ones with little business experience. Although one would reasonably expect experience to affect liquidity preferences, there are no theoretical bases upon which to predict the direction of the relationship.

Market structure is measured by the natural log of the number of branches, agencies, or home offices of other banks operating in the bank's concession territory. The national banks (Banamex, the Banco de Londres y México, the Banco Central, the Banco Internacional Hipotecario, and the Banco Mexicano de Comercio e Industria) were assigned a value for this equal to the number of competitors in the most competitive market in which they operated. In addition, the two national banks of issue (only Banamex and the Banco de Londres could issue banknotes) and the Banco Central are each given a dummy variable, since each occupied a special position within the banking system. In addition, dummies are included to separate out the few banks denied the right to issue banknotes but allowed to offer long-term credit without the need to resort to the subterfuges used by the banks of issue.

A priori, one would expect the national banks to hold lower liquidity ratios than the non-national banks, since their ability to branch nationally would allow them to better diversify their asset portfolios and spread their risks. The Banco Central, however, would be expected to hold higher liquidity ratios due to its mission of supporting the note issues of the state banks. However, if Banamex or the Banco de Londres were indeed exercising market power, then the coefficient on their dummies should be positive.

Finally, one exogenous economic variable is included: the gold price of silver (SP). Since Mexico was on a bi-metallic standard, fluctuations in the silver price could cause large inflows and outflows of specie. Therefore, banks had to guard against changes in the exchange rate. Given that the primary circulating medium in Porfirian Mexico was the silver peso, one would expect that increases in the silver price would cause the banks to try to increase their specie reserves in order to guard against sudden withdrawals by speculators.

In addition, three variables multiplying the individual bank dummies by time were added to determine if the effects particular to the national banks changed over time.

To summarize, we have the following specification, assuming linear additivity:

$$R/A = \beta_0 + \beta_1 \text{ (safe assets/risky assets)} + \beta_2 \text{ (equity/liabilities)} + \beta_3 \text{ (silver price)} + \beta_4 \text{ (age)} + \beta_5 \text{ (total assets)} + \beta_6 \text{ (market structure)} + \beta_7 \text{ (individual bank dummies)} + \beta_8 \text{ (no-issue dummy)}$$

Table 3.5
Random-Effects Specification

	Spec 1	Spec 2
CONSTANT	0.475	0.478
	(13.760)	(11.504)
ARISK	−0.128	−0.124
	(−7.457)	(−7.123)
LRISK	−0.118	−0.119
	(−7.298)	(−7.132)
LN SIZE	−0.0266	−0.279
	(−6.114)	(−6.453)
MARKET	−0.0139	−0.0140
	(−1.971)	(−1.969)
SILVERPRICE		0.0128
		(0.447)
NOISSUE	−0.0388	−0.0386
	(−3.163)	(−3.124)
BANAMEX	0.203	0.206
	(5.850)	(5.848)
B LONDRES	0.145	0.147
	(4.241)	(4.238)
B CENTRAL	0.106	0.070
	(2.568)	(2.104)
BANAMEX$_{time}$	−0.00818	−0.00795
	(−3.824)	(−3.711)
B LONDRES$_{time}$	−0.00697	−0.00665
	(−3.170)	(−3.029)
B CENTRAL$_{time}$	−0.00333	−0.00470
	(−1.416)	(−1.412)

SOURCE: Asset accounts taken from financial data submitted to the Secretaría de Hacienda and published in *El Economista Mexicano*, selected issues. Dividend payments taken from *Boletín Financiero y Minero*.
NOTE: t-statistics are in parentheses; Spec 1: Obs = 316, N = 34, R^2 = 0.5788; Spec 2: Obs = 316, N = 34, R^2 = 0.5451

THE RESULTS

Table 3.5 presents the results of a random-effects specification using unbalanced panel data.

The coefficients back up the predictions of the model. A bank facing no competition, with all its earning assets invested in risky loans and no equity, would be expected to hold 48 percent of its assets as specie reserves. The more of its earning assets it shifted into safer loans, the lower the reserves it would choose to hold. Similarly, the less a bank depended on deposits for finance, the more of its resources it would lend out.

The results also indicate real, if not overwhelming, economies of scale in banking. The coefficient for the natural log of a bank's total assets is negative and strongly significant. The larger a bank was, the less of its total assets it chose to hold in reserve. Doubling a bank's size decreased its liquidity ratio by roughly 2.5 percentage points. The presence of scale economies means that Porfirian policies limiting how large the state banks could grow imposed real costs on the banking system's efficiency, and therefore on economic growth.

Variations in the price of silver had little effect on bank behavior. The most likely explanation is that the banks considered the silver market so unpredictable that they chose to hold a fixed amount of specie to cover potential upsets and withdrawals, without reference to silver's specific level. Age also had little effect. The liquidity preferences of older and younger banks were basically indistinguishable.

For our purposes, the most important coefficients are attached to the market structure and individual bank dummy variables. Competition had an effect. For every doubling of the number of banks, branches of out-of-state banks, and banking companies operating in a state, R/A ratios declined slightly over one percentage point. This, of course, was not costless. It resulted in more profit volatility and greater risk for the banks facing higher competition. But it meant that these banks transferred more of the savings and other resources entrusted to them to borrowers, who could then put them to productive use. Since Porfirian banking law restricted competition by limiting banking start-ups and placing interstate branching at the discretion of the finance secretary, these results imply that Porfirian policies directly lowered financial efficiency.

Both of the national banks of issue (Banamex and the Banco de Londres) exhibited very high liquidity ratios. This is not what would have been expected, considering that they could branch across the country, enjoyed economies of scale, were free from many of the practical and legal restrictions that hampered the smaller banks, and could freely issue new stock on the Mexico City market. They faced lower risks than their competitors and should therefore have demonstrated lower R/A ratios.

Before analyzing this coefficient, how well does this model predict actual observed bank behavior? Quite well, actually. Figures 3.8, 3.9, and 3.10 show the actual and predicted values for the state banks, Banamex, and the Banco de Londres y México. The fit for the state banks is remarkably close

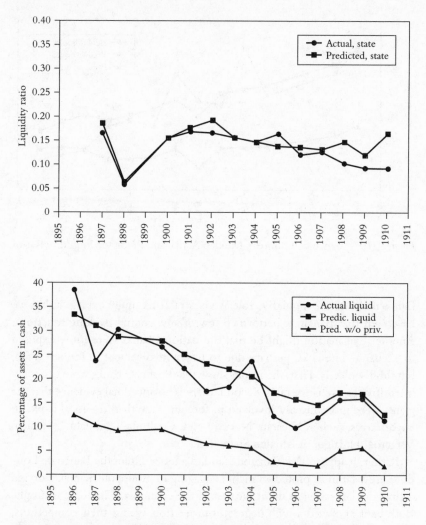

Figure 3.8. (above)   Actual and Predicted State Bank Liquidity Ratios
Figure 3.9. (below)   Banamex Actual and Predicted Liquidity Ratios

through 1908, as is the fit for the Banco de Londres y México; the results
for Banamex are fairly tight throughout the entire period. Whether or not
bankers actually held our model of bank liquidity ratios in their head while
making decisions is, of course, unknowable, but they certainly behaved as
though they did, at least until 1908.

How can we explain the high specie reserves held by Banamex and the

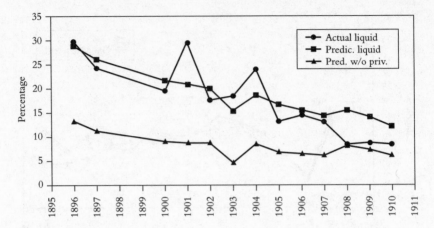

Figure 3.10. Banco de Londres y México Actual and Predicted Liquidity Ratios

Banco de Londres? A putative role as a central bank might explain it, but we have seen that Banamex performed few, if any, central banking functions. Another explanation might be that the national banks were more exposed to exchange rate risks, perhaps due to heavy involvement in foreign trade, but this is unlikely. First, the results show that Porfirian banks were generally insensitive to exchange rates. Second, there is no anecdotal evidence that the giants were more heavily involved in foreign trade than the local banks in export areas, such as Yucatán, Nuevo León, Coahuila, Chihuahua, Sinaloa, Veracruz, Hidalgo, or Mexico State.

Rather, it appears that Banamex (and to a lesser extent the Banco de Londres) grew fat in its protected niche, engaging in monopolistic behavior and acting as a large weight upon the rest of the economy. The logic is simple. Both banks enjoyed a high degree of protection against their competitors, which were limited in their ability to grow. Porfirian banks relied heavily upon equity for resources, far more so than contemporary banks, so the limits placed upon their ability to issue new stock greatly constrained them. In addition, new entrants were restricted by high capital requirements and the tax on banknotes applied to the second bank of issue to start up within any given state: this meant that the financial system could not grow extensively. Therefore, the national banks were the dominant firms of a dominant firm and fringe model, but to a certain extent they were protected from the fringe.

They used this advantage to act like classical monopolists, restricting their "output"—loans and credits—in order to drive up prices. Now, banks may have an incentive not to raise interest rates in order to reduce moral hazard problems among their clientele: they might ration credit to favored (i.e., less risky) borrowers instead. As discussed earlier, this should not affect the present analysis. Banks using legal protections to reduce their risks by rationing credit should produce the same patterns we see in the data: less lending, less risk, and higher profits than their competitors.

There is additional evidence to support this analysis. Unfortunately, interest rate data for the individual banks is unavailable, even on an annual basis, because Porfirian profit-and-loss statements followed the unusual convention of netting out interest payments to depositors before booking interest income on the statements. Because Porfirian banks began offering deposit interest in 1899 (the Banco Mercantil de Monterrey began the practice, engaged in a competitive battle with the well-established Banco de Nuevo León), and the practice had become universal by 1903, we cannot use profit-and-loss statements to reliably estimate average market interest rates.[51] Even if we could, using the gross return on earning assets as a proxy for market rates, it is not clear that a difference in the interest rates charged by the state and national banks would demonstrate anything. Consistently lower interest rates offered by the national banks would support a hypothesis of monopolies engaging in credit rationing, while higher interest rates would indicate firms abusing their pricing power, and no significant difference would indicate capacity-constrained fringe firms taking advantage of the price leadership of the national banks. If any possible pattern in the data can be used to support the market power hypothesis, then the test is useless.

However, the timing of the introduction of deposit interest by the state and national banks can be used to support the argument that Banamex, at least, enjoyed a strong degree of market power in the credit market, but not in the market for deposits. Banamex was among the last banks to introduce deposit interest, in 1903, due to worries about declining deposits.[52] If Banamex had complete market power over its depositors, then the other banks' introduction of deposit interest would not affect Banamex's depositors' inelastic demand for Banamex deposits. As Figure 3.11 demonstrates, however, that was not the case. Banamex's share of total deposits in the banking system began to decline in 1898, and continued falling until Banamex began to introduce deposit interest. The decline reversed itself as soon as Banamex began offering interest.

Banamex's strategy was to attempt to control as much of the resources available to the banking system as possible, and then use that control to limit the supply of credit. The other banks' introduction of deposit interest enabled them, for a time, to get around the limits on their expansion and be-

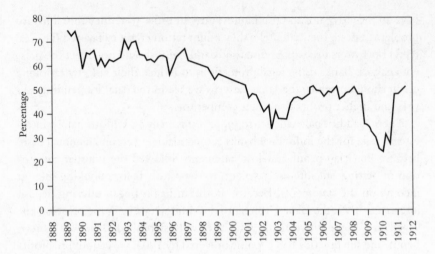

Figure 3.11.   Banamex Share of Deposit Market

gin to threaten Banamex's control over the credit market. So Banamex introduced deposit interest in order to reestablish that control. Had Banamex possessed no advantages on the credit side, then its introduction of deposit interest should have at best stanched the decline in its share of total deposits or negatively impacted its relative profitability. Instead, it allowed Banamex to claw back share and had no effect on its profits.

However, the introduction of deposit interest did change the calculus facing Banamex's directors. In essence, the opportunity cost of holding reserves rose. This meant that in order to maintain its profits, Banamex needed to lend to more borrowers, lend to a higher class of borrowers, or both. The evidence is that Banamex was already lending to the highest class of lenders it could find—its own directors—and so it needed to make more loans to break even.[53] That, however, would risk eroding its market power, if indeed Banamex was acting as a monopolist.

So what kind of behavior should we expect? Well, Banamex should not lend out all of the new resources that its deposit interest payments cause to flow into its vaults, so its overall loan/deposit ratio should fall. However, for any given level of deposits, Banamex should need to make more loans, so its loan/deposit ratio holding deposits constant at their pre-1903 level (or holding them to a counterfactual rate of growth without deposit interest) should rise, and rise substantially. Figure 3.12 calculates Banamex's actual loan/deposit ratio, loan/deposit ratio holding deposits constant, and loan/deposit

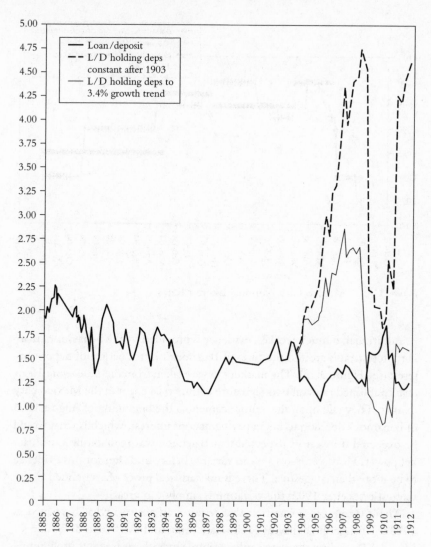

Figure 3.12.　Banamex Loan/Deposit Ratios

ratio holding deposits to their pre-1903 percentage rate of growth. The last overestimates Banamex's counterfactual deposits, since the growth rate was declining over 1900–1903 and most likely would have continued to decline had Banamex not matched its smaller competitors in the market for deposits, in which it enjoyed far less monopsony power than it possessed monopoly power in the market for credit. The pattern shown supports the hypothesis.

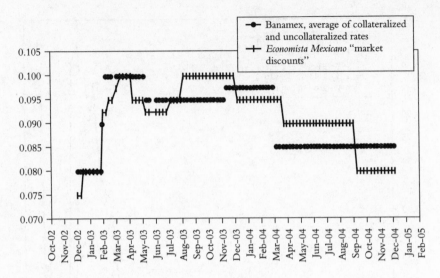

Figure 3.13. Mexico City Nominal Interest Rates

Additional, if much weaker, evidence is provided by the behavior of market interest rates around the time of Banamex's introduction of deposit interest (see Figure 3.13). The market rates are taken from the *Economista Mexicano*'s published rates on two-signature commercial paper in the Mexico City market. They rise upon the announcement at the beginning of August 1903 of Banamex's decision to begin paying deposit interest, which is what would be expected if investors expected that Banamex was reestablishing its market power. However, rates are too variable before and after for this evidence to be more than suggestive. There is no statistical proof of a sustained rise in interest rates after 1903: the variation is simply too great.

There is one other question that requires an answer: what happened in 1908 to change the behavior of the state banks and the Banco de Londres y México? Regarding the state banks, a simple hypothesis presents itself: moral hazard caused by a banking bailout. In 1908, the federal government took out a foreign loan of 50 million pesos and used the money to capitalize a state-owned lending institution with the tongue-twisting name of the Caja de Préstamos para Obras de Irrigación y Fomento de la Agricultura, which then rediscounted the banks' most illiquid loans.[54] Although the Caja was ostensibly created to aid small farmers in obtaining credit to make long-term investments, it actually functioned as a mechanism to allow the commercial banks to remove problematic loans from their books. After 1908, the state banks were simply less risk averse than before. The same argument applies to the Banco de Londres y México, which was very hard hit by the 1907–8 financial crisis, but which received massive aid from the Caja de Préstamos. In fact, the Banco de Londres y México was the second largest single recipient of rediscounts from the Caja after the Banco Central.[55]

Conclusions

How big was the effect of Banamex's privileges on Porfirian economic growth? Figure 3.14 displays the difference between the actual amount of gross credit extended by the banking system (expressed as a percentage of GDP) and the counterfactual amount that would have been extended in the absence of Banamex's market power. On average, gross lending would have been roughly 1.6 percent of GDP higher in every year over the period. This is a substantial amount. In other terms, gross lending would have been 17 percent higher in 1897 and 6 percent higher in 1910 had the national banks not been privileged under Porfirian law.

This is, of course, a minimum estimate. During the 1897–1910 period, the state banks typically reinvested one-third of their net earnings, so they would have most likely grown significantly faster than they did had they not been prohibited from branching across state lines or going to the equity markets to raise capital after 1905, and some would have been bought by competitors, meaning that overall reserve ratios would have dropped more than predicted here as the state banks enjoyed more economies of scale.

A 17 percent increase in gross lending does not translate into a 17 percent

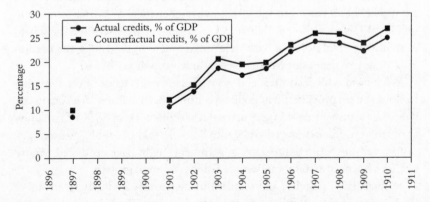

Figure 3.14.   Gross Bank Lending as a Percentage of GDP

increase in net capital formation. For that we would need to know how big a net increase in capital was generated from a given amount of gross lending during the Porfiriato, and that information we do not have. Nor do we know how much capital was raised through the formal financial system, as opposed to informal arrangements, retained earnings by firms, and foreign capital inflows. There is evidence that bank capital was very important in Mexican industrial growth during the period, and participated heavily in the growth of certain lines of export agriculture, especially northern cotton.[56] But we simply lack the data to produce a realistic counterfactual that goes beyond simple guessing.

Nevertheless, the chances are good that such changes in bank behavior would have produced fairly significant effects on the country's long-term economic growth. The new growth theory suggests that very small changes in investment can produce rather dramatic differences in growth over time. In addition, research into insider lending during the Porfiriato and the effects of access to bank credit on the textile industry suggests that increases in the simple number of banks would have produced further increases in the amount and effectiveness of investment.[57] The final conclusion is that a regulatory structure that permitted two banks to exercise monopoly power in the credit market had significant negative effects on the growth of the Mexican economy over the last thirteen years of the Porfiriato.

In Banamex, Mexico saddled itself with a massive bank, protected from competition, unhesitant to exercise its market power, and lacking any commensurate public responsibilities. In fact, Mexico derived few benefits from Banamex after 1894. It appears to have done little to knit the nation into a unified economic entity. Nor was it more deeply involved in financing Mexico's industrialization than the state banks.[58] Banamex certainly did not act as a central bank: it is hard to argue that its presence increased macroeconomic stability. In short, although Banamex's creation may have satisfied the short-term instrumental needs of the federal government in the 1880s, the persistence of its privileges did Mexico's economic growth no favors.

What lessons for institutional theory does the experience of the Porfirian banking system provide? First, political centralization matters. Without it, the federal government could never have stacked the deck in favor of Banamex as much as it did, or limited entry into banking as thoroughly. A more decentralized and more democratic government might have produced a more efficient financial system and with it faster economic growth.

Second, laws, policies, and regulations measurably and concretely affect the banking system's ability to carry out its functions. Bank regulation is neither peripheral nor easily contracted around. Inefficient regulations produced an inefficient financial system. Not only did federal regulations allow Mexico's national banks to exercise market power, they allowed a quasi-monopoly to persist over a significant period of time.

Third, ironically, political centralization can exacerbate regional economic differences. In regions with less competition, banks operated less efficiently, but the federal laws and regulations governing Mexican banking meant that regions with little banking competition were unlikely to experience much founding of new banks or the entry of banks from other regions. This meant that places with little competition and inefficient banks were likely to remain places with little competition and inefficient banks.

In conclusion, institutions make a difference, and efficient institutional structures do not inexorably emerge where they are needed. Even over the short term (thirteen years in the case of this study), the costs to growth can be substantial, and it is not clear that the losses can be easily made up. Today's gaping distance between the GDP of most Latin American nations and that of the developed world is the result of slowly widening income differentials, and not (even in the case of Argentina in the twentieth century) sudden and dramatic divergences. In the words of economic historian Richard Salvucci, "Falling behind was easy. Catching up is much harder to do."

Notes

1. Conant 1910: 24.
2. Conant 1910: 26.
3. Conant 1910: 24.
4. Goodhart 1988: 39–42.
5. Gorton 1985.
6. Conant 1910: 39–40.
7. Conant 1910: 101.
8. Secretaría de Hacienda y Crédito Público 1884: 90–91.
9. Fraas 1974: 449. The specific tools the Second Bank of the United States used to carry this out are mentioned later in the chapter.
10. Rockoff 1996: 204.
11. AHBNM (1901), *Informe annual*: 7–8.
12. AHBNM (1902), *Informe annual*: 7–8.
13. AHBNM (1908), *Informe annual*: 17–18.
14. Since Banamex notes could not be legally used as required reserves by the banks (although they could of course be used as excess reserves), lending out its specie reserves was Banamex's only way to provide liquidity to the other banks.

15. Temin 1969: 46.

16. AHBNM (1894), *Actas de consejo*, vol. 4, December 20.

17. AHBNM (1905), *Actas de consejo*, vol. 6, November 14.

18. Conant 1910: 87, 103.

19. Secretaría de Hacienda y Crédito Público 1906: 212–13. Under the General Banking Act of 1897, banks' note issues could not exceed three times their paid-in capital, or twice their specie reserves. This meant that limits on new stock issues also functioned to limit note issues.

20. Derived from figures published in the *Boletín Financiero y Minero* and GDP estimates cited in Cárdenas 1987: 190.

21. Conant 1910: 86–87.

22. The mint ratio is the official ratio at which gold can be exchanged for silver at the government's mints.

23. Conant 1910: 75.

24. The sharp decline in Banamex's specie reserves in mid-1905 was due to a 10-million-peso loan to federal government, in silver pesos. The bank had advance notice of the loan, and had been bolstering its specie reserves for a year in preparation.

25. AHBNM (1905), *Actas de consejo*, vol. 6, November 28.

26. AHBNM (1905), *Actas de consejo*, vol. 6, November 14. The reason for this agreement was that the government, as required by law, had deposited the receipts from the huge foreign loan of that year in Banamex's vaults and wanted to ensure they remained liquid.

27. Temin 1969: 48–49.

28. The Banco Central Mexicano, a private institution, did an effective job of maintaining the value of the state banknotes after 1899. In that sense, if there was a central bank during the Porfiriato, it was the Banco Central, not Banamex. The financial press ceased reporting the discounts on state banknotes after 1900.

29. AHBNM (1901), *Actas de consejo*, vol. 5, November 26. In debating the 1901 loan to the Banco Oriental, Banamex board members made it clear that they considered the loan to be a commercial investment in the Puebla textile manufacture, many of whose most important entrepreneurs sat on the Banco Oriental's board.

30. AHBNM (1904), *Actas de consejo*, vol. 6, June 14, August 26, November 8, and November 15. The Banco Central was a private institution created to insure the national clearing of the state banknotes at par.

31. AHBNM (1907), *Actas de consejo*, vol. 6, June 18 and September 10.

32. This information is derived from Banamex's monthly balances as submitted to the federal government. Credit lines were shut in 1908 and reopened in 1910 on a piecemeal basis, and not as part of a consolidated strategy on the part of the bank.

33. AHBNM (1908), *Actas de consejo*, vol. 7, June 9.

34. AHBNM (1908), *Actas de consejo*, vol. 7, August 25.

35. AHBNM (1908), *Actas de consejo*, vol. 7, November 24. The slight increases in Banamex's commercial discounts provoked by these moves did not outweigh the continuing reduction in the bank's secured credit lines. Why secured credit lines took the brunt of the credit reduction, and whether Banamex restricted them or whether firms decided to reduce their borrowing due to elevated interest rates, is unclear. These loans were secured by deposits at the bank, and these deposits fell in line with credit, but the chain of causality is not clear.

36. AHBNM (1910), *Actas de consejo*, vol. 7, May 24. This move also appears to have prompted Banamex to expand or reopen the secured credit lines it had restricted or shut in 1908.

37. Conant 1910: 208.

38. Unfortunately, Porfirian accountants netted out interest payments to depositors and bondholders from interest earnings from debtors before booking net interest earnings in the profit-and-loss statement. This made it impossible to add back in payments to depositors in order to estimate gross real returns.

39. The Gómez-Galvarriato price index for the Porfiriato can be found in Gómez-Galvarriato 1998: 353.

40. The Banco de la Laguna has a lower average, but this Coahuila-based bank was only founded in 1908. In 1909 and 1910 its stock yielded significantly more than Banamex.

41. Two of the very profitable northern banks, in Sonora and Nuevo León, also exhibited high yields, indicating that their profitability was to some extent a compensation for risk.

42. Tobin 1969: 15–29.

43. If a firm's only source of capital is the equity market, then this measure captures the same information as the ROA versus the yield rate. If a firm, on the other hand, uses much debt finance, then q is more accurate measure of the ratio between its overall cost of capital and its profits than the ROA/yield ratio. This is because yields capture only the cost of equity finance.

44. See Lindenberg and Ross 1981: 1–32 for a discussion of the reasons why a firm's q-ratio might differ from one even in a competitive market.

45. Lindenberg and Ross 1981: 2.

46. The Banco Central was not a bank like the others. Rather, it was a private note-redemption scheme established in 1900 and intended to allow the par circulation of state banknotes across the national territory. Inasmuch as Porfirian Mexico had a central bank, it was the Banco Central, not Banamex. Nevertheless, there were serious limitations to the Banco Central scheme, as discussed in Maurer 1997: chap. 4; and Robitaille 1997.

47. Regressing Banamex's q-ratio on time produced no statistically signifi-

cant results. [$R^2 = 0.03$, a $= 1.32$ (36.4), b $= -0.002$ (-0.50), t-statistics in parentheses.] Regressing the Londres y México's ratio produced a slightly positive trend [$R^2 = 0.33$, a $= 1.11$ (40.8) , b $= 0.008$ (2.11)].

48. At least after Mexico balanced the federal budget in 1894. Before then, Banamex charged the federal government below-market interest on its credits. Afterward, nominal market yields on federal debt fell below the 6 percent statutory ceiling on Banamex credits to the federal government.

49. This model is based on one presented in Hinderlitter and Rockoff 1976: 379–98, but departs from it in its use of variables for market structure and its interpretation of what liquidity ratios signify.

50. See Maurer 1999. On the surface, these two assets appear as though they should be considered relatively safe. Commercial discounts, after all, putatively represent real short-term transactions and collateralized loans are guaranteed by the collateral. In practice, however, this was not the case. The vast majority of commercial discounts actually financed long-term loans and were continually rolled over at the end of their six-month term, whereas collateralized loans were generally made to individuals (almost always with some personal connection to the bank), and the "collateral" was made up of shares in the new industry being financed. Both were ways to avoid the Porfiriato's legal restrictions on long-term loans, and were considered riskier than credit lines secured by cash deposits or mortgage loans secured by real property.

51. Maurer 1999.

52. AHBNM (1903), *Actas de consejo*, vol. 6, June 9 and July 23.

53. Maurer 1999.

54. AGN (1908), *Sesiones Administrativas de la Caja de Préstamos*, box 1, gal. 2, November 3.

55. The Banco de Londres y México rediscounted 6,105,180 pesos at the Caja de Préstamos between its creation in November 1908 and June 1910. This came to 10 percent of the Caja's gross lending over the period. Data from AGN (1908, 1909, 1910), *Sesiones Administrativas de la Caja de Préstamos*, box 1, gal. 2.

56. Maurer 1999 and Chapter 2 of this volume.

57. Maurer 1999 and Chapter 2 of this volume.

58. See Maurer 1997: chap. 5.

References

[AGN] Archivo General de la Nación, Galería 2. Mexico City.

[AHBNM] Archivo Histórico del Banco Nacional de México. Mexico City.

Atack, J., and P. Passell. 1994. *A New Economic View of American History from Colonial Times to 1940*. New York.

Boletín Financiero y Minero. Mexico City.

Cárdenas, E. 1987. *La industrialización mexicana durante la Gran Depresión.* Mexico City.

Conant, C. 1910. *The Banking System of Mexico.* Washington, D.C.

El Economista Mexicano. Mexico City.

Fraas, A. 1974. "The Second Bank of the United States: An Instrument for an Interregional Monetary Union." *Journal of Economic History,* vol. 34, no. 2: 447–67.

Gómez-Galvarriato, A. 1998. "The Evolution of Prices and Real Wages in Mexico." In J. H. Coatsworth and A. Taylor, eds., *Latin America and the World Economy Since 1800,* pp. 347–78. Cambridge, Mass.

Goodhart, C. 1988. *The Evolution of Central Banks.* Cambridge, Mass.

Gorton, G. 1985. "Clearinghouses and the Origin of Central Banking in the United States." *Journal of Economic History,* vol. 45, no. 2: 277–83.

Haber, S. 1997. "Financial Markets and Industrial Development: A Comparative Study of Governmental Regulation, Financial Innovation, and Industrial Structure in Brazil and Mexico, 1840–1930." In S. Haber, ed., *How Latin America Fell Behind: Essays on the Economic Histories of Brazil and Mexico, 1800–1914,* pp. 146–78. Stanford.

Hinderlitter, J., and H. Rockoff. 1976. "Banking Under the Gold Standard: An Analysis of Liquidity Management in the Leading Financial Centers." *Journal of Economic History,* vol. 36, no. 2: 379–98.

Lindenberg, E., and S. Ross. 1981. "Tobin's q Ratio and Industrial Organization." *Journal of Business,* vol. 54: 1–32.

Mariscal, E., and A. Muñoz. 1995. *Inflación y políticas de estabilización durante el Porfiriato.* Licentiate thesis, Instituto Tecnológico Autónomo de México.

Maurer, N. 1999. "Banks and Entrepreneurs in Porfirian Mexico: Inside Exploitation or Sound Business Strategy?" *Journal of Latin American Studies,* vol. 31: 331–61.

———. 1997. "Finance and Oligarchy: Banks, Politics, and Economic Growth in Mexico, 1876–1928." Ph.D. dissertation, Stanford University.

Maurer, N., and S. Haber. 1998. "The Efficiency Consequences of Financial Regulation: Overcoming Liquidity Constraints in the Mexican Cotton Textile Industry, 1888–1913." Paper presented at the Conference on Institutional Change and Economic Performance, December 18–19, 1998, Stanford University.

McCaleb, W. F. 1920. *Present and Past Banking in Mexico.* New York.

Razo, A., and S. Haber. 1998. "The Rate of Growth of Productivity in Mexico, 1850–1933: Evidence from the Cotton Industry." *Journal of Latin American Studies,* vol. 30, no. 3: 1–37.

Robitaille, Patrice. 1997. "Private Payment Systems in Historical Perspective: The Banco Central System of Mexico." Board of Governors, Federal Reserve System, International Finance Discussion Paper no. 599.

Rockoff, H. 1996. "Money, Banking, and Inflation: An Introduction for Historians." In T. Rawski, ed., *Economics and the Historian*, pp. 177–208. Berkeley.

Secretaría de Hacienda y Crédito Público. 1884. *Memoria 1883–1884*. Mexico City.

———. 1906. *Memoria 1905–1906*. Mexico City.

Temin, P. 1969. *The Jacksonian Economy*. New York.

Tobin, J. 1969. "A General Equilibrium Approach to Monetary Theory." *Journal of Money, Credit, and Banking*, vol. 1: 15–29.

Chapter 4

The Construction of Credibility: Financial Market Reform and the Renegotiation of Mexico's External Debt in the 1880s

CARLOS MARICHAL

The analysis of institutional change in the nineteenth century has traditionally focused on how variations in "national" or "local" institutions affect economic performance. In the study of foreign debt, however, it is important to consider that domestic debtors are generally obliged to conform to international institutional norms. Loan contracts signed abroad commonly require the debtor (public or private) to effect interest and amortization payments in a foreign currency and to resolve disputes in a foreign court of law. As a result, the analysis of external debt policy provides a particularly interesting though complex case within the history of economic and institutional change.[1]

In the case of nineteenth-century Mexico, the subject of foreign debt is of special interest because it reveals the potentially negative political and economic consequences suffered by a government that does not conform to international financial market norms. The Mexican government's suspension of payments in 1828 on its early British loans (issued in 1824 and 1825) led to a traumatic six decades of conflict with foreign creditors. Worse still, the payment moratorium led to military interventions, the most notorious being the invasion and occupation of Mexico by French troops between 1862 and 1867—the famous Empire of Maximilian. The nonpayment of public debts made foreign creditors wary of new investments in Mexico, effectively shutting Mexico out of international capital markets until the 1880s. The costs to the Mexican economy were high, particularly in light of longstanding domestic capital shortages.[2]

In the mid and late 1880s, the restructuring of outstanding Mexican public debt and the renewal of debt service were successfully accomplished, ending the Mexican government's exclusion from international financial markets. The conversion of Mexico's external debt, however, should not be seen merely as an attempt by the government to get foreign bondholders off its back by complying with their demands. Mexican public officials had long demonstrated their imperviousness to the demands of foreign creditors, despite the costs such conduct implied.[3] Such behavior was not due to nationalism so much as to fiscal and financial constraints that made the maintenance of foreign debt service difficult. The fundamental cause of Mexico's extremely long moratorium on external debt service, which lasted from 1826 to 1886—the longest of any nation in Latin American and perhaps in modern world history—was the chronic revenue weakness of the government.

Given these antecedents, the fact that Mexico did break out of the debt quandary in the 1880s could suggest that fiscal reform led to the resumption of external debt service. But, the restructuring and renewal of service on the old debts was not due to the elimination of deficits. Rather, I argue, they were the result of domestic, financial reforms, in particular the creation of a large private bank, the Banco Nacional de México (Banamex), which took over basic responsibility as the unofficial government bank, carrying out the negotiation and service of external debts. Banamex's stockholders included a large number of influential European and North American financiers and investors. This contributed to the notable increase in confidence in the debt policies subsequently adopted by the Mexican authorities. The establishment of Banamex almost single-handedly reestablished the international credibility of Mexican public finance. It also contributed to greater efficiency in tax collections and public disbursements, and to the institutional modernization of Mexican finance. Thus, in a critical sphere, a private agency proved crucial to the transition from a weak to a strong state.

The establishment of an agency that could serve as banker to the government was a critical step in the modernization of the state itself. It signaled to investors that political authorities had accepted the need for more specialized organizations to exercise influence over the administration of public finance with some autonomy vis-à-vis the finance ministry. Moreover, as banking historians have argued, the functions of banker to the government (holding and administering public bank accounts, servicing and issuing public debt) in most late-nineteenth-century European countries resembled the functions most characteristic of central bankers today, albeit not the functions today considered most important.[4] Equally important, the creation of this privately owned "national" bank—with excellent connections abroad—assured foreign bondholders that they could now expect compliance of the Mexican government with international financial norms.

In sum, fiscal reforms were not the key to the Mexican government's success in regaining credibility in international financial markets in the 1880s. Indeed, public deficits increased phenomenally in that decade. Rather, a series of institutional and organizational reforms in financial markets, impelled by the innovative functions of new banking actors, particularly the Banco Nacional de México, played a more important role. Without such actors, the forging of a new public debt policy would not have been possible.

The Burdensome Legacy of Unpaid Debts in Nineteenth-Century Mexico

The history of nineteenth-century Mexican debt policy has been the subject of a fair number of studies, ranging from classic contemporary accounts, three or four descriptive but detailed studies, to a few recent analytical studies by two economists, Luis Téllez and Vinod Aggarwal.[5] To underline my own particular and different focus, I will briefly comment on the latter two contributions. First, however, it is important to present a brief factual account of the trajectory of Mexican public debt from independence forward.

After independence in the early 1820s, the new government of Mexico found itself burdened with a public debt it could not pay off. The debts included approximately 30 million pesos (1 peso = 1 dollar) of old colonial debts that were recognized, but not paid off.[6] More important, in 1824 and 1825, the new authorities took on two large loans in London totaling £6.4 million (32 million pesos). Debt service was met for only two years. In late 1827, payments were suspended and were not renewed on a regular basis until the 1880s.

For decades, this external debt was a bone of contention between foreign creditors and the Mexican Republic. The history of debt-related conflicts, and the failure of various debt conversions, has been well covered in the literature mentioned above. By the 1870s, the total nominal value of the old London debt due (plus arrears in interest) exceeded £24 million (U.S.$120 million) (see Table 4.1). In addition, the Mexican government owed some $5 million to various United States bankers and investors who had supported Benito Juárez during the armed struggle against the French during the Empire of Maximilian (1863–67).

After 1867 and the triumph of the liberal forces under Juárez, the reinstated parliamentary regime resolved to suspend payments on the bulk of

Table 4.1

Mexican Conversion of Foreign Debt, 1885–1886
(in thousands of pounds sterling)

External Debts[a] Outstanding	Total[b] Recognized	Net[c] Saving	Net
Bonds of 1851	10,241	10,241	—
Coupons of 1851 bonds	6,144	922	5,223
Bonds of 1864	4,864	2,432	2,432
Bonds of 1837	434	87	347
Certificates of 1851	180	36	144
Baring certificates	75	15	60
Bonds of 1843	200	58	142
English conv. debt	1,180	824	357
Bonds of 1846	21	11	11
Totals	23,343	14,626	8,717

SOURCE: Secretaría de Hacienda y Crédito Público 1886–88; Council of Foreign Bond-holders 1886–88.

[a]The exact definition of each kind of debt may be found in the *Memoria*, but it should be noted that the first three categories listed (1851 bonds, unpaid coupons of 1851 bonds, and the bonds of 1864) all derived from the original foreign loans of 1824 and 1825 and subsequent unpaid interest.

[b]Debt outstanding according to number of bonds in circulation before June 22, 1885.

[c]Amount of debt recognized by the government on basis of decree of June 22, 1885, and agreements signed with Corporation of Foreign Bondholders on June 23, 1886.

foreign debts. In light of the nominal support provided by Great Britain to France during the French occupation of Mexico, the suspension included not only the spurious external debts taken on by Maximilian, but also the old debts held by English bondholders. Diplomatic ties with the British government were broken off, stretching bondholders' patience. Meanwhile, in sharp contrast to the treatment meted out to European investors and bankers, Juárez ordered the ministry of finance to do its best to service the government's American loans (in particular the advances his army had received from the Washington-based Corcoran Bank). The sums actually paid out, however, were relatively small.

In a well-documented econometric exercise, Luis Téllez has demonstrated that, despite the long suspension of regular service on the Mexican external debt (held in Great Britain), a secondary market for Mexican bonds existed in London through the middle decades of the nineteenth century.

That sophisticated investors bought and sold this apparently worthless paper reflected two factors: first, that the Mexican government occasionally did pay some interest; second, that fluctuations in bond prices did allow for some profitable transactions, as long as investors correctly evaluated future trends of the Mexican economy and polity. For example, the acquisition of bonds shortly before the conversions of 1830, 1837, and 1850 could have allowed for speculative gains on rising bond prices. (Since none of these conversions led to renewed debt service on a regular basis, however, bondholders would have had to sell the Mexican paper before it subsequently fell in price, if they were to realize gains.)

On one propitious occasion, however, bondholders did receive some payments. A major windfall occurred after the U.S. invasion of Mexico in 1847, when Washington paid $15 million to Mexico for the acquisition of California, Nevada, and most of Colorado and New Mexico. The Mexican government transferred approximately $2.5 million of these funds to British bondholders.[7]

By analyzing monthly quotations between 1846 and 1886, Téllez calculates the risk premium of holding Mexican bonds versus British consols. He demonstrates that fluctuations in the risk premium were closely related to economic and political developments. This reflected a fair knowledge on the part of British investors of events in Mexico. Téllez, however, does not adequately analyze the enormous costs that extremely irregular debt service implied, such as the four-year occupation of Mexico by French troops between 1863 and 1866.[8] He also does not explain why the Mexican government finally decided to convert its old, external debt, and, most important, to establish regular debt service from the mid-1880s.

A different analytical approach is adopted by Vinod Aggarwal, who also explores long-term trends in Mexican external debt, particularly the dynamics of the various debt conversions. Aggarwal constructs a game-theoretic model that predicts the probable results of debt negotiations by examining the relative strengths and constraints of the principal actors, namely bondholders and the government. He focuses more specifically on the 1880s debt negotiations and on the conversions of 1830 and 1850, as well as the more recent debt restructuring of the 1980s. He offers a mathematical/political science model to evaluate the negotiations. Contrasting debtor and creditor strategies, he argues that by blocking access to foreign capital (in the early and mid-1880s), bondholders forced the Mexican government to make major adjustments. In fact, however, foreign capitalists continued to invest in Mexico during these years, and it would appear doubtful that bondholders had much influence in the principal fiscal/financial measures adopted by

Minister Dublán in the period reforms.[9] Moreover, Aggarwal makes many factual errors that weaken his argument.[10] Finally, because Aggarwal's brief study neglects analysis of fiscal and expenditure trends and ignores the short-term debt policies of the Mexican government in the 1880s, it appears to be largely conjecture.

Nonetheless, the rigid dichotomy established by this researcher with regard to creditors and debtors (which is also common among other authors dealing with debt resolution) may be useful, if analyzed critically. It points to a need to broaden habitual perspectives, paying special attention to the neglected role of domestic and/or foreign intermediaries (particularly the principal banking firms involved) and to focus on changes in the institutional framework of domestic finance. For this reason, it can be useful in explaining the principal trends of Mexican public finance in the years immediately preceding the conversion of the mid-1880s.

The Legacy of a Weak State: Mexican Fiscal and Financial Policies in the Late 1870s and Early 1880s

During the 1870s, the Mexican finance ministry effected no payments on the old British debt, but it did amortize almost a third of the internal debt. It should be underlined that this was actually the first period in the nineteenth century when the government reduced its domestic debt. However, it should also be observed that annual payments were not large, which helps explain why there were practically no public deficits at the time (see Figure 4.1).[11] Retiring domestic debt, however, did not imply that Mexican authorities were not also interested in regaining access to international markets for new foreign loans. Foreign loans were considered potentially attractive because there were virtually no domestic alternatives in terms of loans (there was only one medium-sized commercial bank in the capital).[12]

As the former finance minister Matías Romero would comment in 1880, the government wanted to renew service on the external bonds, but, due to limited fiscal resources, it could not do so. In response to foreign critics who argued that Mexico was an unrepentant debtor, Romero published a detailed study of the Mexican economy and public finance in which he elucidated the strategy gaining favor among the political elite. This strategy consisted of growing out of debt by stimulating foreign investments in railroad and other modern enterprises, with the intent of promoting economic development and impelling an increase in fiscal revenues that could be used to service the debt. Romero affirmed in 1880:

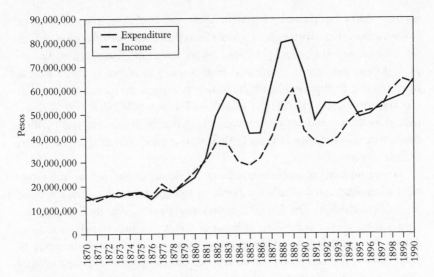

Figure 4.1. Income and Expenditure of the Mexican Government, 1870–1900

It does not appear too hazardous to assert that, if railroads were constructed in the center of the country, and between the principal towns, extending them to the Pacific, in combination with the Veracruz road, in order to have access to both oceans, the nation would receive an impulse such as that its wealth would be sensibly augmented, and with it the income to the Federal Treasury, which would admit of the punctual payment of the interest on the national debt. The creditors of the country appear to have recognized the truth and force of these considerations . . .[13]

Romero was referring in the last sentence to arrangements celebrated with British bondholders and other creditors on December 6, 1878, linking railroad development to the future renewal of debt service and to a possible conversion of the external debt.

The order of priorities, therefore, was to attract foreign direct investment, which would have a positive impact on the economy and on fiscal revenues, and make it feasible, then, to proceed with renegotiation of the foreign debt. During the first years of the administration of General Manuel González (1880–84), United States entrepreneurs and investors did begin to channel a considerable volume of funds into Mexican railroads and mines.[14] Most significantly, between 1880 and 1882, there was a burst of investment in two major railroads, the Central and the National lines, which were promoted basically by United States investors. European capitalists proved more reticent to commit as large a quantity of funds. But it should be noted that Europeans already had made important investments in the Ferrocarril Mexicano (1873), the Banco de Londres y México (1863) (controlled by British and Mexican investors), and in the Banco Nacional (1881) (owned by a wide range of French, British, German, and Mexican financiers and/or rentiers).[15]

The promotion of ambitious railway development projects by the González administration depended not only on foreign direct investment but also on public subsidies. This led to rapidly rising deficits, despite a gradual increase in fiscal revenues.[16] The volume of direct subsidies to private railway enterprises exceeded 7 million pesos in 1882–83 and 3 million pesos in 1883–84. This money went to various private companies, the most important being the Ferrocarril Central, Mexicano and Interoceánico. These subsidies, and additional sums for port works and shipping companies, were paid with *certificados de aduanas*, promissory notes to be paid by different customs offices. This was risky fiscal policy insofar as a great percentage of customs revenues came to be mortgaged to privately owned firms and their financial agents.[17]

The new system of economic development project financing, adopted from the early 1880s, implied a radical shift from the balanced budget policies of the 1870s. Since the new projects required subsidies at a time when it was not yet possible to issue long-term bonds domestically or abroad for this purpose, the finance ministry resolved to mortgage its customs revenues—clearly a dangerous move. The scissors effect of reduced tax revenues and burgeoning expenditures created pressures for the authorities to gain access to new sources of revenue or credit. The situation reached a critical level by mid-1883 as a result of ballooning government deficits.

Not surprisingly, during 1883, the federal government began to pressure the recently established Banco Nacional to provide it with larger short-term loans, including a 2-million-peso bond issue, once again using promissory notes on customs as guarantees. The Banco Nacional had been set up only two years before by a broad-based group of European investors to take advantage of new opportunities in Mexican financial markets. As of 1880, there were still only three banks in the entire nation, one in the capital and two in the northern state of Chihuahua.[18] Although the directors of the Banco Nacional wanted to take a share in government finance, they initially refused to engage the firm's own capital in loans as large as those requested by the government. They conceded an advance of 150,000 pesos only in May 1883. Nonetheless, falling customs revenues forced the finance ministry to keep pressing. In November 1883, the Banco Nacional, in conjunction with seven allied merchant houses in Mexico City and the Paris-based Banque Franco-Egyptienne, finally agreed to advance 700,000 silver pesos to the treasury in exchange for 1 million pesos in customhouse certificates.[19] Curiously, the finance authorities did not seem to be too concerned that the short-term loan was expensive, nor that it transferred to the Banco Nacional control over a portion of government customs revenues in the Pacific ports and the northern frontier customs offices of Nuevo Laredo and Paso del Norte.

The increasingly difficult financial position of the government, however, could not be resolved merely with one loan. The government authorities, therefore, resorted to more "floating debt," taking additional advances provided by the Banco Nacional. During 1884, the treasury requested the bank to provide the huge sum of 5 million pesos in exchange for which the bank was to take over virtually the entire administration of customhouse certificates.[20] But without additional capital, the bank could not meet these extraordinary demands. A solution was found in the merger of the Banco Nacional with the Banco Mercantil, creating one larger company known henceforward as the Banco Nacional de México (Banamex). Edouard Noetzlin, representative of the European stockholders and president of the European board of directors of the bank, arrived in Mexico in February 1884 for the express purpose of signing the final agreements for the merger.[21] He met with President Manuel González, who suggested that an official commission be named for the merger under the auspices and direction of General Porfirio Díaz. Noetzlin, who maintained good relations with Díaz, quickly drafted a contract for the new banking company, and by May it was officially ratified.[22]

The establishment of Banamex represented a major change in Mexican finance. Although it remained privately owned and administered, Banamex formally became the government's bank. Banamex opened a large account for the finance ministry, through which the ministry could draw a total of 4 million pesos during the year. In exchange, the government allocated 15 percent of all customs revenues to the bank on top of the longstanding allocation of income from the national lottery and the stamp tax, which had been standing practice since 1881. Apart from short-term credits, Banamex was also expected to arrange long-term financing for the government. This function, however, did not appear viable without substantial reform of the already existing long-term debt. In turn, this problem implied initiating negotiations with foreign bondholders to see if conversion of the old London debt was feasible.

Banamex and the Initial Failure of Foreign Debt Negotiations in 1883–1884

In order to convince European investors that Mexico was a creditworthy nation, public authorities were obliged to adopt new financial instruments that could guarantee the future service of debt and assure interest payments to bondholders. The most important initiative taken in this regard was the ratification of Banamex as agency for the transfer of interest payments abroad.[23]

Edouard Noetzlin, head of the European board of Banamex, was personally charged by President González to be financial agent for Mexico in Europe and to arrange a foreign loan of £6 million, accompanied by the conversion of the outstanding foreign debt.[24] The interaction of public and private finances was thus not only institutionalized, but internationalized.

The role of Banamex was key here in two ways. First, it could provide local capital resources to assist the government with short-term credits for current account. Second, Banamex maintained excellent financial connections in Europe. Its overseas stockholders included an impressive roster of prominent financiers in Paris, London, and Berlin. Most important, from the point of view of British bondholders, Banamex had close ties with various merchant banks in London (in particular Glyn, Mills and Baring Brothers, on whom it could draw a large volume of funds) and with banks in other European financial centers and New York.[25]

When Noetzlin returned to Europe in the summer of 1884 he had little difficulty putting together a financial plan that quickly received the support of European bankers and bondholders. According to the plan, the bulk of the outstanding Mexican debt (dating from as far back as 1824) was to be converted into new bonds payable in gold. In order to carry out this plan, the Mexican government would negotiate with foreign bankers the issue of £6 million in bonds, the bulk of which would then be handed over to the bondholders.

The news was welcomed by the Council of Ministers in Mexico City. But, surprisingly, when the proposal was presented to the national Congress, an acrimonious and impassioned debate broke out lasting almost three weeks and stymieing approval of the so-called Noetzlin contract.[26] Several pro-government deputies—including the prestigious intellectual Justo Sierra—attempted to sway the Congress by insisting that a loan from European bankers would reduce dependency on United States capital. But the opposition counterattacked, emphasizing the high costs of the transaction. Criticism was directed in particular at a clause calling for the payment of a series of huge commissions totaling more than 13 million pesos, 10 million of which presumably would go to Noetzlin.[27]

Opposition from the press and popular outcry became so intense that, before a final vote could be carried out, popular demonstrations forced suspension of the discussion in the legislature. Hundreds of students took to the streets railing against the government, shouting, "Muera Manuel González! Muera el Manco! Muera Noetzlin!"[28] González was affectionately known as *el manco* because he had lost an arm in the battle of Puebla in 1863. As a result of the visibly corrupt practices of his government, however, he had lost much of his prestige. During the demonstrations, there was massive police intervention, and two persons were killed and hundreds injured; at the same time, the government ordered several newspapers temporarily closed. Nonetheless, the protests were ultimately effective, and González was forced to retire his proposal from Congress, leaving the debt conversion unresolved.

Opposition to the loan plans was not entirely surprising. It took place as the González administration was drawing to a close, in the midst of extended and bitter in-fighting among the elite to determine who would be president in 1885. Indeed, Porfirio Díaz, who was bent on returning to power, presumably did not have an interest in allowing his predecessor a major financial triumph. After the accession of Díaz in early 1885, his new finance minister, Manuel Dublán, wasted no time in sending a telegram to Noetzlin advising him of the suspension of the proposed contract and loan negotiations.[29]

In any case, it is likely that any debt transactions would have failed, for the fiscal situation of the government was becoming increasingly desperate. The government suffered a dramatic fall in revenues (resulting from declining foreign trade in late 1884 and early 1885) and a rise in short-term debts, creating an inability to meet ordinary budgeted expenditures. Nearly 80 percent of customs revenues were pledged to cover subsidies to private railway firms or to Banamex, making it impossible to cover essentials, such as the payment of salaries to army officers, soldiers, and tax officials.

In June 1885, Finance Minister Dublán took emergency action. On June 22, he declared that the government faced a potential deficit of 25 million pesos. He announced a suspension of payments on all short-term government debts, a 10 to 15 percent reduction in the salaries of all state employees, and the establishment of a new plan to convert the entire internal and external debt.[30] The first and most dramatic measure was the suspension of payments on short-term debt. This included a huge backlog of credits due to Banamex, to the three leading foreign-owned railway companies, and to a wide array of public contractors and local creditors. Dublán's emergency measures created a furor both in Mexican and foreign money markets. Nonetheless, the suspension of payments on short-term debts and obligations allowed the Mexican government a considerable respite, and shortly thereafter, public deficits declined. The railway investors received a considerable amount of new internal bonds (*certificados de construcción de ferrocarriles*) to guarantee future payments on their subsidies.[31] Banamex worked out a series of new financial arrangements with the government that assured it a regular percentage of fiscal income to liquidate a portion of the money it had advanced to the government.[32] As a result, the financial situation gradually stabilized, and the prospect of raising a large foreign loan improved markedly.

Despite opposition, therefore, the drastic fiscal/financial reforms of June 1885 proved relatively successful and laid the groundwork for the debt conversion operations of 1886–88, as well as for a string of foreign loans over the following two decades. But it should be underlined that it was Banamex that saved the government by not pressing for immediate reimbursement of all debts and by ceding control of most of the tax revenues that the government had mortgaged to the bank in previous years in exchange for short-term loans. Moreover, it was to Banamex that the government had to turn to renegotiate its foreign debt. In this regard, a private agency was critical in the restructuring of public finance and proved to be the instrument and guarantor of the new foreign debt policies.

The Debt Conversion of 1886–1887 and the Key Role of Banamex

For some time, foreign investors remained extremely wary of any proposals by the Mexican government to invest more money in private enterprises or in a prospective loan. The effects of the crisis of June 1885 did not really subside until June 1886. It was then that, after prolonged negotiations, the financial agent of Mexico in London, General Francisco Z. Mena, reached an agreement with the Corporation of Foreign Bondholders to recognize and convert the outstanding foreign debt of Mexico.[33] The bondholders now accepted the clauses of the June 22, 1885, decrees, whereby they exchanged their old 6 percent bonds for new 3 percent bonds on which they would soon begin receiving cash interest payments. The government was to establish a financial agency in Mexico to supervise the conversion of the debt, and designated the prestigious London firm of Glyn, Mills, Currie and Co. as banker in charge of receiving interest payments from the Mexican government beginning January 1887. It should be noted that Glyn, Mills were the main correspondents of Banco Nacional de México in London, and that the latter had a large account with the London firm.

The debt conversion of 1886 represented a major step forward in the resolution and reduction of the complex financial quandary that had brought six decades of anguish to Mexico. The complex negotiations led to a sophisticated financial solution, providing substantial relief through a reduction of the recognized capital of the outstanding debt. The exact nature of the benefits has long been a subject of debate. But, *grosso modo*, it can be argued that the Mexican government obtained a savings of some 8 million pesos in the form of debt capital reductions on the foreign debt (see Table 4.1) and additional savings on the internal debt.

The outstanding foreign debt was composed of a variety of bond issues, the most important being derived from the old Mexican loans issued in London in 1824 and 1825, plus the interest backlog on them. The previous conversion of 1851 had established that Mexico owed £10.2 million to the British bondholders. But since then, an additional debt had accumulated in the form of interest unpaid between 1851 and 1861 (before the European invasion of Mexico) and interest unpaid from 1867 to 1886. Dublán's decree of June 22, 1885, established that the conversion agreement of 1851 would be recognized in full (that is, £10.2 million), but that the greater part of the interest backlog from 1851 would be struck from the books. Thus a savings of £7.7 million was established by the finance ministry and accepted by the British bondholders. The remaining foreign debts included a potpourri of bonds, the value of which also was reduced substantially.[34] In all cases, the foreign bondholders were to receive new 3 percent bonds payable in gold.

It should be observed, however, that the Mexican government conducted negotiations not only with the foreign bondholders. There was also a long list of local creditors who requested payment on their claims, some dating as far back as 1850, but most stemming from financial advances made to the armies of Benito Juárez and to administrations in power from 1867 to 1880. In total these claims were estimated at 57 million pesos and were converted to approximately 25 million pesos in 3 percent bonds—but it was stipulated they were payable only in silver. This internal debt consolidation—in combination with the foreign debt conversion—marked a substantial step forward in the stabilization of Mexican finances. It projected a new image that modified the views of foreign bankers and investors with respect to the creditworthiness of the nation.

To guarantee the external debt conversion, Dublán made arrangements

with Banamex for the transfer, from 1887 onward, of the bi-annual debt
payments from Mexico to the London merchant bank of Glyn, Mills for
payment to bondholders.[35] It was from this time that Banamex became the
formal agent for the government for all its foreign debt operations and payments, a role it continued to exercise for more than two decades. For foreign investors, the role of this private agency in guaranteeing public debt
service was absolutely fundamental for regaining confidence in Mexico. In
other words, here we find fulfillment of the first essential conditions for the
recovery of international financial credibility by the Mexican government
during the Porfiriato. It consisted not only in recognition of international financial norms, but also in actual observance of them in day-to-day practice.

The 1888 Foreign Loan: Gaining Access to European Money Markets

The renewal of debt service was not the only contribution of the bank to
the restructuring of Mexican finance. The ubiquitous Noetzlin, head of the
Banamex board in Paris, was charged by the Mexican government with the
negotiation of a great loan abroad, intended to consolidate the entire outstanding foreign debts of the Republic. In contrast to his previous bitter experience of 1884, Noetzlin was now able to pull off a major financial coup
by arranging the issue of the 1888 conversion loan in London and Berlin.

The overall merits of the debt restructuring must be measured in terms
of the cost/benefit relation of the conversion itself. In the case of the huge
foreign loan for Mexico issued in Europe in 1888, the following benefits and
costs are particularly relevant: (1) the benefits of converting the huge volume of non-paying old outstanding bonds to a smaller volume of interest-
paying new bonds, (2) the financial savings gained by replacing short-term
debt with long-term debt, (3) the costs of the financial operation itself in
terms of discounts and commissions, (4) the costs of dependence upon one
large bank and its foreign financial allies for debt issue and service, and (5)
the benefits of reentry into international capital markets.[36]

There were several striking aspects to the new foreign loan. First, it had
a positive impact on the overall credit situation of the Mexican government.
The nominal value of this loan was £10.5 million, with a net return for Mexico of approximately £8.2 million. With the latter sum, Dublán was able to
convert the bulk of the outstanding foreign bonds (which were acquired at
40 percent of their face value).[37] In his annual financial report, Dublán argued that, together with the previous conversions of 1885–86, this transaction reduced the outstanding Mexican foreign debt from £23 million to

£14.6 million. On paper this represented a major reduction, but it should be recalled that the 3 percent Mexican external bonds had been quoted at not more than 40 percent on the market. Therefore the government was able to exchange the bulk of the old bonds for the new 6 percent bonds at a total cost of approximately £6 million, leaving a portion of proceeds to pay off domestic debts.

The extra money remaining from the foreign loan was utilized to cancel most of the short-term debts due to Banamex from 1885 onward, including some 12 million pesos in floating debts. This had the double advantage of relieving the treasury of its dependence on the powerful bank, while at the same time freeing its customhouses and other tax sources of most mortgages. The terms and funding made this the most favorable debt renegotiation in the history of the nation.[38]

Nonetheless, contemporaries in Mexico and abroad argued that the loan arrangement was not as satisfactory as Dublán maintained. In the first place, the financial juggling involved in the acquisition of outstanding bonds (to be exchanged for the new gold bonds) provided extremely attractive opportunities to both bankers and politicians for profitable speculation. In fact, these transactions strongly resemble modern-day "swap" operations with Latin American debt, in which the profit margins tend to be quite high. In the second place, the 1888 loan placed Mexican finance increasingly under the sway of European bankers, the most important being the German syndicate headed by the famous firm of Bleichroeder, banker to Bismarck (see Figures 4.2 and 4.3). How Noetzlin was able to convince Bleichroeder to participate is not known. But, because the Berlin banker had long been a major stockholder in Banamex, he was presumably well informed of the state of Mexican finances.[39]

Certainly, the financial terms were singularly attractive to the European bankers. They were to take the first tranche of £3.7 million of the loan at the low price of 70 percent of the loan, and a second tranche of £5.8 million at 85 percent. Given that Bleichroeder was able to sell the bonds corresponding to these two issues at 85 percent and 92 percent, respectively, it can be estimated that his consortium garnered earnings of over £700,000 by simply selling the Mexican securities on the European markets. The money, however, did not go only to the German bankers, but also to other financial houses participating: 62 percent went to the Bleichroeder syndicate, 20 percent to A. Gibbs and Sons of London, and 18 percent to the Banamex branch in Paris.[40]

Other individuals reaping benefits from the Mexican loan included

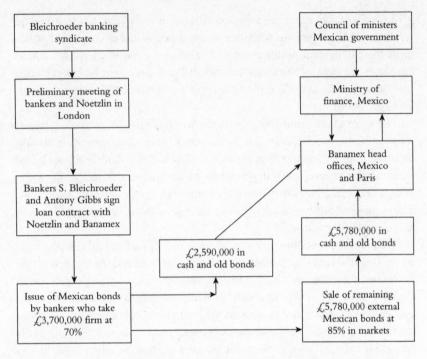

Figure 4.2. Negotiation and Issue of the 1888 Mexican Foreign Loan
(£10.5 million)

Edouard Noetzlin, who received a payment of 1 million pesos for his services as intermediary with the European bankers; Benito Gómez Farías, head
of the Mexican public debt office; and Joaquín Casasús, financial advisor to
the government, both of whom received large commissions. It was also
argued that an indirect but major benefactor was former president Manuel
González, who had purchased large amounts of old bonds before the conversion and the loan.[41] Evidently, the great conversion loan not only contributed to the stabilization of Mexican finances but also proved to be a gold
mine for numerous financiers and politicians on both sides of the Atlantic.

The London *Times* severely criticized the entire loan transaction. It
pointed out that the Mexican government had been facing severe difficulties as a result of the large floating debt and that previous solutions had not
been successful. It further commented that Noetzlin appeared to maintain an
extremely warm relationship with Bleichroeder, despite the fact that the
French banker himself was the official agent of the Mexican government for

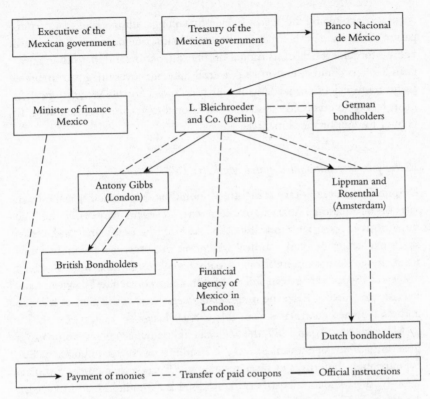

Figure 4.3. Debt Service on the 1888 Mexican Foreign Loan (£10.5 million)

the renegotiation of the public debt. But the London newspaper especially criticized the advantages Bleichroeder enjoyed by being able to exchange devalued bonds of 1851 and 1862 (albeit at a discount) for new gold bonds. The possible speculative gains were enormous. It added:

> Such an arrangement is manifestly very advantageous to the contractor, and much in opposition to the interest of Mexico . . . To raise money to pay off a floating debt upon which a Government pays even as much as 12 percent upon such terms as these is not good finance . . . The only explanation is that the Mexican government are greatly harassed by the persistent demands of the National Bank of Mexico to repay loans made to the Government which are of long standing.[42]

It should be underlined, nonetheless, that the contribution of Banamex to the issue of the 1888 bonds in various European markets was not as per-

verse as suggested by the *Times*. In fact, by taking a substantial direct participation in the issue of the Mexican bonds, Banamex demonstrated that it was
willing to stake much of its capital on the transaction and that other European bankers could count on its powerful influence over the government to
assure regular debt service. Again, this was crucial for the Mexican government to regain credibility among international investors, and, therefore, to
reenter foreign financial markets.

Reentry to International Capital Markets, 1889–1893

Despite the contemporary criticism, it should be emphasized that the bond
sales on international financial markets were successful. Moreover, the high
quotations of Mexican bonds after 1888 on both the Berlin and the London
stock exchanges marked a radical change in the prospects for raising new
loans. Indeed, negotiations for new loans began shortly thereafter. Between
1889 and 1893, the Mexican federal government returned to European markets for three loans. Even the municipal government of the City of Mexico
and state-owned enterprises were able to raise loans.

More specifically, in 1889, the Mexican Tehuantepec railway company (a
government-run operation) issued £2.7 million of mortgage bonds in Europe through the offices of the Dresdner and Darmstadter Banks. Simultaneously, the Mexico City government raised a £2 million loan in London
for major drainage works. Soon after, in 1890, Bleichroeder returned to the
fray, leading a consortium for the issue of £6 million of bonds for the Mexican federal government to help with railway finance.

However, despite the influx of foreign gold, in 1891–93, the Mexican
government was confronted with another crisis situation that was in many
ways more severe than that of 1885.[43] Following his return to the finance
ministry in late 1890, Matías Romero found it impossible to sell domestic
debt securities. Nobody wanted to buy bonds payable in silver at a time of
falling silver prices. His only solution was to request renewed assistance from
Banamex, which was clearly the pillar of the state financial edifice (although
it continued to be entirely privately owned). On August 1, 1892, Banamex
advanced £600,000 in conjunction with a syndicate of bankers in Berlin,
London, and Paris. Ten percent of customhouse taxes were mortgaged to
the loan. Then, in March of 1893, a new advance of 2.5 million pesos was
made, in exchange for which Banamex took over the administration of the
Casa de Moneda (mint) in both Mexico City and San Luis Potosí. Finally,
in June 1893, a short-term loan of £267,500 was made to pay pending railway subsidies. In this case, Banamex obtained a mortgage on 4 percent of all

import taxes, and the entire proceeds of the stamp taxes on alcoholic beverages sold throughout the republic.[44]

By this time, it appeared that Banamex was, once again, on the verge of
becoming an old-style moneylender with a stranglehold grip on the national
treasury and its fiscal offices. Nevertheless, it should be noted that the interest rates charged were no longer truly usurious, but rather determined by
market conditions, locally and internationally. Furthermore, the directors of
the bank were aware that if the government were pressured into a desperate situation, then payments would again be suspended, as they had been in
June 1885. For Banamex, therefore, it was clear that more money could be
made by continuing to serve as loyal government banker. This was manifest
in the issue of the £3 million foreign loan in late 1893. Despite extremely
low quotations for Mexican bonds on European markets, new finance minister Limantour was obliged to go through with the transaction. He needed
to obtain the proceeds necessary to pay off Banamex, Bleichroeder, and other
financial houses that had advanced sums in the years immediately preceding.
Mexican bonds had been declining since mid-1891, but by 1893 the 1888
bonds had fallen on the Berlin stock market to 65. The bankers (Bleichroeder and the European office of Banamex) took £1,650,000 of the loan firm
at 60 and £950,000 at 65. The sale of the bonds was postponed until early
1894 because the markets remained weak. But, once again, the direct participation of Banamex was key to the international operations of the Mexican finance ministry.[45]

Conclusions

The foreign loan of 1893 demonstrated—as had the great conversion loan
of 1888—that Mexican finances were as heavily influenced by short-term
revenue factors as by long-term development objectives. Both of these international financial operations indicated the degree to which domestic and
international finance were now intertwined, and the extent to which this
was due to the innovative and dominant role of Banamex as ex officio government banker. For international investors, this represented a significant
move toward financial modernization in a country in which foreign debt
had long been tied to frequent shifts in political (and fiscal) cycles. It was not
the state that gave credibility to the bank, but the reverse: the finance ministry acquired respectability because of its close ties to a powerful private
banking enterprise that had a dual, domestic/international structure.

Not surprisingly, reliance on one bank (which was not strictly a central
bank, but was certainly a government bank) implied high costs. In the case

of the 1888 conversion loan, most of the funds raised by the sale of the bonds in Europe were used simply for refinancing existing long-term debt, as old bonds were exchanged for new. But much of the revenue was also used to pay off a large array of short-term debts owed to Banamex. Thirty-eight percent of the 1893 loan's net proceeds went to pay off Banamex's short-term advances to the government; another 35 percent went to cover interest payments on the foreign loans of 1888 and 1890 and toward the anticipated service on the 1893 loan itself.[46]

Nonetheless, it is also clear that the 1888 conversion loan did allow both the Mexican government and private enterprise access to European capital markets, stimulating a flow of funds for productive investment. Similarly, 20 percent of the 1893 loan was used to finance the Tehuantepec Railway, and a portion of the debt service covered by the same loan went to similar investment objectives. Both these "revenue" and "development" objectives were essential to the financial equilibrium of the Porfirian regime. It is in this sense that Banamex proved to be a most important agent in facilitating the Mexican government's access to international financial markets.[47]

In general terms, the conversion and renegotiation of the foreign debt in the late 1880s marked an important watershed in the financial history of the nation. What I have attempted in this chapter is quite simply to describe and explain the symbiotic relation between the strategies of the Mexican government and those of the government's banker—Banamex—in the negotiation of the loans of the 1880s and early 1890s. Future research on the impact of these financial operations on the Mexican economy and society requires a different and broader focus. However, perhaps the perspective presented here can be of use for such studies and can suggest the need to simultaneously analyze national and international norms in the financial realm and the degree to which they are interlocked.

Notes

I would like to thank Lance Davis and other commentators at the Stanford University Conference, "Institutional Change and Economic Performance in Mexico," December 1998, for their observations on an earlier version of this chapter.

1. For a review of the legal complexities of Mexican foreign debt in the twentieth century, see Marichal 1999b.

2. Analysis of the weak capital markets in early nineteenth-century Mexico can be found in Marichal 1997.

3. The almost continuous moratorium from 1828 to 1862 was continued

after 1867, when President Juárez declared a new suspension. Hence, no payments were forthcoming to European bondholders on Mexican foreign debts until early 1886. See Bazant 1981.

4. See Aceña 1994. This raises a debate with Noel Maurer's argument in the essay included in this volume (see Chapter 3), although he focuses attention on Banamex's role in the financial market rather than on its administration of public finance.

5. Among the classics, see Casasús 1885; Bulnes 1885; and Ortíz de Montellano 1886. The three most detailed studies are McCaleb 1921; Turlington 1930; and Bazant 1981. Luis Téllez 1992 is based on a doctoral thesis presented at MIT, and Vinod Aggarwal 1989 is an essay in Eichengreen and Lindert 1989.

6. These colonial debts were actually loans advanced by wealthy Mexicans to the Spanish colonial government. Much of the money was later transferred to Spain. For a review of these curious debts, which were never paid back, see Marichal 1999a.

7. Téllez 1992 has less information than Tenenbaum 1986 on this question.

8. British and Spanish troops that had accompanied the French soon retired from Veracruz, while the French army of thirty thousand soldiers remained in Mexico for more than three years.

9. He argues that the British Council of Foreign Bondholders was very strong at this time, an assertion belied by its failure to prevent increasing flotation of Mexican private stock on the London market before and during the years of the debt negotiations.

10. For instance, he argues that the Mexican economy was stagnant in the early 1880s and that there was a terrible balance of payments problem, both of which claims are untrue.

11. Carmagnani 1994: chap. 5 argues that the treasury used 1 million pesos per year to retire a total of 20 million pesos in domestic debt, buying on the market at half of nominal value.

12. As argued in Marichal 1997, the old pattern of depending on domestic moneylenders who charged outrageous prices was no longer acceptable, but the lack of banks and the lack of depth of financial markets created a financial bottleneck.

13. Romero 1880: 41.

14. The biggest enterprise in which they invested was the Ferrocarril Central Mexicano, established in 1880 mainly by Boston capitalists. See Kuntz Ficker 1996.

15. For a detailed analysis of the stockholders of the Banco Nacional 1881 and of the Banco Mercantil 1882 promoted by Spanish merchant residents in Mexico, see Ludlow 1990.

16. For data see Marichal 1988.

17. In his financial report, Minister De la Peña stated in September 1884 that 60 percent of the cutoffs revenues of the port of Campeche, 90 percent of those of Tampico and Matamoros, and 84 percent of the income of the cutoffs house of Veracruz were mortgaged to railway companies, merchant houses, and the Banco Nacional. Secretaría de Hacienda 1884: lxxx–lxxxix.

18. Ludlow 1990 provides information on the original stockholders, who included a large number of Paris-based private bankers as well as the German banker Bleichroeder and the English financier Ernest Cassell.

19. For the contracts on these and other government loans extended by Banamex, see the materials in AHBANAMEX B.

20. See discussion by the bank directors of the government proposal in Banco Nacional de México 1881–1884: January 24, 1884.

21. Edouard Noetzlin was a Swiss-born banker who became a key administrator of the Bischoffseihm banking interests in France. As head of the Banque Franco-Egyptienne he was a chief promoter of the creation of the Banamex and served as head of the Banamex Paris board for decades. He later became president of Banque de Paris et Pays Bas.

22. The details of the contract establishing the Banco Nacional de México (May 31, 1884) as well as additional clauses relating to the financial relationship between the government and the bank are in Castillo 1903: 19–52. Also see Ludlow 1986: 299–346.

23. With nominal capital of 20 million pesos, Banamex was considered a most solid institution, capable of servicing the debt. In 1883, the European directors of the old Banco Nacional repeatedly urged the Mexican managers and directors to take up the issue of the debt service in Europe. They thereby exercised their option to take charge of the management of the Mexican foreign debt, as established in the original contract of the bank. For extremely interesting observations, see bank directors' minutes in AHBANAMEX A.

24. For the text of the legislative decree authorizing the foreign loan, see Castillo 1903: 17–18.

25. Information on relations with London merchant banks can be found interspersed in the directors' minutes, AHBANAMEX A. The bank also maintained close ties to J. P. Morgan in New York, a shareholder of Banamex. For a detailed list of original shareholders see Ludlow 1990.

26. According to the congressional finance commission this was the first public debate on the question of the foreign debt in thirty years, the last major legislative discussion having taken place in 1850. Cámara de Diputados 1885: 178–79.

27. It should be recalled that Noetzlin was acting in the name of the Banco Nacional de México, and that the commissions were probably intended to cover the huge advances the bank had been forced to make to the government on account of the future proceeds of the loan. These surpassed 5 million pesos between May and October, and 2 million pesos in previous months. Nonethe-

less, on being informed of the popular opposition, Noetzlin wired the government his renunciation of the commissions mentioned. The Noetzlin contract was analyzed critically by contemporary financial specialists, although the exact nature of the commissions was never clarified. On Banco Nacional de México advances, see the contracts signed between November 24, 1883, and October 10, 1884, AHBANAMEX B. For critical interpretations of the Noetzlin contract see Casasús 1885: 457–80; Ortíz de Montellano 1886: 101–15; Bulnes 1885: 461–551.

28. For details, see Pérez Siller 1995.

29. Copy of communication dated January 21, 1885, in Castillo 1903: 54–57.

30. On paper, the new debt conversion plan reduced commissions, but actually was not so different from the old González/Noetzlin project; however, new political and economic circumstances changed its impact dramatically.

31. For regulations on amortization of these *certificados*, see Secretaría de Hacienda 1886: 250–51.

32. See AHBANAMEX B, contracts 9, 10, and 11 between Banco Nacional de México and the government, signed October 21, 1885, January 11, 1886, and February 4, 1886.

33. For the text of the agreement signed June 23, 1886, with E. P. Bouverie, president of the corporation and with H. Sheridan, president of the Committee of Mexican Bondholders, see Secretaría de Hacienda 1886: 275–78.

34. On the labyrinthine negotiations related to these additional external bonds, there is abundant contemporary literature, including the previously cited works of Casasús, Bulnes, Ortíz de Montellano, and Bazant. Additional information can be found in the annual reports of the Secretaría de Hacienda and in those of the Corporation of Foreign Bondholders. It should also be observed that there was a large block of outstanding "Mexican imperial bonds" held in France, issued by the regime of Maximilian (1863–67), but subsequently repudiated by Mexico, since they served mainly to finance the invasion and occupation of Mexico by French troops.

35. See AHBANAMEX B, contracts 12–17, between November 27, 1886, and January 2, 1888, which relate to these debt service payments.

36. This type of analysis may be of interest for similar evaluations of the massive conversion of Mexican external debt that took place one century later, namely the conversion undertaken under the so-called Brady plan in 1988–89.

37. It should be noted that, in the agreement signed with the bondholders in September 1886, Dublán managed to extract as a concession the ability to acquire all outstanding bonds at a future date at 40 percent of their nominal value. In practice, the 3 percent bonds sold at approximately this price on the London market.

38. Secretaría de Hacienda 1889: xxxiii.

39. It should also be noted that a large circle of German merchants in Mexico had major interests in Banamex. For details on stockholders of the bank, see Ludlow 1990.

40. Bleichroeder also received an additional commission of £130,000 for taking charge of the whole transaction. Details are in Secretaría de Hacienda 1888–89, 1889–90.

41. On commissions to Noetzlin and González's speculation, see Bazant 1981: 124–25.

42. Economist Intelligence Unit 1954: 180–81.

43. The causes of the economic downturn in the early 1890s were basically three. First, there was the agrarian crisis, which led to bad harvests during two successive years. Second, the dramatic fall in the international price of silver, still the principal export. Third, the weakening of international financial markets, initially as a result of the 1890 Baring crisis in London, and later, in 1893, as a result of the crash in New York. The agrarian crisis required some extraordinary expenditures, but it was the declining price of silver that hit the government hardest, since it led to a steep fall in the foreign trade of the nation. Import tax revenues (still more than 40 percent of total ordinary revenues) dropped precipitously.

44. For data on the loans, see AHBANAMEX B, contracts 26, 28, 29.

45. For details see Wynne 1954: 52–53.

46. See detailed figures on the 1893 loan in chart 29 of Bazant 1981, which summarizes the data from Secretaría de Hacienda 1893–94.

47. The theoretical analysis of "development" and "revenue" loans was developed by Fishlow 1985.

References

Aceña, Pablo Martín. 1994. "La formación de la banca central en España, siglos XIX y XX." In Carlos Marichal and Pedro Tedde, eds., *Formación de la banca central en España y América Latina*, vol. 1, pp. 122–40. Madrid.

Aggarwal, Vinod. 1989. "Interpreting the History of Mexico's External Debt Crises." In Barry Eichengreen and Peter Lindert, eds., *The International Debt in Historical Perspective*, pp. 140–88. Cambridge, Mass.

[AHBANAMEX A] Archivo Histórico de Banamex. *Libro de Actas-Acuerdos del Consejo de Administración, 1881–1886.* Mexico City.

[AHBANAMEX B]. *Libro de Contratos Originales con el Gobierno Federal, 1883–1914.* Mexico City.

Bazant, Jan. 1981. *Historia de la deuda exterior de México.* Mexico City.

Bulnes, Francisco. 1885. *La deuda inglesa.* Mexico City.

Cámara de Diputados (Mexico). 1885. *Diario de Debates, Cámara de Diputados (Doceava Legislatura) 1884–1885.* Mexico City.

Carmagnani, Marcello. 1989. "El liberalismo, los impuestos internos y el estado federal mexicano, 1857–1911." *Historia Mexicana*, vol. 38, no. 3: 471–496.

———. 1994. *Estado y mercado: La economía política del liberalismo mexicano, 1857–1911*. Mexico City.

Casasús, Joaquín. 1885. *Historia de la deuda contraída en Londres*. Mexico City.

Castillo, Juan. 1903. "Colección de leyes, decretos, reglamentos, contratos, supremas resoluciones y noticias referentes al crédito público, 1883–1903: Época del arreglo definitivo de la deuda nacional." Mexico City.

Cerda, Luis. 1991. "Exchange Rate and Monetary Policies in Mexico: From Bimetallism to the Gold Standard, 1890–1910." Working paper DT-9, November 1992, Instituto Tecnológico Autónomo de México.

Cerutti, Mario. 1992. *Burguesía, capitales e industria en el norte de México: Monterrey y su ámbito regional, 1850–1910*. Mexico City.

Cerutti, Mario, and Carlos Marichal, eds. 1997. *Historia de las grandes empresas en México, 1880–1930*. Mexico City.

[CFBH] Council of Foreign Bondholders. Newspaper Clippings on Mexico, 1873–1940. Microfilm. El Colegio de México.

Coatsworth, John. 1984. *El impacto económico de los ferrocarriles en el Porfiriato: Crecimiento contra desarrollo*. Mexico City.

———. 1990. *Los orígenes del atraso: Nueve ensayos de historia económica de México en los siglos XVIII y XIX*. Mexico City.

Cosío Villegas, Daniel. 1964. *Historia moderna de México: Vida económica*. 2 vols. Mexico City. [Several additional volumes of this work deal with the political and diplomatic history of the Porfirian regime.]

Davis, Lance E., and Robert J. Cull. 1994. *International Capital Markets and American Economic Growth, 1820–1914*. Cambridge, England.

Davis, Lance E., and Robert E. Gallman. 1994. "Savings, Investment and Economic Growth: The United States in the Nineteenth Century." In John James and Mark Thomas, eds., *Capitalism in Context*, pp. 202–29. Chicago.

Dickinson, P. G. M. 1967. *The Financial Revolution in England: A Study in the Development of Public Credit, 1688–1756*. New York.

D'Olwer, Nicolau. 1974. "Las inversiones extranjeras." In Daniel Cosío Villegas, ed., *Historia moderna de México: Vida económica*, vol. 2, pp. 973–1177. Mexico City.

Economist Intelligence Unit. 1954. "British Investment in Mexico, 1869–1911." Manuscript. Library of Banco de México.

Eichengreen, Barry, and Peter Lindert, eds. 1989. *The International Debt Crisis in Historical Perspective*. Cambridge, Mass.

Fishlow, Albert. 1996. "Latin American Nineteenth Century Public Debt: Theory and Practice." In Reinhard Liehr, ed., *La deuda pública en América Latina en perspectiva histórica*, pp. 23–45. Frankfurt.

————. 1985. "Lessons from the Past: Capital Markets During the Nineteenth Century and the Interwar Period." *International Organization*,
vol. 39, no. 3: 420–60.

Haber, Stephen. 1989. *Industry and Underdevelopment: The Industrialization of
Mexico, 1890–1940*. Stanford.

————, ed. 1997. *How Latin America Fell Behind: Essays on the Economic Histories of Brazil and Mexico, 1800–1914*. Stanford.

Kuntz Ficker, Sandra. 1996. *Empresa extranjera y mercado interno: El Ferrocarril
Central Mexicano, 1880–1907*. Mexico City.

Lewis, W. A. 1983. *Crecimiento y fluctuaciones, 1870–1914*. Mexico City.

Liehr, Reinhard, ed. 1995. *La deuda pública en América Latina en perspectiva
histórica*. Frankfurt.

Ludlow, Leonor. 1990. "El Banco Nacional y el Banco Mercantil Mexicano:
Radiografía social de sus primeros accionistas, 1881–1882." *Historia
Mexicana*, vol. 34, no. 4: 979–1028.

————. 1986. "La construcción de un banco: El Banco Nacional de México
(1881–1884)." In Leonor Ludlow and Carlos Marichal, eds., *Banca y
poder en México, 1800–1925*, pp. 299–346. Mexico City.

Ludlow, Leonor, and Carlos Marichal, eds. 1986. *Banca y poder en México,
1800–1925*. Mexico City.

Ludlow, Leonor, and Jorge Silva, eds. 1993. *Los negocios y las ganancias: De la
colonia al México moderno*. Mexico City.

Marichal, Carlos. 1999a. *La bancarrota del virreinato: La deuda colonial del Mexico
borbónico, 1780–1810*. Mexico City.

————. 1999b. "Coacción y coerción en el manejo de la deuda externa de
México en el siglo XX: Una perspectiva económica-jurídica." In Ricardo Forte, ed., *Coacción y coerción en América latina: Ensayos de política,
economía e historia*. Mexico City.

————. 1988. "La deuda externa y las políticas de desarrollo económico durante el Porfiriato: Algunas hipótesis de trabajo." In F. Rosenzweig et al.,
Pasado y presente de la deuda externa de México, pp. 85–102. Mexico City.

————. 1997. "Obstacles to the Development of Capital Markets in Nineteenth-Century Mexico." In Stephen Haber, ed., *How Latin America Fell
Behind: Essays on the Economic Histories of Brazil and Mexico, 1800–1914*,
pp. 118–45. Stanford.

McCaleb, Walter. 1921. *The Public Finances of Mexico*. New York.

Ortíz de Montellano, Mariano. 1886. *Apuntes para la liquidación de la deuda contraída en Londres*. Mexico City.

Pérez Siller, Javier. 1995. "Deuda y consolidación del poder en México, 1867–
1896: Bases para la modernidad porfirista." In Reinhard Liehr, ed., *La
deuda pública en América Latina en perspectiva histórica*, pp. 293–335.
Frankfurt.

Riguzzi, Paolo. 1994. "La conexión de México con la economía atlántica, 1880–191: El caso de las inversiones extranjeras." Paper presented at the Reunion of Mexican and American historians, Mexico City.

Riley, James C. 1980. *International Government Finance and the Amsterdam Capital Market, 1740–1815.* Cambridge, England.

Romero, Matías. 1880. *Report of the Secretary of Finance of the United States of Mexico of the 15th of January 1879 on the actual condition of Mexico and the increase of commerce with the United States, rectifying the report of the Hon. John W. Foster, Minister Plenipotenciary in Mexico.* New York.

Secretaría de Hacienda y Crédito Público. 1880–93. *Memoria.* Mexico City.

Semana Mercantil, La. 1884–85. Mexico City.

Stallings, Barbara. 1987. *Bankers to the Third World: U.S. Portfolio Investment in Latin America, 1900–1986.* Berkeley.

Stern, Fritz. 1977. *Gold and Iron: Bismarck, Bleichroeder and the Building of the German Empire.* New York.

Téllez, Luis. 1992. "Préstamos externos, primas de riesgo y hechos políticos: La experiencia mexicana en el siglo XIX." In Enrique Cárdenas, ed., *Historia económica de México*, vol. 3, pp. 327–90. Mexico City.

Tenenbaum, Barbara. 1986. *The Politics of Penury: Debt and Taxes in Mexico, 1821–1856.* Albuquerque.

Topik, Steven C. 1993. "Controversia crediticia: Los 'azulitos' del período de Maximiliano." In Leonor Ludlow and Jorge Silva, eds., *Los negocios y las ganancias de la colonia al México moderno*, pp. 445–70. Mexico City.

Turlington, Edgar. 1930. *Mexico and Her Foreign Creditors.* New York.

Wynne, William. 1954. *State Insolvency and Foreign Bondholders.* New Haven.

Zabludowsky, Jaime. 1992. "La depreciación de la plata y las exportaciones." In Enrique Cárdenas, ed., *Historia económica de México*, vol. 3, pp. 290–326. Mexico City.

Chapter 5

The Legal System, Institutional Change, and Financial Regulation in Mexico, 1870–1910: Mortgage Contracts and Long-Term Credit

PAOLO RIGUZZI

Mexico, in the second half of the nineteenth century, represents a good historical case for the analysis of obstacles that interpose themselves and block interrelations between potentialities for growth. At that time, Mexico's was a backward rural economy with few individual property rights and replete with communal and corporative rights, practices, and values. During the two decades between 1870 and 1890, a process of institutional change, based on the principles of constitutional liberalism, started to transform the legal system and modify economic practices. The liberal program adopted private contracts as the principal mechanism for exchange restructuring, as a means of liberating economic energy, and for the opening of spaces for private interests.

In this context, my objective is to analyze aspects of Mexican institutional change relevant to answering two central questions in neo-institutional economic theory: (1) How do variations in institutional arrangements affect economic outcomes, or the production of wealth? (2) How do variations in the institutional framework affect practicable forms of economic organization available to economic actors?[1] In order to do this, I have selected a contractual area of particular relevance to Mexican institutional change: the mortgage contract. This was one of the principal domains in which institutional modifications restructured the exchange of property rights. In this regard, institutional change affected extensive portions of the Mexican economy.

The chapter is organized in five sections. The first one presents the legal

120

features of mortgage before 1870 and describes the place mortgage credit occupied within the larger credit landscape. The second section analyzes the legal reform of the mortgage contract as a process of institutional change, beginning with the enactment of the Civil Code and Civil Proceedings Code of 1870–72. It is argued that this reform considerably reduced the transaction costs in mortgage contracts and created a more adequate set of guarantees and incentives for the development of long-term credit in Mexico. The third section examines the impact of institutional change upon the mortgage credit market, measuring the transformations produced in the structure of the market and identifying the actual beneficiaries of these changes. The findings indicate that financial intermediaries could not establish themselves as relevant organizations in this sector and that mortgage credit continued to organize around personal links and private moneylenders.

The fourth section explores the reason behind this continuity and focuses on the relationship between financial intermediation, the banking sector, and mortgage credit. The aim is to discern those constraints that imposed limitations and obstacles to banking institutions in the field of mortgage activities. I argue that ad hoc financial regulation, in the form of the first mortgage bank's charter, provided an institutional counterdevelopment that minimized the favorable impact of institutional change and inhibited the transformation of the mortgage market. The last section examines the consequences of the lack of financial intermediation in the field of mortgage credit, with the purpose of identifying those sectors primarily affected. The distortion in the use of banking resources on the one hand and the strangled channeling of credit to the agricultural sector on the other emerge as the most salient obstacles to the potential for economic growth during the period.

The Mortgage Contract in Nineteenth-Century Mexico

In this section I analyze the legal structure of the mortgage contract and its significance for the Mexican economy. Mexico was a predominantly rural country, where agriculture accounted for the main portion of the gross product, and where, toward the end of the nineteenth century, two-thirds of the labor force resided in the countryside.[2] The mortgage was probably the main mechanism of financing private economic activity in the primary sector. Owing to the lack of banking institutions and financial instruments, mortgages filled a substantial gap and fulfilled a variety of functions. This kind of contract was commonly used both in urban real estate and agrarian credit (haciendas and ranches) and the financing of manufacturing plants.[3] The only sector of activity that managed without recourse to mortgages was mining, and this was principally due to the fact that its assets were usually owned in a complex partnership, the *avío*.[4] The primitive characteristics of the Mexican financial system were such that the use of mortgages extended well beyond what is traditionally conceived of as mortgage credit. The entire temporal range of credit, from the financing of working capital to that of short-, mid-, and long-term financing predominantly depended upon this form of credit.[5]

During most of nineteenth century, mortgages in Mexico were caught up in that blend of economy, moral rules, and law typical of societies of the ancien régime. Regulation of mortgage activity was established by the medieval Spanish *partidas* laws and essentially reflected the forms of Roman law. The legal status of mortgage continued to be that of *censo consignativo,* or consignment rent, which disguised interest-bearing loans in order not to break with the traditional Catholic moral condemnation and prohibition of usury.[6] The forms and procedures of mortgage contract involved extremely high transaction costs, risks, and the dissipation of resources. Its predominant aspects—informality, uncertainty, and secrecy—encompassed the entire sequence of the contract, from the stipulation to the enforcement of its legal provisions.

There were two salient characteristics of this situation: first, mortgages were tacit agreements in the sense that they were not formally registered. They were, therefore, secret. The obligation to register was required for only one type of mortgage that represented a minority of cases. Registries were not, properly speaking, public offices. "Mortgage bureaus" (*oficios de hipoteca*) were established in 1778; however, the persons in charge of these were not public officials but rather private individuals who had acquired their position through purchase.[7] Second, the mortgage could be general. That is, it was not necessary that it constitute a real guarantee against a specific property. Instead, it could encumber the totality of a debtor's assets, including future ones. If, on the one hand, it froze debtors' patrimony, it would, on the other hand, drastically reduce the possibility of asserting claims in case of forfeiture. The absence of guarantees led lenders to the practice of including in mortgage contracts a non-transferability agreement: the prohibition both against selling and against the stipulation of successive mortgages on the encumbered property without the consent of the creditor.[8] For lenders, this meant that even if they could not know of the existence of prior liens, they could at least block future mortgages, freezing the debtor's property rights.

From the point of view of contract enforcement, conditions were equally precarious. Identifying all creditors, establishing total liability, and fixing the priority of creditors' rights to an insolvent debtor's properties were all very time-consuming procedures given the high cost of information. Moreover, these procedures were usually held up in labyrinths of technical loopholes for unpredictable periods of time. For example, even after a creditor had obtained a foreclosure decision on a mortgage, the debtor could appeal and request a reversal of the decision in the context of an ordinary trial, holding up the procedure for years. At the end of proceedings, the sale of seized properties was regulated in an ambiguous and confusing manner, making room for further legal loopholes. Following the sale, the debtor's relatives (to the fourth degree) could request an annulment and acquire the property by making use of the *retracto*.[9] In these circumstances, the sale could be delayed for months or even years, tying up capital and causing the accelerated depreciation of the properties involved.[10] The economic consequences of this institutional arrangement were extremely negative: the strangulation of credit, depression of the real estate market, a marked segmentation in the rates of interest (with a high frequency of rates between 10 and 15 percent and with peaks much higher), and an orientation of the mortgage contract toward the short- and medium-term (one to three years) to the relative exclusion of long-term credit.[11]

In Mexico, the structure of interest rates was such that a reference rate was not set for long-term credit. The analysis of mortgage foreclosure suits (*juicios hipotecarios*) for the period 1873–96 demonstrates the prevalence of a wide dispersion, with a polarization around nominal rates of 6 and 12 percent.[12] Even allowing for the limitations of this source of information, this polarization of the structure of rates around such extreme values indicates the existence of isolated and self-sufficient segments of the market that represent two sets of interests responding to different economic and extra-economic factors. The weakness of intermediate rates suggests that explanatory factors other than a structure adjusted according to criteria of risk must be taken into account. Indeed, there is no evidence of a distribution of the mortgage rate according to parameters of risk, such as the size of a loan in relation to the value of a property, terms of the loan, or its transaction costs. The problem resided in the great heterogeneity of the mortgage market, within which customs, attitudes, and social aspects of credit of diverse kinds (e.g., enduring reciprocal obligations) were blended together. On the one hand, there was a sector that complied with the tradition (derived from a religious precept) of a 6 percent limit on interest. This sector was constituted by credit circuits made up of personal relations wherein the qualification of the borrower was a function of the degree of ethnic or familial affiliation or of his position in a social network.[13] In these cases we are confronted with a market structured within the radius defined by social influence and prestige, as is visible both in the case of rural properties and in that of urban real estate in Mexico City. This is the credit segment in which the longest term loans occur, most of them medium term. Yet this is the only segment where terms longer than three to four years appear. At the other extreme, in the class of highest rates, there was what, according to the definition of the times, was called a "usurer" credit segment, which had different characteristics. First, it fulfilled monetary requirements outside the sphere of personal relationships, or at least where these relationships did not have an essential role. Second, it provided emergency loans with short- or medium-term maturities. Third, and most importantly, it offered to maintain the secrecy of the transaction, in deference to debtors' moral codes and preferences.

These unusual conditions—unspecified property rights, ambiguous legal regulation, and differentiated universes of social obligations—had driven the only existing banking institution prior to 1880, the London Bank of Mexico, out of the mortgage business.[14] In the government's view, deficient mortgage legislation was the principal obstacle to the creation of banks that would operate in this sector.[15] From the restoration of the Republic (1867), the attention of policymakers was focused on this issue and, accordingly, the congressional agenda included a collection of legislative reforms: suspension of taxes on mortgages, special mortgage legislation for the Federal District, and the creation of mortgage banks.[16] The modification of the mortgage legal status was studied by the commission that elaborated Mexico's Civil Code. Indeed, institutional innovations regarding mortgage contracts were derived fundamentally from the Civil Code, since the governmental initiatives on mortgage contracts drafted between 1869 and 1875 were never passed into legislation.

Institutional Change in the Mortgage Contract

The single most important contribution of the Civil Code of 1870 to the economy was the modification of the mortgage contract. The code was intended to diminish transaction costs, to specify creditors' property rights, and to endow mortgage credit with contractual certainty. The ultimate objectives of the code were the mobilization of the real estate market, the expansion of credit, and the reduction of interest rates. Table 5.1 contrasts the legal status of the mortgage contract prior to and following changes made via the Civil Code and the Proceedings Code between 1870 and 1872.

Beginning in 1872, the principle regarding the obligation to register mortgages was affirmed, which effectively put an end to the tradition of tacit and general mortgages that had previously been the cause of drawn-out and costly

Table 5.1

Variation in the Legal Aspects of the Mortgage

	Old Legislation	Codes 1870–72
Registration	None	Obligatory
Mortgage duration (max.)	Unspecified	20 years
Statute of limitations	30 years	20 years
Priority of mortgage credit	Unknown	10 years
Sufficient reason for calling back a loan	Unspecified	Bankruptcy, insolvency, failure to pay interest
Non-transferability agreement	Valid	Invalid
Judicial ruling	Mortgage decision was not final judgment; reversion to ordinary trial	Decision final (no appeal)
Duration of suit	Unforeseeable	2 months
Sale of seized goods	66% estimated value; annulment of the sale was possible	Progressive discounts of 10%, max. 30%, above this payment 66%

SOURCE: Lozano 1873; *Código Civil* 1870; *Código de Procedimientos Civiles* 1872.

lawsuits. Inscription in a public agency became the requisite without which a mortgage could not take legal effect; at the same time, the specificity of the mortgage operation was defined, in the sense that encumbrances could be placed only on certain and specified properties.[17]

Other essential features of the new legislation included the establishment of a legal period of time for the mortgage (which had previously been left unstated); term limits for the exercise of legal action; and guarantee of payment of back interest (retrospective for five years) and not just principal. On the whole, the code set the following important advancements: the specification that foreclosure proceedings be initiated without delay and that the decision be final (irreversible); the improved definition of the term limits of the encumbrance; and the establishment of rules determining creditors' priority to debtors' assets. Of special importance was the innovation regarding mortgage suits, which fixed a relatively brief period for sentencing and eliminated the possibility of appeal. With the old legislation, the confiscation of an insolvent debtor's goods could take years. From 1872 onward, the institutional innovations in mortgages guaranteed a much reduced waiting

Table 5.2

Mortgage Loans Registered at the Federal District Mortgage Office
(monetary values in thousands of current pesos)

	Mortgage Values	Number	Avg. Value
1871	2103	394	53.4
1877	2933	661	44.4
Variation, 1871–77	39%	68%	−17%
1882	n.a.	868	n.a.

SOURCES: Secretaría de Justicia, various years; calculations based on *Memoria Estadística* 1888.

period, that is, a maximum of two months between filing suit and the court-ordered sale of the mortgaged property. Furthermore, instead of selling off the confiscated property at an immediate discount equivalent to one-third of the appraised value, the new procedures established sale at public auction, with progressive discounts from 10 percent to a maximum of 30 percent.[18]

These innovations constituted substantial progress regarding guarantees of compliance with terms, increased access to information, the reduction of ambiguity, and a decrease in the time and costs necessary for legal action. All things considered, it can be assumed that the reduction of transaction costs relative to mortgage transactions was considerable.[19] Although lack of information makes a precise calculation impossible, the available figures confirm positive effects with regard to the expansion and mobilization of mortgage operations, as well as with regard to specialization in long-term credit. Table 5.2 shows an increase of almost 40 percent in mortgage values and 68 percent in the absolute number of transactions between 1871 and 1877 in Mexico City. However, between these two dates, the available economic indicators (foreign commerce, fiscal revenue, population) do not demonstrate signs of sustained growth. Therefore, my hypothesis is that the relevant increase both in the total value and in the number of mortgages derives directly from institutional change and the consequent reduction in levels of risk.[20]

In this case, what is expanding is not the demand, but rather the supply of mortgage financing, which had attained greater and more secure guarantees and so could meet a greater share of the (already existing) demand. The significantly lower average value of mortgages in 1877 as compared with 1871

(−17 percent) appears to confirm that what is at issue is that fraction of the demand for credit which consisted of small- and medium-scale property owners who were previously unable to find credit.

Even so, the formal redesign of mortgage contracts left some important areas undefined, and it took a dozen years of trial-and-error to complete the corresponding adjustments. The first general area left undefined by the new reforms involved the legal jurisdiction of the mortgage settlement. This happened to be concentrated in the Federal District and had limited and fragmentary application over the national territory, given that the majority of states did not adopt the Code of Proceedings.[21] The second was of a more technical nature and involved the duration of the preference of mortgage credit following the due date for payment. Until the Civil Code of 1884 provided a solution to this problem, the ambiguity of the text gave rise to conflicting legal interpretations in the proceedings to establish creditors' priority to an insolvent debtor's assets. The third area involved the relationship of the mortgage contract to specific activities. Between 1870 and 1884, legal certainty was lacking regarding the inclusion of livestock in the mortgages of haciendas and farms. This produced opposing jurisprudence on the matter. As a consequence, an entire sector of properties (mostly in the north of the country) were in fact excluded from mortgage credit because of the absence of legal guarantees.[22]

The Civil Code of 1884 solved most of these regulatory problems in the mortgage contract.[23] From the point of view of national uniformity, the code extended its jurisdiction by means of its wider adoption by states. Still, its jurisdiction was selective and incomplete. Following 1884, the available evidence points to the strengthening of legal guarantees and unambiguous rules that enabled the expansion and improvement of mortgage activity. A reflection of this is found in the specialization of this financial operation, which tended to reduce substantially the short-term component of contractual stipulations. Table 5.3 presents information on loan terms on mortgages that were later foreclosed. The data refer to three five-year periods in three different decades after the new legislation came into effect. As Table 5.3 shows, the percentage of contracts with a one-year expiration date moves from more than a quarter of the total between 1874 and 1878 to just 11 percent in 1886−90. Thus, we can conclude that the decrease in levels of risk produced a displacement in the temporal structure of credit.

The perception of investors was that in Mexico, real estate mortgages, especially in the urban context, had become an uncomplicated and safe business, and so the investment of funds in mortgages became one of the favored uses of money for individual private investors with available funds.[24] Proof

Table 5.3

Presence of Short-Term Credits (1 year or less) in
Foreclosed Mortgage Contracts, 1874–1900

	YEARS OF REGISTRATION		
	1874–78	*1886–90*	*1896–1900*
1-year contracts	27%	11%	14%
No. observations	168	141	149

SOURCE: Calculations based on *Diario Oficial* (judicial section), 1875–1910.
NOTE: The data refer to foreclosures proceeding from mortgages between private individuals in the Federal District available for the year of registration and represent the majority number of a subgroup, that of foreclosures. The relationship between my observations and the total number of registered mortgages oscillates between 2% and 3%. Only loans greater than 999 pesos are taken into account.

Table 5.4

Timing of the Establishment of Mortgage Banks
in Mexico and Argentina

	Argentina	*Mexico*
Legal reform of mortgage contract	1871	1872
First mortgage bank	1872	1882
(location)	Province Buenos Aires	Federal District
Second mortgage bank	1886	1900

SOURCE: Ferrari 1996 for Argentina; for Mexico, see text.

of this is the increased number of private lenders and, above all, the presence among them of those typically searching for sure investments: widows, executors of minors, clergy, and real estate salesmen.

Institutional change did not reach the sphere of organizations until the first years of the 1880s, toward the end of the cycle of modifications of the legal rules, when a mortgage bank was established (1882) with the stimulus and support of the federal government. The lag in time separating institutional change from the emergence of a specialized bank is considerable. Comparison with the Argentine case is very illustrative in this regard (see Table 5.4), given that the two countries introduced legal changes in the mortgage contract at almost the same time, reforming the same Spanish and colonial legal tradition.

In Argentina the repercussions of institutional change on banking organizations were almost immediate and originated within a growing agricultural area known as the Buenos Aires province. In Mexico the response of the market was much delayed and was confined to the Federal District. In fact, the Banco Hipotecario Mexicano was created long after banks of this sort had already appeared in the principal South American countries.[25]

What was common to the first experience of the Mexican mortgage bank and that of the other Latin American cases was that all followed the French example of the Crédit Foncier, which served as a general model for the establishment of their own systems, although they did not include the state in management.[26] The objective was the creation of a bank of large dimensions, one that would be capable of boosting the supply and reducing the cost of long-term credit. The Mexican mortgage bank (Banco Hipotecario Mexicano) was awarded the exclusive legal monopoly over mortgage activity for twenty years, although it did not have the privilege of issue. Together with the legal monopoly, a series of extraordinary contractual incentives accompanied the concessions given to the Banco Hipotecario. The most relevant of these was that its mortgage operations were always given priority and were not subject to judicial proceedings. In cases of insolvency, the mortgaged properties immediately came under the bank's control and were put on auction through its offices.[27]

Mortgage Contract and Financial Institutions

My purpose is to assess the impact of institutional change on mortgage credit: to what extent did it modify the structure of the mortgage market, and who were the beneficiaries of these changes? The questions are whether there were adequate conditions and incentives for the mortgage credit to be channeled toward financial intermediaries, and whether in this way mortgages were able to change from a civil contract into a commercial instrument. Accordingly, the present focus is on those specialized financial institutions whose structures of assets and liabilities compensated for the risks inherent in mortgage activity. Principal among these risks were those of liquidity problems—that is, the immobilization of the portfolio in long-term loans—and the risk of borrowers' failure to pay. During the second half of the nineteenth century and the beginning of the twentieth century, the intermediaries capable of maintaining long-term liabilities were fundamentally mortgage banks, by means of issuing mortgage bonds guaranteed by the value

Table 5.5

Percentage of Foreclosures Involving Financial Institutions,
Registered at Federal District's Public Property Archive, 1890–1910

	1890–99	1900–1910	1890–1910
No. foreclosures (total)	633	1,026	1,659
% banking institutions	6	7	6.1
% non-banking institutions	0.0	2	1.6
% all financial institutions	6	9	7.7

SOURCE: Calculations based on *Diario Oficial* (judicial section), 1890–1910. Percentages are rounded off. Mortgage loans smaller than 1,000 pesos are excluded.

of the property as collateral. Also, in Mexico, financial regulation adopted the idea of a banking system with specialized functions, in which long-term credit would be the responsibility of mortgage banks. Prior to 1897, it was difficult for banks of issue to carry out mortgage operations, depending upon the terms of their respective concessions.[28]

First, I will try to ascertain the general presence of financial intermediaries, bankers, and others within the mortgage market. Next, the relative importance of mortgage banks and their role in long-term credit will be assessed. Table 5.5 presents information about mortgage foreclosures during the period 1890–1910 in order to detect the presence of banks and finance companies. As we can see, the proportion was less than 8 percent of the total; and even though it indicates an increase in the second decade relative to the first, it remained lower than 10 percent of the total.

However, in order to judge the validity and significance of these data, two questions must be resolved. First, there might be a problem with geographic representativeness. Although the data refer exclusively to operations registered in the Federal District, this was the area with the highest density of banking activity and where the existing finance companies were concentrated; and about 20 percent of the mortgage transactions considered here even affected properties situated outside of the Federal District. Therefore, the Federal District is the location where we would expect to find the greatest number of mortgage transactions realized by means of the financial sector.

Second, it might be thought that data on foreclosures tend to underrepresent the presence of banks, if only because of the better positioning of these in the financial market in contrast to that of private lenders. Economies of scale, privileged conditions with regard to information, security, and margin of risk might be thought to entail a much lower rate of foreclosures by banks than by other creditors.[29] However, the proportion of banks present is so low that perhaps this explanation should be ruled out. Otherwise it would be difficult to explain why financial institutions would not maximize this advantage over the long term and why lenders would not abandon a field so extremely inefficient for their operations.

In order to measure more accurately the participation by banks in the mortgage market, I have gathered in Table 5.6 information on the position of mortgage activities in the Mexican banking system, as well as estimates of the encumbrance ratio with respect to the fiscal value of property and of the level of farm mortgage debt in 1900 and 1910.

Table 5.6 illustrates three points. First, the development of mortgage banks was minimal, whether calculated in terms of resources or in absolute

Table 5.6

The Presence of Banks in the Mortgage Market, 1890–1910
(monetary values in millions of current pesos)

	1890	*1895*	*1900*	*1905*	*1910*
No. mortgage banks	1	1	2	2	2
Paid-in capital ($)	3.5	3.5	4.5	5.5	8.5
% of banking capital	23	18	7	4	5
Mort. loans by all banks ($)	n.a.	n.a.	10.2	19.4	64.6
Mort. loans by mortgage banks ($)	1.1	2.5	6.7	14.3	46.4
% loans by mortgage banks	n.a.	n.a.	66%	74%	72%
Encumbrance ratio (bank mortgages on real estate fiscal value)	0.3	n.a.	0.9	2	4
Estimates of farm mortgage debt ($)	n.a.	n.a.	200	n.a.	500

SOURCE: Calculations based on *Estadísticas bancarias* 1985; *Memoria de las instituciones de Crédito* 1897–1910; *Cuadro Sinóptico* 1900. The data on farm mortgage debt are rough estimates coming from García 1910 and Viadas 1911.

NOTE: The second mortgage bank was legally founded in 1900, although it did not commence operations until the following year. The data on banks' mortgage loans include all federally chartered banks, but not the quasi-public Caja de Préstamos (for 1910). For the banks of issue I have aggregated mortgage loans and loans on real estate from the balances.

numbers. Mexico had only one mortgage bank in operation until 1900, with headquarters in the capital and without branch offices in the states.[30] The high initial percentage of capital with respect to the total banking system is deceptive, given that the only mortgage bank after 1889 diversified its operations and took on characteristics of a commercial bank. Second, the extremely limited presence of mortgage banks was not even partially made up for by other banking institutions. Prior to 1897, banks of issue required authorization in their charter in order to operate in the mortgage sector. Up until that time, banks contributed a fraction of the supply of mortgage credit, but it was significant only in relation to the small size of the mortgage banks.[31] Although the banking law of 1897 maintained the restrictions on mortgage credit controlled by the banks of issue, it envisaged certain legal possibilities: banks of issue had a growing participation in the amount of mortgage credit granted by the banking system.[32] Indeed, the policy of allowing the banks of issue to operate selectively in the mortgage market was based on the manifest weakness of the mortgage banks.[33] However, the sustained increase of mortgages conceded by banks of issue during the first decade of the twentieth century, rather than constituting a reflection of economic expansion, in reality reflected an emergency intervention. The rescue of a large number of large rural properties in financial difficulties in the wake of the Crisis of 1907 (most of them in Yucatán) almost entirely accounts for the increase.[34]

To the number of institutional lenders calculated must be added a small group of non-banking financial institutions, which operated without federal concession and which were dedicated to long-term credit at the local level. These appear to have been new enterprises and were organized predominantly in the form of cooperative and mutualist societies. They filled a fraction of the void left by the scant presence of mortgage banks. I have been able to identify at least eight such firms for the period between 1895 and 1905, with a total capital that is estimated at around 5 million pesos for 1905.[35] The importance of these firms was considerable in some localities, especially in the north.[36] Nevertheless, in aggregate terms, their significance to the supply of mortgage credit was relatively small, given the meagerness of the financial means available to them.[37]

Third, the vacuum left by financial institutions in the area of mortgage credit was filled by other forces, as shown by the low ratio of outstanding mortgage loans by banks to the stock of farm mortgage debt. Individual moneylenders supplied approximately 94–95 percent of this debt in 1900, and at least 85 percent in 1910. Despite the decrease, the percentage was still very high, considering that the year 1910 represented the maximum height of banking activity in Mexico before the revolution seriously impaired banking business for more than a decade. What institutional change was unable to achieve, then, was the transformation of the structure of the mortgage market and its "financialization." That is, the mortgage market continued to be dominated by credit relations of a personal kind, and its protagonists were individual private lenders and notaries.[38]

The following can be asserted about the structure and functioning of this type of personal credit. In Mexico City, as in the state capitals, there was a circle of well-known persons who were professionally dedicated to the lending of money on mortgage. Besides, mortgage financing existed as part of a buying and selling transaction: the outfitter system in rural areas, in which merchants advanced funds at harvest time, against farming implements and lands as collateral; and the real estate market, where the mortgage often guaranteed the unpaid portion of a property sale. Moreover ecclesiastic elements, in some regions more than others, functioned as channels of access to clerical funds or other funds assembled through the clergy. Finally, as in other sectors, it is likely that notaries played an important role as go-betweens for seekers of credit and persons disposed to provide it, thus overcoming problems of asymmetry in access to information and transaction costs.[39]

Mexico displayed a marked peculiarity when compared to other Latin American countries, such as Argentina, Chile, Peru, and Uruguay, where it was financial institutions, in the form of mortgage banks, that dominated strong credit markets.[40] In any case, Mexico was one of the few countries where, despite repeated attempts, it was never possible to establish a bank properly specialized in agrarian credit until the 1930s of the twentieth century.

Mortgage Banks and the Lack of Long-Term Credit

In Mexico's predominantly rural economy, wherein capital was tied up in real estate and liquid assets were extremely scarce, the insufficient supply of agrarian credit caused financial repression. The demand for long-term financing lacked adequate channels and agencies, and the personal market was able to compensate in only a partial and faulty manner. Unspecialized intermediaries, the banks of issue also had to absorb a part of the demand for mortgage credit. A considerable factor of politicization was introduced into the allocation of the financial system's resources, whereby the intervention of political power or social influences was key to obtaining bank loans. All of this resulted in a profound distortion of the financial structure and the banking system, and the ultimate consequences were extremely negative for the Mexican economy.

What remains to be explained is why the better specification of property rights, the reduction of transaction costs, and the growth of mortgage transactions were not sufficient to attract the participation of banks and other formal financial institutions capable of offering more and better credit to the agrarian economy. My purpose, then, will be to identify the set of disincentives that intervened to constrain within a limited radius the externalities brought about by the improved definition of property rights. I will try to explain this bottleneck, which established a very clear limit to the reaches of institutional change. In order to do so, I will try to evaluate the relative importance of the main obstacles presented to banks in the mortgage credit sector, taking into account all aspects of regulation, whether formal or informal.[41] I have grouped together such obstacles under three rubrics: those relative to demand, to supply, and to the regulation of the banking system.[42]

DEMAND

The first category of obstacles refers to those failures in the demand for mortgage credit on the part of the public that might have played a negative role over the long term, inhibiting the development of a financial market in this sector. Apparently, this involved three essential factors: the preference of rural owners for non-public modalities of mortgage, the problem of defective titles to property, and the limited acceptance of mortgage bonds on the part of savers and investors. What follows is a discussion of these three points.

In the Mexican rural milieu, in some regions more than others, a negative view of credit activity was very widespread. To ask for loans was considered a disgrace and symptom of shameful social and economic difficulties, to the point that many practiced the *préstamo mudo*, or silent loan: borrowers agreed to pay higher amounts on mortgages contracted with "usurer" lenders in exchange for the guarding of secrecy about the transaction.[43] This involved an informal rule, with roots in the moral codes and traditional anti-financial prejudices of a culture that separated the ownership of land from the rules of business.[44] What is relevant from our point of view is the resistance that this informal rule was able to exercise in opposition to the expansion of the mortgage banks' activity. One clear instance of this is the written request of an important landowner in the state of Veracruz to Treasury Minister Limantour regarding the concession of a loan from a mortgage bank. He asked that the usual procedure of appraising the property to be mortgaged by surveyors be dispensed with: "[the question of surveyors] is one of the reasons why so many people abstain from recourse to them, the mortgage lenders . . . The presence of the inspector always speaks unfavorably of the interested party, and it is always noticed by others."[45]

Nevertheless, this factor need not be interpreted as an absolute constraint. Its importance probably varied to a great extent according to region. Moreover, it is possible to hypothesize that rather than being an independent variable, this informal rule was instead a function of the scarce activity of the mortgage banks outside the capital city. The fact that the loans made by these banks were always substantially inferior to the credit demands that they received is a good indication in this regard. In light of this fact, it is reasonable to suppose that a greater density of mortgage transactions made by these banks in the regions would have been able to significantly reduce the influence of this informal rule as well as the mentality underlying it.

The fact that a wide sector of rural property in Mexico was not provided with indisputable and complete titles of ownership was a notable imperfection in the formal rules that prevented the enjoyment of full property rights. Obviously this involved a complex problem with deep historical roots (which I cannot go into here) and about which there is an evident lack of studies and knowledge. Even so, there is plenty of evidence that the institution of private property in the countryside was precarious, ambiguous, and imperfect.[46] The "meandering evolutionary development" of property in Mexico had arrived at a point at which property rights over that land were characterized by extremely high transaction costs, including surveying and appraisal, information, legal title, and the possibility of stipulating and enforcing contracts. The frequency and duration of legal litigation over land was the clearest reflection of this. One of the main agrarian reformers, Andrés Molina Enríquez, considered deficient titles to property as the main obstacle to agrarian credit and to the activity of mortgage banks.[47] In fact, a considerable sector of properties was excluded from recourse to credit from the mortgage banks precisely because of the imperfection of those titles that the banks required in order to grant a loan. In order to evaluate the effect and significance of this constraint, it is necessary to view the problem within the context of concrete credit relations. The sector of private lenders (and to a lesser extent, banks of issue) did not impose the same requirements as the mortgage banks and accepted imperfectly titled properties as guarantees. This suggests the existence of a trade-off between the risk derived from title and the information available to lenders. Private lenders and banks of issue operated, respectively, at the local level and through branch offices, such that they had direct access to firsthand information that helped them decide whether to approve or turn down an application for credit. That is, risk could be substantially reduced through the knowledge and evaluation of local conditions. The situation was quite the opposite for mortgage banks, which lacked regional branch offices and conducted activity from Mexico City, something that did not allow for the lowering of levels of risk. Even so, the very low percentage of mortgages granted by these banks, given the number of existing rural properties, brings into question the relative importance of this factor.

Finally, among the demand factors that serve to explain the marginality of mortgage banks in long-term credit is the lack of acceptance on the part of the public of the mortgage bonds with which the banks had to finance their loans. Here we touch upon a key point regarding the very possibility for a financial institution's ability to deal in long-term credit: the capacity to issue bonds and mortgage obligations that would finance the tying up of capital in long-term investments and that would have characteristics of negotiability and liquidity. This was a constant weakness of Mexican mortgage banks, which before the monetary reform of 1905 did not manage to open a market for their bonds either domestically or abroad. Only the stabilization of the exchange rate and the linking of the monetary system to the gold standard were able to solve this problem, by opening the doors to European stock exchanges between 1905 and 1911 for this class of securities. At the same time, this made possible a rapid expansion of mortgage credit in the period under consideration.[48]

In static terms, the lack of demand for their bonds experienced by mortgage banks appeared to be an absolute barrier, capable of constraining the mortgage activity of financial institutions within narrow limits. In reality, what must be explained is why individual private lenders preferred to continue operating directly instead of going public as fixed-income bondholders, and so avoid the higher levels of risk implicit in personal loans. The structure of interest rates described above (in the first section) is part of the explanation. Mortgage bonds, with nominal rates of 6 percent, rendered average yields slightly above 7 percent in the 1880s and 6.7 percent in the following decade. I have already stated that a polarization between two universes of social credit affected interest rates. If this is correct, it is clear that anyone who could easily levy money on a mortgage at 12 percent would not be much interested in those yields. At the same time, those who accepted loans at rates of 6–7 percent interest probably represented a sector associated with very traditional practices and mentalities, and, therefore, would have had little inclination toward the symbolization of capital in titles. In this context, then, the supply of mortgage bonds was not met by any demand.

The explanatory possibilities are strengthened when we shift from the perspective of demand to that of supply, that is, if we pose the question of why mortgage bonds constituted a supply unable to establish a corresponding demand. It is relatively simple to verify that before the turn of the century the only existing mortgage bank did not undertake to commit sufficient efforts to create a market for its bonds. Year after year, its reports simply confirmed the fact that no market existed for securities. Until 1889, the bank was unable to improve matters, given the meagerness of financial means as reflected in the maintenance of all of its activities in Mexico City. Later, mortgage credit was simply relegated to second place in the bank's portfolio, as we shall see below. It should be added that this issue was relatively secondary because the bank could off-load the problem onto its clients: the federal charter allowed the bank to make loans with its bonds rather than in currency. Consequently, it was the borrowers who had to resell the bonds in order to acquire cash. Given this arrangement, mortgage bonds, instead of financing the bank's portfolio, took on the role of primary means of operation: and so the problem of finding a market for them was the clients' concern and not the bank's.[49]

INFLUENCES ON SUPPLY: THE BANKS' STOCKHOLDERS
AND THEIR INTERESTS

Under this rubric I have grouped together some factors relevant to the mortgage banks' structure and functioning that may have worked to the detriment of their performance, thus blocking the growth of their relations with the broader economy. I will first discuss the role of the preference for urban real estate, and then the composition of stockholders in the mortgage banks and the influence of foreign control. Regarding the first aspect, the bias toward the concentration of mortgage activity in urban areas (and for the most part in capital cities) was a common trait among mortgage banks during the second half of the nineteenth century.[50] In Mexico, everything we know suggests that this bias was present. The fact that the only mortgage bank in existence prior to 1900 did not have branch offices outside Mexico City is relevant evidence in itself. In this regard, the extent of the correlation between the Banco Hipotecario's credit activity and the value of property in the Federal District would appear to be a good indicator by which to detect the urban bias. Nevertheless, the facts do not support this interpretation. Between 1885 and 1900, urban property values in Mexico City increased three times over, but the ratio of amounts loaned with respect to them remained very low: it was 3 percent at the beginning and 5 percent at the end of this period.[51] This indicates that the growth of the capital city was not financed to any significant extent by a mortgage bank. Even supposing that all loans by the Banco Hipotecario were made on urban real estate in the Federal District, the low proportions observed allow us to exclude the likelihood that the bank's efforts to expand its mortgage activities were impeded by an exclusive attention to the urban market.

Regarding the second aspect, Latin American historiography has most often paid attention to the composition of stockholders in businesses, the nationality of investors, and the level of external control over decisions. What is to be ascertained here is whether these elements taken together represented a factor capable of negatively influencing the proper functioning of Mexican mortgage banks. The first such institution (Banco Hipotecario) was founded without the assistance of capital from outside the country only because its promoters were not able to obtain funds in foreign markets. Rather than trying to establish a national company, Mexican businessmen aspired to act like brokers of privilege: to obtain a favorable concession from the government for the undertaking of a particular enterprise and then to transfer this privilege to other groups interested in operating the business. Significantly, because of this, Mexican shareholders refused to commit more than a minimum amount of the bank's capital.[52] In 1889, the bank obtained an expansion of its charter, changed its name to Banco Internacional e Hipotecario, and finally succeeded in placing its stocks on foreign markets; a New York financial syndicate acquired the majority shareholding. This event coincided with the stage at which the Banco Hipotecario acquired the characteristics of a commercial bank and substantially abandoned long-term credit functions. The coincidence between these two events would seem to confirm that foreign control was a variable crucial to the explanation of the first mortgage bank's marginality.

Nevertheless, a closer examination of the issue reveals that this argument has extremely limited explanatory power. Starting in 1889, the bank's board of directors was divided between Mexico City (eight seats) and New York (seven seats). The Mexican board enjoyed decisional autonomy over loans up to 100,000 pesos, and beyond that amount the New York section would have to be consulted to approve the operation. Given the volume of real estate businesses in Mexico, this limit was relatively high and so could not have constituted a mechanism of effective control; loans of more than 100,000 pesos made up a very small part of the bank's portfolio.[53] The problem with the

Banco Internacional e Hipotecario did not, then, reside in foreign control over its activities, but rather in the commercial orientation of the main foreign shareholders. The financial syndicate that controlled a majority shareholding included some figures operating in the silver market and currency exchanges in New York, and they pushed the bank to dedicate the main part of its resources to this sphere of activity. Nevertheless, this substantial change was not exclusively the result of private deals made among shareholders. Rather, the Mexican government had approved and favored such an outcome. The modification of the bank's charter, allowing it to diversify its operations, was conceived as part of a plan to promote international bi-metallism, and the cooperation between Mexican and American silver interests. In this context, the Banco Internacional e Hipotecario had to operate in coordination with a United States bank both in the issuing of silver deposit certificates and in the attempt to move the center of the silver market from London to New York.[54] Clearly, we can appreciate that for Mexican decision makers the defense of silver was thought to be a more important objective of national interest than was mortgage credit.

A confirmation of the hypothesis that foreign stock control was not the main obstacle to the development of the mortgage bank in Mexico is found in the case of the second credit institution, the Banco Agrícola Hipotecario. This bank was established by the initiative of a coalition of regional businessmen who later on were unwilling to invest the previously agreed upon amount of capital. Because of this, the bank operated at a low level of activity during the first five years of its operation.[55] Afterward, a group of large French banks acquired control and injected considerable resources into the bank, and this pushed up the volume of mortgage business to an extraordinary degree. During the five-year period of 1905 to 1910, the total of loans granted rose almost ten times, from 2.8 to 27.4 million pesos.[56] Development, then, rather than obstacles to it, was, at least in this case, a function of the presence of foreign investors and capital.

FINANCIAL REGULATION AND CONTRACTUAL ARRANGEMENTS

The analysis to this point allows us to rule out the idea that the demand factors of mortgage credit and the predominant interests involved in mortgage banks might have been the most substantial constraints inhibiting the development of a market for and specialized institutions in long-term credit. It becomes necessary, then, to consider banking regulation in order to find out whether and to what extent it negatively affected the supply of this kind of

Table 5.7

Main Features of the Regulation of Mortgage Banks
in the Law of 1897

- Banks can make loans only on properties located in states where they have branch offices (Article 46)
- Total sum of mortgages may not exceed 20 times the amount of paid-in capital of the bank (Article 50)
- Banks may not loan to any single person or company more than ⅕ of their capital (Article 50)
- The issue of mortgage bonds may not exceed the amount of loans (Article 55)
- There must be a guarantee fund in the bank sufficient to cover at least two quarters of interest on mortgage bonds issued (Article 70)
- Deposits may not exceed ⅕ of paid-in capital (Article 75)

SOURCE: Ley general de instituciones de crédito, in *Legislación bancaria* 1957.

financial service. In this regard, it should be noted that my conclusions are opposed to the interpretation of the planners of the banking law of 1897, who argued that official bank regulation was a minimal hindrance to the development of mortgage banks. In the official view, the problem was almost exclusively with informal rules. The lack of "enterprising spirit" and of public knowledge about financial mechanisms were considered to be the key factors impeding the emergence of a mortgage bank sector.[57]

The examination of financial regulation must cover two very differentiated phases: before and after the appearance of federal legislation concerning banks. The banking law of 1897 was the first general regulation of the banking sector. Before the banking law, the regulatory framework for credit institutions was based on an ad hoc regime in which each bank was governed by the special terms of its own charter. I will begin with an analysis of the aspects of the law of 1897 relative to mortgage banks and to the granting of mortgage loans. Table 5.7 provides a list of the limitations to which mortgage banks were subjected after 1897, chosen from among those that were not previously included in the existing mortgage bank's concession.

This regulation does not seem to have adversely affected the functioning of mortgage banks. The majority of these measures were oriented toward guaranteeing the security of mortgage bonds as financial assets and toward preventing the concentration of credit activity. Included alongside these rules was the principle of correlation between the making of loans and the presence of the bank in the same location, the intention of which was to distribute the supply of credit across the country. Furthermore, limitations on the amount of loans in relation to paid-in capital were not a constraint; the proportion of loans never came near the limit (its maximum value was 1:6 in 1910), and these banks were not financed by the accumulation of deposits but rather by the issuing of bonds. However, in order to evaluate the importance of the 1897 law it must be taken into account that it was only partially applied. Of the two institutions in existence prior to 1910, one was not run according to the law, but rather by the clauses in its own charter, which preceded the law. The law, then, instead of applying to the entire sector affected only half of it.[58]

In light of these facts, a better understanding of the contractual arrangement behind the creation of the first mortgage bank (the only element of regulation available prior to 1897) takes on special significance. As noted, the mortgage bank was created in Mexico with characteristics of an "essential enterprise," thanks to a package of exceptional concessions and privileges. What must be tested is the possibility that the contractual arrangement between the government and the bank restricted the proper development of a mortgage market and of specialized financial institutions. It will also be important to evaluate its coherence with the process of institutional change that led to the reduction of transaction costs involved in mortgage contracts.

The Banco Hipotecario was established in 1882 by a Mexican financial group that obtained the federal exclusive concession to mortgage banking activity for a period of twenty years.[59] As we have seen, the governmental purpose was to establish a supply of long-term credit especially directed toward the agrarian sector, through the creation of a bank of large dimensions. The means to this end was the protection of the first firm, and this was achieved by imposing barriers of entry to the sector. But from the outset, the creation of this mortgage bank had at its core a contract in which the legal monopoly over mortgage lending was received in exchange for preferential access to credit for the federal government.[60] Thus, in reality, the supply of mortgage credit to the market turned out to be only a secondary function. In terms of the theory of regulatory origins, it would be possible in this case to affirm that the protection of the industry (i.e., of the Banco Hipotecario) and bureaucratic interests (in the possibility of financing an expanding federal budget) intervened and came together toward the realization of the same purpose.

Around this core of the initial contract emerged a series of arrangements that fixed the limits and functions of the bank, as shown in Figure 5.1. The set of features that stemmed from this contractual root defined the position and role of the bank within the broader Mexican financial system for two

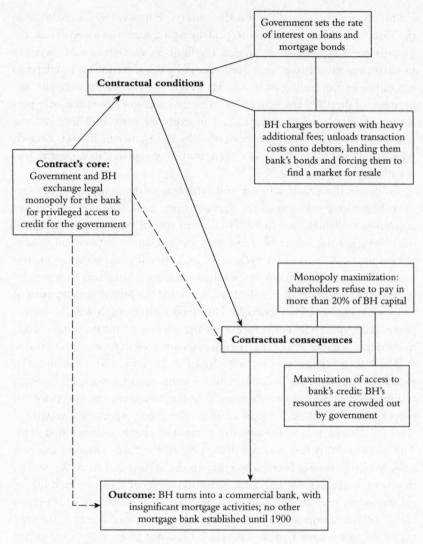

Figure 5.1. Banco Hipotecario

decades. The most obvious consequences were the reduction of investments, crowding-out, rigid and high interest rates, and institutional barriers to the mobility of capital. The combination of formal and informal rules with the institutional environment distorted the significance of the financial innovation and minimized the role of the mortgage bank. We shall see how and why.

To begin with, the shareholders, maximizing their legal monopoly, refused to pay in more than 20 percent of the nominal capital, since the concession specified only the minimal amount necessary for the starting of operations.[61] For its part, the government, maximizing its preferential access to credit, obtained a loan greater than the paid-in capital of the bank, and for the first eight years immobilized more than 50 percent of the total amount of contracted mortgage loans.[62] The government practice of regulating the rate of interest was set in the bank's contract law regarding nominal rates for loans and mortgage bonds. The bank offset these restrictions by charging commissions and by off-loading onto its debtors transaction costs for the sale of the mortgage bonds with which the bank had made the loan. In this way, at the same time that the bank satisfied the principles of government regulation over prices, the Banco Hipotecario's actual active rates turned out to be quite high. As a result, effective costs of around 13–14 percent were not competitive with those of a broad sector of individual moneylenders, and this put the bank's rates in a very limited margin of the market. The opinion of observers that only those who were unable to find a better financing option resorted to the Banco Hipotecario appears to be confirmed by the costs of credit.[63] Finally, the unresolved tension between the states and the federal government limited the bank's contracts to those states in which legislation from the Federal District was currently in effect. State governments' pretensions to imitate the federal government and to obtain credit in exchange for a charter prevented the bank from expanding its operations by means of branch offices beyond the limits of Mexico City.

This configuration of institutional constraints resulted in a very marginal institution with regard to the supply of credit, to the financial market, and to territorial presence. As a consequence of this situation, the Banco Hipotecario diversified. Thanks to its nature as an "essential enterprise," starting in 1889 it obtained the modification of its charter necessary to extend its operations to include commercial discounts and international currency exchange. As noted, the new sectors of operation became the most important sphere of activity of the bank, displacing mortgage credit as a priority. In the period from 1890 to 1896, commercial discounts and resources employed in the currency exchange market were, respectively, eight and nineteen times greater than the gross amount of loans.[64] The new Banco Internacional e Hipotecario (BIH) was committed exclusively to the first component of its business purpose (international), while the second (mortgage) almost disappeared. Of the bank's 3.5 million pesos of capital, only a small part could be considered to be that of the mortgage bank as such. In spite of the fact that the bank could legally lend out up to ten times the total sum of its capital, between 1889 and 1897 the average annual quotient of stock of mortgage loans vis-à-vis capital was inferior to unity (0.7).[65]

All things considered, the contractual arrangement of 1882 represented an institutional "counterdevelopment." It meant the establishment of rules and the erection of an organization whose logic and functioning contradicted the principles that had guided the institutional change in mortgage legislation in the first place (the reduction of transaction costs, low risk, and facility of access to credit). Notwithstanding its marginality, the Banco Hipotecario was relatively efficient at preventing the emergence of other banks of the same type by means of the legal barrier to entry. It was possible to establish a second mortgage institution only once the expiration date of the first's exclusive concession drew near.[66] The negative impact of the legal monopoly, for as long as it lasted, is brought out in relief when contrasting the behavior of the BIH before and after the appearance of a competitor bank. Within just the first eight months of 1899, the total value of mortgage loans suddenly increased 49 percent, going up from 4.3 to 7 million pesos. At the same time, even without establishing branch offices, beginning in 1900 the BIH extended its presence and activities in the states via the employment of company representatives.[67] In the following years, it began to make loans in cash and not (as before) only in bonds, and even to combine the two forms at the discretion of the client. It also implemented a policy to reduce interest rates. It is clear that the reorientation of resources, the respecialization of functions, the territorial extension of activities, and the improvement of service to the public were all causally linked to the appearance of a competitor.[68] Although the second mortgage bank did not live up to the expectations that its establishment had generated, the scenario of competition clearly put in motion a dynamic conducive to a better and greater supply of credit. What seems clear is that, despite political rhetoric, the years 1882–99 did not witness any development in mortgage credit activities by means of financial institutions.

Lack of Financial Mediation and Long-Term Credit: The Consequences

The classification of the credit granted by the banking system indicates that long-term credit represented less than 10 percent of the total between 1882 and 1907 and around 20 percent from 1908 to 1911.[69] Nevertheless, such a calculation derives from a partial consideration of the matter that obscures an important fact. Faced with the lack of financial institutions dedicated to long-term credit, and with a banking system formally organized for short-term credit only, the relationship of "social credit" transformed the criteria for allocation from within. An important part of the banking system's credit activities tended to extend in time along sequences of rollovers. This was true in the case of commercial discounts, and especially for short-term or current account loans granted to rural landowners and industrial firms, which were in this way converted into medium- and long-term financing. Social pressure and the force of demand in a structure based on social prestige severely distorted the functioning of commercial banks. The ministry of the treasury observed that owing to the lack of institutions for the financing of long-term credit, these functions "have had to be carried out by means of other organs that, although not intended fundamentally for this purpose, are capable of providing the service in question in an incidental manner."[70] A tacit agreement between bank and customer, based on the lack of specialization and an undefined period of the loan, constituted a kind of informal rule capable of significantly altering the formal rule. Part of the expectations of the two parties (borrowers and lenders) was the transformation of a short-term operation into one of indeterminate duration by means of rollover.

All of this became especially obvious when, in 1907–8, the coincidence of the international crisis and the internal agrarian crisis disrupted the Mexican economy, revealing a high degree of immobility in the structure of banks' portfolios. The institutional response was the adoption of reforms in banking legislation that would allow for the correction of alleged anomalies that were in reality an established mode of functioning. State intervention was the key to the effort to rescue the banking system, with the creation of a quasi-official institute of credit, the Caja de Préstamos para Obras de Irrigación y Fomento de la Agricultura (lit. trans., Fund for Irrigation Works and the Promotion of Agriculture).[71] The objective was to absorb that portion of the portfolios of the banks of issue immobilized in non-performing assets (almost all of which was tied up in loans to agricultural properties) and to turn it into mortgage credit backed up by the issuance of long-term bonds. After two years of activity, the Caja had awarded loans for 25 million pesos, equivalent to 54 percent of the outstanding loans by the two mortgage banks. If in the short term this was sufficient to save the banks of issue, it is worth mentioning that the Caja's intervention also had significant political consequences. It was seen as direct support from the government for a sector of privileged large landholders and as a discriminatory measure taken against small- and medium-sized agricultural landowners or others not aligned with the regime.[72] This phenomenon was one among several sources for the discontent of a large group of medium-scale farmers in certain regions of the country and at various levels of public opinion that finally culminated in the Revolution of 1911.

The lack of specialized long-term credit in Mexico had very negative consequences with regard to the efficient use of resources and the extent of exchange. On the one hand, it produced a deep distortion in the credit market and substantially affected the banking system. Significantly, in the face of this phenomenon of market failure, it was extra-economic institutions, the state and the Church, that tried to fill the vacuum. The legacy for the twentieth century was the belief that private financial institutions were unable, given their very nature, to provide long-term credit, and that the state had to both come up with the necessary funding and organize it.

On the other hand, the lack of specialized long-term credit had an even more significant impact on Mexico's agrarian structure. What stood out, in this sphere, was the absence of positive relations of any significance between rural production units and long-term credit. Owing to the weakness of mortgage banks, haciendas and ranches had to resort to loans made by individual private lenders (frequently at ruinously high interest rates and short terms) and to gamble on undefined extensions with banks of issue.[73] In aggregate terms, the financing of agriculture did not allow for important improvements with regard to the increase of crop production, irrigation projects, or the optimization of the production units' dimensions. The latter, especially, represented one of the most serious problems in the Mexican countryside. The contrast between the existence of large landholdings and the small size of cultivated lands constituted an obstacle to the efficient allocation of resources. The few experiments with the division of haciendas into smaller lots prior to the revolution testify to the benefits achieved with regard to increased productivity and the expansion of the sector of medium- and small-scale landowners. But agrarian credit was unable to stimulate positive modifications in land tenure; this process was carried out only by destruction, decapitalization, and, later, by the expropriation of haciendas, but without any significant credit supply to farmers. The overall picture indicates that the net cost to the Mexican economy was very high.

Conclusions

The mortgage contract was a relatively simple arrangement, in which institutional change through legislative reform succeeded in defining the property rights exchanged, with the result that levels of trust were increased and the supply of credit was stimulated. The limits to change were the incapacity to encourage the commercialization of mortgage credit, its depersonalization, or its specialization as long-term credit. The lack of financial intermediation on the part of specialized organizations explains this incapacity. What came between institutional change and the financial system was a constellation of political decisions taken on the assumption that the Mexican public would not have responded satisfactorily to incentives produced by institutional change. The government's strategy was, therefore, to structure a financial regulation that awarded exclusive privileges and preferential rights to a small number of organizations and actors; these, given their size, would be in the position to ensure immediate outcomes, offering at the same time relief to the government's fiscal needs. This involved an attempt at a shortcut that actually hindered the goals of mobilizing resources, stimulating growth and strengthening its base, and reducing transaction costs. This strategy conveyed a message highly contradictory to the rationale of institutional change and minimized the potential beneficial effects of the latter. It also allowed for the strengthening of forces that conflicted with the principles of free competition and that were capable of eroding the more innovative aspects of the new institutional rules. Therefore, and notwithstanding the traditional chronology of national banking history, Mexico did not have proper mortgage banks during the nineteenth century. From 1882 to 1899, the existence of a financial institution of this sort was merely nominal. The development of private banks specializing in long-term credit began and ended during the first decade of the twentieth century. The outbreak of the revolution represented the end of these banks' activities and the disappearance of institutional channels for long-term credit.

Notes

I wish to thank Barry Weingast for his comments and suggestions. Jeffrey Bortz, Lance Davis, Aurora Gómez, Carlos Marichal, Jean-Laurent Rosenthal, and an anonymous referee also made several useful comments. The responsibility for errors is, of course, mine alone.

1. Eggertson 1996: 8–10.

2. Reliable information regarding GDP does not exist. According to national census between 1895 and 1930, around two-thirds of the labor force was employed in the agriculture and livestock sector. See Keesing 1969.

3. The textile sector, in particular, resorted to mortgage financing on a large scale, at least until the 1880s. A similar phenomenon has been confirmed in the case of Prussia, where until 1840 industrialists had commonly employed

this instrument. But then this was replaced by the sale of shares and bonds. Cameron 1974:193. For a broader view of the financing of the Mexican textile industry, see Haber 1998.

4. See Riguzzi 1999b. In fact, mortgages on mining properties were extremely rare. The contract of *avío*, an ancient and complex form of partnership, was the main form of financing mining activity.

5. Literature on nineteenth-century mortgage credit in Mexican regions includes Lindley 1983; Greenow 1983; Wiemers 1985. The latter presents an idyllic picture of agricultural credit in the Orizaba-Córdoba area, in contrast to that presented here.

6. Consignment rent (*censo consignativo*) was considered the sale of an annual pension by the real estate owner, the price of which was to be paid in cash. Escriche y Martín 1979: 431–32. In this way, the interest on money did not appear in the transaction. Only mortgages with simple interest were possible.

7. Offices for purchase continued to exist in liberal Mexico. A law was passed in 1861 decreeing their abolition, but later, in 1867, the government allowed the posts to continue until the death of their owners. Secretaría de Justicia 1868: 14.

8. *El Foro*, July 4, 1873: 101.

9. Roa Bárcena 1869: 245. The legal form of the *retracto* can be found in book 5 of the *Recopilación de Indias*.

10. Secretaría de Justicia 1867–68: 19.

11. Prieto 1989: 342; *El Foro*, July 4, 1873. The Mexican mortgage was, indeed, a very strict form of mortgage. However, even in nineteenth-century United States, mortgage was not a proper long-term instrument of credit. See Atack and Passell 1994: 402–5.

12. This section about interest rates is based on Riguzzi 1999a: 360–64.

13. On the social aspects of credit, see the contributions in Chamoux et al. 1993.

14. The difficulties with judicial proceedings and problems with selling the seized properties forced the London Bank of Mexico to abandon mortgage operations before 1870. Lozano 1873: 19.

15. Secretaría de Hacienda 1868–69: 9.

16. The tax on mortgage contracts in the Federal District was abolished in 1868. A federal charter for a mortgage bank was issued in 1875, without results. Secretaría de Hacienda 1876–77: doc. 7. The urgent need for mortgage and banking legislation was frequently alluded to in presidential communications to the Congress during the period 1869–75. See Cámara de Diputados 1966, book 1: 470, 493, 497, 513.

17. Articles 1942, 1979, and 1980 of the Civil Code of 1870. According to Article 2016, the mortgage took legal effect only from the date of register, disregarding the moment of stipulation of the private contract.

18. See Mexico, Código 1872, Title 8, Chapter 4, and Title 17, Chapter 2 of the Civil Proceedings Code of 1872.

19. The contribution of the 1870–72 codes to the improvement in the legal frame of the mortgage has gone entirely unnoticed. Coatsworth 1978: 98, for instance, argues that at the time Díaz seized power (1877), "no mortgage-credit law existed to protect long-term investment and replace the spiritual sanctions on which the Church relied."

20. The information in Table 5.2 corresponds to mortgages realized during the years when the new system (the obligation to register) was in effect. It is unlikely that the increase would be linked to the registration of transactions that previously were not registered.

21. *El Foro*, July 15, 1879: 139. In this source, it is possible to locate several cases of conflict between federal and state legal provisions with regard to mortgages.

22. Another problem involved properties owned by groups of individuals in an undivided manner. The code of 1870, in the attempt to regularize the access of these properties to credit, declared it possible for individual co-owners to mortgage parcels of these properties. Mexico, Código 1870: Article 1978. The impossibility of measuring and specifying the limits of such parcels led to contractual ambiguities and legal confusions.

23. See Mexico, Exposición 1880 and Macedo 1884: 19–20.

24. *El Economista Mexicano*, September 3, 1887: 49. On Mexican investors' strong preference for mortgage loans see also Busto 1877, vol. 1: 219.

25. Between 1855 and 1872 mortgage banks were founded in Chile, Peru, Bolivia, Argentina, and Uruguay. Jones 1977: 46. In Brazil during the same period, there were no mortgage banks. But beginning in 1866, the banking laws created a section of mortgage loans in the Bank of Brazil. See Lobarinhas Pineiro 1996.

26. Ferrari 1996: 222; see Casasús 1890 for a discussion of the applicability of European mortgage bank models. The Crédit Foncier was created in 1852, with private capital and contributions from public funds. The government appointed the president of the board of directors, in which officials from the ministry of finance were also present. See Herrick and Ingalls 1926: 114–27.

27. Banco Hipotecario 1882.

28. Studies on banking in Mexico have focused almost exclusively on the problem of regulation of banks of issue, largely ignoring the status of mortgage banks. For one of the few contributions to the study of mortgage banks, see the brief note by Ludlow 1996.

29. In the absence of land registry values, mortgage banks required that an inspector appraise the value of mortgaged properties prior to granting a loan. They would not make loans against properties with defective titles, and they fixed a ceiling on loans at 50 percent of the land's value. Nevertheless, prior

to 1901, the only existing mortgage bank did not have branch offices in the states and therefore did not have access to information about local agricultural conditions.

30. I refer here to the Banco Hipotecario Mexicano (BH), which in 1888 changed its name to the Banco Internacional e Hipotecario (BIH). In 1900, the Banco Agrícola Hipotecario was founded, which in 1907 became the Banco Hipotecario de Crédito Territorial. The first regional bank offering long-term credit appeared in 1911, the Banco Hipotecario y Agrícola del Pacífico. See *Memoria de las Instituciones de Crédito,* various years.

31. It is exceedingly difficult to ascertain the amount of long-term credit, since mortgage loans did not appear in banks of issue balance sheets, being instead classified as loans on collateral. However, information pertaining to the main bank's (Banamex) portfolio indicates the presence of several mortgage loans for considerable amounts, granted exclusively to important clients. See Cerda 1994, vol. 2, "Extracts from the Board Weekly Acts."

32. The law of 1897 prohibited banks of issue to grant mortgage loans, with two exceptions. The first was in cases wherein an authorization was obtained from the Secretaría de Hacienda. The other was the ability of banks to accept the mortgage as collateral whenever the borrower's credit that guaranteed the loan was about to diminish. In cases of authorization, the maximum term could not exceed two years; in the other case there was no such limit (Article 30 of the banking law, in Mexico, *Legislación bancaria* 1957).

33. Treasury Secretary Limantour gave the following explanation: "In the charters of the banks of issue we had to authorize, even if extraordinarily, mortgage transactions only because of the fact that mortgage banks are absolutely insufficient, and it is not convenient to preclude the public from obtaining this kind of credit." Archivo Limantour (hereafter AL), roll 46, file 18, Limantour to Noetzlin, October 14, 1907.

34. Mortgage loans granted by banks of issue rose 118 percent between December 1906 and June 1908, from 4.7 to 10.3 million pesos. At the end of this period, almost half of these mortgage loans (in the amount of 4.9 million pesos) were concentrated in the Yucatán's Banco Peninsular. The severe fall in sisal plant prices provoked the collapse of several export houses engaged in highly speculative transactions and severely disrupted the Yucatecan plantation economy. Martínez Sobral 1911: 362–63.

35. The partial census is based on *Diario Oficial* 1897–1908; *Boletín Financiero y Minero* 1903–8.

36. The most indicative case is that of the state of Coahuila. In addition to the several financial institutions established there, mortgage loans were also obtained from financial societies in Monterrey, largely because mortgage activity was taxed in the state of Nuevo León but not in Coahuila.

37. Together with these, it is possible to mention also the case of the Compañía Bancaria de Obras y Bienes Raíces (Banking Company of Real Es-

tate and Public Works), founded in 1905. This was an enterprise protected by the government, which dedicated part of its capital of 10.6 million pesos to mortgage loans linked to the construction sector. On the whole, the share of non-banking financial institutions in the mortgage market for the year 1910 should be less than 2 percent of the level of farm mortgage debt.

38. See Riguzzi 1999a.

39. See the fiscal recognition of lenders' activity in Secretaría de Hacienda 1878–79: 270. About the outfitter system, see Cerutti 1998: 61–62, and *Economista Mexicano*, October 10, 1900: 114–15. Wiemers 1985: 528–29 describes the use of mortgage in real estate sales. Concerning the role of notaries as brokers in France, see the study by Hoffman, Postel-Vinay, and Rosenthal 1998.

40. Riguzzi 1999a: 355; Marichal 1998.

41. In order to reconstruct the functioning of mortgage banks in existence during the period, I have consulted their annual reports and balance sheets: for dates prior to 1897, in the journals *Economista Mexicano* and *Mexican Financier*; for later dates, in the collection of banking system documents *Memoria de las Instituciones de Crédito*, published by the finance department.

42. These are separations made for classificatory purposes, not as analytic distinctions that would ignore the interrelation between financial regulation and the structure of supply of credit.

43. *Boletín de la Sociedad Agrícola Mexicana*, September 30, 1890: 579.

44. This traditional culture was reflected in the legal system, in the division between the Civil Code and the Commercial Code. The aspects relative to agricultural businesses dealt with civil legislation.

45. AL, role 70, file 20, J. Mirón Mosquera to Limantour, April 26, 1910. See also the letter from the same landowner to a member of the board of directors of a mortgage bank: "These inspections that never escape the attention of neighbors, who are usually narrow-minded, are, in my humble opinion, one of the reasons that mortgage credit for agricultural businesses could not have become so widespread in the nation." Ibid., J. Mirón Mosquera to Emilio Pardo June 15, 1910.

46. The leading economic journal stated in 1908: "There are few properties about which their owners can say with certainty: this belongs to me, and so many that are exposed to litigation without end." *Economista Mexicano*, July 18, 1908: 318. The rarely cited but valuable study by Holden about public lands is replete with evidence of this sort. See Holden 1994: chaps. 1 and 4.

47. See the long section concerning territorial credit in his book, *Los grandes problemas nacionales* (first published 1909). Molina Enríquez 1978: 200–38. For the same topic, see García Granados 1910: 38.

48. The 1905 report of the Banco Internacional e Hipotecario stated that its mortgage bonds had been sold in Great Britain, France, and Germany. During the first half of that year, their value rose from 90 to 101.5. *Economista Mexi-*

cano, April 28, 1906: 81–82. The other mortgage bank sold its bonds in France, beginning in 1906.

49. The bank made loans exclusively with bonds, which the borrowers then had to resell in order to procure cash. Since there was no stock exchange, nor a secondary market for these titles, it was very difficult to sell these, as the bank itself acknowledged in its reports. The value of these bonds was merely nominal, and those who sold them had to accept lower sale prices in order to dispose of them. See the bank's reports in *Mexican Financier*, March 28, 1885: 414; *Economista Mexicano*, March 31, 1888: 103.

50. See the case of the Crédit Foncier and those of German banks, in Kindleberger 1988: 151; Born 1983: 105.

51. Information concerning the value of real estate property in the Federal District derives from the Foreign Office 1886, annual series no. 28: 48; Mexico, Cuadro 1900.

52. The identity of shareholders in the Banco Hipotecario during the period 1883–89 is unknown. The first board of directors was formed by three merchant/lenders, two landowners, and two persons linked to government circles. See *Mexican Financier*, March 28, 1885.

53. Banco Internacional e Hipotecario 1889: 34–39. During the decade 1886–95 the number of the bank's loans to fall into insolvency was eighteen: only three were for more than 100,000 pesos (information obtained from *Diario Oficial*).

54. The project had been elaborated by U.S. Treasury Secretary Windom, even though it was not backed by the United States government. The Western National Bank and the Banco Internacional e Hipotecario were to be the instruments that would make possible the retention of silver produced in these two countries, issuing certificates of deposit against silver in order to reduce supply on the world market. Casasús 1896: 131–33. See the BIH prospectus in *Diario Oficial*, October 10, 1889. The repeal of the Sherman Act and the end of a silver policy in the United States meant the definitive failure of this project.

55. Banco Agrícola Hipotecario (BAH) applied to the Secretaría de Hacienda for a series of extensions in order to come up with the capital planned in its charter. See *Memoria* 1904–6, vol. 3: 371, 376. It took five years to raise the capital from 1 to 2 million pesos.

56. Union Parisienne and Comptoir d'Escompte were the principal members of the French financial group that had controlled the BAH since 1906. AL, roll 37, file 4, J. Y. Limantour to Julio Limantour June 18, 1906. The bank changed its name in 1908 and obtained the listing of its shares on the Paris stock exchange, where a French section of its board of directors was created. *Memoria* 1907, vol. 1: 773–74. See Ramírez Bautista 1985 for the loans granted. As an additional benefit, the opening of the French market allowed for the reduction of interest rates on mortgage bonds from 6 to 5 percent.

57. See the government's report accompanying the 1897 law in Mexico, *Legislación bancaria* 1957: 61–97.

58. A similar problem involved the principal bank of issue, the Banco Nacional de México, with regard to the rest of the banking system. Ludlow 1998: 169–73.

59. In Article 2 of the 1882 contract, the government agreed not to grant other concessions for a period of twenty years, "as long as the bank fully satisfies the conditions of operation for which it was created." The concession was heavily debated in the Congress, but obtained a sufficiently strong majority. Cámara de Diputados, 10 Congreso, vol. 4: 740–41.

60. In the Congress, the bill specified that in exchange for the exemptions and concessions conceded to the Banco Hipotecario, the government would receive a line of credit of up to 2 million pesos, with a mortgage on national properties. Cámara de Diputados, 10 Congreso, vol. 4: 740–41.

61. This group attempted to issue one-fifth of the bank's capital in New York, but was unable to acquire funds. In fact, of the 5 million pesos in nominal capital, only 4 million were actually subscribed, paying in only 20 percent. *Diario Oficial*, March 8, 1883.

62. The federal government mortgaged properties in order to obtain a loan of 888,000 pesos in 1884. Secretaría de Hacienda 1884–85: 8. The amount of capital paid-in to the Banco Hipotecario up until 1889 was 800,000 pesos. Ramírez Bautista 1985, table 36. A similar case is that of the Banco Hipotecario in Spain, which during its first twenty years of operation lent out more to the state than to private borrowers. Tortella 1994: 145.

63. The bank charged 8 percent (initially 9 percent) interest and 2 percent annual amortization on twenty-year loans, plus 1 percent security. From the nominal total of capital must be subtracted the sale of bonds (which implied an average discount of 15–20 percent) the commission (2 percent), and the cost of appraisal of the property (estimated at 1 percent); see the charter in Banco Hipotecario 1882. Additional costs for the debtor were represented by processing of the entire operation in Mexico City and delays for approval. See Macedo 1905: 165.

64. Information about the bank's portfolio are derived from calculations based on the annual reports published in *Mexican Financier* and *Economista Mexicano*.

65. Standard deviation is 0.20. Calculations based on Ramírez Bautista 1985.

66. The BIH pressured the Secretaría de Hacienda in various ways against the authorization of a second bank, charging violation of its privilege and even going so far as to threaten diplomatic protests by foreign investors. AL, roll 3, file 8, H. B. Hollins and Co. to Limantour July 13, 1900; see Limantour's strong reaction, in Limantour to Hollins, July 6, 1900.

67. *Memoria* 1897–99, vol. 1: 130–38.

68. The second mortgage bank appeared in May 1900. My hypothesis, considering the slow processing of banking concessions, is that beginning in 1899 information regarding the imminent entrance of a competitor would have been available to the administrators of the Banco Internacional e Hipotecario. Furthermore, the programs of the new institution, the Banco Agrícola e Hipotecario, were to set off a very intense competition with the BIH: to exceed its supply of credit, to reduce rates of interest, and to create branch offices in the states.

69. Calculations based on El Colegio de México n.d.: 190.

70. Mexico, *Legislación bancaria* 1957: 113. The government had direct knowledge about this phenomenon. Because of the politicization of credit, intervention by its members in the renewal and extension of credit was not unusual. See the exemplifying case that involved Treasury's Secretary Limantour, the Bank of London and Mexico, and an important hacendado. AL, roll 6, file 4, Limantour to Waters, February 26, 1900; Waters to Limantour April 8, 1901.

71. About the reforms to the banking law see Casasús 1908. One-fifth of the seats on the Caja de Préstamos board of directors was occupied by government officials. Most important, they had right of veto over any proposed mortgage loan. This was possible owing to the fact that the Mexican government guaranteed the payment of the interest and capital of the Caja's bonds issued abroad. Oñate 1991: 41–44. Unless specified, information on Caja de Préstamos is based on this source.

72. In its first year of activity, the average amount of Caja's loans was the huge sum of 600,000 pesos. The manager informed Secretary Limantour that, because of the structure of financial costs, the minimum amount loanable by Caja de Préstamos was 200,000 pesos, which excluded medium and small landowners from access to credit. The result was that this banking institution was seen as "antidemocratic and unfriendly by the public opinion." AL, roll 58, file 7, Manuel de Zamacona to Limantour June 14, 1909. See also the treasury's worried statement in *Diario Oficial*, August 23, 1909.

73. Curiously, even the best recent studies about agriculture in the nineteenth century ignore this problem or pay only marginal attention to it. See, for example, Tortolero 1995.

References

Agencia Mercantil de la República Mexicana. 1888, 1890. *Memoria Estadística enero a diciembre 1888 y Memoria Estadística de los meses de julio a diciembre de 1890*. Mexico City.

Archivo Limantour, Condumex. Mexico City.

Atack, Jeremy, and Peter Passell. 1994. *A New Economic View of American History.* New York.

Banco Hipotecario Mexicano. 1882. *Contrato de concesión: Ley de aprobación y estatutos.* Mexico City.

Banco Internacional e Hipotecario. 1889. *Leyes: Contrato de concesión y estatutos.* Mexico City.

Born, Karl Erich. 1983. *International Banking in the Nineteenth and Twentieth Centuries.* New York.

Boletín Financiero y Minero. 1903–8.

Boletín de la Sociedad Agrícola Mexicana.

Busto, Emiliano. 1877. *Estadística de la República mexicana.* 3 vols. Mexico City.

Cámara de Diputados (Mexico). 1878–1908. *Diario de los Debates de la Cámara de Diputados.* Mexico City.

———. 1966. *Los presidentes de México a la nación: Informes, manifiestos y documentos.* Book 1. Mexico City.

Cameron, Rondo. 1974. *La banca en la primera etapa de la industrialización.* Madrid.

Casasús, Joaquín. 1896. *Estudios monetarios.* Mexico City.

———. 1890. *Las instituciones de crédito en México.* Mexico City.

———. 1908. *Las reformas a la ley de instituciones de crédito.* Mexico City.

Cerda, Luis. 1994. *Historia financiera de Banamex, 1884–1910.* 2 vols. Mexico City.

Cerutti, Mario. 1998. "El préstamo bancario en el noreste de México: La actividad de los grandes comerciantes de Monterrey (1855–1890)." In Leonor Ludlow and Carlos Marichal, eds., *La banca en México: Lecturas de historia económica mexicana.*

Chamoux, Marie Nöelle, Danièle Dehoùve, Cécile Gouy Gilbert, and Pepin Lehalleur, Marielle, eds. 1993. *Prestar y pedir prestado: Relaciones sociales y crédito en México del siglo XVI al siglo XX.* Mexico City.

Coatsworth, John. 1978. "Obstacles to Growth in Nineteenth Century Mexico." *American Historical Review,* vol. 83, no. 1: 80–100.

El Colegio de México. n.d. *Fuerza de trabajo y actividad económica por sectores.* Mexico City.

Diario Oficial de la Federación. 1870–1910. Mexico City.

Eggertson, Thráinn. 1996. "A Note on the Economics of Institutions." In L. Alston, Thráinn Eggertson, and Douglass C. North, eds., *Empirical Studies in Institutional Change,* pp. 6–24. Cambridge, Mass.

El Economista Mexicano. 1884–1910. Mexico City.

Escriche y Martín, Joaquín. 1979. *Diccionario razonado de legislación civil, penal, comercial y forense.* Mexico City.

Ferrari, Marcela. 1996. "El Banco hipotecario de la Provincia de Buenos Aires y el estímulo a la producción rural, 1872–1890." *Anuario del IEH* (Tandil), vol. 10: 219–42.

El Foro: Periódico de Jurisprudencia y Legislación. 1873–1884. Mexico City.

García, Rafael. 1901. *El presente y el porvenir económico de la República*. Mexico City.

García Granados, Alberto. 1910. *El crédito agrícola en México*. Mexico City.

Greenow, Linda. 1983. *Credit and Socioeconomic Change in Mexico: Loans and Mortgages in Guadalajara, 1720–1820*. Boulder, Colo.

Haber, Stephen. 1998. "Financial Market Regulation, Imperfect Capital Markets, and Industrial Concentration: Mexico in Comparative Perspective, 1830–1930." *Economía Mexicana*, vol. 7, no. 1: 5–46.

Herrick, Myron, and R. Ingalls. 1926. *Rural Credits, Land and Cooperatives*. New York and London.

Hoffman, Philip, Gilles Postel-Vinay, and Jean-Laurent Rosenthal. 1998. "What Do Notaries Do? Overcoming Asymmetric Information in Financial Markets: The Case of Paris, 1751." *Journal of Institutional and Theoretical Economics*, vol. 153, no. 3: 499–530.

Holden, Robert. 1994. *Mexico and the Survey of Public Lands: The Management of Modernization, 1876–1911*. De Kalb.

Jones, Charles. 1977. "Commercial Banks and Mortgage Companies." In D. C. M. Platt, ed., *Business Imperialism, 1840–1930: An Inquiry Based on British Experience in Latin America*, pp. 17–52. Oxford.

Keesing, Donald B. 1969. "Structural Change Early in Development: Mexico's Changing Industrial and Occupational Structure from 1895 to 1950." *Journal of Economic History*, vol. 29, no. 4: 716–38.

Kindleberger, Charles. 1988. *Historia financiera de Europa*. Barcelona.

Lindley, Richard. 1983. *Haciendas and Economic Development: Guadalajara, Mexico at Independence*. Austin.

Lobarinhas Pineiro, Théo. 1996. "Política e crédito agrícola no Brasil do século XIX." In *América Latina en la Historia Económica: Boletín de Fuentes*, no. 6.

Lozano, José M. 1873. *Derecho hipotecario comparado*. Mexico City.

Ludlow, Leonor. 1998. "La formación del Banco Nacional de México: Aspectos institucionales y sociales." In Leonor Ludlow and Carlos Marichal, eds., *La banca en México: Lecturas de historia económica mexicana*, pp. 142–80. Mexico City.

———. 1996. "Un tema por explorar: Los bancos hipotecarios del período porfiriano." *América Latina en la Historia Económica: Boletín de Fuentes*, no. 6.

Ludlow, Leonor, and Carlos Marichal, eds. 1998. *La banca en México: Lecturas de historia económica mexicana*. Mexico City.

Macedo, Miguel. 1884. *Datos para el estudio del nuevo Código Civil del D.F. y Territorio de la Baja California*. Mexico City.

Macedo, Pablo. 1905. *La evolución mercantil: Comunicaciones y obras públicas: La hacienda pública*. Mexico City.

Marichal, Carlos. 1998. "El nacimiento de la banca mexicana en el contexto latinoamericano: Problemas de periodización." In Ludlow Leonor and Carlos Marichal, eds., *La banca en México: Lecturas de historia económica mexicana*, pp. 112–41. Mexico City.

Martínez Sobral, Enrique. 1911. *Estudios elementales de legislación bancaria.* Mexico City.

Memoria de las Instituciones de Crédito. 1897–1911. Mexico City.

Mexican Financier. 1884–97. Mexico City.

Mexico. Código. 1870. *Código Civil del Distrito Federal y Territorio de la Baja California*. Mexico City.

Mexico. Código. 1872. *Código de Procedimientos Civiles del Distrito Federal y Territorio de la Baja California*. Mexico City.

Mexico. Cuadro. 1900. *Cuadro Sinóptico y Estadístico de la República Mexicana, año de 1900*. Mexico City.

Mexico. Exposición. 1880. *Exposición de motivos de las reformas, adiciones y aclaraciones hechas al Código de Procedimientos Civiles del Distrito Federal*. Mexico City.

Mexico. Informe 1897. "Informe sobre el uso de la autorización concedida al Ejecutivo para expedir la ley general de instituciones de crédito." In *Legislación bancaria 1957*.

Mexico. *Legislación bancaria*. 1957. Book 1. Mexico City.

Molina Enríquez, Andrés. 1978. *Los grandes problemas nacionales*. Mexico City.

North, Douglass C. 1990. *Institutions, Institutional Change and Economic Performance*. Cambridge, England.

Olson, Jr., Mancur. 1996. "Big Bills Left on the Sidewalk: Why Some Nations Are Rich and Others Poor." *Journal of Economic Perspectives*, vol. 2, no. 2: 3–24.

Oñate, Abdiel. 1991. *Banqueros y hacendados: La quimera de la modernización*. Mexico City.

Prieto, Guillermo. 1989. *Lecciones elementales de economía política*. Mexico City.

Ramírez Bautista, Elia. 1985. *Estadísticas bancarias*. Recopilación de estadísticas económicas del siglo XIX. Vol. 3. Mexico City.

Riguzzi, Paolo. 1999a. "Mercado financiero en México, 1880–1925: Las razones de su ausencia." In Marcello Carmagnani, Alicia Hernández, and Ruggiero Romano, eds., *Para una historia de América Latina*. Vol. 2, pp. 344–74. Mexico City.

———. 1999b. "Un modelo histórico de cambio institucional: La organización de la economía mexicana, 1857–1910." *Investigación Económica*, vol. 59, no. 229: 205–35.

Roa Bárcena, Rafael. 1869. *Manual razonado de práctica civil forense mexicana*. Mexico City.

Secretaría de Hacienda y Crédito Público. 1868–69, 1878–79, 1884–85. *Memorias*. Mexico City.

Secretaría de Justicia. 1868–1909. *Memorias*. Mexico City.

Tortella, Gabriel. 1994. *El desarrollo de la España contemporánea: Historia económica de los siglo XIX–XX*. Madrid.

Tortolero, Alejandro. 1995. *De la coa a la máquina de vapor*. Mexico City.

Viadas, Lauro. 1911. *El problema de la pequeña propiedad: Informe presentado al Secretario de Fomento*. Mexico City.

Wiemers Jr., Eugene. 1985. "Agriculture and Credit in Nineteenth-Century Mexico: Orizaba and Córdoba, 1822–1871." *Hispanic American Historical Review*, vol. 65, no. 4: 519–46.

Part II

Foreign Trade Reforms During the Porfiriato

Chapter 6

Institutional Change and Foreign Trade in Mexico, 1870–1911

SANDRA KUNTZ FICKER

La enfermedad en las costas, los precipicios en las serranías,
se oponen al tránsito de las mercancías y los hombres,
pero deben desaparecer bajo los rieles del ferrocarril,
bajo las alas del vapor y bajo la presión combinada de las ciencias
y las artes. Hasta que el terreno se amolda a las necesidades humanas,
aparecen pueblos como la China, Inglaterra y los Estados Unidos.
No esperen este prodigio esos empleados que convierten la oficina
en buque de piratas y que escriben tomos para cotizar las ligas
a cincuenta centavos por kilogramo.

—Ignacio Ramírez[1]

It is common wisdom that protectionism fosters domestic production and import substitution by making imports more expensive than they would be under free-trade conditions. This allows local producers to sell at higher prices in the domestic market. In less developed countries in the nineteenth century, industrial activities were a favorite target for protection. The purpose of protectionist policies was to "[keep] manufacturing competition from more advanced countries at bay while [infant industries] incur[red] the high initial costs of getting started."[2] Nobody questions the general validity of this idea. However, if the model is applied a-critically, it loses most of its explanatory power. In nineteenth-century Mexico, protectionism was common, and, for eight decades, was the most conspicuous feature of commercial policy. But it proved unable to foster any significant industrial growth for the first six decades of that period. Between the late 1820s and the 1880s, Mexico's tariffs were very high, but still rather ineffective at generating industrial activity. The only exception was the textile sector, which experienced tottering growth from the 1830s onward, thanks not only to high tariffs and import prohibitions, but also to the Mexican government's temporary policy of active promotion.[3] Even this industry, however, though heavily protected and subsidized, had become small and weak by the 1870s.[4]

If protectionism was not enough to foster industrialization in Mexico through the 1870s, it would be difficult to argue that protectionism alone explains industrial growth from the late 1880s to the eve of the Mexican Revolution in 1910. On the contrary, Mexico's first period of significant industrial growth coincided precisely with the liberalization of trade policy and the lowering of barriers to import trade. For, as we shall see, it was only in the last years of the century that the tariff and some non-tariff barriers to trade began to recede. Mexico's import trade grew at an unprecedented pace, and the Mexican economy became much more open than it ever had been before. Does this mean that the classic theory of international trade does not hold for the Mexican case? Certainly not. This only means that it does not hold in such a simple way. The distinctive feature of policy implemented after the last decade of the nineteenth century was not its protective stance against imports, but rather its embrace, for the first time in Mexico's history, of a broad range of measures that generated certainty, encouraged investment of both foreign and domestic capital, expanded the domestic market, *and* contributed to the country's integration into the international economy. Thus growth in manufactures was coincident with, though not as rapid as, growth in the mining–metallurgical sector, foreign trade, and export agriculture. However, it was certainly more rapid than growth in the domestic agricultural sector.[5]

Rather than examining the overall process of late-nineteenth-century Mexican economic growth or a particular aspect of the growth process, this chapter instead focuses on commercial policy implemented in late-nineteenth-century Mexico, particularly on those policies that relied on tariffs and customs regulations. The findings of this preliminary survey, however, do address more general concerns about the rationale underlying commercial policy and the way commercial policy affects the process of growth. It is usually argued that Mexican industry began to develop in the 1890s because it enjoyed high levels of protection.[6] Such assertions are true, but they put the emphasis in the wrong place. Mexico's industry developed at that time *in spite of lower* tariff levels *because*, for the first time, tariff protection was framed within a wider developmentalist commercial policy. The government selectively protected some industrial activities, while at the same time lifting many of the restrictions that, to the detriment of both consumers and producers, had kept the domestic market closed. Though in a strict sense less "protectionist" than before, commercial policy was more balanced and achieved its goals more efficiently.

The purpose of this chapter is to present evidence of the liberalization of some important aspects of Mexican commercial policy in the last decade of the nineteenth century. I argue that during most of the century, foreign trade was seriously hindered not only by high duties and prohibitions, but also by a regulatory framework that increased transaction costs and created powerful disincentives to participate in foreign trade. These barriers were at their highest in the late 1880s, when ad valorem tariffs on some products reached historical peaks, and customs regulations became "intricate beyond all precedent."[7] I then argue that levels of protection implied by the tariff and barriers imposed through regulation both began to decline in the last decade of the nineteenth century. Several indicators of tariff protection fell sharply in 1891 and 1892 as a result of legislated changes in the tariff schedule. The downward trend continued at a slower pace during the next thirteen years, driven in part by currency devaluation.[8] However, as I will try to show, Mexico's greater openness toward foreign markets was made possible not only by a lower degree of tariff protection, but also by a more liberal regulatory environment that considerably reduced the transaction costs incurred in international trade.

This chapter summarizes the evolution of Mexico's tariff system. It analyzes the different elements that informed the tariff policy, presents new estimates of the average tariff level, and refers briefly to other factors that influenced the protection actually granted to domestic industries. Next, it deals with the regulatory aspects of the tariff. It describes the norms and procedures that regulated customs operations in the beginning of the period and analyzes the subsequent changes that gave way to a more efficient institutional framework. I propose that at some point in the 1890s, institutional change combined with tariff liberalization to radically improve the environment for trade development, and this, in turn, contributed to the country's closer integration with the international economy.

Tariffs and the Levels of Protection

For the first fifty years after independence, Mexico was a closed economy: external trade was scant and grew at a very slow pace. The available evidence indicates that Mexican imports averaged 16 million pesos per year between 1825 and 1872. In fact, during this forty-seven-year period, the total value of imports increased by less than 6 million pesos, or by an annual rate of 0.7 percent.[9] By the mid-nineteenth century, imports per capita amounted to only 2.3 dollars.[10] Not only was Mexico's foreign trade small, but it was also highly concentrated in a very limited number of trading partners. Fifty-five percent of Mexico's imports originated in Great Britain, and the remaining 45 percent in only three or four other countries. High transportation costs, poorly developed links with international commercial transport, and a lack of financial institutions made Mexico a difficult country with which to trade. Furthermore, the composition of Mexico's import trade was poor: textiles, haberdashery, and wines jointly accounted for 79 percent of the total value of imports in 1856.[11] This kind of import basket is typical of a traditional, premodern society in which foreign trade usually does not play an important role in the domestic economy. Instead of contributing to the expansion of productive capacity or complementing the domestic supply of goods for general consumption, Mexico's imports were mainly oriented toward the concentrated and inelastic demand of the upper classes.

High tariffs and other restrictions were crucial factors limiting the growth and diversification of import trade. Even though no reliable data are available for years prior to 1870, it is likely that between 1825 and 1870, customs duties averaged 50 percent of the total value of imports.[12] Common to tariff laws within this period were import prohibitions covering a wide range of products. The number of prohibited items increased from fifty in the late 1820s to seventy in the mid-1840s.[13] Licenses for the importation of otherwise banned products sometimes would be granted to particulars, as was the case with raw cotton during the 1830s and 1840s. Alternatively, such products might be reserved for state monopoly, as was the case with tobacco until the 1850s.

Was the goal of this restrictive policy to protect particular economic activities from foreign competition? If so, then the protectionism of the early Mexican government was hardly consistent with this goal.[14] Lists of prohibited goods changed from one tariff to another, and the criteria on which prohibitions were based are not always easy to discern. It is clear that one aim was the protection of some handicrafts, for the import of Mexican shawls, spurs, and other riding implements "of the Mexican type" were often banned (although one must wonder from whom they were being protected).[15] But none of these activities ever reached the level of an "industry," nor were they supported by any other means. Although the import ban on most basic foodstuffs might indicate a protective stance toward the agricultural sector, the ban was accompanied at times by prohibitions on the import of plows and all other agricultural implements not produced domestically. The only industry consistently protected by the tariff throughout the period was the cotton textile sector, which benefited from high tariffs and sometimes even from the prohibition of foreign cotton manufactures. However, even in this area, protective policy was not fully consistent. The conflicting interests of cotton producers and cotton manufacturers pushed a weak

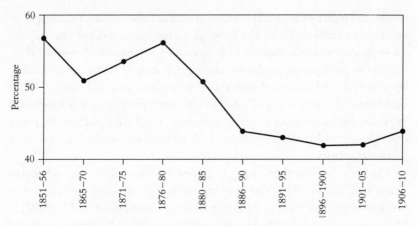

Figure 6.1. Customs Duties as a Percentage of Public Revenue (five-year averages, current pesos)

SOURCES: Tenenbaum 1986: 212; Carmagnani 1994: appendix 3.
NOTE: 1851–56 and 1865–70: average of available years.

government for some years to ban the importation not only of cotton fabrics but also of raw cotton, seriously hampering the industry's development.[16]

In short, the Mexican government's restrictive stance in these years can hardly be explained by purely protectionist motives. To make better sense of it, we must look to other factors, the most important of which was the government's heavy dependence on customs duties for its own survival. As Figure 6.1 shows, up until the 1880s, customs duties provided more than 50 percent of the public revenue. Several reasons explain this dependence. Federalism and a low penetrative power due to the lack of infrastructure forced the Mexican state, from early on, to rely mostly on indirect taxation rather than on property or income taxes. For a state with poor administrative capabilities, customs duties represented the easiest and cheapest alternative among indirect sources of revenue because they are gathered at only a few ports of entry and at relatively low cost.[17]

Mexico imposed high tariffs on most of its imports because it was not very import dependent and relied heavily on customs revenue to meet the fiscal requirements of the state. For this reason, the state "had to levy high tariff rates on scarce imports in order to accumulate sufficient income."[18] This was possible because most of the imported goods were quite price inelastic. For the most part, imports consisted of luxury goods supplied to the upper classes, and high tariffs could be imposed without diminishing consumption. In sum, the tariff policy of the national period was informed not only by somewhat inconsistent motives of industrial—or agricultural—protection, but also by fiscal policy, by the size and composition of trade, and ultimately by what Hobson has termed the level of "state power accumulation."[19] More significantly, because the tariff's design was constrained by such a wide range of factors and was subject to many, sometimes conflicting, influences, it was difficult to calculate precisely how much protection was needed to foster a particular activity.

The arrival of the liberal party in power was followed by the issuance of a new tariff law in 1856. The new law claimed to represent a relaxation of previous restrictive policies regarding external commerce. The list of prohibitions was reduced to only 18 items, and the duty-free list was expanded to include plows, coal, and machinery. Motives other than protection were still powerful at the time, however, and were reflected in a somewhat incoherent tariff structure.[20] Except for plows, all agricultural implements were subject to a high duty, as were artisan tools, raw cotton and wool, and many other inputs necessary for the nascent manufacturing sector. It is not possible to estimate the average level of the tariff for these years, but in cases where the law prescribed ad valorem tariffs, formal import duties ranged from 30 to 60 percent of the invoice value of imports.[21] However, these were only part of the duties levied on imports. A large share of regular customs duties was used to pay the heavy public debt. For this reason, the law also established so-called additional duties, which were essentially surcharges on the nominal tariffs, and amounted to about 80 percent of the nominal tariff value.[22] Assuming that the 30 to 60 percent ad valorem was representative of the overall tariff structure, and taking into account the 80 percent of additional duties, total customs duties for dutiable imports may be estimated at between 54 and 108 percent of invoice value.[23] Clearly, then, as long as customs incomes were tied to the payment of debt obligations, the tariff could not serve as an instrument for economic development.

A new, relatively more liberal, tariff law was enacted in 1872. It eliminated import prohibitions, expanded the duty-free list (to forty-seven products), and fused nominal and additional duties together, facilitating their payment. The average level of the tariff for this period is measurable, and, according to my estimates, represented about 48 percent of the total value of imports during the decade (see Figure 6.2). Apparently, there was a consensus among the political elite about the need to reduce import duties, which were too high and lacked a clear justification from the point of view of industrial protection. However, fiscal motives again prevented the politi-

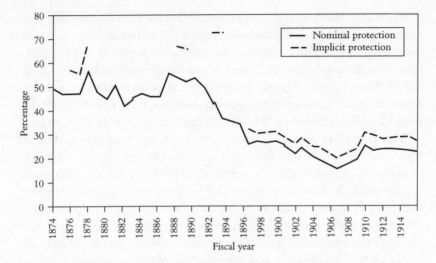

Figure 6.2. The Average Height of the Tariff: Nominal and Implicit Protection Levels

SOURCES: Import figures from Kuntz Ficker forthcoming; customs duties from Secretaría de Hacienda 1880–1910. A complete series of customs revenues (with slightly different figures) is provided in Carmagnani 1994.

NOTE: Nominal protection: import duties to total imports; implicit protection: import duties to dutiable imports.

cal elite from acting accordingly.[24] Addressing the Congress in 1879, the treasury minister emphasized the need to reduce the tariff on some cotton fabrics that were by then being produced domestically, apparently implying that they no longer needed protection. He went on to acknowledge that the tariff in force was higher than necessary for whatever protectionist purposes might be claimed. The reason those duties could not be reduced, therefore, was completely divorced from protectionist motives. As the minister acknowledged, the government simply could not do without the 5 million pesos that tariffs on cotton imports yielded each year, an amount that represented half of all customs revenue at the time.[25]

Several circumstances impeded the liberalization of tariff policy in the following decade, and, largely for reasons other than protectionism, tariffs were pushed even higher in the 1880s. First, seeking to reestablish itself in international credit markets and to make its commitments credible, the government renegotiated its external debt, resuming payment after six decades of insolvency. Second, in an effort to attract foreign resources for the construction of a much longed-for and long-delayed railroad system, the government granted financial subsidies to foreign railroad companies. These undertakings—both critical prerequisites for economic growth—put a heavy burden on the state's finances. Since customs duties continued to provide the largest share of public revenue, import duties were adjusted to meet the increased requirements of the government. Revenue from import duties rose from 12 million pesos in 1879 to about 22 million pesos only ten years later.

This growth in customs revenue took place at a time when Mexico's trade patterns were undergoing major changes. The traditional composition of foreign trade was weighted heavily in favor of luxury consumption goods. Capital goods, however, mostly railroad equipment and mining machinery, began to play an increasingly more important role. The geographic profile of Mexico's import trade also changed dramatically. Great Britain, traditionally Mexico's most important trading partner, was suddenly and definitively displaced by the United States, which became the supplier of more than 50 percent of Mexico's imports in 1889.[26] U.S. investment in the largest railroad lines provided not only financial resources and managerial capabilities, but also unprecedented amounts of capital goods, underscoring for the first time the importance of vicinity. All this produced remarkable growth in Mexico's import trade, which nearly doubled in value in the space of a single decade.[27] However, the growth in imports did not automatically produce an increase in customs duties. Massive imports of railway equipment took place within the context of concessions granted to investing companies, which included duty-free provisions for the introduction of all capital goods engaged in the projects.

Reconciling this feature with the increased need for revenue was not an easy task, particularly since "revenue maximization was an art, not a science."[28] Three different tariff laws were in force during the 1880s—a good reflection of the efforts made by the government to adjust to the new realities brought about by the onset of railroad construction and foreign investment. In order to follow changes in the average tariff level during this period, two standard measures have been adopted to express ad valorem equivalents. The first is the ratio of import duties to the total value of imports, hereafter referred to as the nominal level of protection. The second is the ratio of import duties to *dutiable* imports, hereafter referred to as the implicit rate of protection.[29] The evolution of both rates is presented in Figure 6.2. As the figure shows, the tariff schedules issued in 1880 and 1885 produced a slight increase in the level of nominal protection compared with the previous decade, whereas the 1887 tariff law instigated a downward trend that continued into the 1890s. The most significant feature of the 1880s tariff changes, however, was that they tried to make up for the revenue loss attributable to the duty-free importation of capital equipment by raising the duties paid on other goods. As a result, the level of implicit protection was significantly higher in the 1880s compared with the previous or subsequent years. This means that although a lower percentage of imports was dutiable, payments on dutiable imports were greater than they were before.[30] This trend peaked in the late 1880s, when the ratio of duties collected to total imports was falling while duties collected on dutiable imports amounted to between 73 and 85 percent of their invoice value.[31]

The 1887 tariff law reflects the delicateness of the situation the Mexican government faced as it engaged in broad economic promotion without diversifying sources of revenue. The government continued to rely primarily on customs duties, but its financial needs increased considerably with the resumption of external debt service and the subsidizing of railroads. At the same time, customs revenues were squeezed by the exemption of railroad equipment from duties. As a result of these influences, the 1887 tariff was influenced by budgetary considerations more than ever had been the case in the past. These considerations, combined with traditional protectionist claims, created extremely high tariffs for a wide range of goods subject to import duties. Table 6.1 compares the effects of the 1871 and the 1887 tariffs by estimating the implicit ad valorem for the main groups of imports in the 1872 and 1889 fiscal years. In the first year, 87 percent of Mexico's imports were dutiable. As a result, nominal and implicit levels of protection were very similar (59 and 67 percent, respectively). In contrast, by 1889, 41 percent of Mexico's imports entered duty-free, and as little as 43 percent of imports (by value) provided more than 80 percent of customs revenue. Consequently, nominal and implicit levels of protection diverged. Nominal protection was much lower than in 1872 (43 percent), whereas implicit protection reached 73 percent ad valorem. In all but one of the headings subject to comparison, ad valorem equivalents were considerably higher in 1889 compared with 1872, revealing the increased fiscal needs underlying commercial policy.

In 1889, the highest duties were imposed on cotton goods, with an overall ad valorem equivalent of 106 percent. In order to provide a more detailed picture of the tariff structure, Table 6.1 includes some individual items, most of which are related to the cotton industry. White coarse cotton cloth traditionally had been the favorite target of protection, but by the late 1880s the domestic cotton industry was diversifying into dyed cloth as well. As the table shows, the 1887 tariff provided a wide umbrella of protection for both: ad valorem duties in 1889 amounted to 134 and 148 percent, respectively,

Table 6.1
Imports, Duties Paid, and Ad Valorem Equivalents, 1872–1873 and 1889–1890

Main Headings of the Tariff	1872–73			1889–90		
	A	B	C	A	B	C
Cotton goods	7,036,913	4,992,004	71	7,677,131	8,109,445	106
Wool and silk fabrics	1,433,284	936,344	66	3,085,034	3,051,961	99
Crystal and china	279,216	172,154	62	667,593	743,389	111
Groceries and foodstuffs	3,613,162	2,184,376	60	5,954,813	4,627,228	78
Iron and steel				2,034,625	1,507,561	74
Paper products				1,359,417	1,154,446	85
Drugs and chemicals	178,259	141,181	79	1,737,395	1,036,989	60
Total sample	12,540,834	8,426,059	67	22,516,008	20,231,019	90
Total dutiable imports	17,736,504	11,833,118	67	30,780,058	22,454,155	73
Duty-free imports	2,429,508			21,238,599		
Total imports	20,166,012	11,833,118	59	52,018,657	22,454,155	43
Individual items						
Raw cotton (3)				1,582,398	540,144	34
Cotton thread (23)				628,070	439,340	70
Coarse cotton cloth, white (37)				1,213,313	1,628,008	134
Coarse cotton cloth, dyed (39)				2,052,951	3,047,211	148
Fine cotton cloth (41)				843,576	1,076,368	128
Nails, screws, and nuts (235)				217,257	243,775	112

A: Invoice value (pesos)
B: Duties paid (pesos)
C: Ad valorem equivalents (percentage)

source: Secretaría de Hacienda 1880: passim; 1892: 134–208.
note: Due to changes in the tariff classification between 1872 and 1889, some headings as well as the individual items are not comparable, and thus were not included for 1872. Ad valorem equivalents are calculated as the ratio of duties paid to the f.o.b. value of imports according to the official import figures. The fiscal classification of the tariff for individual items is included in parentheses. Import values provided in this table were taken from Mexican official statistics and thus may underestimate the actual value of imports.

for the white and dyed varieties.[32] Even if one accepts the claim that protection was the primary goal of these heavy duties, it is hard to ignore that imports of the three main types of cotton fabric alone yielded tariff revenue of more than 5 million pesos, or 20 percent of total customs revenue in 1889.[33] Moreover, the effective protection granted to this industry was affected by the structure of a tariff that was designed to provide revenue.[34] Thus, important inputs for the cotton industry, such as raw cotton and cotton thread, were subject to duties of 34 and 70 percent of their invoice value, respectively, in 1889.[35] Both inputs were produced in Mexico, and protectionist motives could be cited for both. However, domestic production grew slowly and was never enough to satisfy the demands of the textile industry. In fact, even though imports of raw cotton declined over time, imports of cotton thread tripled between 1889 and 1907.[36]

This example highlights the fact that the government was benefiting both by granting high nominal protection to domestic industries and by imposing duties on inputs used by these industries. This tariff structure reduced effective protection and revealed instead its fiscal motives.[37] Fiscal motives are manifest in most of the headings of the tariff, also included in Table 6.1. Drugs and chemicals, for which no protectionist motives could be claimed, were subject to an ad valorem equivalent of 60 percent. Typical imports for luxury consumption, such as wool and silk fabrics and china, were subject to duties of 99 and 111 percent of their value, respectively, in 1889, an increase of 50 and 80 percent, respectively, compared with 1872. The only potentially legitimate protectionist claim related to some wool fabrics manufactured on a small scale in Mexico. The highest ad valorem duties, however, were placed on goods that were not produced in the country, such as fine wool cloth and fabrics. In 1889, duties on those articles averaged 114 percent of their invoice value.[38]

Iron and steel products provide a final example of the fiscal motives of the 1887 tariff. Before 1903, hardly any iron goods were manufactured in Mexico. The industry consisted of "small foundries that produced a limited range of finished products and employed the most archaic production techniques."[39] The only large iron and steel foundry did not begin operations until 1903, and it concentrated on the production of structural shapes and steel rails.[40] Before then, steel was not produced domestically. Thus there was little reason (apart from the need to respond to the leverage of a small group of iron manufacturers) to protect the domestic market from imports that were necessary inputs for other industrial activities, such as construction. In spite of this, the 1887 tariff imposed an implicit ad valorem of 74 percent on iron and steel products. Growing demand allowed the government to levy an even higher duty on the importation of particular iron goods, such as nails, screws, and nuts.[41] In 1889, these items were subject to an ad valorem of 112 percent.

Several circumstances helped to rationalize the tariff policy in the last decade of the century. The government proved increasingly successful at renegotiating the terms of its fiscal policy with the states and with the upper classes. It thereby managed to diversify its sources of income and achieved a higher degree of fiscal autonomy. The government's ability to collect excise taxes on production was also enhanced by the construction of a railway network that gave it greater penetrative capacity over the territory. Clearer definition and better enforcement of property rights allowed the government to sell patrimonial lands and to broaden the fiscal base. As a result, the contribution of customs duties to the public revenue shrank from an average of 53 percent before 1890 to about 42 percent between 1890 and 1910 (see Figure 6.1). Even if the process was slow and not trouble-free, less dependence on customs revenue certainly provided the government more room to maneuver in designing commercial policy.[42]

The 1891 tariff law reflected the new stance of the Mexican government. The law represented a crucial step toward the liberalization of import trade and stood in neat contrast to the restrictive policies implemented before.[43] The new tariff continued the declining trend in the nominal protection rate that had started in the late 1880s; more important, it produced a sharp fall in the level of implicit protection, which dropped from 73 to only 32 percent between 1889 and 1892 (see Figure 6.2). The average height of the tariff continued shrinking during the 1890s due to the devaluation of Mexican currency, reaching its lowest levels in 1902. In this year customs duties represented 16 percent of the total import value, and 20 percent of that of dutiable imports. After 1903, upward revisions of the tariff put an end to this declining trend and reestablished the average levels that had prevailed in the mid-1890s but that were far below the historical peaks of the late 1880s.[44] By 1911, the ratios of nominal and implicit protection amounted to 23 and 27 percent, respectively, having declined 40 and 63 percent, respectively, compared to 1889 levels.

The progressive liberalization of Mexican tariff policy in the 1890s had nothing to do with the "compulsory economic liberalism" supposedly imposed on less developed countries by the developed world.[45] Nor did it signal the abandonment of a protective policy toward import-competing industries. Rather, it reflected the Mexican state's achievement of a greater degree of autonomy and financial strength, which allowed it, for the first time in Mexico's history, to design and implement a consistent developmentalist commercial policy. By lowering tariff levels, the government created more favorable conditions for the development of Mexico's foreign trade and fostered the country's greater openness. At the same time, the government selectively granted high levels of protection to some domestic industries, thereby preserving the revenue-producing benefits of the tariff. The diversification of revenue sources in the 1890s allowed the government to reduce the overall burden imposed on import trade and to draft a tariff law that was more heavily influenced by economic promotion goals.

Tariff liberalization and industrial protection were compatible because the developmentalist character of the tariff was not necessarily the result of higher levels of nominal protection. In fact, specific duties for several finished goods that competed with domestic production were reduced from levels set by the 1885 and 1887 tariffs. This was the case for paper, beer, candles, soap, coarse cotton cloth, and glass products. Along with the reduction in tariffs for finished goods, some important inputs also benefited from lower import duties. These included raw cotton and cotton thread, wool, tobacco, some chemicals, and artisans' instruments. The loss in revenue was partially offset by the imposition of small duties on machinery, iron tools, and explosives. Duties were imposed on these imports in retaliation against the McKinley tariff of the early 1890s, but levels were generally innocuous from the point of view of protection. Other increases in tariffs for revenue purposes affected fine wool and silk fabrics and the finest types of paper. Higher specific tariffs with strict protectionist purposes were imposed in the 1890s on tobacco products, fiber sacks, and, in the early 1900s, on iron and steel manufactures.[46]

To provide a rough account of the evolution and structure of the tariff, Table 6.2 presents a comparison of the 1889, 1898, and 1903 ad valorem equivalents for a sample of finished products and some of their inputs. All the finished products included competed at some point with domestic industries. In cases where only one product of a particular kind is considered, the product with the highest demand within the Mexican market was chosen.[47]

First, notice the substantial reduction in ad valorem duties across the sample: considering only dutiable imports, these duties fell, on average, from 78 percent in 1889 to 37 percent a decade later, and to only 29 percent by 1903—a cumulative fall of 63 percent. Three factors explain this downward trend. The turning point was the 1891 tariff (and its reforms in 1892), which produced the sharpest decline in tariff levels, and particularly in the level of implicit protection (as shown in Figure 6.2). The downward trend continued after 1892, mainly as a result of the devaluation of the currency. Between 1898 and 1903 the exchange rate was relatively more stable,[48] and

Table 6.2

Ad Valorem Equivalents on Selected Finished Products and Their Inputs (percentages)

Fraction*	Article	1889–90	1898–99	1903**	% Change 1889–1903	% Change 1898–1903
	Cotton					
3/125	Raw cotton	34	28	17	−50	
679	Dye products		18	13		−31
23/448	Cotton thread	70	30	18	−75	
37/458	Cotton cloth (coarse, white)	134	62	48	−64	
39/460	Cotton cloth (coarse, dyed)	148	62	48	−67	
41/462	Cotton cloth (fine)	128	58	42	−67	
	Leather					
397/72	Prepared hides	82	35	26	−69	−26
394/68	Leather goods	64	48	37	−43	−24
400/90	Boots (adult)	81	44	35	−57	−20
413/98	Shoes (adult)	40	40	32	−19	−20
	Wool					
25	Raw wool		11	12		2
110/557	Wool fabrics	84	47	42	−50	−11
	Yute					
128a	Yute		4.4	4.2		−4
19/231	Hemp cable	df	20	14	+	−31
30/233	Yute sacks	df	59	44	+	−25
305/237	Cordage	46	24	19	−58	−19
	Iron and Steel					
228/307	Wire	3	40.5	41	1268	1

23/317	Pipes	df	9	7	+	−19
225/322	Pig iron	72	42	22	−69	−46
239/323	Hoop iron	45	63	52	15	−18
305	Steel bars		36	20		−45
238/326	Iron and steel sheets	100	30.0	31.1	−69	4
34/332	Iron and steel rails	df	df	df	df	df
246/333	Iron beams	36	13.3	13.9	−62	4
235/340	Nails, screws, etc.	112	68	50	−55	−26
	Paper					
67/198, 239, 246/742	Paper pulp and waste	df	df	df	df	df
388/743a	Print paper	86	36	27	−69	−26
387/746	Pack paper	126	39	43	−66	12
	Average ad valorem on dutiable goods in the sample	78	37	29	−63	−22

SOURCE: Secretaría de Hacienda 1892: 134–208; 1899a: 381–546; 1899b: 965–81; 1904: 1–15. For tariff laws and their reforms see Dublán and Lozano 1877–1910: passim.

NOTE: Due to changes in the tariff classification, some items included for 1898 and 1903 do not have an exact equivalent in 1889, and therefore were not included for this year. For the same reason, the definition given for each fraction may not be identical in 1889 with respect to the other years. Due to changes in the sources, two different methods were employed to calculate ad valorem equivalents. For 1889, these are estimated as the proportion of duties paid to the f.o.b. value of imports. As for the following years, ad valorem equivalents are calculated as the ratio of the specific tariff in force to the unit value of imports. Unit values were obtained by dividing the invoice value by the quantity imported according to the Mexican official records.

* According to the classification in force in 1889/1898/1903 (omitted when fraction does not change).

**Unit values estimated from the import figures in the second semester of the 1902–3 fiscal year.

df: duty free

+Indicates the change from duty-free to dutiable import.

there were few legislated reforms of the tariff. Therefore, most of the decline in ad valorem equivalents between these years is explained by the increase in the gold price of imports.

The first rows of Table 6.2 present the evolution of ad valorem equivalents for the most traded goods related to the cotton industry, the traditional
target of tariff protection. Nominal ad valorem duties on some important inputs, such as raw cotton and cotton thread, fell by 50 and 75 percent, respectively, between 1889 and 1903. Those imposed on dyes fell by 31 percent between 1898 and 1903. This decline did not necessarily increase levels
of effective protection because duties on finished goods fell by 65 percent
on average between 1889 and 1903. However, the trend toward lower duties, evident across the sample with few exceptions, did not deprive import-
competing industries of considerable levels of tariff protection. In fact, imports bearing duties near or above 40 percent by 1903 are easy to identify as
targets of protection. What changed, and in a rather drastic way, were the
average level of the tariff and the perception on the part of the Mexican government of what should be considered a reasonable level of tariff protection.
As we have seen before, relaxation of the fiscal motives underlying commercial policy played a crucial role in these changes. As a result, some "protective" duties that in the late 1880s stood in the range of 80 to 150 percent
were reduced to between 30 and 50 percent. Such was the case with duties
on cotton and wool fabrics, some leather goods, and pack paper. Some in-
fant industries, led by entrepreneurs who possessed leverage over the government, benefited from some of the highest new duties, as illustrated here
in the cases of yute sacks and wire. But even the nascent iron and steel industry had to make do with lower levels of nominal protection for several
goods. In 1903, pig iron, iron and steel sheets, and iron beams were subject
to ad valorem duties that were 60 percent lower than in the late 1880s, and
actually lower than those granted to other protected industries.[49]

In short, beginning in the 1890s, Mexican tariff policy continued to provide protection for some industries and to produce revenue, but it did so
within the context of liberalized commercial policy. Influenced less by fiscal
motives, the tariff granted selective protection for domestic industries that
were undergoing technological modernization, reducing marginal production costs, and enhancing their ability to compete with foreign goods. For
industries still in their infancy, the tariff generally offered higher levels of
nominal and effective protection. But, whether considered high or low, the
level of protection granted between 1891 and 1911 was probably the lowest ever provided by a Mexican tariff.

The total actual protection enjoyed by the domestic market was also affected by non-tariff factors, the most important of which between 1892 and 1904 was currency devaluation.[50] Devaluation increased the silver value of imports and thus created an overall shelter against foreign goods. The effect on particular industries, however, was determined by their degree of dependence on imported fuels, machinery, and inputs, and, therefore, it differed across domestic activities.[51] In 1905, the devaluation stopped playing a role, as monetary reform established a fixed exchange rate for the Mexican peso. An upward revision of the tariff in the same year counteracted the effect of the currency stabilization, but only to some extent. As a result, the total actual protection enjoyed thereafter by the domestic market was lower than in the years of the sharpest currency devaluation.

The second most important non-tariff factor that influenced import prices in the domestic market was transportation costs. Thanks to a vast railroad construction program, inland transportation costs fell sharply in the 1880s: on average, railroad freight rates in the north-south lines were about 70 percent lower than average wagon rates.[52] Later increases in railroad rates affected particular commodities and journeys, but, even then, transportation by railroad was considerably cheaper than the most efficient available alternative. Lower transportation costs partially counteracted the impact of currency depreciation in the 1890s, and, to the benefit of domestic industries, added to the dramatically enhanced conditions provided by railroads for the transportation of bulky commodities, such as capital goods and fuels.[53] The third most important non-tariff factor affecting import trade was the institutional structure, which is the subject of the next section.

The Evolution of the Institutional Framework

The tariff constituted a conspicuous but largely predictable barrier the costs of which could be estimated by merchants and producers. By contrast, the regulatory aspect of the tariff laws imposed a series of less visible and less predictable hindrances that considerably raised the transaction costs incurred by economic agents in import trade operations, preventing them from realizing "the gains from trade."[54] Most of these costs cannot be quantitatively estimated, and their impact upon trade is not easily isolated and measured. With the available data, however, I will try to show how inefficient institutions—mainly customs regulations and procedures—constituted an obstacle at least as serious as high tariffs. A real reduction in the barriers to trade could take place only when a fall in duties was accompanied by a substantial liberalization and better specification of the rules of the game related to foreign trade.

This part focuses on formal institutions, namely the set of laws, rules, and procedures defined by the government and by the customs administration to regulate import trade operations. Informal institutions, that is to say, the set of codes, norms, and conventions that regulates human interaction,[55] are considered here only implicitly, to the extent that they influenced the subjective interpretation of the law or oriented the actual application of customs procedures. The purpose of this section is twofold. First, it describes the institutional setting that regulated import trade in late-nineteenth-century Mexico and examines the means by which that setting affected trade operations. Second, it traces the timing and pace of institutional change and estimates the extent to which such change actually contributed to a lowering of barriers to trade.

INSTITUTIONAL FRAMEWORK AND TRANSACTION COSTS

The first modern tariff law in Mexico was issued in 1872. This was not only the first non-prohibitionist law enacted since the 1820s, but was also the first attempt to seriously confront the reality of import trade and the need to carefully regulate its operations. More important, this was the first time in Mexico's national history that a uniform set of rules and customs administration was effectively enforced throughout the territory.[56] However, the 1872 tariff law did not represent a true liberalization of customs operations in Mexico. In many senses, the law continued the tradition of conceiving trade as a luxury and potential threat. Accordingly, it was much more focused on preventing smuggling and securing public revenue than it was on fostering international trade. There was broad consensus among traders that excessive and inefficient customs regulation was more of an obstacle to trade than were tariffs themselves. Arguing against a 10 percent rise in import duties projected in 1875, the Mexico City Cámara de Comercio complained that the projected increase "was enormous, not so much because the duties would be raised, but because the current regulation is vile and obscure, the wording is diffuse and confusing and the customs procedures are tyrannical."[57]

Starting in the late 1870s, import trade grew in volume and importance, but the administrative capacity of the Mexican government did not keep pace. The treasury ministry estimated the value of contraband at 3 to 4 million pesos, or one-fifth of the total value of imports in 1878. In an attempt to check smuggling and to secure the revenue to which the government was entitled, authorities issued a series of decrees affecting import trade operations. Imprisonment and heavy fines were established for smugglers and cheaters, and monetary rewards were granted to informants and customs employees for reporting illegal practices. In the mid-1880s, a special armed corps was created (the *gendarmería fiscal*, or fiscal police) by fusing military squadrons with rural police in order to control the northern territory. This corps was granted ample faculties to apprehend and prosecute contraband suspects. Any merchandise circulating within the Mexican Republic had to be accompanied by a passport (*guía*).[58] Anyone carrying merchandise anywhere within the territory without the required documentation could be imprisoned according to the law by the authority of the fiscal police.[59]

Attempts to control contraband and to increase customs revenue affected not only enforcement mechanisms, but also the regulatory aspect of import trade. The rules enacted in the late 1880s were regarded by some as "the most complicated Customs regulations human ingenuity is capable of devising."[60] In the following pages, I analyze the different means by which the regulatory framework that prevailed until the 1890s increased transaction costs and itself became a barrier to the development of import trade.

Information

The procedures implied in an import trade operation required that all participants possess full information about Mexican tariff law. The acquisition of such information, however, was an impossible task, as the British representative complained:

> Having devoted seven months to the study of the intricate customs regulations and tariff in force here . . . I venture to draw attention to some of the most salient facts of the subject; for . . . to discuss with due advantage the treatment received by the 696 specific articles comprised in the tariff would require a greater measure of technical knowledge of all trades than one individual can be expected to possess.[61]

The remittent of goods in a foreign country was required to fill out an invoice containing not just the particulars of the lot, but also the exact tariff classification applicable to each of the goods exported. This requirement was not easy due to the intricate nature of the law and was compounded by the fact that the law was subject to frequent changes sometimes announced with very short notice. Neither the law nor its reforms were publicized broadly either within the country or abroad. It could take the *Diario Oficial* several months to publish the full details of a new tariff. In the decade from 1890 to 1900 alone, more than sixty reforms to the tariff law were enacted in Mexico, affecting tariffs and procedures to varying degrees.[62] To become acquainted with all of them was almost impossible, but failure to do so led invariably to heavy fines and even the risk of confiscation.

The information problem was aggravated by the fact that in addition to the law itself there were different interpretations of the law. The proliferation of confusing and misleading opinions, created by the vagueness of regulations, is illustrated by a note published by the *Board of Trade Journal* that stated:

> Several importers of foreign goods and various members of the administration have held the opinion, that the interpretation which ought to be placed upon the Article 40 of the [*ordenanza*], which inflicts double duties upon all goods, the bill of lading of which is found to inaccurately describe the quality, is that the sum of the double duties should be calculated, not on the total of the duties which the goods ought properly to pay, but only on the difference between those imposed upon the article incorrectly described, and that which actually applies to the goods themselves. There is no foundation for this opinion, and it is opposed to the text of the article itself. The President of the Republic, therefore, to avoid all further misconception, has decided that the following rules are to be observed . . .[63]

Only in 1908 did the foreign ministry issue a "practical guide of the *Ordenanza*" and distribute it among Mexican consuls abroad. However, the Dirección de Aduanas soon declared that this guide "was not an official document, and, thus, the provisions offered by it are only assessments, more or less founded, by its author, that cannot be taken into account to solve any doubt stemming from the application of the *Ordenanza*."[64] For these reasons, the information available to the public about customs regulations was always imperfect and could never be complete.

Costly and Complicated Procedures

Even full availability of information, however, did not guarantee safe clearance of goods at customs. Procedures themselves were complicated, and it was difficult to comply with customs officials' demands. The assumption was "that all importers are guilty unless they can pass unscathed the severe ordeal of . . . [a] labyrinth of perplexing and complicated regulations."[65] Even customs administrators complained about the "useless procedures that increase the work that has to be done by importers, which are already less preoccupied by the duties they have to pay, than about the requirements that they are forced to fulfill."[66] The bureaucratic ordeal can be summarized as follows. Every participant in an import transaction, from the exporter to the ship captain and the consignee, had to carry out from three to seven procedures, some at different administrative offices. All of them had to write up from two to seven different documents, each in two to five identical hand-written copies. The instructions given for the fulfillment of these requisites reflect neatly the spirit that guided the law:

> [Article] 125 . . . [The pediments] should be presented in quadruplicate form, all completely alike, without abbreviations, flaws, corrections or erasures. They should be written legibly so the reader experiences no doubts, with horizontal lines from the end of each written period to the end of the line, so that no additional information can be added later. Each request should have sufficient space in the margin for custom's business. In case all of the above is not included, the customs agent should not accept them, but rather the information should be replaced with the proper clarity.[67]

Most of the transactions involved in an import operation included the payment of some kind of fare or duty (consular duties, several port taxes, import duties, stamp taxes, international duties), and many included the risk of fines. The impact of transaction costs upon prices becomes transparent if one considers that sale prices "have to be so regulated as to cover fines and the complicated clearing arrangements."[68]

Even so, this was the simplest standard procedure available, assuming that no major contravention was found. Otherwise, a whole set of further transactions had to be carried out: from resorting to the treasury ministry to initiating an administrative or a judicial lawsuit in the Mexican courts. When a major contravention was found, the defendant was allowed to choose between an administrative or judicial procedure. Administrative procedures were held within the customs office with the administrator acting as a judge; the defendant had the right to appeal to the treasury, which issued the final decision. Judicial procedures required the prosecution of a lawsuit in a federal court with the intervention of all the judicial instances required, and with the customs administrator having the right to appeal. Both procedures were time-consuming. A lawsuit also implied monetary expenses. In either case, the outcome was uncertain.[69]

This complicated system created bottlenecks at customhouses in the delivery of goods, a situation that was often aggravated by deficient organization. In 1904, at a time when regulations had been eased and procedures for the dispatch of goods greatly loosened, the treasury ministry was informed by the Tampico customs administrator of occasions when as many as three hundred delivery requests were waiting to be dispatched.[70]

Offenses and Fines: The Problem of Measurement

Mexican customs regulations were extremely severe in the definition of faults
and offenses, and offenses were heavily penalized. There were "enormous
fines for (morally speaking) trivial offenses," and the severity of penalties
made uncertainty a factor in every goods clearance. The transaction costs
implied by fines were a common component of the final price of merchandise, even if the amount of fines was not easy to predict. "The fines [are] so
unduly heavy and so uncertain as to the number of them any particular cargo
may incur, they become a most difficult factor in the question as to what
profit, duty paid, the goods may be expected to realize."[71] There were times
when uncertainty neared the limits of acceptable risk. As a U.S. consul at
Matamoros warned in the early 1880s, "very severe laws have taken effect
which make doing business in this country very risky, as a clerical error may,
if it be over $300, make one liable to imprisonment."[72]

Consider so-called trivial offenses. Exporters, ship captains, and consignees could be fined for filling out their respective documentation with era-
sures or amendments, for providing "incomplete" information, or for not
having written the exact tariff classification of goods otherwise rightly declared. According to the 1872 tariff law, additions and corrections to invoices were allowed within twenty-four hours of a ship's arrival. However,
if those corrections were "considerable," the payment of double duties applied.[73] The treasury minister justified this measure with the awkward statement that "it cannot be said that this rigor is onerous to *bona fide* trade, for
accuracy is one of the conditions of a merchant."[74] In 1885, a decree slightly
loosened the penalty for additions and corrections by excepting those cases
in which they were made on involuntary mistakes and did not affect the payment of duties. Minor faults were indeed costly and time-consuming, but
were not likely to affect seriously the completion of an import transaction.
This was not, however, the case with major offenses, such as contraband,
fraud, or supplantation.

There were several incentives for contraband in late-nineteenth-century
Mexico, particularly in the early years of the period. The first was the weakness of the national government and its inability to monitor the huge coasts
and frontiers and to enforce the law.[75] In addition, the extreme complexity
of tariff regulations, the high duties levied upon imports, the degree of discretion enjoyed by customs authorities, and the high penalties imposed on
the infringement of the law acted as powerful incentives to risk illegal importation.[76] The chances of getting away with contraband were good and the
potential gains so high that "enormous profits" could be expected "even if

25 percent of their consignments are seized en route."[77] In an effort to check contraband, the government imposed severe penalties that were strengthened over the years. The penalty for trafficking in plain contraband included the confiscation of goods and the vehicles conducting them. The penalty for some minor varieties of smuggling included the payment of double duties. The 1880 tariff law tightened the rules by adding, on top of economic penalties, imprisonment of five years in cases where duties on contraband exceeded 200 pesos.[78] The 1891 law eliminated the minimum duties requirement as a condition for imprisonment and set sentences of one to five years according to the seriousness of the crime.[79] The law was so absurdly formulated that small imports of less than 100 pesos in value were subject to excessive and strict procedures, and the failure to comply with them was punished in the same way as any other case of smuggling.[80] In 1901 a customs administrator complained that to "form a smuggling suit for each tiny thing seized" was "a more or less impracticable procedure":

> Not only does the customs house waste a lot of time in forming the respective file and all of its copies, but it is also the case that the judicial authority has to employ valuable time on its prosecution. The cost of paper is sometimes more than the duties on the seized merchandise. This does not even take into account the additional expense of 20 pesos daily for the cost of maintaining one prisoner in jail.[81]

The combination of severe regulations with an enhanced capacity to control the territory and enforce the law allowed the government to progressively eliminate contraband. An indicator of this trend is the declining number of confiscation suits, which fell from 780 in 1873–74 to only 278 in 1885.[82] By the early 1890s, plain smuggling had been practically wiped out.

According to the law, however, contraband had a broad definition. It included not only the clandestine introduction of goods, but also omissions and inaccuracies in customs declarations. Perhaps one of the most vexatious of the regulations concerned supplantation—that is, the attempt to defraud the treasury through the inaccurate declaration of goods imported, be it in quantity or quality. According to the 1872 tariff law, the punishment for supplantation was payment of double duties on the supplanted goods; for omissions it was payment of three times the duties due according to the tariff.[83] As somebody pointed out, "the fine of double duties is virtual confiscation, if not worse; for the single duties generally exceed 100 percent ad valorem."[84] The 1880 tariff law added to this pecuniary penalty corporal punishment of two months to five years in prison, according to the amount of duties not paid.[85] This extreme measure was not relaxed until the 1891 ordenanza, which specified an administrative fine of double duties for sup-plantation, but not corporal punishment. Corporal punishment did apply, however, if the offense was consummated.

All this wouldn't be so serious if the crime of supplantation hadn't been so easy to commit. The possibility that either the certified invoice sent by the exporter or the importer's declaration of goods differed from the exam-ination made by the customs official was very likely, given the complicated regulations and the space left to personal interpretation. A serious problem of measurement and specification arose here, because the specific duties im-posed by the tariff implied that the difference between one fiscal fraction and another was often determined by the weight, length, width, or thickness of merchandise.[86] Some examples illustrate the point. Fractions 444 and 445 of the tariff schedule set the duties for cotton strings at $1.50 or $0.15 per le-gal kilo, respectively. This huge difference in duties depended on whether the strings were less than or greater than 10 millimeters thick. Another ex-ample is provided by a supplantation lawsuit from 1884 in which the judge found it difficult to determine to which fraction a lot of paper belonged. Witnesses and experts gave discrepant opinions—justified by the fiscal pros-ecutor himself, who argued that "in the fiscal classification [of different types of printing paper] there is always place for the appreciation of experts *for this is not a qualification subject to exact principles*."[87] The difference in duties pay-able was not negligible, however, ranging from 10 to 43 cents per kilogram; nor was it negligible that the verdict in the case depended on the judge's de-termination and could send the importer to prison. As a final example, du-ties on cotton cloths varied depending on the smoothness of the fabric, on the number of yarns, and on the color, amount, class, and material of adorn-ments. The difficulty of measuring, weighing, and stating the quality of goods is obvious. Even so, if the statement of the exporter or the declaration of the consignee failed to agree with the customs official's assessment (and was not corrected in a timely fashion), the importer could be charged with supplan-tation, face heavy penalties, and, before 1891, imprisonment.

The Vicious System of Fines Distribution (and Some Ways to Avoid It)

In order to create incentives for customs agents to enforce the law and not to accept bribes, the government established the practice of dividing the funds received from confiscations and fines among customs employees, after first deducting that share of the fine that was owed the treasury. This proved to be profitable for the state, particularly in the early years of the period, be-cause it tied together the interests of the treasury with those of the customs employees. The system was complemented by terrible punishments for officials who defrauded the government. Punishment included imprisonment, lifelong disqualification from public employment, and the publication of the official's name and crime. However, this system had a number of unintended consequences. First, it created an incentive to find major contraventions of the law in what were, at times, minor errors in customs declarations. Second, it generated controversies about the correct way to share this extraordinary income among the various officials and between them and the treasury. This gave rise to a great deal of further regulation and negotiation.[88] Third, the government's attempts to loosen procedures and eliminate fines for rather trivial faults were resisted by customs officials, who saw such reforms as a threat to their income.

Perhaps the most important implication of this system was that customs officials were interested parties who obtained material benefits from the imposition of fines. More than serving the public or improving efficiency, they sought to find offenses in every transaction or to allege a major infraction where only a trivial mistake had been made. It is telling that in 1874–75, 1,154 dossiers for fines and confiscations were opened at the treasury ministry.[89] This is a very high figure if one considers that in those years there were only about 1,250 port and border operations recorded by all customhouses.[90] Customs officials considered their participation in fines a part of their regular income. Even the British consul felt obliged to apologize for his complaints by saying: "No one would suggest that they should be deprived of these fines, constituting as they do the greater part of the customs officials' emoluments, without compensation."[91] As Table 6.3 illustrates, the amount of this additional income was far from negligible. In the Veracruz customhouse, it was equivalent to between 70 and 90 percent of customs officials' salaries during the 1890s—a time when customs procedures already had been somewhat rationalized, and income from this source had been reduced by more than 80 percent compared to the previous decade.

It is also worth noting that things may well have been worse in other customhouses that were less crowded and less important than Veracruz, and, therefore, less subject to federal government control. In this respect, an astonishing figure is available for the Tampico customhouse, which in 1887–88 obtained 97,500 pesos from fines and confiscations. After considering the amount of import duties collected there in the same year, it turns out that fines imposed an extra burden of 20 percent on the imports introduced through that port.[92]

There is evidence that in the early 1890s, the treasury minister tried to eliminate "the direct personal interest which the customs officials at present have in the imposition of fines for trifling errors."[93] However, vested inter-

Table 6.3

Confiscations and Fines and Salaries of Customhouse
Officials, Veracruz Customhouse, Selected Years

Fiscal Year	(1) Confiscations and Fines*	(2) Salaries of Customhouse Officials	(1) As a Percentage of (2)
1885-86**	146,030	n.a.	
1887-88	101,965	n.a.	
1891-92	79,766	88,493	90
1897-98	68,766	96,958	71
1898-99	66,725	92,222	72

SOURCES: *Mexican Financier,* July 16, 1892; Secretaría de Hacienda 1897–98,
Memoria de Hacienda: 363; 1898–99: 263–64; *Diario Oficial,* January 8, 1886;
El Economista Mexicano, September 2, 1888: 89.
*The figures include only the types of fines that were set aside for further
distribution among customhouse officials.
**Calculated from the figure for the first half of the year.

ests within the customs administration limited what could be done in this
respect. When in 1893 the treasury abolished fines imposed on additions to
consular invoices, it also raised the fine on supplantation by 25 percent in an
effort to compensate for the loss in extraordinary income that previously had
been divided among customs employees. The proportions in which that income was to be shared also changed, tending to favor lower officials and informants relative to customs administrators.[94] However, the practice as such
held until the end of the period.

Each vicious practice, however, created incentives for its own compromise. Because customs officials had an incentive to find faults in the declaration of goods, importers ran a serious risk of being accused of supplantation. To avoid this risk, importers engaged in the practice of overrating their
imports, even if they had to pay higher duties as a result, making it impossible for the customs official to charge them with supplantation. Mazatlán
merchants testified in a lawsuit that they used to declare some wool clothes
as fraction 126 (which implied higher duties) even though everybody knew
that they belonged to fraction 103, "only to avoid trouble and lawsuit expense."[95] The practice was officially acknowledged in the 1890s, when a reform in the law allowed importers to request, before the treasury ministry,

a reimbursement of the excess duties paid at the customhouse. This solution was far from perfect, because it implied the payment of higher duties and the need to carry out additional procedures before the treasury. There is no way to measure the impact of this costly remedy, for excess duties were added to regular customs accounts. However, it is clear that this was the cost of avoiding the risk of being charged with supplantation—and many were ready to pay it. Trying to discourage this practice, the treasury ministry in 1897 mandated careful revision of those lots not accurately declared by the consignee and the imposition of fines on inaccurate (even if upwardly biased) declarations. The practice did not cease, however, as a "reminder" of this order dated 1900 makes evident.[96]

Undue Importance of Brokers

The excessive amount of information needed to fulfill the numerous requisites imposed by the customs law, and the uncertain circumstances involved in the clearance of goods, made it preferable for merchants to incur the additional costs of hiring agents to do the job: "Merchants shipping into Mexico must employ at ports of entry brokers versed by long experience in technicalities, who levy upon all goods passing through their hands and without whose aid shippers are liable to incur heavy fines. Simple and reasonable customs regulations would do away with all this."[97]

Although this procedure seemed to be safer than taking personal charge of the introduction of goods into Mexico, it did not guarantee safe clearance of the imported goods. The possibility remained of "fines which brokers incur, for not knowing the merchandise they receive."[98]

Merchants bore two transaction costs: the fines imposed by customs authorities and the costs of intermediation by customs brokers. Brokers not only charged a percentage of the imports' value as a commission for their services, but also found every possible way to overcharge their customers for everything from alleged maneuvers, including unloading, deposit, and transport of the goods to the railway station. The common practice, however, was to leave the lots free of charge at the customhouse yard (where bundles were always subject to small theft) until the time arrived to send the cargo by railway.[99]

Apparently, using brokers was a better alternative than facing the bureaucracy, even if brokers' honesty left much to be desired. A broker in Veracruz was fined for "a very clear case of supplantation." He persuaded the owners of merchandise in Mexico City that a fine was fair and had to be paid. Once he received payment, he then applied for and was granted reimbursement of the fine from the treasury ministry. The broker did not notify his clients, keeping the reimbursement for himself. Thus, "the equity exercised by the Ministry benefited the rascal broker and not the owner of the effects."[100] This kind of double cheating may not have been uncommon at all, for the whole system offered powerful incentives for it. The intricate nature of the law placed many merchants in a defenseless position, but gave brokers a crucial role in managing customs procedures. The search for extraordinary income encouraged customs officials to find inaccuracies that could be interpreted as offenses. The right to appeal customs decisions before the treasury ministry—*after the business was settled and the fines paid*—made brokers the potential beneficiaries of their patrons' losses.

Brokers played an intermediary role that was crucial for the completion of import trade transactions. Brokers were, perhaps, the most finished creation of the regulatory framework in the sense that "the kinds of skills and knowledge that will pay off will be a function of the incentive structure inherent in the institutional matrix."[101] They diverted part of the gains from trade and closed the vicious circle of constraints that for so long had suffocated import trade and thwarted its development in Mexico.

THE PACE OF INSTITUTIONAL CHANGE

Tariff reform and institutional liberalization did not occur simultaneously, nor did they unfold at the same pace. Although in the early 1890s some important provisions were made that relaxed some of the most pernicious practices, change in the regulatory framework was slow, and liberalizing measures were often counteracted by renewed attempts to control and secure public revenue.[102] On the whole, the beginning of a more consistent trend toward liberalization began somewhere in the mid-1890s. This process of institutional change slowed by the end of the century and then experienced a huge jump with the vast reform of 1904. Between 1905 and the outbreak of the Mexican Revolution, no major changes in the regulatory aspect of the tariff law took place.

In order to capture the timing and pace of change in the regulatory framework, I have quantified the changes in the procedural part of the tariff laws from 1887 to 1905.[103] I selected sixty reforms of the law of differing scope, containing every kind of modification to rules, practices, and procedures in the customs field. Also included are some circulars issued by the treasury ministry that did not constitute a reform to the law but amounted to an actual (and often significant) change in the interpretation given to it.[104] Next, I assigned a quantitative value to every change affecting regulation, according to the following criteria. For changes that

A. Improved information and efficiency within the customs administration, provided better specification of the rules, or enhanced control mechanisms: [105] −3

B. Unified or facilitated procedures, eliminated discretional or arbitrary practices by customs officials: [106] −2

C. Lightened barriers to trade: [107] −1

D. Increased regulation or procedures, raised fines, and made trade more difficult: [108] +2

E. Reestablished old, onerous regulation: [109] +3

It is important to note that according to the criteria adopted, a decrease in the regulatory burden does not necessarily mean that deregulation was taking place. Many of the progressive changes were actually due to an *increase* in regulation, in the form of better specification, more uniform procedures, and the like. In total, I recorded ninety-five changes within this eighteen-year period. The exercise is rough and has many shortcomings arising from the difficulty of assigning a quantitative equivalent to qualitative changes of various degrees of importance and scope. Many isolated reforms of the early years are overestimated compared to the radical and comprehensive reform enacted in 1904. Every isolated change in each single rule produces a full value in the scale created above, while the massive reforms of 1904 are not coded individually but grouped and weighted by the type of change they implied. Thus, the results presented in Table 6.4 may not pass statistical muster, but are still quite suggestive.

Change was rather slow in the first eight years, and its incremental nature was affected by the important number of regressive reforms (columns D and E) that partially offset the trend toward liberalization. After 1895, the liberalizing changes became more numerous, and after 1901 they affected more significant aspects of the regulations (columns A and B as compared with column C). In fact, almost 60 percent of the changes accumulated during the period took place between 1901 and 1905.

The significance of institutional change in the customs field is indicated by the extent to which such change facilitated import trade operations, thereby reducing barriers to trade. In this sense, institutional change played a role similar to, and in fact complementary to, that of liberalization of the tariff burden. How did the timing and pace of regulatory change couple with that of tariff liberalization? The only way to match both dimensions is by looking at the evolution of nominal and implicit protection levels (see Figure 6.2) and comparing them with the incremental changes in regulation as presented in the last column of Table 6.4. Some differences are apparent. First, whereas

Table 6.4

Quantitative Values of Change in Customs Regulations, 1886–1905

Period	Number of Changes	NUMBER OF CHANGES WITHIN EACH CATEGORY					Total Value of Changes within the Period
		A (−3)	B (−2)	C (−1)	D (+2)	E (+3)	
1887–90	5	1	2	2	0	0	−9
1891–95	22	6	2	7	3	4	−11
1896–1900	29	5	5	11	8	0	−20
1901–05	39	15	12	4	8	0	−57
Totals	95	27	21	24	19	4	−97

NOTE: For sources and method see text.

nominal and implicit protection levels exhibited the steepest decline before 1893, the regulatory burden showed a very slow decline up to 1895. After 1895, the evolution of protection levels and regulatory change matched more closely, producing a moderate convergent trend toward liberalization. Between 1901 and 1905, the evolution of both variables separated again: the average level of the tariff declined slightly but then rose and returned to the point achieved by the mid-1890s, while changes in regulation provided the steepest reduction in the regulatory burden throughout the period. On the whole, if the data presented capture with acceptable precision the timing of both trends, it can be stated that liberalization in one dimension took place precisely when the other dimension held steady, and vice versa. Thus, waves of tariff liberalization are to be found in 1891–92 and 1898–1902, whereas surges of regulatory change are perceptible in 1895–98 and 1901–5. Significantly, the last drop in the regulatory barrier was accompanied by the last rise in tariff protection in the period.

Conclusions

In the fifty years after independence, Mexico followed a restrictive commercial policy designed to provide the resources necessary for the survival of a very weak state and to protect, albeit in a rather inconsistent manner, small economic groups with significant leverage over the government. Noneconomic motives seem to have played a crucial role during this period as well, for the restrictive stance toward "foreign influences" extended beyond external trade.[110] There were severe restrictions on foreign investment in mining activities in spite of a persistent shortage of capital to develop the sector. Traditional patterns of business organization, based on family networks and interpersonal relations within the context of a heavily politicized economy, created a general climate that favored the participation of natives or longtime residents over foreigners in economic activities.[111] It was as if, in the view of the political elite, the process of nation-building required that the doors to the outside world be locked—at least temporarily. In this respect, the restrictive stance—along with a variety of deterring conditions—served its purpose. By 1870, Mexico had developed very scant connections to the international economy, with extremely low levels of foreign trade, foreign investment, external debt, and immigration from abroad.

The strengthening of the state after the definitive triumph of the liberal party in the late 1860s created the conditions for a progressive opening of the Mexican economy. These conditions translated into a lightening of restrictions on foreign investment and the integration of the country into international capital markets, a double process that unfolded clearly from the 1880s. However, the new policy increased the financial needs of the government without eliminating its dependence on customs revenue. This dependence coupled very well with continuous demands for protection from emergent industrial groups. The result was a commercial policy that tried to reconcile the different challenges the government faced. The loss of revenue attributable to the duty-free importation of capital goods was offset by higher tariffs for dutiable imports, providing both revenue and protection. It is likely that the levels of implicit protection reached in the late 1880s were, as some scholars have pointed out, "among the highest in the world."[112] This background provides the lens necessary for understanding the liberalization of commercial policy implemented through the 1891 tariff law and its subsequent reforms. The average level of the tariff declined considerably after the historically high levels reached in the late 1880s: nominal protection fell by 40 percent and implicit protection by 63 percent between 1889 and 1911. It is likely that effective rates of protection also declined, for in many cases the reduction in ad valorem duties affected both finished goods and their inputs.

High duties were not the only barrier to foreign trade in nineteenth-century Mexico. At least as onerous was a set of customs regulations that increased the costs and risks of international trade operations and deterred actors from engaging in them. Customs regulations were often considered even more harmful to trade than duties. Not only were regulations intricate, time-consuming, and subject to widely different interpretations and discretionary application, but they also created powerful incentives to obstruct the straightforward clearance of goods, promoted inefficiency, and generated uncertainty among merchants. Economic agents could more easily calculate the cost of tariffs than they could the costs of delays, losses, thefts, fines, bribes, and lawsuits. During the 1880s, import operations were also risky in a more radical sense: whoever undertook them ran the risk of being imprisoned if his judgment and that of the customs official did not coincide.

In the early 1890s, the regulatory dimension of commercial policy began to liberalize. More uniform and simple procedures, lighter regulation and penalties, and a more efficient customs administration gradually enhanced conditions for international trade by facilitating transactions and lowering the degree of uncertainty involved in import operations. However, the fear of contraband and free-riding kept the government from rapidly relaxing regulatory barriers, and the process of liberalization unfolded slowly in the first years. The most consistent trend toward liberalization in this field took place only after 1895, and it culminated in 1904 with a major modification in the regulatory aspects of the tariff law. During these years, both dimensions of the liberalization process converged to create a very favorable environment for the development of foreign trade: the lowest tariff burden converged with the least onerous regulation ever achieved in Mexico's history. In spite of a moderate increase in the tariff in 1905, this favorable setting held until the end of the period.

The different timing of tariff and regulatory liberalization produced a relatively slow opening of the Mexican market to foreign trade. The slow pace of this opening better enabled the government to gain control of smuggling, to enhance its administrative capabilities, and to improve its ability to enforce the law. This pace also provided the time necessary for the export sector to develop, preventing the growth in imports from translating into an uncontrollable outflow of specie. By these means, trade deficits were contained within reasonable levels. In sum, the fact that both processes were not entirely simultaneous had the effect of smoothing the transition from a rather closed economy to one moderately opened and integrated into the international market. But the overall result of this process is unequivocal: per capita imports doubled in value between 1895 and 1910,[113] and in the three decades between 1880 and 1910, imports grew at the very respectable rate of nearly 5 percent per year. This rate not only was unprecedented by Mexico's standards, but also compares favorably with the main trends in world trade at the time.[114]

Notes

I wish to acknowledge the valuable comments provided by Stephen Haber, Paolo Riguzzi, and Luis Jáuregui on a previous version of this chapter. I also thank the Social Science History Institute at Stanford University for its support and all the participants in the conference "Institutional Change and Economic Growth: A New Economic History of Mexico" for their comments.

1. From an article published in *El Siglo XIX*, September 9, 1871, reproduced in Banco Nacional de Comercio Exterior 1976: 345.

2. Lindert 1986: 157.

3. This policy included direct subsidies and the provision of imported machinery sold on credit to investors by a promotion bank financed by the government. Potash 1983.

4. Thomson 1989.

5. Although quantitative data for this period is scant and must be taken with reservation, some annual rates of growth give a rough indication of the performance of the Mexican economy between 1895 and 1907. Population: 1.2 percent; GDP: 3.9 percent; domestic agriculture: 2.5 percent; export agriculture: 5.8 percent; manufactures: 4.6 percent; mining/metallurgy: 6.7 percent; commodity imports: 8.1 percent; commodity exports: 7.4 percent. All production figures calculated in 1900 pesos according to Coatsworth 1989: 41; El Colegio de México 1961; Instituto Nacional de Estadística Geografía y Estadística 1985. Foreign trade values estimated in current dollars in Kuntz Ficker forthcoming.

6. Rosenzweig 1989: 152; Beatty (Chapter 7 in this volume). Rosenzweig's work is one of the few studies that deal with economic policies during the Porfirian period (1877–1910) within the framework of Mexican conventional historiography. On the other hand, Ted Beatty provides a systematic attempt to apply international trade theory to Porfirian Mexico. In contrast to the conventional view, he proves that the commercial policy of this regime was driven by consistent developmental goals rather than by the leverage power of some interest groups upon the government. Our chapters coincide in asserting that the government selectively protected some industrial activities, but then they follow different routes. Beatty's chapter highlights tariff protection and its impact upon industrial investment, whereas this chapter emphasizes the progressive liberalization of commercial policy after a long tradition of restrictive and even prohibitionist policies toward international trade.

7. Foreign Office 1886: 3.

8. The two works that have recently addressed the issue of tariff protection during the Porfirian period evaluate correctly the crucial role played by currency devaluation in eroding the levels of nominal protection after 1892. However, in both cases the analysis starts after the most important decline in those levels had already taken place (thanks to legislative action). As a result, what's

underscored is the moderate downward trend once the overall level had fallen, and the significance of the 1891 fall with respect to the historical trends is underplayed. See Beatty (Chapter 7 of this volume); Márquez 1998.

9. Lerdo de Tejada 1967; Herrera Canales 1977: 26, 82; Secretaría de Hacienda 1880: 6.

10. The figure corresponds to 1856. Exports per head, though higher, were also rather small, amounting to 3.2 dollars circa 1850. This ratio compares very negatively to the rest of Latin America, being higher than that of only Colombia, Ecuador, Guatemala, and Paraguay. Bulmer-Thomas 1994: 38.

11. Herrera Canales 1977: 26.

12. An estimate for some years is presented in Salvucci et al. 1995: 103. However, as the authors state, discrepancies in the data offered by different sources impede a more accurate calculation.

13. Cosío Villegas assumes that prohibitions accumulated from one tariff to another, achieving the amazing number of 334 by the mid-1840s. Cosío Villegas 1989: 25–29. For an analysis of prohibitionism and protectionism in nineteenth-century Mexico, see Riguzzi 2000.

14. A similar answer to this question is given in Cosío Villegas 1989: 80 ff.

15. See, for instance, the ordenanza of 1856, in Dublán and Lozano 1877, vol. 8: 45.

16. The ban on raw cotton was suspended in 1846, only to be replaced by a high tariff. Potash 1983: 138.

17. "In determining the optimum tax mix, say, between tariffs and excise taxes, differential collection costs may weight the scales heavily in favor of tariffs in spite of the production distortion cost that may result from the protective effects of tariffs." Corden 1997: 50. Just to illustrate this point for Mexico, in 1875 customs duties for 10 million pesos were gathered in thirty customhouses, by a total of 830 employees at a cost of 8 percent of the amount collected. The cost was relatively low if one considers that duties provided 50 percent of the entire revenue of the Mexican government in that year. Sierra and Martínez Vera 1973: 171.

18. Hobson 1997: 214.

19. Hobson 1997: 218–20.

20. As Lerdo de Tejada stated, there were some "essential mistakes in the bottom of the law, that contradicted its main purpose." Quoted in Banco Nacional 1976: 324.

21. The 1856 tariff law established ad valorem tariffs for some products, and specific rates for most. Ad valorem tariffs are expressed as a percentage of the invoice value of imports, whereas specific rate tariffs are set at a fixed rate per physical unit, such as the quantity or weight of the goods. In the ensuing years, Mexico's tariff structure shifted completely to a system of specific tariffs in an effort to avoid contraband via the underinvoicing of imports. For our purposes, specific duties must be converted into ad valorem equivalents in or-

der to calculate the nominal rate of protection. Due to data limitations, this can only be done for the period after 1870. For the 1856 ordenanza, see Dublán and Lozano 1877, vol. 8: 42–94.

22. The express purpose of this division between import duties and additional duties was to diminish the share of the customs revenue that had to be set aside for external debt payments. See Banco Nacional 1976: 323.

23. According to Treasury Minister Matías Romero, total customs duties for some products actually may have reached 150 percent ad valorem, but this is probably an overstatement. See Dublán and Lozano 1882, vol. 12: 4–5.

24. As Romero explained, "a wise reduction in import tariffs" could only take place "once the internal revenue had been systematized." Banco Nacional 1976: 320.

25. Secretaría de Hacienda 1880, *Memoria de Hacienda.*

26. Regarding the evolution of relations among this "threesome," see Riguzzi 1992. For the long-term trends in the bilateral trade between Mexico and the United States see Kuntz Ficker 2001.

27. Mexico's imports grew from $23 million in 1879 to $44 million by 1889. Kuntz Ficker forthcoming.

28. Bulmer-Thomas 1994: 33.

29. To calculate these ad valorem equivalents of the tariff I have used my own reconstruction of the yearly value of Mexico's imports, which in some years differs greatly from that provided by Catáo 1991. The latter constitutes the basis of Ted Beatty's estimate (see Chapter 7 of this volume, Table 7.1 and Figure 7.1). My import series provides the f.o.b. value of imports in current dollars, and was converted to pesos at the nominal exchange rate. Regarding the reconstruction of import figures see Kuntz Ficker forthcoming; for the exchange rate, see El Colegio de México 1960: 36.

30. According to available official figures, the share of dutiable imports to total imports decreased from an average of 86 percent in the 1870s to an average of 63 percent in the fiscal years 1888–89 and 1889–90. It rose again to more than 80 percent from 1892 onward. See Secretaría de Hacienda, *Memoria de Hacienda,* passim.

31. The levels of nominal and implicit protection presented in Figure 6.2 have been calculated according to my reconstruction of import values (see note 29, above), which corrects some deficiencies present in official statistics. However, whereas nominal protection could be estimated for the whole period, the ratios of dutiable to total imports needed to calculate implicit protection are not available for many years before 1892. According to Cosío Villegas' estimates, implicit protection reached its highest levels between 1883 and 1891, averaging 82 percent of dutiable imports. This ratio is consistent with my own figures for those years. His calculation for the following decade, however, is biased by the mistaken assumption that customs duties were paid in gold. See Cosío Villegas 1989: 57 ff.

32. Secretaría de Hacienda 1892, fractions 37 and 39 of the tariff.

33. Fractions 37, 39, and 41 of the tariff, included in Table 6.1. Fine cotton cloth paid an ad valorem of 128 percent, even though it was not produced within the country.

34. Effective protection is defined as "the percentage effect of the entire tariff structure on the value added per unit of output in each industry." Simply stated, it measures the nominal protection rate imposed on finished goods *less* the nominal protection rate levied on the inputs necessary to produce those goods. Lindert 1986: 141. In this chapter no attempt is made to measure effective protection, but only to give some rough indication of its apparent trends over the period. A more thorough analysis of the structure of the tariff with the aim of calculating effective protection is provided by Beatty (Chapter 7 of this volume). His exercise is limited by the availability of data to the period after 1891, a year in which the levels of protection were already at a historical low point.

35. Secretaría de Hacienda 1892, fractions 3 and 23, respectively.

36. These went from 0.5 million pesos in 1889 to 1.9 million in 1907. Secretaría de Hacienda 1892: 172; 1909.

37. The importance of "fiscal" duties in a supposedly protective tariff has been proved for the Italian case in Federico and Tena 1998.

38. Ad valorem duty for fractions 106 and 110−12 on imports from the United States, France, Great Britain, and Germany. Secretaría de Hacienda 1892.

39. Haber 1989: 45.

40. Beato and Síndico 1992: 196; Haber 1989: 46; Gómez-Galvarriato 1997.

41. Imports of these products grew from 1,400 tons in 1889 (fraction 235 of the tariff) to 6,500 tons in 1907 (fraction 257). Import figures from Secretaría de Hacienda 1892, 1909.

42. Carmagnani 1994: 213−18, 248−61. A significant indicator in this respect is that, in the first decade of the twentieth century, an internal tax (the *timbre*, or stamp tax) became the primary source of federal revenue.

43. The 1891 tariff was subject to significant adjustments that consolidated this trend, which were published in the first reform to the tariff law enacted in 1892. Other reforms of lesser importance were issued in the following ten years.

44. In this sense, my estimates coincide with Márquez's conclusion that "the erosion of the 1890s was not fully reversed [by the upward reforms], generally leaving ad valorem rates below their 1892 level." Márquez 1998: 417.

45. Bairoch 1993: 41, 53.

46. Wire was granted a very high and clearly protective duty beginning in 1897, when the specific tariff jumped from 1 to 4 cents per kilogram. See Dublán and Lozano 1898, vol. 27: 92−93 and Table 6.2.

47. Often the Mexican tariff broke down generic products into several tariff fractions according to the size, quality, and other particular features of the items. The specific duty imposed could vary greatly from one fraction to the other; thus it was necessary to decide which particular fraction was relevant from the point of view of the commercial policy. In these cases I chose the fraction that had the highest demand in the Mexican market, which also was (or became) the most traded within its kind. To illustrate the application of this criterion, consider the following. Within the heading "boots" the tariff included eight different fractions (girls', boys', women's, men's, with or without silk or adornments, etc.). In 1891 the specific tariff applied in either case varied from 30 cents to 2.50 pesos per pair. However, only one fraction was of high demand in Mexico: adult men's leather boots, which was therefore chosen to study the actual impact of the tariff upon imports. Due to the application of this criterion, and to the use of different years and sources to estimate ad valorem equivalents, the figures presented in Table 6.2 differ from those provided by Beatty in Chapter 7 of this volume.

48. Except for 1902, between 1898 and 1904 the Mexican currency was subject to less fluctuation than in previous years. The exchange rate of the silver peso in dollars was .47 in 1898–99 and .44 in 1903, a difference of 6 percent between the two years.

49. An upward revision of the tariff to provide somewhat higher protection for the iron and steel industry took place only in 1904. See tariff reform of February 4, 1904, in Dublán and Lozano 1908, vol. 36: 109–15. Treasury Minister Limantour defended this "shy exercise at protection" against the claims of the British business attaché in AJYL, roll 24, box 6/29, 1904.

50. Beatty (Chapter 7 of this volume); Márquez 1998.

51. For the effect of currency devaluation upon prices in the domestic market, see Zabludowsky 1984.

52. Coatsworth 1981: 94–99; Kuntz Ficker 1996: 125.

53. Besides, machinery and coal were transported at the lowest rates available throughout the period.

54. North 1985: 558.

55. North 1993: 54.

56. Riguzzi 2000.

57. Secretaría de Hacienda 1875: 124.

58. Sierra and Martínez Vera 1973: 179–81, 197–98.

59. For the British Consul, the system of passports necessary for the circulation of merchandise was retained "as part of the complicated and costly machinery for suppressing the smuggling which the high tariff encourages." *Board of Trade Journal*, vol. 2, January–June 1887: 548.

60. *Board of Trade Journal*, vol. 2, January–June 1887: 399, 545.

61. Foreign Office 1886: 1.

62. See Dublán and Lozano 1877–1910: passim.

63. *Board of Trade Journal*, vol. 1, July–December 1886: 314.

64. Circular of July 11, 1908, in Dublán and Lozano 1910, vol. 40–1: 387.

65. *Board of Trade Journal*, vol. 2, January–June 1887: 544–45.

66. AJYL, first series, roll 1, box 3, doc. 721, Javier Arrangoiz to José I. Limantour, Mazatlán, May 2, 1893.

67. Ordenanza of 1887, in Dublán and Lozano, 1887, vol. 18: 59.

68. Foreign Office 1886: 4.

69. For judicial lawsuits, the law granted up to four months to go from one instance to another, but there is evidence that it could take much longer for them to get to a final decision.

70. AJYL, second series, roll 26, box 12/29, Limantour to Guillermo Curtis, Mexico City, November 19, 1904.

71. Foreign Office 1886: 3.

72. U.S. Department of State, no. 12, 1881: 164.

73. Articles 66 and 29 of the 1872 ordenanza.

74. Secretaría de Hacienda, *Informe de Hacienda*, 1873–74: 6.

75. Enforcement was particularly difficult for the government in the 1870s and 1880s. Among the difficulties faced, one of the more documented is the scant support provided by district judges. In a telling case, an inspector sent by the federal government to monitor the activities of a customhouse found anomalies and fired some local employees. The people affected accused him before the local judge, who decided in favor of the employees and *imprisoned* the treasury inspector. Secretaría de Hacienda, *Informe de Hacienda*, 1874–75: 9. Similar cases are cited in Secretaría de Hacienda, *Informe de Hacienda*, 1873–74: 5.

76. See U.S. Department of State, no. 19, May 1882: 60–61.

77. Foreign Office 1886: 3.

78. See the 1880 ordenanza, Article 87, in Secretaría de Hacienda, *Memoria de Hacienda* 1881: 61.

79. Ordenanza of 1891, Articles 510 and 535, in Dublán and Lozano 1898, vol. 21.

80. "Those interested in importing goods should present before the customhouse four copies of an application to get an import permit. Once authorized, the permit should be brought to the nearest Mexican consul for certification. Duly certified, the merchandise should be presented at the customhouse for examination within three days after the expedition of the import permit." See ordenanza of 1891, Articles 468–74.

81. AJYL, first series, roll 7, box 7/19, Carlos Mertens to Limantour, Cd. Porfirio Díaz, January 14, 1901. Mertens recalls having made the same complaint in 1889, to no avail.

82. Secretaría de Hacienda, *Informe de Hacienda* 1873–74: 11–12; Secretaría de Hacienda, *Memoria de Hacienda* 1888: 31.

83. Except for the fine of triple duties, those provisions remained in force, with slight variations, in every tariff law from 1872 on.

84. Foreign Office 1886: 3.

85. In 1885, a man was accused of supplantation by faulty declaration of the quantity imported and immediately paid 705 pesos as double duties of the supplanted merchandise. In the lawsuit that followed, the defendant claimed that he had not attempted to defraud the treasury, neither had he participated in the offense, for "the consular invoice was not formed by him, but by the sender of the merchandise, in the city of Bordeaux." The judge considered that it was not the deliberate will of cheating that was to be punished, but the offense itself. Thanks to some attenuating circumstances, the defendant was "only" sentenced to forty days in prison. *El Foro*, March 12, 1885: 174.

86. A common warning in U.S. consuls' reports was that "a small deviation from the width in the invoice or import declaration will not only make very heavy fines and vexatious delays, but subject the really innocent importer to imprisonment." U.S. Department of State, no. 3, January 1881: 13.

87. *El Foro*, October 24, 1885: 323. Emphasis in the original.

88. At least six decrees or circulars were issued between 1888 and 1905 concerning the ways in which the *reparto* should be carried out. Dublán and Lozano 1877–1910: passim.

89. Secretaría de Hacienda, *Informe de Hacienda* 1874–75: 5. The excessive number of cases brought some trouble to the ministry, for 425 files were pending resolution at the end of the year.

90. The latter figure corresponds to 1876–77 and includes the number of ships that arrived at port plus the number of import operations carried out at the border customhouses. The relation is made in Secretaría de Hacienda, *Memoria de Hacienda* 1877: 68. The next year the reported figure amounted to 1,569, from which 445 were ballast ships, 777 loaded ships, and 347 border operations. Of course, it must be understood that the arrival of one loaded ship implied more than one import operation. *Memoria* 1879: 76.

91. Foreign Office 1886: 3.

92. *El Economista Mexicano*, September 22, 1888: 89.

93. *Board of Trade Journal*, vol. 13, July–December 1892: 695.

94. Decrees of April 20, 1893, and March 29, 1904, in Dublán and Lozano 1898, vol. 23: 103, and 1908, vol. 34: 294.

95. *El Foro*, no. 45, March 10, 1887.

96. Circulars of November 8, 1897, and October 29, 1900, in Dublán and Lozano 1898, vol. 27: 363, and 1904, vol. 32: 752.

97. U.S. Department of State, no. 142, July 1892: 574. Apparently, the system of distributing fines also contributed to the indispensability of brokers. "The omission of certain formulae incurs fines, and these fines are divided between the Government and the employee who discovers and reports the omission. This has made the system so painfully exact that the principal business of

the customs house agent is to rewrite the necessary documents and put them in the required form, and thus avoid fines for his principal." *Board of Trade Journal*, vol. 27, December 1899: 687.

98. AJYL, first series, roll 1, box 3, doc. 703, Arrangoiz to Limantour, Mazatlán, August 11, 1892.

99. AJYL, first series, roll 1, doc. 771, Arrangoiz to Limantour, Veracruz, March 23, 1895. About the "inveterate custom" of small theft among customs officials, commerce employees, and carriers, see AJYL, first series, roll 1, doc. 806, Arrangoiz to Limantour, Veracruz, September 20, 1895.

100. AJYL, first series, roll 1, doc. 771, Arrangoiz to Limantour, Veracruz, March 23, 1895.

101. North 1992: 10.

102. Some important steps toward a more efficient customs regulation were the progressive elimination of fines for trivial offenses and elimination of imprisonment as a penalty for supplantation. An 1893 law organized the customhouses and established their jurisdictions, improving their internal operations. In 1896 the "vigilance zone," in which the fiscal police were granted ample powers, was limited to 100 kilometers from the border, unless there was "founded suspicion" of smuggling. Later on, the vigilance zone was further narrowed, and the faculties of the fiscal corps were reduced. In 1900 a special agency, the Dirección General de Aduanas (which reported to the treasury ministry), was created to improve control and service in customs administration. Some inefficient practices remained until the end of the period, however. Among them were the discretionary powers granted to customs officials, and the authorization to take "all the time required" to qualify additions or corrections and to fine consignees when the latter were too numerous. Additionally, some fines for major offenses were increased to compensate for the suppression of other penalties. See Dublán and Lozano 1877–1910: passim.

103. A similar attempt at quantification of legal change may be found in Libecap 1978.

104. It is worth mentioning that the sample is not exhaustive, particularly in regard to small and isolated changes that were not included in the legislative collection compiled by Dublán and Lozano 1877–1910: passim.

105. Some examples are the authorization not to consult the treasury ministry in the taking of particular decisions and the establishment of the customhouse jurisdictions.

106. For example, the specification of the faculties enjoyed by the fiscal police or the regulation of the way in which fines should be divided among customs officials.

107. For example, the authorization to make additions and corrections to consular invoices without incurring fines and the reduction or suppression of penalties.

108. For example, the order to check the entire load when packages were declared as a whole, or the imposition of high sureties, fines, and onerous procedures for transit trade.

109. For example, detraction from the agreement to eliminate a second revision of merchandise at the Mexico City treasury office.

110. Cosío Villegas 1989: 26–27.

111. A fascinating portrait of this environment is presented in Walker 1986. As for the politicization of economic activities, see also Tenenbaum 1986.

112. Salvucci 1991: 722, 726.

113. They went from 3.4 to 6.8 dollars between 1895 and 1910. Kuntz Ficker forthcoming.

114. The world rate of imports growth was 3.5 percent per year between 1881 and 1913. Bulmer-Thomas 1994: 54.

References

[AJYL] Archivo José Yves Limantour, Condumex. Mexico City.

Bairoch, Paul. 1993. *Economics and World History: Myths and Paradoxes.* Chicago.

Banco Nacional de Comercio Exterior. 1976. *Colección de documentos para la historia del comercio exterior de Mexico City. VII: Del centralismo proteccionista al régimen liberal, 1837–1872.* 2d series. Mexico City.

Beato, Guillermo, and Doménico Síndico. 1992. "El comienzo de la industrialización en el noreste de México." In Enrique Cárdenas, ed., *Historia económica de México: Lecturas.* Mexico City.

The Board of Trade Journal. 1886–99. London.

Bulmer-Thomas, Victor. 1994. *The Economic History of Latin America Since Independence.* Cambridge, England.

Cámara de Diputados (Mexico). 1966. *Los presidentes de México ante la nación: Informes, manifiestos y documentos de 1821 a 1966.* Vol. 3. Mexico City.

Capie, Forrest H. 1994. *Tariffs and Growth: Some Illustrations from the World Economy, 1850–1940.* Manchester and New York.

Carmagnani, Marcelo. 1994. *Estado y mercado: La economía pública del liberalismo mexicano.* Mexico City.

Catáo, Luis. 1991. "The Transmission of Long Cycles Between 'Core' and 'Periphery' Economies: A Case Study of Brazil and Mexico, c. 1870–1940." Ph.D. dissertation, University of Cambridge.

Coatsworth, John. 1989. "The Decline of the Mexican Economy." In Reinhard Liehr, ed., *América Latina en la época de Simón Bolívar: La formación de las economías nacionales y los intereses económicos europeos, 1800–1850,* pp. 27–54. Berlin.

———. 1981. *Growth Against Development: The Economic Impact of Railroads in Porfirian Mexico.* De Kalb.

El Colegio de México. 1960. *Estadísticas económicas del Porfiriato: Comercio exterior de México, 1870–1910.* Mexico City.

———. 1961. *Estadísticas económicas del Porfiriato: Fuerza de trabajo y actividad económica por sectores.* Mexico City.

Corden, W. Max. 1997. *Trade Policy and Economic Welfare.* 2d ed. Oxford.

Cosío Villegas, Daniel. 1989. *La cuestión arancelaria en México.* Mexico City.

Diario Oficial. 1886. Mexico City.

Dublán, Manuel, and José María Lozano. 1877–1910. *Legislación Mexicana o Colección completa de las disposiciones legislativas expedidas desde la independencia de la República.* Vols. 8–42. Mexico City. The specific volume and year are provided in the notes. Title may vary.

El Economista Mexicano. 1888. Mexico City.

Federico, Giovanni, and Antonio Tena. 1998. "Was Italy a Protectionist Country?" *European Review of Economic History,* vol. 2, no. 1, April: 73–93.

Foreign Office. 1889. *Mexico.* Annual Series, no. 604. London.

———. 1886. *Mexico: Report from Veracruz on the Railway Rates and Customs Duties at that Port.* Miscellaneous Series, no. 13. London.

El Foro. 1885–87. Mexico City.

Gómez-Galvarriato, Aurora. 1997. "El desempeño de la Fundidora de Hierro y Acero de Monterrey durante el Porfiriato." In Carlos Marichal and Mario Cerutti, eds., *Historia de las grandes empresas en México, 1850–1930,* pp. 201–44. Mexico City.

Haber, Stephen H. 1989. *Industry and Underdevelopment: The Industrialization of Mexico, 1890–1940.* Stanford.

Helleiner, G. K. 1972. *International Trade and Economic Development.* London.

Herrera Canales, Inés. 1977. *El comercio exterior de México, 1821–1875.* Mexico City.

Hobson, John M. 1997. *The Wealth of States: A Comparative Sociology of International Economic and Political Change.* Cambridge, Mass.

Instituto Nacional de Estadística Geografía y Estadística. 1985. *Estadísticas históricas de México.* 2 vols. Mexico City.

Kuntz Ficker, Sandra. 2001. "El comercio México-Estados Unidos, 1870–1929: Reconstruccíon estadística y tendencias generales." *Mexican Studies/Estudios Mexicanos,* vol. 17, no. 1: 71–107.

———. 1996. "Ferrocarriles y mercado: Tarifas, precios y tráfico ferroviario en el Porfiriato." In Sandra Kuntz Ficker and Paolo Riguzzi, eds., *Ferrocarriles y vida económica en México, 1850–1950: Del surgimiento tardío al decaimiento precoz,* pp. 99–165. Mexico City.

———. Forthcoming. "Nuevas series del comercio exterior de México, 1870–1929." *Revista de Historia Económica.*

Lerdo de Tejada, Miguel. 1967. *Comercio exterior de México desde la conquista hasta hoy.* Mexico City.

Libecap, Gary D. 1978. "Economic Variables and the Development of the Law: The Case of Western Mineral Rights." *Journal of Economic History*, vol. 38, no. 2: 338–62.

Liehr, Reinhard, ed. 1989. *América Latina en la época de Simón Bolívar: La formación de las economías nacionales y los intereses económicos europeos, 1800–1850*. Berlin.

Lindert, Peter H. 1986. *International Economics*. 8th ed. Homewood.

Márquez, Graciela. 1998. "Tariff Protection in Mexico, 1892–1909: Ad Valorem Tariff Rates and Sources of Variation." In John H. Coatsworth and Alan M. Taylor, eds., *Latin America and the World Economy Since 1800*, pp. 402–44. Cambridge, Mass., and London.

Mexican Financier. 1892. Mexico City.

North, Douglass C. 1984. "Government and the Cost of Exchange in History." *Journal of Economic History*, vol. 44, no. 2, June: 255–64.

———. 1993. *Instituciones, cambio institucional y desempeño económico*. Mexico City.

———. 1985. "Transaction Costs in History." *Journal of European Economic History*, vol. 4, no. 3, September–December: 557–76.

———. 1992. *Transaction Costs, Institutions, and Economic Performance*. Occasional Paper no. 30. San Francisco: International Center for Economic Growth.

Potash, Robert A. 1983. *Mexican Government and Industrial Development in the Early Republic: The Banco de Avío*. Amherst.

Riguzzi, Paolo. 2000. "Constitución, libertad económica y libre cambio en la experiencia mexicana, 1850–1896." In Marcello Carmagnani, ed., *El orden liberal en América Latina, 1850–1930*. Turin.

———. 1992. "México, Estados Unidos, Gran Bretaña: Una difícil relación triangular, 1867–1911." *Historia Mexicana*, vol. 3, no. 41, January–March: 365–436.

Rosenzweig, Fernando. 1989. *El desarrollo económico de México 1800–1910*. Mexico City.

Salvucci, Richard J. 1991. "The Origins and Progress of U.S. Mexican Trade, 1825–1884: 'Hoc opus, hic labor est.'" *Hispanic American Historical Review*, vol. 4, no. 71: 697–735.

Salvucci, Richard J., Linda K. Salvucci, and Aslán Cohen. 1995. "The Politics of Protection: Interpreting Commercial Policy in Late Bourbon and Early National Mexico." In Kenneth J. Andrien and Lyman L. Johnson, eds., *The Political Economy of Spanish America in the Age of Revolution: 1750–1850*, pp. 95–114. Albuquerque.

Secretaría de Hacienda y Crédito Público. 1875. *Documentos anexos al informe de Hacienda*. Mexico City.

———. 1892. *Importaciones 1889 a 1890: Primer semestre-segundo semestre-año fiscal*. Mexico City.

————. 1880. *Noticia de la importación y exportación de mercancías en los años fiscales de 1872 a 1873, 1873 a 1874 y 1874 a 1875.* Mexico City.

————. 1899a. *Estadística Fiscal: Importación año fiscal de 1895–96.* Book 2, no. 181. Mexico City.

————. 1899b. *Boletín de Estadística Fiscal,* no. 194. Mexico City.

————. 1904. *Boletín de Estadística Fiscal,* no. 254. Mexico City.

————. 1909. *Boletín de Estadística Fiscal,* no. 327. Mexico City.

————. 1872–73, 1873–74, 1874–75. *Informe de Hacienda.* Mexico City.

————. 1877, 1880, 1881, 1888, 1897–98, 1898–99. *Memoria de Hacienda.* Mexico City.

Sierra, Carlos J., and Rogelio Martínez Vera. 1973. *Historia y legislación aduanera de México.* Mexico City.

Taussig, F. W. 1967. *The Tariff History of the United States.* New York.

Tenenbaum, Barbara A. 1986. *The Politics of Penury: Debts and Taxes in Mexico, 1821–1856.* Albuquerque.

Thomson, Guy P. C. 1989. "Traditional and Modern Manufacturing in Mexico, 1821–1850." In Reinhard Liehr, ed., *América Latina en la época de Simón Bolívar: La formación de las economías nacionales y los intereses económicos europeos, 1800–1850,* pp. 55–86. Berlin.

U.S. Department of State. 1881–1904. *Reports from the Consuls of the United States on the Commerce, Manufactures, etc., of Their Consular Districts.* Washington, D.C. The specific year and number are provided in the note.

Walker, David W. 1986. *Kinship, Business and Politics: The Martínez del Río Family in Mexico.* Austin.

Zabludowsky, Jaime. 1984. "Money, Foreign Indebtness, and Export Performance in Porfirist Mexico." Ph.D. dissertation, Yale University.

Chapter 7

Commercial Policy in Porfirian Mexico:
The Structure of Protection

EDWARD BEATTY

Growing levels of investment in domestic manufacturing in Mexico between 1880 and 1910 should surprise us.[1] Not only did these decades witness increasingly aggressive efforts by foreign firms to capture sales markets around the world—and especially in Mexico—but falling international and domestic transport costs also brought foreign goods to Mexican markets at ever-lower prices. Salesmen from North Atlantic firms crisscrossed Mexico, new department stores carried foreign products, U.S. and European consular agents actively promoted the interests of the import trade, and foreign firms adopted aggressive sales strategies to capture shares of the Mexican market. Meanwhile, oceanic and overland transportation advances reduced the prices of foreign goods facing Mexican consumers. The historian, then, is confronted with something of a paradox: rising (and mostly new) investment in domestic industry in the face of increasing foreign competition.

Most recent studies of Porfirian industry have not satisfactorily addressed this issue, but have implicitly suggested one of three explanations. The first sees early industrialization as the result of export-led growth that broadened consumer demand and stimulated linkages to industry. The export boom determined the rate and direction of investment, and "the rest, to a certain extent, was a by-product."[2] The problem, however, is that this does not explain why rising demand was not satisfied through increased imports. Why not continue buying low-cost, high-quality goods from abroad? Furthermore, the only systematic study of export linkages in Mexico found them few and ineffective.[3] The second views new and expanding industries as the result of government patronage and protection granted on an ad hoc and personalistic basis, favoring those with close political connections.[4] The third argues that the depreciation of Mexico's silver currency stimulated investment in domestic manufacturing and, by raising the price of imports, constituted "the true factor of protection in the face of foreign competition."[5] Each view implicitly denies the existence of a coherent, impersonal, and consistent federal policy to promote investment in a wide range of domestic industries.[6]

This chapter examines one federal policy that aimed to induce investment in domestic industry: the tariff schedules that levied duties on imported goods. I argue that tariff-based protection was substantial from the 1880s to 1910 and covered a wide range of traditional and new industries, that tariff reforms were increasingly designed to favor developmental rather than fiscal objectives, that federal officials aggressively and proactively countered the effects of the peso depreciation, and that there is a strong correlation between tariff levels and the early, concurrent process of import-substituting industrialization.[7] Indeed, it would be difficult to imagine or explain any significant industrial growth in the last decades of the nineteenth century without protective tariffs designed to stimulate investment in industries ranging from soap and beer to cotton textiles and steel.

At the same time that the Porfirian government conferred substantial protection to domestic industry, it also reduced the overall burden of import duties and non-tariff regulations on the country's foreign trade, as Sandra Kuntz Ficker demonstrates in this volume. The result was an economy both more industrial and more closely integrated with the North Atlantic economies. Indeed, an increasingly open economy was a necessary complement to industrial protection, as an expanding industrial sector depended on imported inputs, which were in turn purchased with the foreign exchange earned through expanding exports.[8] In this case, an open economy and industrial protection were not incompatible.

There has long been anecdotal evidence that levels of protection were substantial throughout nineteenth-century Mexico. From independence most Mexican policymakers imagined an industrial future and adopted tariff schedules more or less appropriate to that end.[9] The refrain of classically liberal, free-trade rhetoric found little expression in formal legislation, despite its use by several administrations from the 1820s through the 1880s. As Miguel Lerdo de Tejada remarked somewhat sarcastically concerning the tariff of 1829,

This law, which can be described as one of the most severe in terms of prohibitions, has nevertheless been issued by a government which espouses the most exaggerated principles of liberty and social progress; we can only presume that its authors, sacrificing all the ideals they proclaim, have no other object than to acquire popularity, cajoling those who believe that this is how they must protect national industries and arts.[10]

Half a century later, when Finance Minister Matías Romero publicly argued for lower tariffs during the 1870s and 1880s and pursued bilateral trade treaties with the United States, tariff reforms actually increased legislated rates.[11] Yet from independence through the 1880s the fiscal needs of an unstable and frequently embattled state overwhelmed any protectionist objectives. Although high tariffs yielded some coincident protection, this was erratic, unpredictable, and inconsistent. Only the cotton textile industry benefited significantly.[12]

By the late 1880s, however, tariff reforms increasingly sought to achieve developmental goals by conferring substantial protection to a range of traditional and new industries. By the 1890s, a strong consensus in favor of a protectionist, pro-industrial policy pervaded Díaz's advisors and ministers, and tariff policy was also increasingly freed from the fiscal concerns of the state.[13] Matías Romero's successor, José Yves Limantour, consistently acknowledged the protectionist and import-substituting consequences of tariff reforms, writing in 1905 that "the natural consequence of higher tariffs will be a reduction in the importation of certain articles," while *La Semana Mercantile* concluded (albeit with some degree of overstatement) that tariff protection constituted "the actual generator of our [material] progress."[14]

Contemporaries agreed, in short, that Porfirian protectionism was neither accidental nor ad hoc. Yet no work has examined the structure of protection in Porfirian Mexico since Daniel Cosío Villegas's classic study of 1932, and that presented no systematic analysis of late-century tariff protection. Consequently this chapter examines several aspects of tariff-based policy: the breadth of protection across Mexican industries, the level of protection conferred to particular industries, the impact of the peso depreciation on industrial protection, and the structure of protection, that is, the balance of low and high tariffs on industrial inputs and finished products. The chapter continues with a brief discussion of the political and economic interests affected by tariff policy. Together, these issues provide an explanation for the new pattern of investment in domestic industry after 1880, demonstrated at the end of the chapter by comparing tariff levels with extant data on industrial production and import flows. This does not mean, however, that tariff protection and the kinds of industrial investment it induced were necessarily good for Mexico, only that tariff protection began to alter the economic and social character of a country that had long been dominated by subsistence agriculture and export production.

Levels of Protection

Tariffs, by levying a tax on imported goods and thus increasing their price to domestic consumers, allow domestic producers to charge a higher price than would be possible otherwise. Because new industries in late developing countries frequently face production costs higher than those in already industrialized countries, these industries would not likely survive foreign competition in their home markets in the absence of tariff protection. This is particularly true for new industries that have not yet had sufficient experience to reduce production costs, or that have not yet achieved significant economies of scale, or that face relatively high input costs (for materials, technology, or labor, for instance). In Porfirian Mexico, all industries, including both the newest and the most developed (steel and cotton textiles), faced higher production costs than their foreign competitors for one or more of these reasons.[15] Without tariff protection, investment in such industries would have been foolhardy, and conversely, tariffs attracted investment to domestic industry and allowed domestic producers to expand their market share relative to competing imports.[16]

The level of protection conferred by a nation's tariff schedule is not always self-evident, however. The Díaz administration levied *specific* tariffs on imported goods. Throughout the century legislated duties were generally specified as an amount, in pesos, payable per unit of the imported commodity, usually in kilos. While specific tariffs are generally more enforceable—less easily evaded by such devices as false invoicing—than the ad valorem alternative, they also fail to establish a stable relationship between the tariff and the value of an imported good. As a consequence, periods of inflation (or deflation) among imports will act to decrease (or increase) the protection granted by a specific tariff as the tariff constitutes a smaller (or larger) portion of the final imported commodity price facing consumers. Specific tariffs, then, do not provide a meaningful measure of protection. The ad valorem equivalent tariff rate, on the other hand, measures the increased price a domestic producer can charge consumers over free-trade prices and still compete with foreign producers. The ad valorem measure of protection is defined as the legislated, specific tariff as a percentage of the pre-tariff price of the dutiable import.[17]

Ad valorem rates indicate the tariff's impact on prices facing *consumers*, but they do not necessarily reflect the actual level of protection granted by a tariff schedule to domestic *producers*. For producers, what matters is the price they receive in domestic currency for their products, relative to the price they pay for production inputs. When tariffs increase the price of those goods that constitute their inputs—like raw material and semi-manufactured goods—producers' costs are increased and these increases need to be subtracted from the ad valorem tariff on the final product in order to measure the overall protection conferred to the industrial process in question. Furthermore, protection conferred by tariffs to an industrial activity is best measured in relation not to its final output, since a portion of this is comprised of inputs purchased from other industries, but rather in relation to the value added in its own production processes. The conventional measure of protection that accounts for both tariffs on purchased inputs and the portion of value-added in an industry's final product is the *effective* rate of protection. A detailed description of the methods and sources for calculating ad valorem and effective tariff rates is presented in the endnotes and the appendix. Finally, as Daniel Cosío Villegas pointed out nearly seventy years ago, the uncertainty of many trade statistics leads to conclusions that can only have relative value. Because the specific tariffs were set by law, sources of variation or misrepresentation come primarily from the unit price component of the tariff calculations.[18] But this glass can also be viewed half-full: the ad valorem and effective rates of protection reported here are valuable precisely because they indicate relative levels of protection across industries.

Implicit Protection

How high were Mexican tariffs? The answer depends on how protection is measured and whether it is measured on individual commodities or as an average across a range of importable goods. The implicit level of protection measures the average weight of the tariff across the entire range of Mexican imports and is calculated here as the ratio of collected duties to total imports.[19] Thus the implicit rate does not provide a meaningful measure of industrial protection, but rather gives a broad indication of the burden of import tariffs on a country's foreign trade. Implicit tariff burdens can, for instance, stand at high levels, close to 100 percent, while a particular industry is protected by very low or negligible duties. The reverse could also be the case.

As Table 7.1 and Figure 7.1 illustrate, implicit rates had been high since Mexico's independence in the 1820s, averaging over 40 percent until the

Table 7.1

Implicit Protection: Import Duties as a
Percentage of Total Import Value,
Average by Decade, 1820–1910

Decade	Implicit Protection (%)
1820s	36
1840s	45
1870s	46
1880s	46
1890s	29
1900s	21

SOURCE: 1820s and 1840s are averages for the years
1821–23 and 1841–45 taken from Salvucci, Salvucci,
and Cohen 1995: 103, and 1870–1910 are calculated
from import duties, taken from Carmagnani 1994:
appendix 3 (fiscal years); and total import values in
U.S. dollars are from Catáo 1991: table A.2.2, converted to current Mexican pesos using the exchange
rate in INEGI 1994: table 20.6.
NOTE: Calculated by dividing total import duties
by total import values.

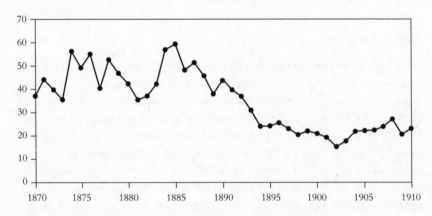

Figure 7.1. Implicit Protection in Mexico, 1870–1910 (percentages)
SOURCE: See Table 7.1.

1890s.[20] This measure, in fact, displays remarkable consistency from the 1820s through the 1870s despite the extreme instability that characterized the Mexican government.

Implicit measures of over 40 percent through most of the century represent high levels of aggregate protection, but they are not unusually high by world standards. In the United States, with one of the most protectionist regimes among the industrialized North Atlantic countries, implicit rates averaged roughly 40 percent from 1875 through 1913, and in 1845 rates on particular goods ranged from 22 percent to over 100 percent.[21] Among the developing countries of the late nineteenth century, including Russia and Brazil, tariff rates exceeding 50 percent and often 100 percent were not uncommon.[22] Indeed, during the 1880s and 1890s Great Britain, France, Germany, Russia, and the United States all raised levels of protection in response to international conditions. Although the implicit rates calculated here locate Mexico's tariff-based protection among the world's highest in 1890, the rates were far from exceptional relative to other countries bent on stimulating domestic industry.

More to the point, however, the implicit rate (whether measured as a percentage of total trade or of dutiable imports) says little or nothing about the protection conferred on specific industries. Instead, by assessing the weight of tariff duties on foreign trade, it provides one measure of the openness of an economy to foreign trade.

Protection and the Peso Depreciation

After 1885, Mexico's implicit tariff level fell steadily and dramatically for seventeen years before leveling off after 1904 at a level less than half of its previous average (Figure 7.1). This decline was not the result of legislated reductions in specific tariff rates. Neither the major tariff reforms of 1891 or 1905 nor numerous intervening minor reforms substantially altered the aggregate level of protection levied on Mexican imports. Whereas the new rates in the 1891 schedule tended to reduce average rates by about 10 percent, the 1905 schedule increased them by about 5 percent. In short, there was no significant *across-the-board* change in protection levels due to formal, legislated tariff reforms before the revolution. Furthermore, declining implicit rates indicate that foreign trade was becoming less burdened by tariff duties, but does not indicate that protection to domestic industries was declining, as we shall see.

Declining implicit tariff levels were the result of an increase in the denominator of the tariff calculations: increased import prices. Either rising commodity prices or a depreciating currency would effectively raise the peso cost of imports, leaving Mexico's specific tariffs a smaller percentage of import prices. But commodity prices did not rise significantly during the period, as Mexico's import price index rose less than 1 percent per year.[23] Thus it was the depreciation of the Mexican peso that drove down implicit tariff levels between 1885 and 1905 (Figure 7.1).[24]

As silver prices fell worldwide against gold through the 1880s and 1890s, a currency exchange of 1.27 Mexican pesos per U.S. dollar in 1891 fell to 2.39 in 1902 before stabilizing in 1905, when Mexico effectively converted to the gold standard. This dramatic depreciation overwhelmed any tariff and price changes for particular commodities in the sample, with a few exceptions to which we will return below. As a consequence, implicit protection across all Mexican imports fell by 50 percent. Depreciation also meant that the ad valorem equivalent rates for individual commodities—and hence protection granted to particular industries—declined in those cases where specific tariff duties were not adjusted. Declining implicit and ad valorem tariff levels were thus a consequence of depreciation and not of policy via a broad reduction in the legislated duties of the 1887 and 1891 tariff schedules.

Do declining implicit tariff levels mean that protection declined and that federal tariff policy was passive? Not necessarily. On the face of it, Mexican producers could now manufacture import-substituting products at increasingly "cheap" silver prices, taking advantage of the widening margin between silver and gold. This differential would provide an increasing de facto advantage to balance the declining de jure advantage of the tariff, and would provide Mexican purchasers with incentives to shop at home rather than abroad. Many contemporary observers felt that the depreciation of silver had a more profound and positive effect on industrialization than did tariff protection. Pablo Macedo wrote in 1901 that transportation improvements and the peso depreciation were the most decisive factors in Mexico's industrial development, and Angel M. Domínguez, writing in *La Semana Mercantil*, concurred.[25] As U.S. consular agent Long related from Parral, Chihuahua, in 1901, "On account of the low price of silver and the consequent high rate of exchange on foreign countries, articles that are manufactured in this country . . . are bought in preference to foreign goods."[26] This view has also been the consensus among historians, dating at least from the publication of the *Historia Moderna de México*, where Fernando Rosenzweig concluded, "the fall of silver signified a secure protection for manufactures."[27]

Two factors, however, stood in the way of a facile correspondence between rising import prices and rising levels of de facto protection. First, rising import prices meant that Mexican producers who had to purchase production inputs abroad faced rising costs that undercut any advantage that depreciation gave them in the final product market. Most Mexican manufactures imported heavily from the United States and Europe, including raw materials scarce in Mexico, semi-manufactured inputs unavailable locally, and capital equipment. The import manifests for companies in the files of the federal Industrias Nuevas program reveals in endless detail the extensive sums spent by new manufacturing concerns for imported materials.[28] Trade and production data show that the beer industry imported all its barley and malt; cotton mills imported between one-third and one-half of all raw cotton; and the leather industry purchased nearly all tannin abroad until after 1900. Similarly, 81 percent of all coal and coke, 50–80 percent of all cement and bricks, and nearly 100 percent of all industrial chemicals used in mineral processing and industry were imported. The same was true of course for the lumber, machinery, and structure steel used by new and expanding Mexican industries. The peso depreciation posed an increasing burden to most Mexican producers.

Second, rising import prices would confer an advantage to Mexican producers *only as long as* their costs—both foreign and domestic—did not rise to a corresponding degree. Economic theory predicts that they would. That is, across-the-board increases in import prices (generated either by inflation abroad or by a currency depreciation) would lead relatively rapidly to an increase in general domestic price levels, assuming open and costless trade.[29] This was not unrecognized by contemporary observers. As the American commissioners to the Mexican Monetary Commission of 1903 observed, "the fall in the gold price of silver permits goods to be sold abroad for a falling gold price, *so long as wages and cost of materials at home remain unchanged in terms of silver*" (emphasis added).[30] However, price levels in developing countries of the nineteenth century were not tightly tied to world price levels, because tariff barriers, high transportation costs, and fragmented markets hindered an easy translation of prices across national boundaries. Although Finance Minister Limantour believed that rising import prices did induce a rise in the general domestic price level "in proportion to the loss in value of our currency," this was only true after 1899.[31] Thereafter, domestic inflation caught and surpassed rising import prices and negated any advantage the latter had given Mexican producers.

Domestic price inflation remained well below import price inflation in the 1890s, at 0.7 percent average annual growth versus 5.1 percent for imports (see Table 7.2). Thereafter the situation reversed, with domestic inflation rising to 3.4 percent per year 1900–1910 while import prices fell by

Table 7.2
Price Indices and the Exchange Rates for Mexico and the United States, 1890–1911

	A	B	C	D(A*C)
	Price Index U.S. 1890 = 100	Price Index Mexico 1890 = 100	Nominal Exchange ps/usd	Real Exchange 1890 = 100
1890	100.0	100.0	1.20	100.0
1891	99.4	89.0	1.27	105.3
1892	92.8	94.4	1.44	111.5
1893	95.2	105.2	1.61	127.8
1894	85.2	103.5	1.98	140.6
1895	86.9	98.3	1.92	139.1
1896	82.8	102.6	1.91	131.6
1897	82.8	107.2	2.14	147.4
1898	86.3	99.1	2.17	156.0
1899	92.8	98.6	2.07	160.4
1900	99.7	107.0	2.06	171.6
1901	98.3	120.5	2.11	173.2
1902	104.9	131.9	2.39	208.7
1903	106.3	136.6	2.37	210.4
1904	106.3	128.3	1.99	176.4
1905	106.9	127.0	2.02	179.8
1906	110.0	139.7	1.99	182.5
1907	115.8	145.0	2.01	193.8
1908	112.2	142.0	2.01	188.0
1909	120.5	145.7	2.01	201.9
1910	125.2	160.8	2.01	209.6
Average Annual Growth:				
1890–1910	1.51	2.62	1.88	3.39
1890–1899	−1.60	0.69	6.73	5.14
1900–1910	2.28	3.44	−0.81	1.47

SOURCE: The U.S. index is the wholesale price index constructed by the U.S. Bureau of Labor Statistics, taken from Jastram 1961: 206–7, table 21. The Mexican index was constructed by Zabludowsky 1992: 292–99, which is based on the wholesale price index for Mexico City published in Colegio de México 1960 and adjusted for the exaggerated presence of foodstuffs in that index by introducing an index of Mexican export prices weighted at 17.4% of the composite. The exchange rate is taken from INEGI 1994, vol. 2: table 21.

1.5 percent per year. That Mexican prices rose at rates substantially less than those of import prices before 1899 indicates that the peso depreciation did in fact have real consequences in the 1890s. Import inflation translated into increased de facto levels of protection as Mexican producers stood a greater chance of being able to keep their peso-denominated production costs at levels that would allow them to compete with imported products. This would be especially true for those producers whose production processes required relatively few imported inputs. After 1899, however, Mexican producers were unable to reap the benefits of the peso's depreciation.[32]

Interestingly, the turning point in this trend corresponds closely with contemporaries' views concerning the stimulus granted to Mexican industry by the peso depreciation. Throughout the 1880s and 1890s the erosion of tariff levels by silver's depreciation evoked little debate as prominent Mexicans and foreign observers felt confident that the fall of silver favored domestic activities and rendered tariff protection of secondary consequence. Such optimism, however, was increasingly rare after 1900, and voices critical of depreciation's effect on national industry were heard with greater frequency in the national press, leading eventually to the monetary reform of 1905.

Ad Valorem Equivalent Rates of Protection

The effect of the peso depreciation on implicit protection and its consequences for Mexican producers is ambiguous before 1899 and not helpful thereafter, but we still have no indication of how federal tariff policy affected specific industries. To begin to do this we need to look at the *ad valorem equivalent* tariff rates presented in Table 7.3.[33] In the interest of brevity, the table presents rates for the years 1890 and 1905. These years bracket and highlight the major changes in legislated (specific) and ad valorem tariff levels for the Porfirian era of rising industrial investment. The 1890 estimates use the specific duties of the 1887 tariff schedule and unit prices as three-year averages 1889–91, whereas the 1905 estimates use specific duties from that year's tariff schedule and three-year price averages 1904–6. The estimates in Tables 7.3 and 7.5 thus capture the impact of the legislated tariffs in the 1891 and 1905 schedules and intervening reforms. Note that the ad valorem equivalent tariff will vary positively with the specific tariff (column D) and inversely with the commodity price and exchange rate (columns E and F). It should be noted that any decline in the ad valorem equivalent tariffs on domestic products between the mid-1880s and 1891 came not as a result of legislated action but as a result of the downward pressure of the peso depreciation.[34]

Table 7.3
Ad Valorem Equivalent Rates of Protection, 1890 and 1905, and Percentage Change in Components

	A	B	C	D	E	F
			PERCENTAGE CHANGE IN			
	1890 Ad Val. Tariff	1905 Ad Val. Tariff	Ad Val. Tariff	Spec. Tar.	Comm. Price	XR
Agriculture and food products						
Corn*	37	17	(55)	(20)	6	(37)
Wheat and other grains*	65	152	133	160	(34)	
Wheat flour*	77	96	24	(9)	(56)	
Cattle	0	0			(10)	
Hides	42	8	(82)	(65)	14	
Beef, canned	65	41	(37)	20	19	
Cheese	63	32	(50)	0	19	
Sugar	81	14	(83)	(83)	(42)	
Salt*	148	43	(77)	(33)	72	
Beer, unbottled*	59	112	88	25	(58)	
Beer, bottled*	76	52	(32)	25	9	
Tobacco and products						
Tobacco leaf	79	137	74	205	4	
Cigarettes*	89	82	(8)	60	4	
Leather and products						
Leather	140	210	50	233	32	
Sole leather	140	105	(25)	67	32	
Boots	111	98	42	100	34	
Shoes	33	38	82	156	34	
Fiber and products						
Jute, raw*	78	4	(95)	(93)	(17)	
Hemp cable (>3 cm)*	0	18			1	
Cordage (<1 cm)	0	28			(22)	
Burlap sacks*	0	53			71	
Cotton and products						
Cotton, raw	30	20	(34)	(4)	(13)	
Cloth, uncolored, coarse	87	55	(36)	(11)	(17)	
Cloth, uncolored, fine	106	76	(28)	0	(17)	
Wood products						
Lumber, for building	0	0				
Paper, printing	49	127	157	220	(26)	

Table 7.3
(continued)

	A	B	C	D	E	F
			PERCENTAGE CHANGE IN			
	1890 Ad Val. Tariff	1905 Ad Val. Tariff	Ad Val. Tariff	Spec. Tar.	Comm. Price	XR
Glass products						
Flat glass*	225	58	(77)	(72)	(27)	
Glass bottles*	16	7	3	120	35	
Construction materials						
Cement*	0	30			(15)	(37)
Bricks	13	20	54	53	(41)	
Chemicals and Related Prods.						
Glycerin	0	0				
Cyanides	11	0				
Mercury	0	0				
Caustic sodas	0	9				
Sulfuric acid	0	0				
Dynamite*	0	11				
Paints, powdered*	35	20	(43)	(20)	40	
Ink, writing*	137	30	(71)	(52)	(2)	
Ink, printing	0	0				
Paraffin	64	42	(34)	(10)	(14)	
Candles	80	56	(30)	0	(15)	
Soap	173	143	(17)	39	0	
Fuels						
Coal and coke	0	0				
Petroleum, crude*	27	94	241	230	(43)	
Petroleum, refined*	49	21	(57)	(10)	25	
Smelting and Refining						
Copper bars and sheets	27	17	(36)	22	90	
Copper wire, insulated	0	0				
Blast furnaces						
Pig iron	0	62			(13)	
Steel works and rolling mills						
Iron bars	103	30	(43)	(50)	(48)	
Iron sheets and plates	38	58	54	65	(36)	
Hoop iron*	157	91	(42)	(20)	(18)	
Steel bars and rods*	60	30	(50)	10	(54)	
Steel sheets and plates	46	85	85	65	(47)	

(continued)

Table 7.3
(continued)

	A	B	C	D	E	F
			PERCENTAGE CHANGE IN			
	1890 Ad Val. Tariff	1905 Ad Val. Tariff	Ad Val. Tariff	Spec. Tar.	Comm. Price	XR
Finished iron and steel prods.						
Steel rails	0	36			(27)	
Structural iron and steel*	24	30	26	200	42	
Wire	10	56	435	450	(39)	
Nails, cut	152	136	(11)	20	(20)	
Pipes and fittings	0	9			(3)	
Machinery*	0	5				

SOURCE: See text and appendix for methods and full citations. All unit price data come from the yearly volumes of U.S. Department of Commerce 1890–1911 unless marked by *.
NOTE: Parentheses denote negative change; change in commodity prices are calculated on the basis of U.S. (gold) dollar prices; and the exchange rate (XR) decline is −37% for all imported goods.

Whereas the aggregate (implicit) tariff burden across all imports fell dramatically (Figure 7.1), the ad valorem protection granted to selected manufactured and semi-manufactured goods held constant or actually increased through proactive legislation. If the average (implicit) protection across all imports had fallen to 22 percent in 1905, the ad valorem protection granted to the sample of primary materials, semi-manufactures, and finished goods in Table 7.3 averaged 47 percent, only 9 percent below its 1890 level. If all raw materials and intermediate inputs are removed from this sample, leaving only select semi-manufactures and finished goods, the decline disappears entirely. As Table 7.4 demonstrates, whereas implicit protection fell by 50 percent, manufacturing industries that were the object of import-substituting policy saw their ad valorem protection remain constant at 69 percent in the face of the corrosive influence of the peso depreciation. These results dramatically highlight the difference between alternative measures of protection: falling implicit levels do not indicate declining industrial protection and are wholly compatible with steady or even rising ad valorem rates.

Ad valorem protection on import-competing manufactured goods rose because by 1905 finance ministry officials had increased legislated tariffs on these goods to compensate for the effects of depreciation. Duties on bottled beer climbed from 20 centavos a kilo to 25, cigarettes went from $1.37 per thousand to $2.20, and bricks saw their duties raised by half, from $1.80 per thousand to $2.75. Iron and steel products ranging from pig iron to steel bars to wire had their specific duties raised from between 1 and 5 centavos per kilo to between 2 and 7 centavos, averaging a 140 percent gain. The legislated, specific tariffs on one sample of twenty-three import-competing goods was raised by an average of 91 percent between 1891 and 1905.[35] This was not the result of a narrow, interest-based effort to favor certain manufacturing interests. Although some industries had seen isolated duty changes during the 1890s, sometimes in response to lobbying efforts, the 1905 schedule increased the specific duties on each and every import-competing product.

Two other characteristics are evident in the ad valorem equivalent rates presented in Table 7.3. These rates range widely, from goods wholly exempt from tariff duties to goods dutied at rates exceeding 100 and sometimes 200 percent. With few exceptions, this range is consistent with the import-substituting objectives of Mexican policy: high rates correspond to the products of Mexican industry while low rates are levied on important production inputs. Furthermore, altogether new industries received substantial protec-

Table 7.4

Comparative Average Levels of Protection,
1890 and 1905 (percentages)

	1890	*1905*
Implicit measure	44	22
Ad valorem average, sample 1	53	48
Ad valorem average, sample 2	69	69

SOURCE: See the text and appendix.
NOTE: Implicit measure = total duties collected on imports divided by total import value; see Table 7.1. Ad valorem measure = calculated as the unweighted average of the ad valorem equivalent rates (that is, the specific tariff divided by the commodity price) for the two samples. Sample 1 = all commodities listed in Table 7.3, covering a range of foodstuffs, primary materials, intermediate inputs, semi-manufactures, and finished goods. Sample 2 = all commodities listed in Table 7.5, covering intermediate inputs and finished goods.

tion from the ad valorem tariffs implicit in Mexico's specific duties, some for
the first time as a result of legislated reforms between the late 1880s and 1910.
Among those products that were dutied for the first time or that saw their
legislated, specific duties increased during the period are wheat, canned beef,
bottled and unbottled beer, tobacco, cigarettes, leather and footwear, all wo-
ven fiber products, paper, glass bottles, both cement and bricks, caustic sodas, dynamite, soap, crude petroleum, copper bars and sheets, pig iron, iron
sheets and plates, steel bars and rods, steel sheets and plates, steel rails, structural iron and steel, cut nails, wire, pipes and fittings, and machinery. This
list matches almost exactly the lists of new industries in Mexico mentioned
by both contemporary observers and historians, and moves tariff-based protection well beyond its more limited objectives in the 1830s and 1840s.[36]

In sum, the structure of ad valorem protection levied on imported commodities by the tariff schedule was consistent with import-substituting industrialization objectives in 1890 and remained so in 1905. As noted in
Table 7.4, samples that focus on import-competing products reveal steady
levels of protection in the 70 percent range, in the face of contemporary peso
depreciation! Legislated changes in specific tariff rates effectively negated the
erosive effects of depreciation. Without accounting for the major tariff reform of 1905, these policy-induced changes are not evident.[37] Federal tariff
policy, in other words, worked to counteract the effects of the peso depreciation and aggressively maintained substantial ad valorem rates on a broad
range of import-competing industries.

Effective Rates of Protection

Although ad valorem rates indicate the degree to which tariff policy raised the
price of imports for Mexican purchasers, they do not reveal the full impact
of tariff policy on Mexican producers. Because many producers depended
on imported inputs (including capital equipment, intermediate inputs, fuels,
and sometimes raw materials), tariffs on these inputs increased production
costs and adversely affected producers' profits and their ability to compete
with foreign imports in the final goods market. If we wish to understand the
investment decisions of entrepreneurs operating in the Mexican economy,
the ad valorem equivalent tariff rate provides an unsatisfactory indicator and
the *effective rate* of protection provides a better measure. The effective rate
measures protection on what matters to domestic producers: the value added
by domestic activity. It varies directly with the ad valorem tariff on an industry's output and inversely with the ad valorem tariffs on inputs.[38] In short,
high (or low) ad valorem tariffs do not simply or necessarily correspond to

high (or low) effective rates of protection for particular industrial activities. In Mexico, effective rates exceeded ad valorem rates for most new and expanding industries, often by substantial amounts.

Effective rates highlight the structure of protection conferred by a tariff system by considering the relative duties on inputs and finished goods. In many developing countries, including the United States in the nineteenth century, ad valorem rates on finished goods tended to be higher than rates on raw materials and other inputs. Under such a "cascading" tariff structure, the effective protection granted to the industry will always be higher than the ad valorem rate on the final product. As the ad valorem rate is the more readily visible of the two, the true degree of protection granted to domestic industries is greater than it appears. Conversely, when inputs are dutied at rates higher than finished goods, effective protection will be low or possibly negative.[39]

Did Mexico have a cascading tariff structure? For most industries, the answer is yes. "The most efficient method to facilitate new industries and the development of existing ones," wrote Finance Minister Matías Romero to his counterpart in the development ministry in 1892, "lies in studying the customs tariff, with special attention to the importation of primary materials in relation to duties paid on imported manufactures."[40] Raw materials, with the exception of those that were available domestically, were admitted free of duty. Cotton textiles, steel manufactures, fiber products, candles, and soap all faced a cascading tariff structure (see Table 7.3). Raw cotton, steel bars, raw fibers, wax and tallow, and intermediate soap inputs all were dutied at lower rates than the finished products for which they were inputs. As U.S. Consul William Canada reported in 1898 from Veracruz, for example, the tariff on standard laundry soap, "with the comparatively low duties on the chemicals used in the manufacture of the soap, has been found sufficient to afford ample protection, and numerous factories have been erected in all sections of the country."[41] As one government official wrote in 1903, "we believe that the protectionist policies of the administration to favor the development of industry should not include primary materials, if these are not found in the country."[42] Raw materials, processed or semi-processed inputs, and capital equipment were usually dutied at lower rates than the finished products that were the object of Mexican industries.

As a consequence, effective rates for most selected industries in the present sample exceeded the ad valorem equivalent rates (Table 7.5). Effective rates exceeded ad valorem rates for this sample by 80 percent, granting (on average) a consistent level of protection to Mexican producers of nearly 125 percent in spite of the effects of the peso depreciation. This relationship

Table 7.5
Ad Valorem and Effective Rates of Protection on Select
Manufactures, 1890 and 1905 (percentages)

Product	AD VALOREM TARIFFS		EFFECTIVE PROTECTION		Date First Project*
	1890	*1905*	*1890*	*1905*	
Consumer and light industry					
Wheat flour	206	103	176	−23	
Beer, unbottled	59	112	85	160	1865
Beer, bottled	76	52	192	133	1865
Cigarettes	41	77	23	51	**
Leather	140	210	385	787	
Soap	173	143			1883
Boots	111	98	128	23	1898
Shoes	33	38	−65	−128	1898
Burlap sacks	0	53			1892
Cordage	0	28	−227	102	1896
Cotton cloth, coarse	87	55	163	103	**
Cotton cloth, fine	106	76	207	150	**
Paper	49	127	115	296	1890
Glass, flat	255	53			1909
Dynamite	0	11			1901
Bricks	13	20			
Cement	0	30			1906
Average for group	79	76	107	150	
Petroleum					
Refining	49	21	169	−187	
Blast furnaces					
Pig iron	0	62	0	221	
Steel works and rolling mills					
Iron bars	61	34	151	37	
Iron sheets and plates	38	58	86	104	
Iron hoops	157	91	426	199	
Steel bars and rods	60	31	149	27	1903
Steel sheets and plates	41	85	94	181	1903
Average for group	71	60	181	110	
Iron and steel products					
Steel rails	0	36	−23	41	1903
Structural iron and steel	24	30	46	24	1903

Table 7.5

(continued)

Product	AD VALOREM TARIFFS		EFFECTIVE PROTECTION		Date First Project*
	1890	*1905*	*1890*	*1905*	
Wire	10	56	6	99	
Nails, cut	152	136	412	327	
Sample average	69	69	123	124	

NOTE: See Table 7.3 for ad valorem tariff rates and the text and appendix for sources and methods.

*Date of establishment of first firm dedicated to large-scale production.

**Denotes large-scale production begun early in the century.

held for most industries, but was least pronounced in the consumer and light industry fields. There, effective protection exceeded ad valorem rates by an average of only 29 percent in 1890, as for some industries crucial inputs were the object of significant duties, cutting into the benefits the tariff structure conferred to final producers. This was particularly true for flour milling, cigarettes, shoes, and cordage, where the primary inputs were dutied at ad valorem levels near or above the tariff on the finished product. In two of these— shoes and cordage—effective rates were actually negative in 1890, creating a severe disincentive to invest in their domestic production. By 1905, the excess of effective over ad valorem rates for these fields had grown to 69 percent, but this was largely driven by sharp increases in the effective protection granted to cordage and leather manufactures by new tariffs on their final products.

In the metallurgical industries, effective protection generally favored the heavy part of the industry: pig iron and semi-manufactured products like bars and sheets. Here, effective rates exceeded ad valorem rates by 155 percent in 1890 and 83 percent in 1905. Between the two dates, there is a slight but noticeable movement toward the protection of the light part of the industry: the re-rolling and finishing of iron and steel products. Steel rails and wire received large increases, while cut nails maintained what must have been nearly prohibitive protection.

Four industries experienced sharp reversals in the level of effective protection granted them by the structure of the tariff schedule: flour milling, fiber cordage manufacture, petroleum refining, and the production of steel rails. Each moved dramatically from positive to negative protection, or vice versa. In flour milling, for example, the removal of all protection came with the doubling of the ad valorem equivalent tariff on wheat in 1905, when the administration worked to balance its policy of granting duty-free import to corn and wheat for particular states in times of poor harvests with increasing the general level of protection to the nation's wheat farmers—primarily the rancheros and hacendados of the center-north. For fiber cordage, the movement was even more dramatic, but in the opposite direction. Whereas the ad valorem tariff on fiber imports was legislated progressively down to under 10 percent of its 1890 level by 1898, new duties were levied on finished cordage for the first time in 1891. Together, these moves transformed effective protection from −227 percent to 102 percent, thus granting substantial incentives and protection to the new fiber manufacturing firms in Mérida, Orizaba, and Cuautitlán.

There were exceptions to the cascading tendency that conferred high effective protection. Machinery was the most prominent of those finished products that were admitted free or were dutied at low levels (Table 7.3). Capital equipment provided the mechanical backbone for Mexico's nascent industries, and Mexican producers uniformly purchased their requisite technology abroad. Granting relief to one industry in the form of low tariffs on inputs could mean reducing protection on the output of another industry, or vice versa. Several manufacturers complained that high duties on particular inputs relative to duties on the finished product handicapped their efforts to establish competitive industries in Mexico, and at least one abandoned his efforts when tariff relief on imported inputs was not forthcoming.[43] Those products most favored by high tariff rates were those that required a production process within reach of Mexican manufacturing capabilities. Fully assembled machinery and electrical apparatus, for instance, were not yet the object of investment projects or of government protection. Instead, intermediate goods such as iron and steel rods or finished leather received higher tariff rates than the finished products for which they were inputs. In sum, to the extent that Mexico's tariff schedules exhibited a cascading structure, the effective rates that protected domestic producers were significantly higher than the already substantial implicit and ad valorem rates.[44]

Non-Tariff Factors

Transport costs, internal taxes on commerce, and customs procedures had long imposed high burdens on imported goods through most of the nineteenth century, burdens that were substantially reduced between 1880 and 1910. These reductions, however, did not undermine but instead favored the administration's development objectives.

The cost of carrying foreign goods to Mexican markets fell dramatically over the last third of the century as a result of both oceanic and overland transport developments. Completion of rail lines across the U.S.-Mexican border in the 1880s increased overland imports from negligible levels in the 1870s to 36 percent of total U.S.-Mexican trade in 1880–85 and 53 percent in 1890–95. The new rail lines north to El Paso, to Laredo, and to Piedras Negras, as well as to the gulf port of Tampico, carried tremendous volumes of Mexico's growing export and import trade and served to drive down rates on all rail access to Mexican markets, at least for the duration of the 1880s. Where shipments in 1896 between New York and Veracruz took ten to twelve days by steamer, they took only six by rail.[45] Shorter transport times reduced transport costs in Mexico's foreign trade.

Freight rates for Mexican imports fell steadily through the 1880s and 1890s. Construction of the rail lines in the 1870s and 1880s represented a large one-time reduction in overland freight over the alternative: mule and wagon transport. Once established, however, freight rates on Mexican rails did not fall through the rest of the Porfiriato on all lines, and in many cases were increased.[46] Oceanic rates, however, fell steadily, declining at an annual average of 1.51 percent according to one estimate.[47] The size of freight's burden on imported goods depended not only on changing rates but also on the nature of the good. Freight added a smaller percentage to the cost of high-value, low-bulk goods like cigarettes than to low-value, high-bulk goods like cement, although both rail and shipping rates were structured to partially equalize this impact. This disparity is illustrated in Table 7.6, showing the weight of freight charges on a select group of imported goods which competed against domestic manufactures. At the high end, the combination of oceanic and rail transport charges could increase the price of cement by a factor of three or more; in contrast, the impact on the final price of cigarettes was only marginal. Comparing rates in 1882 and 1899 on the New York to Mexico City route (to Veracruz via ship and overland via rail) shows an average decline of 32 percent on all freight.

Non-tariff burdens on foreign trade were also reduced via Mexican legislation. For most of the nineteenth century the *alcabala*, an internal tax levied by states on interstate commerce, had posed a significant barrier to regional and national commerce as states strove to fill their coffers and compete among themselves for business. These taxes created a large impediment to the development of a national economy and attracted frequent criticism in

226

Table 7.6

Freight Burden on Selected Imports, New York to Mexico City via
Veracruz, 1882 and 1899, Percentage Increase over World Prices

	Cement	Steel Bars	Bottle Beer	Cigarettes
1882	469	34	17	4
1899	249	27	15	2
% Change	(−47)	(−21)	(−12)	(−50)

SOURCE: Oceanic rates from Maria y Campos 1889: 171 for 1889 extrapolated to 1882
and 1899 according to the 1.51% per annum average reduction in oceanic freight rates
cited in Harley 1988: 861. Rail freight rates for 1882 and 1899 for the Ferrocarril Mexicano from Maria y Campos 1889: 217 ff and Maria y Campos 1899: 276. See the appendix for commodity price sources and calculations.
NOTE: Calculated by combining oceanic freight rates from New York to Veracruz with
overland rail rates from Veracruz to Mexico City and dividing by the commodity unit
price in the U.S. foreign trade.

the national press. As a U.S. consular agent reported in 1895, "the interstate
customs . . . are a principal obstacle to the development of the import business of this place."[48] It was not until the 1890s, however, that the balance of
federal-state power permitted their undoing. Although the practice was out-
lawed in the 1857 Constitution, the federal government did not succeed in
finally abolishing it until 1896, when states were compensated with income
from newly legislated federal taxes. Their abolition was enthusiastically welcomed by those engaged in foreign trade.[49]

Finally, Mexican customs procedures were notoriously complex and
opaque through the 1880s. Indeed, the "bewildering array" of regulations
was held by some to be more deleterious to Mexico's foreign trade than the
high duties themselves.[50] As U.S. Consul Warren Sutton wrote from Matamoros, "I am told that . . . the name, description, duties, etc., of each
package of goods arriving and departing from here to the interior have to
be minutely and very carefully written fourteen times, with all sorts of risks
of fines and penalties of imprisonment for errors of even the most trivial
character."[51] Complex and ambiguous customs requirements, coupled with
contraband concerns, frequently caused trans-border shipments to be delayed for days or weeks by customs officials.[52] The federal government was
not unaware of these burdens, and the tariff reforms of the 1880s and 1890s
were partly motivated by a desire to simplify and expedite customs proce-

dures. Hacienda officials explicitly sought to "abolish those practices which hinder trade or weigh heavily on our operations."[53] In this they apparently succeeded. No U.S. consul—the first to hear of and to publicize any obstacle to bilateral trade—related complaints from traders thereafter, and non-tariff taxes on traded goods were also reduced below 1870s levels.[54]

Declining non-tariff costs to trade lowered the cost of imports to Mexican purchasers, but this did not provide an unambiguous advantage to imports over domestic production. First, reductions in overland freight rates and internal taxes also expanded markets for domestic goods, and in fact the regulated structure of freight rates favored medium-haul freight (between 300 and 450 km) over the long hauls more characteristic of the import trade. Indeed, one of the railroad rate commission's stated goals was "the protection of domestic manufactured goods with respect to competing foreign imports."[55] Second, falling trade costs promoted exports, which earned the foreign exchange necessary to support the importation of industrial inputs.[56] Third, if the overall reduction in non-tariff costs to trade did facilitate imports across the board, this in fact promoted the import-substituting aims of the tariff structure. As we have seen, the importation of raw materials, intermediate inputs, and capital equipment was crucial to industrial enterprises, and falling transport costs aided such endeavors. In contrast, the legislated maintenance of high ad valorem equivalent (c. 70 percent) and effective rates (c. 125 percent) of protection on those imported goods that competed against domestic manufactures more than compensated for any reduction in transaction costs.

The Political Economy of Industrial Policy

Porfirian Mexico's protectionist tariff policies were the result of a combination of ideas and interests, funneled through the offices of the federal finance ministry and its minister after 1892, José Yves Limantour. Space prohibits a full treatment of the politics of tariff policy here, but the present conclusions concerning the structure of protection raise three questions. First, did declining aggregate (or implicit) tariff levels mean declining government revenue? If so, this would be surprising, given the importance of trade taxes in government revenue and the increasing pressure to balance the federal budget in the 1890s. Second, was tariff policy the result of policymakers' vision of an industrial future or a response to a set of existing interests? Did tariff protection anticipate or follow financial interests in domestic production? Third, and relatedly, were private interests—individuals, firms, industries, or organizations—active and influential in lobbying for protection? Was federal policy responsive to public input, and if so, who were the winners and losers in the lobbying and tariff reform process?

Through the last decade of the nineteenth century falling silver prices and the consequent depreciation of the Mexican peso resulted in rising import prices and falling ad valorem tariffs, on average, as the specific duties became an ever smaller portion of the final price. While depreciation cut the implicit tariff to half its previous level by 1902 (Figure 7.1), this did not translate into an erosion of government revenue. The ad valorem equivalent and implicit rates measure the tariff as a percentage of import prices, and declining rates were the result of rising prices rather than declining formal duties. Thus these percentage measures can decline while the revenue they produce does not. Furthermore, Mexico's foreign trade expanded rapidly, growing at an average of roughly 7 percent per year between 1890 and 1902. As a consequence, government revenue from import duties grew by 3.3 percent per year even while the implicit tariff fell by 50 percent.[57] At the same time, tax and budget reforms led trade revenue to occupy a relatively smaller place in total government income, from roughly 50 percent to 40 percent of total revenues. Trade growth and budget reforms gave treasury officials increasing room to reduce the overall burden of tariffs on trade while raising tariffs on competing imports.

Did federal officials confer tariff-based protection to industries that in the late 1880s did not yet exist, thus anticipating investment and creating an economic interest where none had existed? Although most of the industries shown in Tables 7.3 and 7.5 that were protected by high tariffs existed *at some scale of production* through the nineteenth century, only a handful were characterized by large-scale, mechanized, and modern processes that were the express object of Porfirian policy. Table 7.5 includes the founding dates of large-scale industrial enterprises for selected products, and most fall subsequent to the initiation of tariff protection. Moreover, the growth of large-scale industry between 1890 and 1910 was not the result of the gradual expansion of small-scale production, but rather marked a discontinuity in the development of production processes. In most cases, all aspects of new Porfirian industry—from finance to technology to management to labor—were the result of individuals, groups, and processes wholly new in the history of Mexican manufacturing. Thus in the production of cement, dynamite, steel, paper, boots and shoes, and soap, Mexican tariff policy conferred protection to activities that either did not yet exist or that were characterized by small-scale facilities geared to local markets. The large-scale, highly financed industries that sprang up after 1890 responded to the possibilities that tariff protection offered, and those involved did not play a significant role in motivating protection in the first place. Federal policymakers, in short, held a proactive vision of a Mexico that substituted domestic manufactures for goods long imported. As Finance Minister Limantour wrote in 1906, "The idea behind the tariff reforms [of 1905] was to consider certain articles considered as competition to similar goods produced in the country. . . . The government has proposed, as all know, to provide protection to national industries that would be . . . [otherwise] annihilated by foreign competition." [58] This does not necessarily imply that they envisioned an industrial Mexico as an alternative to an export-oriented Mexico, but only that there existed a growing consensus among elites that the twin goals of economic diversity and economic independence justified protectionist policies. [59] Through the 1890s dozens of entrepreneurs—large and small, Mexican and foreign—responded to this vision and echoed the goals of government officials.

It is also true, however, that tariffs by 1890 conferred protection to already existing industries and thus to existing financial interests. Cotton textiles, tobacco products, and beer, as well as leather and bricks, were already produced in large-scale facilities. Moreover, once investors responded to tariff protection on "new" industries after 1890, they frequently sought to pressure the government to increase or at least maintain the effective protection they enjoyed. Efforts by individuals representing both existing and new industries to lobby treasury officials for favorable tariff reforms were not uncommon through the last two decades of the Porfiriato, but they did not always receive a favorable response.

Through the 1890s requests flowed into the Mexico City offices of both the development ministry and the treasury, asking for favorable revisions to the tariff schedule or for firm-specific exemptions of tariffs on imported production inputs. [60] Typical of those who sought protection for new industrial projects were the British backers of the Santa Gertrudis Jute Mill, in Orizaba, and their Mexican agent, Guillermo Landa y Escandón. [61] In the early 1890s domestic production was unlikely if not impossible: raw jute fibers were dutied at around 80 percent and manufactured products like burlap sacks were admitted free. Effective protection was thus highly negative and investment foolhardy. Arguing for new tariffs of .13 pesos on sacks and duty exemptions on imported jute, Landa y Escandón suggested the firm could not otherwise compete. With British sacks selling in English ports at the equivalent of .16 pesos, in Mexico imported raw jute alone ran .17 pesos per sack after paying duties. Even after adding 56 percent to the price of British goods for transport to Orizaba and just 44 percent to the cost of jute for production costs in Mexico, no domestic firm could compete with imports and still turn a profit. "We only want to be able to compete," he wrote in 1894, "and in time we will no longer need such protection." The response in this case was favorable, although not to the degree the firm had hoped. Specific duties on raw jute were reduced by 50 percent while a new .02 pesos per kilo tariff on sacks was added, with treasury officials fearing anything higher would "prejudice the interests of agriculturalists" who used the sacks for packing. By 1905 the ad valorem tariff on burlap sacks stood at 53 percent, and Santa Gertrudis and its sister plant, La Aurora in Cuautitlán, were on their way to supplying a good portion of national burlap consumption.[62]

Lobbying also proved decisive in gaining additional protection for the nascent steel industry after 1900. Vicente Ferrara of the Fundidora de Hierro y Acero de Monterrey led the effort to seek increased tariff protection from federal officials, as well as both federal and state tax exemptions. In response (most contemporaries assumed), duties on competing imports were systematically raised in 1901, 1904, 1905, and 1908.[63] By one measure, the average ad valorem tariff on the products of the Fundidora Monterrey, weighted by their importance in the import trade, increased from 8 percent in 1902 to 44 percent in 1909.[64]

Finally, tariff lobbying occasionally came also from industry-specific organizations, although in the years before the revolution these were more likely to be foreign than domestic in origin. In 1905, for instance, the American Association of Mining Engineers assembled in Mexico City, met with government officials, and drafted a list of goods they wanted duty free.[65] Mining interests had few worries, however: nearly all crucial requisites were duty exempt through the Porfiriato.

Not all lobbying efforts were successful, and many were denied by treasury officials, who deemed some requests excessive or prejudicial to other economic interests.[66] This was particularly true for new projects to manufacture various chemical products in Mexico, most of which were crucial inputs for the mining and metallurgical industries. Between 1890 and 1910 over a dozen firms were organized to undertake the production of cyanide, copper sulfate, calcium carbonate, or zinc oxide in order to replace imports. Few undertook production, however, largely because tariffs on competing imports were low and federal officials were unwilling to burden export-oriented mining activities by revising them upward. Such was the case when Trinidad García asked for a .06 pesos per kilo duty on copper sulfate in late 1903, which was refused.[67] It was also the case for the officers of the Roessler and Hasslacher Chemical Company, who, realizing that the domestic production of cyanide could not compete with German imports on a level playing field, conceded defeat since any protective tariff would "elevate the price of [cyanide] and thus prejudice or perhaps ruin the mining industry."[68]

Although some firms and industries were successful in their attempts to gain favorable tariff treatment from treasury officials after 1890, by the late 1880s the tariff schedule had already conferred substantial protection to a wide range of domestic producers and effectively balanced low duties on inputs with high duties on final products (Tables 7.3 and 7.5). Thus most who sought to invest in new or expanding firms through the 1890s and beyond had little cause to seek special reforms through lobbying pressure. Tariff lobbying, in short, played a role in shaping tariff levels for a handful of particular goods, but did not fundamentally determine the structure of protection across industries. This structure was instead the product of policymakers' attempt to create incentives to invest in large-scale manufacturing enterprises, whether or not financial interests in them already existed.

Protection and Production

We have seen that the Mexican tariff schedules conferred consistently high levels of protection to a wide range of manufacturing industries from the 1880s until the onset of revolution. Ad valorem equivalent rates for the present sample of new and expanding industries (Table 7.5) averaged around 70 percent throughout the period, while effective rates of protection averaged nearly 125 percent. We would thus expect to see increasing domestic production and declining imports as domestic producers could effectively compete against imports even with relatively higher production costs. Was this the case? Did substantial tariff and non-tariff burdens effectively attract investment to domestic industry and begin a process of import-substituting industrialization?

Changes in Mexico's import trade would suggest so, especially among consumer goods. Table 7.7 presents rates of growth for imported goods that were also the object of new industrial investment. With few exceptions, the import series either decline or grow at annual rates slower than the average rate for all Mexican imports (7.3 percent). These low or declining rates came despite an expanding domestic market for traded goods: between 1895 and 1910 population growth was 1.2 percent per year, real GDP growth was nearly 3 percent per year, and the population of Mexico's largest cities (and consumer centers) expanded their size by nearly a third.[69] When imports grow slower than demand, import-substituting production is likely filling the gap. Further support for successful import substitution is found in the limited extant data on the output of Mexico's manufacturing industries. In textiles, beer, cigarettes, and cement, domestic production expanded at annual growth rates between 3 percent and 15 percent.[70] More Mexicans were buy-

Table 7.7

Indicators of Import Substitution: Percentage Annual
Average Growth (or Decline) of Selected Commodities
in Mexico's Import Trade, 1895–1908 (volume measures)

Total Mexican Imports	7.3 (.97)
I. Selected consumer goods:	
Total consumer imports	8.1 (.96)
Tobacco products	−5.5 (.28)
Cotton cloth	−4.3 (.44)
Beer	−4.0 (.32)
Paper	3.2 (.11)
Soap	5.3 (.16)
Writing ink	7.6 (.89)
II. Selected producer goods:	
Total producer imports	10.7 (.94)
Natural fiber products	2.3 (.42)
Iron and steel	2.7 (.14)
Explosives	5.6 (.50)
Nails, etc.	7.4 (.53)
Other iron products	8.9 (.93)
Glass	8.9 (.92)
Bricks	9.4 (.67)
Paints	10.6 (.89)
Glass bottles	19.8 (.82)
Cement	19.9 (.94)

SOURCE: All trends are calculated from volume measures of the import series
in Colegio de México 1960 for the sake of consistency, unless otherwise noted.
Total Mexican imports from p. 175, deflated with the price index on p. 63;
total consumer and producer series from pp. 43–45.
NOTE: OLS regressions on volume measures; R^2 in parentheses.

ing more goods, but they were increasingly doing so at home rather than
abroad. Several industries illustrate the close relationship between tariff protection and industrial growth.

Although cotton textile factories had long been the target of tariff-based
protection, this was largely ineffective until the 1880s. Despite high tariffs,
temporary prohibitions on competing imports, and the support of the short-
lived Banco de Avío in the 1830s, it was not until the Porfiriato that cloth
production began a period of rapid and sustained growth. Although con-

temporary observers alleged that some classes of cotton cloth were dutied at over three times their value during the Porfiriato, the evidence here fails to bear this out on the most common and general type of cloth imports.[71] Ad valorem equivalent duties on cotton cloth averaged 96 percent in 1890, with fine cloths dutied somewhat higher than course weaves. By 1905 the ad valorem rates had fallen to a still-substantial average of 65 percent. Legislated changes in the specific tariff contributed to this decline, and cotton textiles were one of the very few import-competing goods to see a net decline in their specific duties between 1890 and 1905.

Low ad valorem equivalent rates on raw cotton combined with the high rates on cloth meant that the effective protection granted the textile industry roughly doubled the ad valorem rates throughout the period, despite the latter's deterioration before 1905. As a consequence, the industry attracted substantial investment during the period, more than doubling its output under the protective umbrella of substantial effective protection. Despite national and urban population growth, imports of unadorned cotton cloth fell 31 percent by value and 49 percent by volume from the 1890s to 1910. Figure 7.2 illustrates the relationship between domestic production, rising at

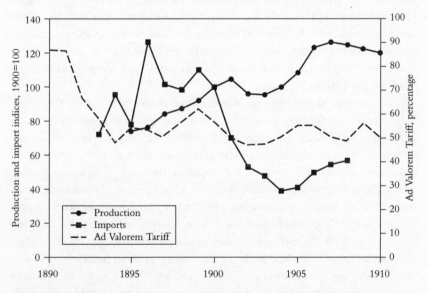

Figure 7.2. Coarse Cloth Production, Imports, and Tariffs

SOURCE: Production calculated from Haber 1989: table 8.1; quantum imports from Colegio de México 1960: 224; tariffs as per appendix.

an average 3.4 percent per year; cloth imports, falling at an average rate of 4.3 percent per year; and ad valorem tariff levels. Despite the substantial erosion in both ad valorem and effective rates through the 1890s, protection levels after the turn of the century continued to confer substantial advantage to domestic producers in the Mexican market. In 1905 tariffs allowed them to sell cloth at prices half again as high as competing imports. Mexican textile producers, in short, succeeded in substituting their products for imports in the domestic market behind this legislated barrier.

If cotton cloth exemplifies one of Mexico's few traditional manufacturing industries, beer represents the experience of a number of emerging new industries. Breweries appeared and grew rapidly between 1890 and 1910 as beer increasingly became the beverage of choice for urban middle-class consumers in Mexico: production grew tenfold and imports fell to a quarter of their previous level.[72] Domestic production, led by the Cervecería Cuauhtemoc in Monterrey, Nuevo León, supplied an ever-increasing portion of domestic demand. Did the industry operate under substantial tariff protection? Ad valorem equivalent tariffs on bottled beer ran at 76 percent of the final product in 1890, but had fallen to 52 percent by 1905 with the peso depreciation.[73] The beer industry also operated under an effective rate of protection over 100 percent higher than these ad valorem rates (Table 7.5). While barley received duties on the level of other grains (see Table 7.3), malt was admitted free until 1905 and dutied at low levels thereafter. In the meantime, beer producers sought to establish domestic barley cultivation and malt production in Mexico, although these projects would not reach fruition until after the revolution.[74]

Glass bottles, hand blown in Mexico through the 1890s, were the other major input cost for beer producers, and ad valorem equivalent duties were reduced in 1891 from 16 percent to 6 percent to facilitate imports. Although formal duties were doubled in 1904 and raised again in 1905, ad valorem rates remained at only 7 percent. Nevertheless, the costs of importing bottles was high, and associates of the Cervecería Cuauhtemoc obtained exclusive rights to the Owens automated glass production machinery in order to undertake domestic production, eventually accomplished under the Vidriera Monterrey. With this technology, they acquired a substantial cost advantage over competitors.[75] In sum, duties on beer along with its inputs were structured to encourage domestic production, and by 1900 or so the beer industry was sufficiently competitive to thrive under reduced ad valorem rates. Figure 7.3 shows the close correspondence between rising import prices (tracked by falling ad valorem equivalent tariffs) and rapidly rising produc-

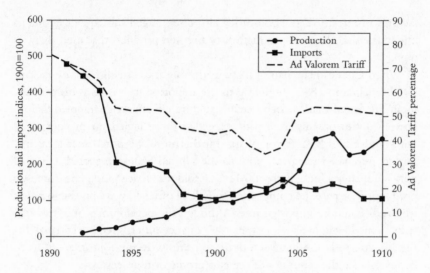

Figure 7.3. Bottled Beer Production, Imports, and Tariffs

SOURCE: Production index calculated from Haber 1989: table 4.3; quantum import index from Colegio de México 1960: 208; tariffs as per appendix.

tion through 1899 or so. From then through 1903 production stagnated as the industry lost its previous advantage of cheap domestic costs, before regaining high growth rates in 1904–6 under a stabilized exchange regime and a legislated increase in the specific tariff.

Policymakers were often caught between conflicting industrial interests when setting tariff levels, perhaps most severe in the iron and steel industry. On the one hand, vital sectors of the Mexican economy relied on a steady and cheap supply of affordable iron and steel products. Firms in the mining, transportation, and construction sectors demanded huge quantities of iron and steel products, and federal policy favored these interests, especially before the 1890s. For example, manufactured articles such as steel rails, fence wire, telegraph and electrical wire, and structural materials for mining were all exempt from import duties in 1891 and thereafter paid relatively low rates. In contrast, many of the intermediate iron and steel products, including rods, bars, and sheets of iron and steel paid relatively higher ad valorem duties as federal policy sought to stimulate and protect nascent foundries and, after 1900, steel mills. Ad valorem equivalent tariffs on the products of foundries and rolling mills averaged 71 percent in 1890 and 60 percent in 1905. However, although high duties on imports may have stimulated domestic manufactures of intermediate goods, they also discouraged subsequent efforts to undertake the domestic production of finished products that used them as inputs.

When Charles Haughan of New York sought to establish a wire factory in Chihuahua in 1896, intending to use imported iron rods as his primary input, he found that Mexico's tariff structure effectively guaranteed failure. Formal duties on imported rods exceeded those levied on manufactured wires and cables by a factor of six. Furthermore, he noted that local importers purchased telegraph wire in the United States, imported it free of duty, and, after adding barbs in Mexico, sold it as fence wire. The domestic production of wire, he complained to federal officials, was impossible unless iron rods could be imported free. Although the development ministry initially denied Haughan's request, in 1897 finance officials reduced formal duties on iron rods and increased duties on thin wire fourfold in an effort to better balance the requisites of the two production processes.[76]

Mexico's tariff structure also made domestic efforts to produce machinery all but impossible. The capital equipment needs of Mexico's incipient industrial sectors dictated low tariffs on machinery, engines, tools, and parts. Machinery, agricultural equipment, and tools entered Mexico on the free list until 1897, when ad valorem equivalent tariffs between 3 and 5 percent were levied for revenue purposes.[77] When investors began showing interest in the manufacture of machines and parts in Mexico after 1900, however, these low rates made their success unlikely. In 1902 Eugenio Mier Ruben began construction of a factory to manufacture parts for looms and other textile machinery in Puebla. Although the plant apparently began operation in 1903, Mier Ruben complained several times to Fomento officials about the competition he faced due to low duties on competing foreign imports.[78] In another case, the success of the Compañía Nacional de Construcciones Mecánicas y Calderas, in Mazatlán, constituted an extraordinary exception to the absence of machine shops in pre-revolutionary Mexico. Founded by Joaquín Redo under a war ministry contract as a shipyard and dry dock in the late 1880s, the firm branched into the production of steam engines and boilers in the 1890s under the rubric Fundición de Sinaloa. By the early 1900s the company was producing machines for mining companies throughout the Mexican north. Yet this exception only confirms the importance of protection: although Redo complained that low tariffs on competing imports and high tariffs on intermediate goods virtually "prohibited Mexicans from making boilers," the firm's success largely depended on direct subsidies from the federal government.[79]

Conclusions

Substantial evidence points to the conclusion that some import-substituting production occurred during the Porfiriato. Overall, consumer goods formed 75 percent of imports in 1876, whereas in 1911 they constituted only 43 percent.[80] We have seen that imports of a wide range of consumer goods either declined or grew slowly in the face of increased foreign competition (Table 7.7). This shift in the distribution of the import trade suggests that the development of Mexican industry was substantial, a suggestion that is made all the more certain by recent studies.[81] Indeed, between 1895 and 1910 manufacturing output grew at nearly 6 percent per year, more than doubling its size, while the national economy as a whole grew by just 50 percent.[82]

Unclear in the historical literature, however, is the degree to which federal policy contributed to this outcome. Was the structure of protection conferred by Mexican tariffs consistent with observed trends in import-substituting development? Calculations of ad valorem equivalent and—most important—effective rates of protection conferred by the Mexican tariff schedules, coupled with evidence on the development of industry and the patterns of Mexico's import trade, indicate the answer is yes: Mexican tariffs were highly protectionist, and the pattern of high and low tariff rates corresponds closely with what we know about the pattern of industrial development (and foreign commerce) in the Mexican economy. This was true in 1890 and remained so in 1905, despite the downward pressure the peso depreciation exerted on tariff rates and the contemporary reduction in non-tariff barriers. Ad valorem equivalent rates on most items did decline from 1890 to 1903 as a result of the peso depreciation, as captured in Table 6.2 of Sandra Kuntz Ficker's chapter in this volume. But once depreciation was halted with the monetary reform, the 1905 tariff schedule raised average tariff levels back to their pre-1891 level (Table 7.3). Tariff protection was also intentional: federal policymakers (led by José Yves Limantour) set and reformed specific duties consistent with a goal of encouraging investment in domestic manufacturing. Given intensifying competition from foreign manufacturers, substantial investment in domestic industry would be highly implausible without the conferral of effective protection.[83]

Tariff protection could not alone induce investment in domestic industry. Tariffs were but one piece of a broader "developmentalist commercial policy," as Sandra Kuntz Ficker argues in this volume. New and expanding industries were indeed dependent on imported inputs and on sufficient foreign exchange to pay for those. Thus lowering the barriers to both imports and exports through a lower overall tariff burden (the implicit tariff level) and through less onerous customs regulations and transport costs comprised necessary complements to industrial protection. Yet tariffs provided the keystone. Without protection, no amount of institutional reform could have been sufficient to allow Mexican industrialists to compete against foreign manufacturers.

That tariff policy during the Porfiriato was protectionist should not be surprising. Not only did Mexico have a long tradition of high trade barriers, but those economic interests prominently represented in the Díaz administration overwhelmingly favored a protectionist regime. Neither traditional nor new agricultural interests had a large voice in the government, and in most cases those with rural economic concerns also had strong interests in extractive or manufacturing activities. Indeed, diversification was the normal pattern in the investments of Mexicans and foreigners alike.[84]

Tariff-based protection was effective, and customs officials apparently administered the federal government's tariff policy in a consistent fashion. We can assume that a certain degree of mistaken invoicing and oversight, intentional or otherwise, did occur, but there is little evidence of local abuse or significant departure from established procedures, as had occurred with regularity in previous decades. Furthermore, the federal government did not frequently grant privileges to individuals or firms that exempted them from customs policies or import tariffs, although there were a few exceptions. One was the Industrias Nuevas program, which granted limited tariff exemption rights on construction materials to less than a dozen firms between 1892 and 1910. Tariff reductions were also offered to support state and municipal projects as well as to railroad construction and similar large public works. Finally, the administration conceded concessions to several large mining and smelting ventures along the northern border during the depression years of 1908–11. Citing a temporary scarcity of fuel that threatened the operations, petroleum imports were temporarily exempted from duties for specified mineral processing companies.[85]

Mexico's protective tariffs did not lead simply or quickly to widespread industrialization. Although tariff protection did protect and stimulate industrial activity in particular sectors, protected industries were not always able to respond readily to the opportunities for market space created by the tariff umbrella. In several cases, investors failed to respond quickly to tariff protection. Demand consequently exceeded available supplies as domestic production levels were low and imports were constrained under nearly prohibitive tariffs. Such was the case, for example, in the newsprint industry in the mid-1890s. Import levels had fallen to a fourth of their previous levels by

1897, and domestic production, though increasing, could not supply demand even in the capital city.[86] Tariff protection, while a necessary condition for the development of industrial activity in late-nineteenth-century Mexico, was not a sufficient condition. Nor was the existence of an adequate consumer market. Access to the requisite technology, expertise, skilled labor, primary and intermediate inputs, and long-term finance was not always cheap or easy. Uncertainty was common and transaction costs, though greatly reduced, were still high and often plagued by uncertainty. Active government policy in the form of protective tariffs compensated many industries for the additional costs posed by these obstacles, but did not alter the underlying conditions.

Appendix

DATA SOURCES AND CLASSIFICATIONS

Calculating ad valorem equivalent tariffs involves three variables: the formal tariff, in this case specific duties, commodity prices, and the exchange rate. Mexican tariff schedules were published yearly in several venues; I have taken the formal specific tariffs from the *Ordenanzas Generales de Aduanas Marítimas y Fronterizas* for 1887, 1891, and 1905, published in the yearly volumes of the *Boletín del Ministerio de Hacienda*, along with minor intervening reforms. Locating serial price data on the commodities in the sample posed several problems. Few reliable and complete price series for Mexican imports exist. Quantum and value series published in *Estadísticas económicas del Porfiriato*, or their original sources in the yearly *Estadística Fiscal* of the Secretaría de Hacienda, offer the most compete source, but do not offer the possibility of extending series before 1889 or after 1911.

Unit prices for most of the commodities examined here are calculated from data published by U.S. Treasury and Commerce Departments in the annual series *Foreign Commerce and Navigation of the United States*. Because the United States provided most of Mexico's imports, these prices best reflect those with which Mexican producers had to compete. These prices are checked against and supplemented by price series taken from Colegio de México, *Estadísticas económicas del Porfiriato*, United States, *Historical Statistics of the United States, The Mexican Year Book*, and the U.S. *Bulletin of Labor* of March 1911. In several cases I estimated values for missing years based on existing trade data and the U.S. export commodity price indices found in Robert E. Lipsey, *Price and Quantity Trends*. The unit prices used to calculate the 1890 and 1905 ad valorem equivalent tariffs in Table 7.3 are three-year averages (1889–91 and 1904–6) taken to minimize the influence of annual variations.

Two distortions are introduced into my calculations. First, ad valorem equivalent tariff calculations should be based on the C.I.F. (cost, insurance, and freight) price of imported goods at Mexican ports; that is, the import price including shipping and freight costs, insurance, etc. As the majority of the prices used here—those taken from U.S. Commerce Department sources—are presumably f.o.b. (free on board) prices, the results will somewhat *overestimate* ad valorem rates. Second, I have not adjusted commodity weights for the three-tiered classification of Mexican tariffs, which levied duties according to net (the weight of the goods alone), legal (the weight of the goods plus inner and intermediate wrappings), or gross (the weight of the goods and all packaging) weights. Thus to the extent that the U.S. prices used here are based on the gross weight of traded items, ad valorem tariffs for those goods dutied per legal and net weights will be *underestimated* (roughly 40 percent of items on the tariff were dutied at legal weights). No attempt is made here to adjust for these distortions, and the ad valorem tariff calculations are to be taken as indicative of relative levels and orders of magnitude rather than as exact measures.

As Mexico's formal tariffs are levied in pesos per kilo and the U.S. prices are in dollars per pound (or other English units), I convert dollars into pesos at the nominal exchange rate (taken from *Estadísticas históricas de México*, vol. 2, table 20.6) and English units into metric units using the appropriate conversion.

The effective rate calculations are based on the ad valorem tariffs on finished products and their primary inputs, most of which are presented in Table 7.3, with input coefficients and value added calculated from data in the 1905 United States Census of Manufactures, *Special Reports on Selected Industries*. This assumes that input-output relations were similar across U.S. and Mexican industries. Because the majority of new and expanding industries in late-Porfirian Mexico—like those listed in Table 7.5—were based on imported technology, imported technicians, and imported managers (see Haber 1989 among others), this assumption is likely not far off. Nevertheless, the effective rates presented here should not be taken as precise measurements, but rather as indications of the relative difference between ad valorem and effective rates and the variation of protection and its impact across Mexican industries.

The following presents the source of commodity prices as well as tariff classifications in the *Ordenanzas Generales* for 1890 and 1905 (as 1891/1905) for the commodities included in Tables 7.3 and 7.5.

Corn: *Estadísticas económicas*, p. 180, maize. Tariff classes 143/103.

Wheat: *Estadísticas económicas*, p. 183, trigo y demás cereales. Tariff classes 146/104.

Wheat flour: *Bulletin of Labor*, 1911, p. 419, buckwheat flour. Tariff classes 175/130.

Cattle: U.S. Department of Commerce 1890–1911 (hereafter *FCNUS*). Tariff classes 1/1.

Hides: *FCNUS*. Tariff classes 34/28.

Canned beef: *FCNUS*. Tariff classes 42/34.

Cheese: *FCNUS*. Tariff classes 49/40.

Sugar: *FCNUS*. Tariff classes 170/125.

Salt: *Estadísticas económicas*, p. 219, sal común molida para mesa. Tariff classes 712/557.

Beer, unbottled: *Estadísticas económicas*, p. 207, cerveza y sidra en barril. Tariff classes 734/573.

Beer, bottled: *Estadísticas económicas*, p. 208, cerveza y sidra y bebidas refrescantes en botellas. Tariff classes 735/572.

Tobacco leaf: *FCNUS*. Tariff classes 166/119.

Cigarettes: *FCNUS*, with weight per 1,000 cigarettes from weighing an unfiltered pack of 20 (Camels), checked against Haber 1989: 49. Tariff classes 244/179.

Leather: *FCNUS*. Tariff classes 68/59.

Boots: *FCNUS* (boots and shoes series). Tariff classes 86/72.

Shoes: *FCNUS* (boots and shoes series). Tariff classes 97/74.

Cotton, raw: *FCNUS*. Tariff classes 125/85.

Cotton cloth: *FCNUS*. Tariff classes 458/333 (coarse); 459/334 (fine).

Yute: *Estadísticas económicas*, p. 258, Yute en rama o rastrillado. Tariff classes 128/90.

Hemp cable: *Estadísticas económicas*, p. 272, cable de aloe, canamo, y demas fibras analogas. Tariff classes 231/168.

Cordage: *Estadísticas económicas*, p. 295, jarcia y cordelería. Tariff classes 237/173.

Sacks: *Estadísticas económicas*, p. 280, costales de yute, pita, henequen, y canamo. Tariff classes 233/169.

Lumber: *FCNUS*. Tariff classes 201/146.

Paper: *FCNUS*. Tariff classes 743/582.

Glass bottles: price per bottle from *FCNUS*, weight per bottle from weighing a one-liter glass juice bottle. Tariff classes 419/303.

Flat Glass: *FCNUS*. Tariff classes 441/321.

Bricks: *FCNUS*. Tariff classes 400/291.

Cement: *Estadísticas económicas*, p. 319, cal común, hidraulica, y cemento de Portland. Tariff classes 359/268.

Cyanides: *FCNUS*. Tariff classes 677/536.

Mercury: *FCNUS*.

Caustic sodas: *FCNUS*. Tariff classes 718/561.

Sulfuric acid: *FCNUS*. Tariff classes 654/518.

Dynamite: *Foreign Commerce and Navigation of the United States*, supplemented by data from *The Mexican Year Book*, 1909, p. 414, and from AGN: *Industrias Nuevas*, box 1, file 1, p. 5, and *Boletín de Secretaria de Fomento*, vol. 2, 1902, pp. 28 ff. Tariff classes 846/642.

Printing ink: *FCNUS*. Tariff classes /713.

Writing ink: *Estadísticas económicas*, p. 232, tinta para escribir. Tariff classes 726/567.

Powdered paint: *Estadísticas económicas*, p. 279, colores en polvo, cristales y preparados. Tariff classes 679/543.

Paraffin: *FCNUS*. Tariff classes 379/277

Candles: *FCNUS*. Tariff classes 396/289.

Soap: *FCNUS*. Tariff classes 899/693.

Coal and coke: *FCNUS*. 371/269, 383/279.

Crude petroleum: *Estadísticas económicas*, p. 244, aceite mineral impuro. Tariff classes 378/276.

Refined petroleum: *Bulletin of Labor*, 1911, p. 442. Tariff classes 379/277.

Copper bars and sheets: *FCNUS*. 267/197.

Copper wire, insulated: *FCNUS*. 271/200

Pig iron: *FCNUS*. Tariff classes 322/239.

Bar iron: *FCNUS*. Tariff classes 322A/240.

Iron sheets and plates: *FCNUS*. Tariff classes 326/243.

Hoop iron: *FCNUS*. Tariff classes 323A/241.

Steel bars and rods: *FCNUS*. Tariff classes 305/228.

Steel sheets and plates: *FCNUS*. Tariff classes 326/243.

Steel rails: *FCNUS*. Tariff classes 322/248.

Structural iron and steel: *Estadísticas económicas*, p. 331, vigas y vigetas de hierro para techos. Tariff classes 333/250.

Wire: *FCNUS*. Tariff classes 307/229.

Nails, cut: *FCNUS*. Tariff classes 340/257.

Pipes and fittings: *FCNUS*. Tariff classes 317/236.

Machinery: calculated from price per weights published in *The Mexican Year Book*, 1909–10, pp. 416–17. Tariff classes 800/612.

Notes

I extend deep thanks for commentary and critique to John Coatsworth, Stanley Engerman, Judith Goldstein, Aurora Gómez, Stephen Haber, Josefina Monteagudo, and Gavin Wright, as well as to conference audiences at Stanford and Harvard Universities and the All-UC Economic History meetings. Research support was provided in part by the Social Science Research Council.

1. For several accounts of this investment and its consequences, see among others Cerutti 1992; Glade 1969; Gómez-Galvarriato 1990; Haber 1989; Mariscal and Cerutti 1997; Rosenzweig 1965; and Saragoza 1988.

2. Aguilar Camín and Meyer 1993: 2.

3. Catáo 1991. Export linkages are ways in which export industries stimulate growth in other parts of the economy.

4. Haber 1989; and Rosenzweig 1965: 474.

5. Rosenzweig 1965: 481, among others.

6. For the ultimate expression of this, see Katz 1991: 30; and Vernon 1963: 42. Note that historians who assert high levels of protection tend to cite each other, with the ultimate source an anecdotal, contemporary reference to a single industry; see Salvucci 1991; and Topik 1990: 109, citing Haber 1989: 39, who cites Graham-Clark 1909, a U.S. Commerce Department agent.

7. For comparison with two other very recent analyses, see Márquez 1998, who presents a systematic analysis of import tariffs 1892–1909; and the estimates of Kuntz Ficker in Chapter 6 of this volume. We all agree that the protection conferred by tariffs to specific industries was substantial, yet we disagree about some aspects of relative levels and trends in protection from the 1880s to 1910. These discrepancies are discussed in more detail below, and my argument that tariffs formed the keystone of an explicit industrial policy after 1890 is laid out in Beatty 2001.

8. This argument is pursued in depth in Beatty 2000.

9. Cosío Villegas 1932: 20 and passim. Potash 1983 provides a thorough discussion of trade policy and commercial interests from 1823 through the 1840s. For subsequent policy, see Rosenzweig, 1965: 474–81; and Platt 1972: chap. 5. New tariff schedules were promulgated in 1821, 1827, 1830, 1842, 1843, 1845, 1853, 1856, 1872, 1880, 1887, 1891, and 1905.

10. Quoted in Cosío Villegas 1932: 26.

11. Rosenzweig 1965: 475; Herrera Canales 1988: 449–51.

12. See the contribution of Kuntz Ficker in this volume for a thorough explanation of the fiscal motives of tariffs before the 1880s.

13. See Cott 1979. Debate between free traders and advocates of protection was stronger in the 1870s and 1880s, both in Congress and the press, including the papers *El Proteccionista, El Hijo de Trabajo, El Partido Liberal,* and *El Tiempo.* See Rosenzweig 1965: 474–81. On the reduction of fiscal constraints on tariff policy, see Kuntz Ficker in this volume.

14. Quoted in Gómez-Galvarriato 1990: 173; *La Semana Mercantil*, May 21, 1900.

15. Gómez-Galvarriato 1997; Haber 1989: 37 ff.

16. For discussions of tariff economics, see Atack and Passell 1994: 123–41; Yarbrough and Yarbrough 1994: chap. 6; and Balassa 1971: chap. 1.

17. Because all Mexican duties after the 1880s were specific duties, the ad valorem tariffs estimated in this chapter are the estimated *equivalents* of a tariff levied on an ad valorem, or percentage, basis. The term *ad valorem* is used in this chapter to mean the percentage increase over the unit import price represented by the legislated specific duties. See the text below and the appendix for a full description of methods and sources.

18. The tariff estimates presented in Tables 7.3 and 7.5 are just that— estimates—and unit price differences explain some of the variation between ad valorem equivalent estimates in this chapter and those of Kuntz Ficker in this volume and Márquez 1998. See the appendix for a discussion of these differences.

19. This measure is the same as the "nominal" tariff calculated by Kuntz Ficker in this volume, and the trends are similar through the century.

20. The variance between these estimates and those of Kuntz Ficker in this volume lies in different sources for Mexico's trade value rather than in duties collected. That uncertainty about the value of Mexico's foreign trade exists for the period before 1870 highlights that it is the *trend* of implicit levels rather than their exact level that we are best able to comment upon.

21. See Yarbrough and Yarbrough 1994: 177 (table 6.1) for late century averages. For 1845 rates, see Atack and Passell 1994: 126 (tables 5.5 and 5.7), 137 (for 1824).

22. Graham-Clark 1909: 38–39; Platt 1972: 82–83.

23. Calculated from a chained Laspeyres index of import prices in the Mexican-U.S. bilateral trade constructed by the author; see Beatty 2000.

24. Declining implicit rates inversely tracked rising import prices and the exchange rate; the correlation coefficient between implicit tariffs and the exchange rate is −1.56 with an R^2 of 0.95 for 1885–1905.

25. Cited in Rosenzweig 1965: 481; *La Semana Mercantil*, May 21, 1900.

26. Report of U.S. Consul W. W. Mills, Chihuahua, October 23, 1902, in U.S. Department of State, Bureau of Foreign Commerce 1902: 505–6. For similar views on the stimulating effect of the peso depreciation for exports and domestic industry, see the reports of U.S. Consul E. C. Butler, Mexico City, March 4, 1995, in U.S. Department of State, Bureau of Foreign Commerce 1894–95: 325; Consul General Andrew D. Barlow, Mexico City, December 1, 1997, in U.S. Department of State, Bureau of Foreign Commerce 1896–97: 473. Many investors also cited Mexico's increasingly devalued silver currency as justification for their projects, which would substitute domestic production for imports that were becoming increasingly expensive as the price of silver

fell. For example, see the Industrias Nuevas application of Ernesto Peláez in 1902 (AGN: *Industrias Nuevas*, box 25, file 5).

27. Rosenzweig 1965: 476. See also Pletcher 1958.

28. AGN: *Industrias Nuevas*, box 30, file 6, pp. 39 ff.; box 9, file 6, pp. 251–56; box 9, file 7, pp. 23–28; and box 28, file 7, pp. 64–73. See also Beatty 2000.

29. The absolute version of purchasing power parity holds that identical goods in different countries would sell at the same price in terms of the same currency; that is, that the exchange rate between two countries is simply a ratio of the two country's price levels (E = P*/P, where E is the nominal exchange rate and P* and P are the price levels in the two countries). The relative version of the theory holds that percentage changes in relative price levels will approximate percentage changes in exchange rates. It thus predicts that the exchange rate and the price ratio will move proportionally. See Krugman and Obstfeld 1991: 380–92.

30. Kemmerer 1916: 480.

31. Cited in Zabludowsky 1992: 291. Zabludowsky tests the response of Mexican prices to silver's depreciation and finds that the absolute version of purchasing power parity does not hold, but leaves open the question of relative price changes; see pp. 291–98.

32. This analysis is confirmed by the independent work of Mussacchio 1998: chap. 3. It also confirms the views of historians who have asserted that Mexican manufacturers benefited substantially from the currency depreciation, but only until 1899. For such assertions, see Platt 1972: 84; Carstenson and Rouzan 1992: 479; Leal 1972: 103; and Pletcher 1958: 40.

33. Ad valorem equivalent tariffs are defined simply as the specific rate (*T*) as a percentage of the price (*P*) which would pertain under free trade, or $T/P \cdot e$, where *e* is the current exchange rate. The conventional method of calculating ad valorem tariff rates is to divide the tariff revenue collected for a product or a group of products by the imported value, but such data is not available for Mexico prior to the revolution. See the appendix for a discussion of sources and method. A similar analysis of ad valorem equivalent rates has been conducted on a sample of products by Márquez 1998. Although she uses Mexican trade data as a source for commodity prices whereas I use U.S. sources, our results differ by an average of only 3 percent over the ten commodities we analyze in common. The differences between our estimates of ad valorem tariffs arise entirely out of unit price variations.

34. For one sample of twenty products, the specific tariffs were lowered in four cases, raised in two cases, and remained constant in fourteen cases. These include raw cotton, cotton thread, coarse and fine weave cloth, wheat flour, beer, cigarette products, shoes, flat glass, printing paper, soap, bricks, iron bars, steel bars and sheets, iron and steel wire, hand tools, and nails.

35. These include those listed in Table 7.5 except for wheat flour, unbottled

beer, petroleum, iron sheets and hoops, and steel rails. See Secretaría de Hacienda: various years 1890–1905.

36. See, for instance, Ruíz 1992: 279; the list includes textiles, paper, beer, glass, soap, dynamite, cigarettes, cement, fiber products, and iron and steel products. For post-independence tariff objectives, see Potash 1983.

37. See, for instance, Kuntz Ficker's Table 6.2 in this volume.

38. The formula for calculating the effective rate of protection is ERP $= (t_o - \Sigma a_i t_i)/(1 - \Sigma a)$; where t_o is the ad valorem tariff rate on the imported finished good, a is the coefficient of inputs as a share of the value of the final good under free trade, and t_i is the ad valorem tariff on imported inputs used by domestic producers. Thus $(1 - \Sigma a)$ is the value added for the industry. For the classic application of this concept, see Hawke 1975: 84–99; and Capie 1978: 399–409.

39. In the simple case of a one-input industry with a 50 percent input coefficient and 10 percent tariffs on both the output and the input, the effective rate will be 10 percent. Raising the tariff on the input *above* that on the final product will lower the effective rate, possibly to a negative figure, whereas lowering it will raise the effective rate.

40. AGN: *Industrias Nuevas*, box 1, file 8, November 23, 1892.

41. U.S. Dept. of State, *Special Consular Reports*, no, 15 March 15, 1898.

42. There were exceptions made to this rule, but the administration's general refusal to consider exceptions is illustrated by the negative responses of both Fomento and Hacienda officials to requests for exceptions made by applicants to the federal Industrias Nuevas program. See (for the quote) AGN: *Industrias Nuevas*, box 25, file 5, p. 77. For similar cases, see the applications of Carlos Banoni, box 35, file 4; David Camacho, box 19, file 6; and Trinidad García, box 21, file 9.

43. See the cases of Charles P. Haughan and the Roessler and Hasslacher Chemical Company, AGN: *Industrias Nuevas*, box 34, file 2; and box 31, files 7–10.

44. Mexico was not alone among Latin American nations in having a cascading tariff structure in the late nineteenth century, but it appears that its was more extensive and aggressive than those of other countries, where vested interests in agriculture favored the cheap entry of a much broader range of manufactured goods. See Glade 1969: 245.

45. Overland imports calculated from data in U.S. Department of Commerce 1890–1911; shipment times from U.S. Department of State 1896–97: 483. See also Kuntz Ficker 1995: 126–69; Coatsworth 1981: 97–103.

46. See Kuntz Ficker 1995: 127–69 for a thorough discussion of the regulated freight rates. Whereas first-class rates on the Mexican Central Railroad (El Paso to Mexico City) were increased by 29 percent between 1889 and 1899, comparative rates on the Mexicano Railroad (Veracruz to Mexico City) fell by 10 percent. See Maria y Campos 1889: 221; 1899: 276.

47. Harley 1988: 861.

48. U.S. Department of State, Bureau of Foreign Commerce 1884–85: 666, 684–86.

49. For the tax consequences of the abolition, see Secretaría de Hacienda 1896, vol. 11: 38–39. For post-abolition enthusiasm, see U.S. Department of State, Bureau of Foreign Commerce 1885–86: 879.

50. Cited in Glade 1969: 246.

51. U.S. Department of State, Bureau of Foreign Commerce 1880–81: 516; 1887–88: 37.

52. Riguzzi 1996: 81.

53. Secretaría de Hacienda 1893, vol. 8: 101–102. See also Rosenzweig 1965: 474–75.

54. U.S. Department of State, Bureau of Foreign Commerce 1895–1905, successive volumes; Cosío Villegas 1932: 47. See the chapter by Sandra Kuntz Ficker in this volume for a systematic and careful effort to quantify these changes.

55. Kuntz Ficker 1995: 131–38.

56. Beatty 2000.

57. Calculated from revenue figures reported in Carmagnani 1994: appendix 3.

58. Cited in Gómez-Galvarriato 1997: 218.

59. See also Cott 1979.

60. Many such requests can be found in the Limantour archives at Condumex. See, for instance, the appeals of Joaquín Redo (March 5, 1895) and J. A. Robertson (February 21) in series 1, roll 12. Requests to the development ministry (Fomento) after 1893 fell within the Industrias Nuevas program; see for instance those of John Bannon, AGN: *Industrias Nuevas*, box 19, file 5, and Maurice Strouse, box 33, file 3. For an analysis of the program and such requests, see Beatty 2001: chaps. 6 and 7.

61. For correspondence between the firm and officials in the treasury and development offices, see AGN: *Industrias Nuevas*, box 1, files 8, 15.

62. Output at La Aurora, for instance, was 36,000 sacks per month from a hydropowered plant of over 2,000 spindles and 600 workers. See *Economista Mexicano*, September 16, 1905: 539; and *The Mexican Herald*, April 30, 1905: 8 and August 1, 1905: 7.

63. See also Gómez-Galvarriato 1997: 215–19; and Gómez-Galvarriato 1990: 174–78. The Fundidora's principle products included steel bars, structural steel, and steel rails. Besides tariff protection, the Fundidora Monterrey received exemptions from state taxes in Nuevo León and, most importantly, a 1907 contract with the National Railroad to supply rails.

64. Gómez-Galvarriato 1997: table 2.

65. *Engineering and Mining Journal*, April 13, 1905: 712.

66. Limantour voiced suspicion about the motivations of many appellants,

writing to Governor Bernardo Reyes in 1898, "It is a marked tendency in all industries to ask the government to increase import duties on similar imported goods and thus to seek the advantage of artificial protection, [an advantage] which in the majority of cases they could achieve through their own efforts." Condumex, Archivo Limantour, series 1, roll 12, September 20, 1898.

67. AGN: *Industrias Nuevas*, box 21, file 9, pp. 1–10.

68. AGN: *Industrias Nuevas*, box 31, file 8, pp. 55–57.

69. INEGI 1994: tables 8.1, 1.1, and 1.4. For further evidence on Porfirian consumer culture, see Bunker 1997.

70. Haber 1989: tables 4.1, 4.2, 4.3, 8.1; and INEGI 1994: table 13.5.

71. Graham-Clark 1909: 38–39.

72. Haber 1989: 53; Hibino 1992: 27–30; Colegio de México 1960: 208; Bunker 1997.

73. The pre-1891 ad valorem equivalent rate was confirmed by U.S. Consul Warner P. Sutton in 1890, who cited an ad valorem rate of about 75 percent of the price of bottle beer at the U.S.-Mexican border. Cited in Hibino 1992: 27.

74. See *Diario Oficial*, March 12, 1904; Secretaría de Fomento 1908–9: 65; *El Economista Mexicano*, December 10, 1904: 206, January 1, 1905: 342, and May 26, 1906: 165; and the *Mexican Herald*, January 3, 1905: 7, and January 12, 1905.

75. Barragán and Cerutti n.d.

76. AGN: *Industrias Nuevas*, box 34, file 2.

77. Ad valorem equivalent duties are calculated from specific rates of from $0.01 to $0.0165 per kilogram for imported machinery using data from *The Mexican Year Book*, 1909–10: 416–17, as well as AGN: *Industrias Nuevas*, box 39, file 4 and box 8, file 14, pp. 9–31. Since machinery imports totaled over $8 million (U.S.) in 1906, the revenue potential of this duty was substantial.

78. AGN: *Industrias Nuevas*, box 39, file 4. See also the case represented by Ernest Peláez before development officials in box 25, file 5, p. 64 ff.

79. Condumex, Limantour Archives, series 1, roll 12, April 24, 1897; AGN: *Industrias Nuevas*, box 14, files 4–6, boxes 15–17, passim.

80. Colegio de México 1960: 43–44.

81. See sources cited in note 1.

82. Cárdenas 1987: tables A1.3, A1.4. It should be remembered that manufacturing in 1910 still comprised a relatively small part of the national economy, contributing between 10 and 12 percent of GDP and employing not much more than 10 percent of the labor force.

83. No attempt is made here to evaluate the welfare consequences of tariff protection, either in terms of higher prices to consumers of protected goods or in terms of yielding inefficient production processes. On the latter, see Gómez-Galvarriato 1997: 219–30; and Haber 1989: passim. Also, the precise

level at which ad valorem tariffs were either effectively protectionist (at the low end) or outright prohibitory (at the high end) is difficult to determine given the weakness of quantitative data for Mexican industry before 1910.

84. See Cerutti 1992: chaps. 5, 7, and 8; Gamboa Ojeda 1985; Haber 1989: chap. 5; and Saragoza 1988: chap. 3.

85. On the Industrias Nuevas program, see AGN, *Industrias Nuevas*; on public works, see Secretaría de Hacienda 1897, vol. 12: 31–39; and on smelting, see *Diario Oficial*, September 16, 1908 and April 1, 1909. Concessions included those to the Companía Cananea Consolidada de Cobre, S.A., the Companía Minera Banco de Oro, and the Calumet and Sonora of the Cananea Mining Company; see *Diario Oficial*, June 11, 1908, December 23, 1908, and January 14, 1911.

86. For import levels, see Colegio de México 1960: 216; for complaints from the newspaper industry, see *El Economista Mexicano*, December 14, 1895: 230.

References

[AGN] Archivo General de la Nación. Mexico City.

Aguilar Camín, Héctor, and Lorenzo Meyer. 1993. *In the Shadow of the Mexican Revolution*. Austin.

Atack, Jeremy, and Peter Passell. 1994. *A New Economic View of American History*. 2d ed. New York.

Balassa, Bela. 1971. *The Structure of Protection in Developing Countries*. Baltimore.

Barragán, Juan Ignacio, and Mario Cerutti. n.d. *Juan F. Brittingham y la industria en México, 1859–1940*. Monterrey, Mexico.

Beatty, Edward. 2000. "The Impact of Foreign Trade on the Mexican Economy: Terms of Trade and the Rise of Industry 1880–1923." *Journal of Latin American Studies*, vol. 32, no. 2.

———. 2001. *Institutions and Investment: The Political Basis of Industrialization in Mexico Before 1911*. Stanford.

Bunker, Steven. 1997. "Consumers of Good Taste: Marketing Modernity in Northern Mexico, 1890–1910." *Mexican Studies / Estudios Mexicanos*, vol. 13, no. 2: 227–70.

Capie, Forrest. 1978. "The British Tariff and Industrial Protection in the 1930s." *Economic History Review*, vol. 31: 399–409.

Cárdenas, Enrique. 1987. *La industrialización mexicana durante la gran depresión*. Mexico City.

Carmagnani, Marcello. 1994. *Estado y mercado: La economía pública del liberalismo mexicano, 1850–1911*. Mexico City.

Carstenson, Fred, and Diane Rouzan. 1992. "Foreign Markets, Domestic Initiative, and the Emergence of a Monocrop Economy: The Yucatecan

Experience, 1825–1903." *Hispanic American Historical Review*, vol. 72, no. 4: 555–92.

Catáo, Luis A. V. 1991. "The Transmission of Long Cycles Between 'Core' and 'Periphery' Economies: A Case Study of Brazil and Mexico, c. 1870–1940." Ph.D. dissertation, University of Cambridge.

Cerutti, Mario. 1992. *Burguesía, capitales e industria en el norte de México, Monterrey y su ámbito regional (1850–1910)*. Mexico City.

Coatsworth, John. 1981. *Growth Against Development: Economic Impact of Railroads in Porfirian Mexico*. De Kalb.

Colegio de México. 1960. *Estadísticas económicas del Porfiriato: Comercio exterior de México, 1877–1911*. Mexico City.

Cosío Villegas, Daniel. 1932. *La cuestión arancelaria en México: III: História de la política aduanal*. Mexico City.

Cott, Kenneth S. 1979. "Porfirian Investment Policies, 1976–1910." Ph.D. dissertation, University of New Mexico.

Diario Oficial de la Federación. March 12, 1904.

Gamboa Ojeda, Leticia. 1985. *Los empresarios de ayer: El grupo dominante en la industria textil de Puebla, 1906–1929*. Puebla, Mexico.

Glade, William P. 1969. *The Latin American Economies: A Study of Their Institutional Evolution*. New York.

Graham-Clark, William A. 1909. "Cuba, Mexico, and Central America." Part 1 of *Cotton Goods in Latin America*. Washington, D.C.

Gómez-Galvarriato, Aurora. 1997. "El desempeño de la Fundidora de Hierro y Acero de Monterrey durante el Porfiriato." In Carlos Marichal and Mario Cerutti, eds., *Historia de las grandes empresas en México, 1850–1930*. Mexico City.

———. 1990. "El primer impulso industrializador de México: El caso de Fundidora Monterrey." Ph.D. dissertation, Instituto Tecnológico Autónomo de México.

Haber, Stephen. 1989. *Industry and Underdevelopment: The Industrialization of Mexico, 1890–1940*. Stanford.

Harley, C. Knick. 1992. "International Competitiveness of the Antebellum American Cotton Textile Industry." *Journal of Economic History*, vol. 53, no. 3: 559–84.

———. 1988. "Ocean Freight Rates and Productivity, 1740–1913: The Primacy of Mechanical Invention Reaffirmed." *Journal of Economic History*, vol. 48, no. 4: 851–76.

Hawke, G. R. 1975. "The United States Tariff and Industrial Protection in the Late Nineteenth Century." *Economic History Review*, February: 84–99.

Herrera Canales, Inés. 1988. "La circulación (comercio y transporte en México entre los años 1880 y 1910)." In Ciro Cardoso, ed., *México en el siglo xix*, pp. 437–64. Mexico City.

Hibino, Barbara. 1992. "Cervecería Cuauhtémoc: A Case Study of Technological and Industrial Development in Mexico." *Mexican Studies/Estudios Mexicanos*, vol. 8, no. 1: 23–43.

INEGI. 1994. *Estadísticas históricas de México*. Mexico City.

Jastram, Roy W. 1961. *Silver: The Restless Metal*. New York.

Katz, Friedrich. 1991. "The Liberal Republic and the Porfiriato, 1867–1910." In Leslie Bethell, ed., *The Cambridge History of Latin America*. Vol. 5. Cambridge.

Kemmerer, Edwin Walter. 1916. *Modern Currency Reforms*. New York.

Krugman, Paul R., and Maurice Obstfeld. 1991. *International Economics: Theory and Policy*. 2d ed. New York.

Kuntz Ficker, Sandra. 1995. *Empresa extranjera y mercado interno: El Ferrocarril Central Mexicano 1880–1907*. Mexico City.

Leal, Juan Felipe. 1972. *La burguesía y el estado mexicano*. Mexico City.

Lipsey, Robert E. 1963. *Price and Quantity Trends in the Foreign Trade of the United States*. Princeton.

Maria y Campos, Ricardo de. 1889. *Datos mercantiles*. Mexico City.

———. 1899. *Renseignements commerciaux sur les Etats-Unis mexicains*. Mexico City.

Mariscal, Carlos, and Mario Cerutti, eds. 1997. *Historia de las grandes empresas en México, 1850–1930*. Mexico City.

Márquez, Graciela. 1998. "Tariff Protection in Mexico, 1892–1909: Ad Valorem Rates and Sources of Variation." In John H. Coatsworth and Alan M. Taylor, eds., *Latin America and the World Economy Since 1800*. Cambridge, Mass.

Mussacchio, Aldo. 1998. "Entre el oro y la plata: Un estudio de las causas de la adopción del patrón oro en México." B.A. thesis, Instituto Tecnológico Autónomo de México.

Platt, D. C. M. 1972. *Latin American and British Trade, 1806–1914*. New York.

Pletcher, David M. 1958. "The Fall of Silver in Mexico, 1870–1910, and Its Effects on American Investments." *Journal of Economic History*, vol. 18, no. 1: 33–55.

Potash, Robert A. 1983. *Mexican Government and Industrial Development in the Early Republic: The Banco de Avío*. Amherst, Mass.

Riguzzi, Paolo. 1996. "Los caminos del atraso: Tecnología, instituciones e inversión en los ferrocarriles mexicanos, 1850–1900." In Sandra Kuntz Ficker and Paolo Riguzzi, eds., *Ferrocarriles y vida económica en México, 1850–1950: Del surgimiento tardío al decaimiento precoz*, pp. 31–98. Mexico City.

Rosenzweig, Fernando. 1965. "La Industria." In Daniel Cosío Villegas, ed., *Historia moderna de México: El Porfiriato: La vida económica*, vol. 1, pp. 311–481. Mexico City.

Ruíz, Ramón Eduardo. 1992. *Triumphs and Tragedy: A History of the Mexican People*. New York.

Salvucci, Richard. 1991. "The Origins and Progress of U.S.-Mexican Trade, 1825–1884: 'Hoc opus, hic labor est.'" *Hispanic American Historical Review*, vol. 71, no. 4: 697–735.

Salvucci, Richard, Linda K. Salvucci, and Aslán Cohen. 1995. "The Politics of Protection: Interpreting Commercial Policy in Late Bourbon and Early National Mexico." In Kenneth J. Andrien and Lyman L. Johnson, eds., *The Political Economy of Spanish America in the Age of Revolution, 1750– 1850*, pp. 95–114. Albuquerque.

Saragoza, Alexander M. 1988. *The Monterrey Elite and the Mexican State, 1880– 1940*. Austin.

Secretaría de Fomento. 1857–1911. *Memoria*. Mexico City.

Secretaría de Hacienda. 1889–1911. *Boletín del Ministerio de Hacienda*. Mexico City.

———. 1880–1910. *Memoria de Hacienda*. Mexico City.

Topik, Steven. 1990. "La revolución, el estado, y el desarrollo económico en México." *Historia Mexicana*, vol. 40, no. 1: 79–144.

U.S. Department of Commerce. 1890–1911. *Foreign Commerce and Navigation of the United States*. Washington, D.C.

U.S. Department of Commerce, Bureau of the Census. 1961. *Historical Statistics of the United States: Colonial Times to 1957*. Washington, D.C.

———. 1908. *Manufactures 1905*. Parts 3–4: *Special Reports on Selected Industries*. Washington, D.C.

U.S. Department of Commerce, Bureau of Labor. 1911. *Bulletin of Labor*. Washington, D.C.

U.S. Department of State. 1890–1912. *Special Consular Reports*. Washington, D.C.

U.S. Department of State, Bureau of Foreign Commerce. 1880–1912. *Commercial Relations of the United States with Foreign Countries*. Washington, D.C.

Vernon, Raymond. 1963. *The Dilemma of Mexico's Development: The Roles of Private and Public Sectors*. Cambridge, Mass.

Yarbrough, Beth V., and Robert M. Yarbrough. 1994. *The World Economy: Trade and Finance*. 3rd ed. Fort Worth.

Zabludowsky, Jaime. 1992. "La depreciación de la plata y las exportaciones." In Enrique Cárdenas, ed., *Historia económica de México*, vol. 3, pp. 290– 326. Mexico City.

Part III

Labor Relations Reforms During the Porfiriato

The Legal and Contractual Limits to Private Property Rights in Mexican Industry During the Revolution

JEFFREY L. BORTZ

Embedded in the concept of private property is the right to appropriate one's own or someone else's labor. The appropriation of labor, as well as goods and services, is a function of legal rules, organizational forms, and norms and behaviors.[1] It is, therefore, a social construct. However, there is a complex interplay between the norms and rules that allow people to appropriate their labor and the norms and rules that govern the social relations of work because the rules of work can conflict with the rules of private property. It is in the interest of property holders in industry to extend the meaning of property to control over the workplace—to hire, to fire, to discipline, to define and control the work process. It is equally in the immediate interest of working people to maximize their own control of the work environment. "Employees' interests conflict with those of their employers even at the moment that they produce goods and services and not just at the end of the day when the fruits of their productive activity are distributed amongst the different factors of production."[2] In every society, the outcome of this conflict between those who work and those who control work establishes the parameters of the social relations of work. These parameters are a subset of the labor regime, the set of organizations and institutionalized behaviors, attitudes, and rules that comprise the social relationships of work, or, what Gordon, Edwards, and Reich label the "socially expected organization of the labor process."[3]

Labor regimes are political and economic. They influence the industrial economy directly and also through the definition and enforcement of property rights. Property rights, the rights of property holders, are not limited to the right to buy and sell property. In fact, these are the least important rights. Property that generates wealth is not passive; rather it is property that directly or indirectly controls the labor of others. The most important right of property holders is therefore the right to command and control the workplace. Although the modern literature on Mexico has placed emphasis on wage and benefits packages implied in the 1917 Constitution, it has not fully addressed the command and control implications of Mexico's twentieth-century labor regime, closely tied to that document. According to North, "the total costs of production consist of the resource inputs of land, labor and capital both in transforming the physical attributes of a good and in transaction—defining, protecting, and enforcing the property rights to goods (the right to use, the right to derive income from the use of, the right to exclude, and the right to exchange)."[4] The right to use capital to control work is a fundamental component of property rights in Mexico and elsewhere.

Mexico's revolution radically transformed the labor regime. In 1910, there existed no body of law that was specifically a labor code. There were no minimum wage or maximum hour regulations. There were no collective contracts. Unions existed but only on the margins of law and power. There were no government labor offices or labor courts. By 1927, following a decade and a half of violent social upheaval and several hundred thousand dead, the country invented the most extensive set of labor laws, regulations, and governmental offices in the western hemisphere. These included but were not limited to an extensive chapter of the 1917 Constitution; lengthy and detailed state labor codes; mandatory collective contracts in the country's major industries; wage, hour, and benefits regulations; federal and state labor offices; arbitration boards; and legal provisions that not only protected unions but ensured union shops.

Interestingly, most historians and social scientists have treated this change as a political rather than economic phenomenon. This has left unanswered three interrelated questions. Where did the laws and rules come from? Did the law constrain private property rights in fundamentally new ways? Did these constraints have an impact on the behavior of workers and managers?

This chapter argues that the Mexican Revolution legally changed the socially expected organization of the labor process in such a way as to fundamentally alter private property rights in Mexico. Property rights in industry has two meanings, the appropriation of product and also the right of the owners to control the labor process. During the revolution, Mexican factory workers in the country's most important factory industry, cotton textiles, successfully challenged the right of owners to run the factory. The result of this revolution in the mills was a completely new set of labor institutions and organizations grounded in labor law and collective contracts. The new legal institutions effectively limited the right of owners to run factories as they wished, therefore constraining private property rights in new ways.

Although Mexico of the revolution was an overwhelmingly agrarian and rural country, revolutionary elites understood that the future of the country lay in its industrialization. Since the 1830s, government and private industrialists had pursued a policy of industrialization. Many of these efforts concentrated on the cotton textile industry. This was Mexico's first factory industry and was still in the 1910s Mexico's leading industrial activity, with 140 factories and 30,000 workers, most concentrated in four industrial zones: Mexico City, Puebla, Atlixco (in Puebla state), and Orizaba (in Veracruz). If Mexico was to continue to industrialize, the dream of many, then the problems associated with an industrial labor force became important. These included training potential workers to the habits of modern industry, minimizing labor costs, and maximizing workplace efficiency.

Labor conflict during and after the revolution could not but have an impact on labor costs and workplace efficiency. Workers, like owners, wanted to maximize incomes and control. Pre-revolutionary Mexico lacked a formal labor relations systems to mediate conflicting interests. Revolutionary Mexico invented one, although many scholars have seen it as a political rather than economic institution.

Mexico's revolution included but was not primarily a workers' revolt. There was more industry in Mexico than just cotton textiles, and rebellious workers were not limited to mill hands. Nonetheless, cotton textiles was the leading factory industry in the country, and events in mills large and small played the critical role in forcing not only legal changes that affected all industrial establishments, but also the emergence of tripartite collective bargaining and industry-wide collective contracts. The formation of a labor relations system in cotton textiles is therefore particularly instructive in understanding the limits to private property in post-revolutionary Mexico.[5]

Law

To understand the dramatic change in labor affairs during the revolution, it is useful to look at labor institutions and organizations just prior to 1910. The cotton textile strike movement of 1906–7 leading to the famous massacre at the large Rio Blanco mill illustrates well Porfirian labor affairs. In response to union organizing in the textile industry in 1905 and 1906, the Puebla textile owners founded the Centro Industrial Mexicano (CIM) in

October 1906. The next month the CIM issued regulations for textile mills in the Puebla area "which were intended to halt increasing labor agitation there."[6]

> The new rules fixed working hours at between 6 A.M. and 8 P.M.; workers had to work the entire week without a break to receive their week's wages; there were to be no objections to the fines levied for defective work; and workers were forbidden visitors in their homes. They were humiliating, to say the least, and completely unacceptable, since fatigue induced by long working hours would make it impossible to avoid mistakes.[7]

Implementation of the new *reglamento de trabajo* led to a strike/lockout in much of Mexico's cotton textile industry and ultimately culminated in the Rio Blanco massacre in 1907. Porfirio Díaz ended the strike through severe and bloody repression in Orizaba (though there was considerably more compromise in Atlixco) and the issuance of a labor decree on January 4, 1907.[8]

Díaz's decree was neither contract nor law but a presidential ruling in a response to a specific problem. In this regard, it more resembled medieval law in which Hispanic kings responded to specific petitions by vassals rather than modern labor law, which applies to all citizens within a certain category. In Atlixco the decree was ignored; Jefe Político Ignacio Machorro fulfilled his promise to labor leaders to not have it posted inside the factories.[9] In Orizaba the decree was implemented; widespread government violence had crushed workers' resistance to owners.[10] The decree was therefore a government-sponsored set of work rules in some factories but not in others.

Article 1 reopened the factories on January 7, 1907, forcing mill hands to return to work under whatever rules the owners wanted. Article 2 committed the owners to study wage unification in the industry and offered merit pay for the best workers, according to "the judgment of the administrator."[11] Article 3 implemented a notebook system in which the factory provided one for each mill hand where supervisors graded the "good conduct, diligence, and skills of the worker."[12] In Article 4, the textile owners offered to study factory work rules in order to "guarantee the interests and good performance of their establishments, and to make better, as far as possible, the situation of the workers."[13] Article 5 allowed workers to file a signed written complaint to anything they objected to. If not satisfied, they could quit![14] In Article 6, the owners agreed to create new schools for workers' children or to improve already existing factory schools. Article 7 prohibited the factories from employing children younger than seven! Article 8 committed the workers to accepting control of the *jefes políticos* over their newspapers, allowing the state's local political leaders to appoint the directors of workers' periodicals "in order to not let slip injustices toward anybody, nor publish subversive doctrines that might mislead the workers."[15] The last article contained a no-strike clause since Article 5 "established the form in which they might complain," meaning the right to resign.[16]

Díaz made a few concessions to workers in the decree, albeit minor ones. Nevertheless, the decree did not raise wages or otherwise improve working conditions. Most important, it ratified the authority of owners to run the mills as they wished. It upheld the power of owners to discipline workers through fear. That was the meaning of the notebook and merit pay system, both of which rewarded obedience and subservience to the firm while threatening workers with the loss of their jobs for bad attitudes.

The ultimate discipline in the workplace is the ability to fire workers. The formal and informal rules of firing are therefore the most important institution in controlling the factory. In this respect, Articles 3 and 5 enumerated rather clearly the core of the Porfirian work world: supervisors judged the loyalty of workers and could punish them at will, while the only recourse that workers might have was to quit. Although the entire decree was not contract or law, it did demonstrate that for factory owners in Mexico, private property rights included hiring and firing at will, while for workers, property rights meant, "the worker . . . can leave . . ."

At the end of the Porfiriato, the formal institutional labor relations system was almost nonexistent. There was no body of labor legislation. Neither unions nor collective contracts existed by law; worker organizations were barely and only sometimes tolerated. Government regulation consisted of the personal interest of local jefes políticos, state governors, or the president himself. In short, the labor regime was little formalized, but what formality existed was that of the owners.

The radical changes in the labor relations system in Mexico from 1910 to 1927 cannot be understood without reference to the country's social revolution and the revolution of textile workers within the surrounding revolution. During the social upheaval, Mexico's underclasses armed themselves. When conflict erupted between those who ruled and those who were ruled, the climate permitted the latter to kill the former, often with impunity. Not all campesinos took to killing hacendados, nor did all workers take to stabbing supervisors. But enough did to embolden others to clamor for taking land away from the rich in the countryside and power away from the owners in the factories.

Mexican cotton textile workers led a revolution of their own inside Mexico's small industrial world.[17] In 1911 mill hands organized the first successful general strike in Mexican history, forcing owners and Madero's revolutionary government to draft the country's first industry-wide collective contract. The owners intended the contract to lessen conflict in the mills and mill towns, which it did not. But it did strengthen labor organizations. In fact, it led to complete unionization of the mills. The contract made unions necessary, perhaps even desirable as a mechanism for managing a collective contract.[18] With unions in place, however, workers challenged authority more easily because the threat of being fired became more distant. Despite the economic travails of civil war, men and women in the mills fought for better working conditions and more control over the factory environment.[19] As the revolution continued, workers and their unions made great progress, though not in a linear fashion. Revolution and civil war often played havoc with the textile and other industries. Many workers lost their jobs, others joined armed bands, while some returned to the countryside to work the land in order to avoid starvation. Nonetheless, there was no decisive defeat of working-class challenges in the factories despite the political defeat of the radical Casa del Obrero Mundial.

With one national government after another collapsing, with no group capable of establishing its own hegemony free of entangling alliances, with a populace armed and angry, it was inevitable that new elites who sought to establish control over the nation would try to change the legal system. Any successful group would have to adapt law to the new social and political realities of revolutionary Mexico while also using it to strengthen their own power. The new social reality of Mexico included mill owners who had lost absolute control of the factories and industrial workers who enjoyed unions and used violence at work to win what law denied them.

Most national political leaders during the revolution—Madero, Huerta, Carranza, Obregón, Calles—were personally ambitious. Madero and Carranza came from wealthy families and positions of power that they never renounced. Once in power, Obregón and Calles did all they could to acquire personal wealth. It is inconceivable that these capitalists or aspiring capitalists had any interest in weakening private property or the control of property holders over the production process. Nonetheless, the owning classes of Mexico had lost their ideological hegemony through the revolutionary process. Therefore the new elites had to reconcile two impossible tasks in law: institutionalize property rights for future economic development while also institutionalizing the rights of social classes who lacked property and who had challenged the control of those who owned it. With social relationships in flux, law could not lag behind, not for any group aspiring to govern what had now become a dangerous country. New elites would have preferred to strengthen property rights, but an armed and dangerous working class wanted more control over the factory environment, which meant weakening traditional property rights.

Even before Madero assumed office, the fall of the Díaz government presaged a change in the social and legal relationships of work. On September 22, 1911, the interim government of Francisco León de la Barra sent a "Proyecto de Ley" to Congress, asking it to establish a labor office as part of the ministry of development to, among other tasks, "arrange fair regulation in cases of conflict between owners and workers, and serve as arbiter in their differences, whenever they might solicit its services."[20]

The Congress approved the Proyecto without modification. Madero assumed the presidency on November 6, 1911, and the law took effect on December 18, 1911.[21] The direct antecedent of the modern Secretaría del Trabajo y Previsión Social, it provided the country's first legal means for government to intervene through institutional rather than personal or military mechanisms in what had previously been considered a private matter, the relations between owners and workers.

Despite the new office, in December 1911, textile workers carried out the first successful general strike in Mexican history,[22] an act they repeated in 1917.[23] In between the two strikes, workers organized permanent unions, assaulted the owners' authority inside the factories, and made it impossible for supervisors to govern the mills under the old rules. The owners responded to the first strike through an industry-wide labor contract. Thereafter, contracts, unions, and worker violence made mill hands stronger and the old labor culture weaker. Between the July 1912 textile convention, which drafted the first national labor contract, and the November 1916 constitutional convention, which drew up a social contract for the entire country, national and regional authorities continued to seek partial remedies to the labor problem through legal and bureaucratic measures.

Mexico's revolution was a violent affair in which much of the country fell under the rule of military commanders at one time or another. As a consequence, many of the initial legal changes in labor affairs came about through military decrees. Military commanders tried to accomplish what Madero could not: to use the legal system to solve Mexico's social problem.

On September 19, 1914, Luis F. Domínguez, "military governor of the State of Tabasco," issued the "Decreto Relativo al Proletario Rural."[24] Arguing that rural peons suffered "true slavery" and in order to "begin to carry out the promises of the Revolution," the decree set minimum wages (75 centavos a day for rural work), maximum hours (eight), abolished rural debts and physical punishment, and permitted the state to observe and enforce the decree. On October 28, 1914, General Gertrudis G. Sánchez, "provisional Governor and Military Commander of the State of Michoacán de Ocampo," issued a decree establishing a rural minimum wage of 75 centavos a day and a maximum workday of nine hours.[25] It also provided rural workers with the right to take care of two animals on the farms, extending that to five animals for sharecroppers.[26]

In Veracruz, Cándido Aguilar, "governor and military commander of the state," issued two decrees (October 19, 1914, and January 24, 1916) to solve the labor problem in his state, which included the mill town of Orizaba. The 1914 measure declared that "one of the primary goals of the Revolution is the betterment of the social and economic condition of the working classes, promoted by means of an adequate legislation . . ."[27] Its eighteen articles established a maximum workday of nine hours, overtime pay of 100 percent, a minimum wage of 1 peso a day for "*peones de campo*," and it made owners responsible for medical care, work accidents, and schools. In a sharp break with the past, it also gave authority to the Juntas de Administración Civil to settle differences among workers and owners, "hearing representatives of unions and societies." Article 16 gave the Juntas the ability to fine or arrest those who didn't abide by its rulings.

By providing the Juntas de Administración Civil authority to intervene in labor conflict and formalizing the rights of unions to present cases to them, the decree introduced unions to the formal labor relations system. It also took some authority for disciplining workers away from the factory and gave it to a supposedly neutral civil authority. Article 18 declared that "the attributes and faculties that the Juntas now have will pass to the municipal governments." Aguilar meant to permanently transfer this authority from the owners to the state.

Meanwhile, in early 1915 Carranza was on the defensive with his government in Veracruz rather than Mexico City. This was the moment when he could least ignore the violence and desires of campesinos and workers. On January 6, 1915, Carranza issued an agrarian law to restore peasant lands, on January 29, a decree to federalize labor law,[28] and on March 22, a generalized wage increase for textile workers through the "Decreto de Aumento de Jornales" for the "Obreros de la Industria Textil."[29] Then on April 12, 1915, at the very height of Mexico's civil war, with the Convention in power in Mexico City and the Constitutionalists in Veracruz, Carranza's secretaría de gobernación, Rafael Zubarán Capmany, published the "Proyecto de Ley sobre Contrato de Trabajo."[30]

Zubarán Capmany noted that the legislation was necessary because

the relationships between Capital and Labor have been taking since then [Constitution of 1857] a character of hostility that before they didn't have, and that have been exacerbated to the degree that the development of the capitalist regime, whose clearest manifestations have been "maquinismo" and the concentration of industry in large factories, has made more frequent occasions of conflict between these two factors of production, whose harmonious participation constitutes today a very distant ideal.[31]

This was official recognition that conflict in the factories demanded a new legal framework for labor affairs. The Proyecto included government-mandated maximum hours of work, minimum wages, and requirements for businesses to provide written work rules that had to be registered with the federal labor office. It promised to legalize unions, protect workers from being fired for joining them, and recognize collective contracts. Although the civil war prevented the proposal from becoming law, it is nonetheless evidence of elite fear of the workers' new challenge to authority and the need to contain it through new labor law.

By mid-1915 Mexico's social revolution appeared to be at a turning point. Obregón inflicted a major military defeat on Villa at Celaya, while U.S. president Woodrow Wilson finally decided to recognize Carranza. Although the Constitutionalists were then able to reassert their control over Mexico City, they were not a unified group. Their military successes depended on the loyalty of hastily assembled troops under the control of semi-independent regional caciques. This made the task of constructing a national government and a new hegemony a high priority. Without a new, revolutionary constitution, it would be difficult to convince the country that revolutionaries had won.

Most scholars argue that while Carranza needed a new constitution to cement the power of the aspiring revolutionary coalition, he neither desired nor implemented radical social provisions. According to Niemeyer, "Carranza's political revolution against Huerta assumed a social and economic character only after Huerta's defeat, when the constitutionalist movement was torn with dissension and Carranza was fighting against Villa and Zapata for the very survival of his cause."[32] It was this need rather than progressive desires that forced Carranza to call a constitutional convention. According to Hart, Carranza then resisted the "forced promulgation of the Constitution of 1917. . . ."[33]

Whatever Carranza's personal beliefs, it was not politically feasible to go back to the status quo ante. Mexican workers had already forced government to cede labor reform. Military governors had codified labor reforms at the state level, and even Carranza's own secretary of government had laid out additional plans for labor relations. The outcome of this process was Article 123 of the Constitution of 1917.

On September 14, 1916, Carranza decreed a constitutional convention, which began its work on December 1. The delegates finished January 31, 1917, and the new constitution became law on February 5.[34] The Congreso Constituyente consciously patterned the document on the 1857 Constitution but stumbled over labor, which lacked precedent in Mexico. Factory workers were not a threat in 1857 but they were now.

The framers of the 1857 Constitution had written a document that responded to the conflicts of the early republic, when Mexico suffered numerous foreign invasions, the loss of half the national territory, and the inability of the country's elites to reach a consensus on a social, economic, or even a political project. The political chaos of the early years of the Republic attested to the difficulties of nation building. When the liberals took power after the Plan de Ayutla, they needed to build and save a nation rather than give voice to the underclasses. Therefore the constitution was addressed to the state rather than to the people. Although it unleashed a decade-long civil war, it was a war among elites for control of the state. It culminated in the absolute victory of the liberals.

The liberals had little to say about workers other than the traditional liberal program of creating and protecting a free market in labor. On labor, they labeled Title 1, Section 1, "Of the Rights of Man," in clear allusion to the revolutionary French document of 1789.[35] In France, "the Revolutionaries believed in the free market, that all must be free to trade on equal terms. . . ."[36] That was pretty much the extent of legal ideas on work in mid-nineteenth-century Mexico. Article 2 of the 1857 Constitution ratified the complete abolition of slavery. Article 4 declared that "every one is free to engage in any honorable and useful profession, industrial pursuit, or occupation suitable to him, and to avail himself of its products." Article 5 affirmed that "no one shall be compelled to render personal services without due compensation and without his full consent. . . ."[37]

By 1917 the liberal project was in clear disarray. The rebellion of the underclasses made a mockery of the ideology of the free market, which to them appeared to benefit the Mexican people little and the wealthy much. On the other hand, the old Porfirian liberal, Venustiano Carranza, had become civilian chief of the most powerful military force in the country. Why would an old liberal want an anti–free market labor code? Some have argued that he did not and that labor reform was somehow imposed.[38]

Although no one argues that Carranza was friend to the common worker, his position on labor cannot be understood without reference to Zubarán Capmany's 1915 proposal. When the old Porfirian political hegemony collapsed, when hundreds of thousands, if not millions, of campesinos challenged traditional property rights in land, when thousands of textile workers repeatedly shut down the industry and contested the owners' traditional rights in the mills, a politician like Carranza could only survive by recognizing reality. In revolutionary Mexico, the broader social revolt and the more localized factory rebellions made labor reform inevitable. The 1915 proposal demonstrated that the most conservative of revolutionaries was entirely ready to concede worker demands, not because he wanted to, but because he had to. It is therefore possible that his original constitutional proposal was a negotiating ploy. In any case, the labor commissions of the Congreso Constituyente used the Zubarán proposal as the original draft for 123.[39] The final product, Article 123, was in fact less extensive than Zubarán Capmany's in some areas. In this light, and given the striking parallels between the 1915 Proyecto and the 1917 Article 123, it is possible to affirm that Carranza and his cronies had prepared for labor reform because the workers' rebellion required that they prepare for it. The mechanism that expressed the need for change was, as Niemeyer phrased it, "a spontaneous demand for the redemption of the Mexican proletariat, an outburst that found poignant expression in debates . . ."[40] Aspiring elites had to support progressive labor institutions as the only road to peace in the factory.

Article 123 contained thirty separate items covering hours and wages, fringe benefits, unions and strikes, and other issues important to Mexican workers.[41] Sections 1 and 2 established the eight-hour day, seven for the night shift. Section 3 set strict limits to the hours of work of minors. Section 4 fixed the seventh day as one of obligatory rest. Section 5, building on Zubarán Capmany's 1915 proposal, extended the paid leave for mothers with newborns to one month, with two half-hour periods when they return to work to breast-feed their babies. Section 6 set up a legal minimum wage. "The minimum wage to be received by a workman shall be that considered sufficient, according to the conditions prevailing in the respective region of the country, to satisfy the normal needs of the life of the workman, his education and his lawful pleasures, considering him as the head of a family."[42] Sections 7 through 11 mandated other aspects of wages. Section 7 required equal pay for equal work, specifically requiring employers to pay women the same as men. Section 9 instituted minimum wage commissions in each municipio, subject to state labor boards.

Sections 12 through 15 mandated housing and health benefits. Section 12 required all businesses employing more than 100 workers to provide comfortable and clean housing for their workers. Section 14 made employers responsible for work-related accidents and illnesses.

Sections 16 through 22 specifically permitted workers to unionize while also allowing owners' associations. Section 18 defined legal strikes as those whose goal was to "achieve the equilibrium between the diverse factors of production." However, strikes were illegal only when the majority of strikers engaged in violence or when workers in military establishments struck during wartime. On the other hand, Section 19 established that owners' lockouts were legal only when an excess of production made it necessary to shut down, and then only with previous approval of the Junta de Conciliación y Arbitraje. The set of clauses was quite illiberal.

Section 20 ordained that "differences or disputes between capital and labor shall be submitted for settlement to a board of conciliation and arbitration to consist of an equal number of representatives of the workmen and of the employers and of one representative of the Government." Section 22 provided that workers fired for joining a union receive three month's salary as compensation. Sections 23–25 dealt with the mutual debts of workers and owners, providing legal protection to workers. Section 25 provided for free employment services.

Section 26 protected Mexican workers who signed labor contracts with foreign owners. Section 27 contained the eight clauses that would make a labor contract null and void, protecting the rights of workers. The last two sections, 29 and 30, provided constitutional provisions for housing, retirement, unemployment, and disability funds.

Many observers have commented that law in general and constitutions in particular have a different meaning in Mexico than in the United States, and not only because of the Hispanic and Napoleonic origins of the Mexican legal system. In the United States, the Constitution establishes fundamental law; in Mexico, it sets fundamental goals. Law in the United States is mostly observed whereas law in Mexico is often ignored. Nonetheless, this does not diminish the role of Article 123 in post-revolutionary Mexico.

First, whatever the defects of law and legislation in post-revolutionary Mexico, the Constitution sets standards that any citizen can claim as just. Article 123 proclaimed to all Mexicans that workers now had rights previously ignored: to organize unions, to strike for better working conditions, to demand a decent standard of living. Before 1917 these rights could not be violated because they didn't exist. Now, even if everybody violated them, they were still fundamental rights of workers according to the ultimate law of the land. The passage from no constitutional rights for workers to many and progressive rights would have been inconceivable if Zubarán Capmany and the Constituyente hadn't observed persistent conflict in the mills and other workplaces. The delegates wrote Article 123 to be a solution to the problem of conflictive workers. In this regard, 123 was a victory for the factory revolt.

Second, Article 123 legitimated workplace standards for Mexican workers. That the standards were not absolute but subject to constant negotiations such as inflation, technological change, and market shifts affecting the economy of industry, did not diminish their importance. It simply meant that the most important constitutional provisions were those concerning the conditions of negotiation rather than specific standards themselves. In this area, 123 ratified what cotton textile workers had won in practice and then in state military decrees, including the right to organize unions, to shut down factories, and to carry out successful strikes. Section 20 formalized what state military commanders had discovered during the civil war: final authority in the factory no longer belonged to the owners. "Differences or disputes between capital and labor shall be submitted for settlement to a board of conciliation and arbitration to consist of an equal number of representatives of the workmen and of the employers and of one representative of the Government."[43] This provision may not have left workers controlling the workplace, but it nonetheless weakened the authority of owners. The 1917 Constitution ratified workers' power to the degree that workers had gained some real power between 1910 and 1917. Once again, law followed practice.

Third, Article 123 established the framework for a new set of labor organizations in Mexico. The law could be ignored but the organizations could not. The constitution provided for worker and employer associations, government inspection and arbitration, and federal, state, and municipal labor bureaucracies. These organizations existed, acted, and constituted a new industrial relations system in the country. For example, in 1918 Puebla governor Alfonso Cabrera decreed state municipal wage commissions with equal representation of owners and workers to carry out the article's mandates on minimum wages and profit sharing.[44]

Although 123 established progressive labor legislation, it was a compromise. Conservative liberals only grudgingly conceded the need to protect labor at all, while radical liberals and Jacobeans were convinced that there could be no social peace in Mexico without legal justice for the working classes.[45] It was an unsatisfactory compromise to many, reflected in the article's notorious lacunae. Mexican constitutional law requires complementary statutory and regulatory law, without which constitutional precepts are a dead letter. Although Carranza had wanted to federalize labor legislation, the Congreso Constituyente left to the states the execution of constitutional mandates through state labor codes. The federal constitution therefore established certain minimum goals/rights for workers but left no practical means for them to be implemented.

Veracruz issued its code in 1918 and it quickly became a model for other state labor laws.[46] To a certain degree, the differences in the state codes— and there were many—came about because workers' challenge to authority varied greatly from region to region, so that state governments felt more or less pressured depending on the depth of the social revolution there. The relative lack of mobility of capital in the early twentieth century compared to today contributed to this pressure.[47]

Veracruz had been the site of Carranza's revolutionary government, violent fighting in the countryside, and sharp conflict between owners and workers in the Orizaba textile industry. It was the perfect place for model state legislation to define the limits of property in the workplace. On January 14, 1918, less than a year after the promulgation of Article 123, Cándido Aguilar issued Decree 52, the Ley del Trabajo del Estado Libre y Soberano de Veracruz-Llave.[48] With eight titles or divisions and 206 articles, it was considerably longer and more detailed than Article 123, from which it received its constitutional mandate.

The law's lengthy and detailed "Title 1" defined the labor contract. Article 21 recognized collective contracts and the right of unions to be signatories to them. Article 22 then limited that right to unions "legally constituted according to this law." Pre-revolutionary Mexico was of course innocent of both collective contracts and legally recognized unions; together, they virtually mandated some form of collective bargaining. Thus, by 1917–18, constitutional and statutory law institutionalized a relatively new form of industrial relations.

Article 33 of the Veracruz code established eleven "common obligations of all owners or in their absence, their administrators or representatives to the workers."[49] These included preferring Mexicans over foreigners; treating workers "with due consideration, abstaining from treating them badly by word or by deed"; providing one-month salary each year as profit sharing; and "listening to workers' complaints about the employees [supervisors] and correcting the problems caused."

Section 7, establishing an extra one-month salary, became noteworthy.

The federal constitution, Article 123, Section 6, instituted profit sharing but left the specific formula to state governments. The Veracruz law translated this mandate into a thirteenth month's salary. This became the famous *aguinaldo*, which Mexican workers still enjoy, paid just before the Christmas holiday.

Article 34 prohibited bosses (*todo patrón, jefe, empleado o maestro de fábricas, talleres y demás establecimientos*) from mistreating workers:[50] The prohibitions included retaining wages for fines, forcing workers to buy items in specific stores (the *tiendas de raya*), demanding or accepting money from workers as payment for allowing them to work, charging interest for wages paid in advance, and forcing workers "through coercion or any other means" to leave the union. It also prohibited the bosses from showing up drunk, carrying arms, or collecting money from workers inside the factories. Lastly, it prohibited "any other action or abuse that might result in prejudicing workers or the freedom of action."

Article 35 covered nine parallel worker obligations, including "behaving well and treating the owner and his representatives with consideration and due respect." It also mandated workers to obey the factory's work rules, which had to be approved by the Junta Central de Conciliación y Arbitraje del Estado.[51]

Articles 33, 34, and 35 represented the overthrow of the old labor regime in Mexican factories. Before Mexico's revolution, owners and their supervisors ran the factories as they wished, subject only to common cultural expectations. The violence of the revolution changed factory operations as workers not only organized unions, but also attacked and sometimes killed recalcitrant bosses without great fear of retribution.[52] Unions, worker violence, and the incapacity of the state to support beleaguered owners changed factories.

The formality of running a factory lay in the reglamento de trabajo, the set of written work rules that established workers' obligations. Before the revolution, owners wrote the reglamentos. The 1912 tripartite convention of the industry introduced some minor limits to owner work rules. However, the deepening violence inside and outside the factories after 1912 brought more worker influence than anybody in Mexico had ever thought possible. By 1918, the Veracruz labor code legalized, formalized, and institutionalized what had happened in practice: the owners were no longer able to command at will. The Veracruz code specifically and strongly endorsed unions and collective contracts, absolutely prohibited companies from firing workers for belonging to unions, forced factories to listen to workers' complaints and to correct wrongs, and unconditionally prohibited companies from physically or verbally mistreating workers. Furthermore, although Article 35 obligated workers to obey factory work rules, it made the factories register the reglamentos with the state government, tantamount to allowing an outside authority (state governments) to intervene in the process. This was not trivial. The set of rules contained in Articles 33, 34, and 35 took away from the owners their absolute dominion over the factory that had prevailed during the Porfiriato. Although it did not directly transfer authority to workers, it did set the state in the middle of the factory through its power to (not) approve work rules.

State legislation backed by constitutional authority mandated new behaviors and work rules in the factory. The law demanded equality, mutual respect, and mutual rights and obligations between workers and owners. Legislation prevented owners from unilaterally exercising control over the work process, inserting state and federal labor offices, unions, and workers in the production process. This was a dramatically new social relationship for Mexican workers, at least on paper. Article 40, Section 4 of the Veracruz code required owners of large industries (more than 100 workers) to have a written *reglamento interior*. Article 41 decreed that the reglamento be drafted by two representatives of the owners and two of the workers, then submitted to the Junta Central de Conciliación y Arbitraje del Estado for approval.[53] Thus, owners of medium and large factories could not even write their own work rules. The law could not be more clear: everybody—owners, workers, and the state—participated in running the factory. This was not socialism, but it was a new limit to the definition of private property rights.

Chapter 9 of Title 1 established the conditions "of the Termination of the Contract." It specified rules for ending the labor contract, effectively limiting the right of owners to fire workers. Most important was Article 96, which stated the only valid reasons for contract termination. Section 1 permitted firing workers when they didn't do the agreed-upon work, "in the judgment of the Boards of Conciliation and Arbitration." Section 2 allowed termination when the workers didn't obey orders, "according to the judgment of the same Boards." Section 5 determined that a worker could be discharged for violating *three times in a month*[54] the *"reglamento interior de la fábrica."* Section 6 allowed owners to discharge workers who damaged their interests "a juicio de las Juntas de Conciliación y Arbitraje." Article 97 prohibited termination for joining a union or participating in a strike.[55] These provisions forced owners to appeal to state labor boards in order to fire workers even if the latter didn't do their work, refused to obey orders, or assaulted supervisors. It specifically permitted workers to violate factory rules twice a month without fear of firing! It protected the unions that assuredly would defend the workers before the state labor boards. It shifted authority in the workplace away from owners and toward unions and state labor boards.

Title 3 implemented the wage aspects of Article 123. Chapter 2 defined the minimum wage as that necessary to "satisfy the normal necessities of the worker's life, individually or considered as the head of a family."[56] Following guidelines laid down by the constitution, it provided for the establishment of Municipal "Comisiones Especiales del Salario Mínimo." With instructions from the Junta Central de Conciliación y Arbitraje del Estado, local commissions would determine the minimum wage in each municipio. Workers (in reality, unions) and owners in each industry sent an equal number of representatives to the comisiones especiales, guaranteeing legal parity.[57]

Title 5, "De los Sindicatos y Federaciones," defined legally constituted unions that could be party to a collective contract. Legality required unions to register with the municipal government and to forward to it the minutes of their initial meeting, the members of the leadership, and a copy of the bylaws. They had to send monthly reports to municipal authorities of the names of workers who entered or left the union. The law prohibited businesses from refusing to work with unions but also prohibited unions from coercing people to join. It further disallowed "in their membership agitators or people that carry out propaganda of subversive ideas."[58]

The law made unions legally powerful but potentially subordinate. The 1918 Veracruz labor code recognized and defended unions but subjected them to requirements that potentially could subordinate them to strong governments. Only legal unions could sign collective contracts and only the state could make a union legal. Furthermore, the state prohibited unions from affiliating with workers who held anti-state ideas, the practical meaning of "*ideas disolventes.*"

Revolutionary practice between 1910 and 1918, and legal changes between 1912 and 1918, took factory discipline away from the owners. Here the workers were victorious. However, although Mexican textile workers were strong enough to weaken owners' control, they lacked the strength to impose workers' control. The new state then took over this middle ground, attempting its own subordination. This was a new subordination, however. Under old law, workers had been subordinate to owners. Under new law, legally defined unions shared power in the workplace with owners and state officials. It was a complex legal arrangement that could not but turn the factory into contested terrain. It was a contested terrain that reflected the true social indefinition of Mexico's revolution, in which no social class, neither in 1920 nor in 1927, had the power to completely implement its own form of property.

Unions (and owners) were not subordinate to an abstract state but to new, concrete institutions. Title Seven established the Juntas Municipales de Conciliación and also the Junta Central de Conciliación y Arbitraje del Estado. The municipal boards were composed of two representatives of the owners, two of the workers, and the Síndico of the Municipio. The state board consisted of three representatives of the owners, three of the workers, and one representative of the state government.[59]

The juntas had the right to approve the reglamentos interiores of the factories as well as rule on conflicts between owners and workers. The municipal boards served the role of conciliation in the first instance. If that failed to resolve a conflict, either party could take the issue to the state board. The state body, the Junta Central, offered arbitration and conciliation. It also interpreted contractual provisions, work rules, and other issues. Arbitration was not subject to the formal rules of Mexican law.[60] In Veracruz, federal and state law had created numerous organizations—municipal, state, federal—to which complaining workers could appeal. What owner would fire an incompetent laborer if a union defended him or her? The cost of various appeals, the time delays, the procedural difficulties, turned the labor world upside down.

By 1917–18, therefore, the institutional and organizational labor relations system was radically different from what had prevailed less than a decade earlier. The federal constitution and state labor codes provided a complex institutional framework that had no Porfirian counterpart.

It is not necessary here to go into detail about the Puebla state labor code, enacted into law on November 14, 1921, by Governor and General José María Sánchez.[61] It was a massive document with 110 pages and 330 articles, demonstrating the complexity of Mexico's post-revolutionary labor institutions. In basic structure and outline, the Puebla law showed the influence of Veracruz.[62] It varied in further strengthening the power of state bureaucracies, removing authority from owners, and amplifying both unions and state control over them. On hiring, the Puebla law introduced a radically new concept, union control, legally creating the union shop and union selection of new candidates.[63] Most of the gains of the Veracruz and Puebla labor codes found their way into the 1931 federal labor law.

In all of this, nothing was more important than the impact of the new labor relations system on the social relationships of the factory. Before the revolution, owners ruled the factory. After the revolution, they did not. Before the revolution, a worker could advance only through increasing his or her skills in the workplace. After the revolution, powerful unions offered a new and better source of social mobility. Before the revolution, the liberal ideal of unfettered property rights determined factory relationships. After the revolution, factory relationships were mediated by layers of new organizations, each with some measure of power and influence. Meanwhile, a complex set of rules ensured that workers could dominate only if they controlled their unions, not easy in the political environment of post-revolutionary Mexico. In 1910, private property rights for industrialists allowed owners to run the factories as they wished. By 1921, constitutional and state law restricted the rights of owners to hire, fire, or discipline workers, and to even write work rules. These were new limits to private property in Mexican industry.

Contracts

A critical component of the liberal concept of private property was the idea of work as an individual matter, one of individual choice and responsibility. Therefore, the labor contract could only be a matter between two individuals acting voluntarily, an owner offering a job and a worker accepting it. A further assault on the old liberalism and its broad definition of property rights came through the replacement of the individual work contract by collective contracts.

In the new labor relations system, the most important role of trade unions was representing workers in their contractual arrangement with owners. Collective contracts changed the social relationships between owners and workers for four reasons. First, these contracts, unlike the individual ones that preceded them, assigned specific payments to specific jobs, with unions determining what workers got what tasks. Second, they permitted unions to participate in formulating work rules, to assign jobs within the factory, and to make decisions previously made by owners. Third, they allowed unions to do what individual workers could never have done, control firing and hiring. Finally, they made workers as a group equal to owners as a group, which workers could enforce through successful strikes.

As with labor law, collective contracts came about because of worker activity in the factory during the revolution. The 1911 general strike in the textile industry forced the Madero government to convene a meeting of the industry. In July 1912, owners, government officials, and labor representatives wrote Mexico's first industry-wide collective contract.

Although the July 1912 agreement survived the revolution, the legal changes from 1917 to 1925 were so severe and had so changed the institutional framework for labor relations in Mexico that another, radically different, contract was called for. In 1925–27, another meeting of the industry wrote a second contract. The two contracts in cotton textiles, 1912 and 1927, set forth the new parameters of Mexico's revolutionary and post-revolutionary industrial relations system, supported by and complementary to the new legal system.

Cotton textile workers had been restive since the late Porfiriato. They took advantage of the dictatorship's collapse to organize labor unions in the mills in late 1910 and early 1911. On December 21, 1911, just weeks after Madero and Jose Pino Suarez took office as the new president and vice president of Mexico, respectively, workers from fifteen Puebla textile factories walked out, in "the first labor action of great importance in the Republic."[64] A week later, Mexico City textile factories shut down as mill hands throughout the country joined the strike, with the notable exception of Orizaba.[65] Even there, however, workers threatened to join the spreading nationwide labor protest.

Newly formed workers' commissions from Puebla and Tlaxcala funneled into Mexico City to lead the growing general strike, joining their counterparts from the capital. Madero now had a problem because he knew he had to resolve the labor conflict in order to gain credibility among the owning classes, yet he lacked the power of Porfirio Díaz to resort to naked repression. Forced to negotiate, he invited textile owners to meet on January 20 with his brother, Gustavo Madero, with his new minister of government, and with the head of the recently established labor department. The workers had proposed a twelve-point program to settle the labor dispute and Madero was interested in negotiating a response.[66]

When they met on the 20th, the government coaxed the owners into signing an accord that reduced the workday to ten hours and increased wages 10 percent across the board. The strike leaders then agreed to go back to work while the owners established a commission to discuss industry problems.[67] All parties agreed that the January 20 settlement was only provisional. Meanwhile, without institutionalized unions or labor laws, textile workers throughout the country had successfully shut down the industry, resisted government pressures, and forced management to concede better work conditions. This was certainly a dramatic contrast with the late Porfiriato, when labor conflict in the Orizaba and Atlixco mills led to the bloody repression in the Rio Blanco mill, the breakup of incipient unions, and the dispersal of labor leaders.

During the month of July 1912, Mexico's most important textile owners met at the first Convención de Industriales. It was in fact a tripartite meeting at which government officials presided and labor leaders intervened, albeit somewhat indirectly.[68] The convention drafted what was labeled at the time the "Reglamento de Fábricas de Hilados y Tejidos en la República."[69] It was actually a national, industry-wide labor contract, not called such at the time because the idea was so new to Mexico that the country lacked an appropriate legal terminology. Of course, it could not be as effective as later industry-wide contracts because contemporary law did not match the changing industrial relations scene. Nonetheless, the reglamento established norms for labor relations in the industry and set standards for hours of work and pay.

New at the business of writing labor contracts, the owners divided the 1912 document in two sections, Reglamento and Tarifa. The reglamento determined work rules, the tarifa, wages. They issued the former on July 17, the latter, August 1. Before this contract, each textile factory had its own set of work rules that formalized the power of owners.[70] Now, there was a government-endorsed set of work rules to which every factory reglamento would have to conform. Although the tarifa was important to workers and owners, the reglamento played an even more significant role in the country's future labor relations system. Whereas the tarifa contributed to income determination, the reglamento subjected labor relations to an industry-wide contract and also established limits to the owners' control of the work process. These initial limits were minimal, but it was the principle that the control of owners was not absolute and could be modified through a contractual mechanism that would affect future property rights.

The reglamento consisted of twenty articles.[71] Article 1 established the ten-hour workday, nine hours for the night shift. It abolished overtime work without extra pay. Overtime became 50 percent higher than regular pay. Article 2 permitted factory administrators to set shift times, but within strict limits. Article 3 stated that "during work hours, each worker will stay in his place in his department, without distracting his attention on matters foreign to his obligations and will not go to another department unless his work requires it, nor will he interrupt the attention of other workers for any reason." It also prohibited dues collections inside the factory.

Articles 4, 5, and 6 established workers' responsibilities for taking care of machinery, for being responsible for damages, and for working the entire week. Article 7 permitted workers to present their complaints in writing to the administrator, outside of work hours. The worker had to continue working while the complaint was pending, but the administrator had to provide a resolution within ten days. Article 8 assured that only workers and their families could occupy factory houses.

Article 9 prohibited the bosses from mistreating "the workers by word or by deed; to demand or accept money from them in exchange for work, or for any other reason. It is also prohibited for them to lend money at interest, or any similar abuse, under penalty of expulsion of both." Meanwhile, Article 10 prohibited workers from going to work drunk. Also, "equally prohibited is smoking inside the factory, bringing matches, flammable materials, newspapers, alcoholic beverages, or carrying arms or any other object that might cause distractions. Workers will leave their hats and coats in the place designated for them, and can only enter the departments with small caps." Article 11 stated that "acts of disobedience, insubordination, and lack of respect toward the administrator, employees, and other bosses, noisy demonstrations, and ineptitude, will cause the rescinding of one's work contract and the separation of the worker, without the necessity of a resolution by any authority." Although Article 12 reduced the indemnity (fines) for defective products, it still maintained a system of fines.

Article 13 established Sunday and holiday rest. The holidays included January 1 and 6, February 5, March 21, Thursday, Friday, and Saturday of Holy Week, May 5, June 29, September 16, November 1 and 2, December 12 and 25, and "*el día de la fiesta local del patrón de la fábrica.*"

In an important step, Article 14 declared that the reglamento constituted a contract between worker and owner. In cases not covered by this contract, Article 15 allowed either party to rescind the contractual relationship with eight days notice. Article 20 established that this contract replaced all previous ones, and that it would be placed in a visible spot in the factories.

Article 16 prohibited children under fourteen from working in the factory. Article 17 prohibited commercial monopolies and mandated payments and loans to workers in cash. Article 18 made the owners responsible for educational expenses and free medical care to workers for work accidents. Article 19 provided that peons or special workers would transport heavy materials rather than the regular workers.

To what degree was the new contract a radical break with the past? Compared to the industry's future contracts, the twenty articles appear to cover a bare minimum of issues. More important than the number of issues was the lack of an enforcement mechanism other than the government's ability to impose a tax on recalcitrant mills. Furthermore, the contract never mentioned unions. Discipline was left to the owners, "without the necessity of resolution by any authority. . . ."[72] Workers were not only prohibited from disobeying orders, but also from "lacking respect for the administrator, the employees, and other bosses."[73] Although wages increased and hours of work decreased, not an insignificant victory for mill hands, owners ran the factory and workers were to do only what they were told.

Certain principles were established, however, that represented a significant break with the past. First, the reglamento not only constrained the behavior of workers, it formally constrained the behavior of supervisors. Article 9 prohibited them from mistreating workers "by word and by deed."[74] Second, Article 5 introduced the concept of parity in contract enforcement through the establishment of a tribunal in which the three representatives of the workers had the same vote as the two representatives of the owners.[75] Lastly, Article 14 virtually declared the new reglamento a kind of collective contract, specifically mentioning the term *contract*: "The labor contract between industrialists and workers will be ruled by the prescriptions of this Reglamento, which is understood to be accepted by the workers upon entering the factory, and not following the preceding articles will constitute cause to end the contract."[76]

The 1912 reglamento was thus Mexico's first industry-wide collective contract. It contained more protections for laborers than had existed in the past. The formalization of rules somewhat rationalized the situation of workers previously dependent on the opinions of bosses. Prior to the reglamento, bosses prevailed over workers. After the reglamento, workers' opinions counted. This was a radical change in the institutional labor relations system that came well before the 1917 Constitution, but after and because of a successful general strike of textile workers. Minister of development Rafael Hernández recognized that the workers had forced a change in the labor relations system:

> Due to the recent political movements in the Republic, there have also been some movements of a social character. Strikes have followed strikes and the Government, worried about this state of things and desirous of finding a solution, agreed to convene this meeting [July 1912] with the object of discussing the general basis of a labor bylaw in the Republic, that the Government proposes to elevate to the category of Law, presenting such to the Federal Legislature.[77]

Madero's minister of development thus admitted that the convention and contract were a direct result of the workers' strike movement. It is interesting to note that despite the many and violent changes in Mexico's governments from 1911 to 1939, every president came to pursue the same solution to the worker problem: tripartite conventions leading to industry-wide collective contracts.[78] It became part of Mexico's labor regime.

The 1912 contract did not solve Mexico's labor problem. The revolution continued. In labor affairs, workers became more, not less, radical, necessitating the changes in Mexican law described above. By 1925, a new federal constitution and state labor codes had dramatically altered the institutional landscape in Mexico. Powerful unions and union leaders exercised control unheard of in pre-revolutionary Mexico. Meanwhile, the textile industry operated under a contract that had been revolutionary in 1912 but that had since been overtaken by social and legal events.

When textile industrialists wrote the country's first collective contract in 1912, there was no labor legislation, only a miniscule federal bureaucracy, and no formal participation of unions in factory life in Mexico. When, on October 6, 1925, Luis N. Morones opened the Convención Industrial y Obrera del Ramo Textil to rewrite the contract, Mexico had a radically different and institutionalized labor relations system. To begin with, Morones himself was the national leader of the Confederación Regional Obrera Mexicana, Mexico's largest labor confederation, and also of the Secretaría de Industria, Comercio y Trabajo, the federal government's agency for regulating labor and industrial affairs. He also headed a powerful political party, the Partido Laboral Mexicano, that got out the vote for his allies, Alvaro Obregón and Plutarco Elías Calles. Meanwhile, federal and state laws mandated regulation not only of the workers' rights and protections, but also of large and growing federal and state labor bureaucracies. The legislation, the regulatory agencies, the bureaucrats, and the lawyers institutionalized not only the existence of unions but also their participation in running the workplace, from discipline to hiring and firing. With a relatively stable government in power in Mexico City and with unions stronger than ever in the textile industry, the old contract was simply outmoded.[79] It was a contract that didn't fit the law or the new social reality of modern Mexico.

The textile convention met until March 18, 1927.[80] The 1912 reglamento was only four pages and twenty articles. The published 1927 contract covered 256 pages, 116 basic articles (there were hundreds more job-specific or miscellaneous articles), and specific rules for an industry-wide system of "comisiones mixtas" for dispute resolution.[81] In the 1912 contract, management and individual workers were the relevant parties. In the 1927 contract, Article 2 stated that "the parties to this Collective Labor Agreement are the owners and the workers' unions."[82] Between the two contracts was more than just fifteen chronological years; there was also a social revolution that cost the country between 5 and 10 percent of the population, a violent alteration of social relations in cotton textile factories, and a completely new legal system in labor affairs. Between them, also, were the emergence of sustained working-class militancy and a radical if corrupt unionization of Mexico's largest industries. The new contract contained within it all the social and legal changes of Mexico's work world between 1912 and 1927, which is to say, a social revolution.

Chapter 1 of the 1927 contract, "Del contrato de trabajo," contained eleven articles, the first of which provided definitions of workers, owners, and unions; made unions the legal party to the contract; and determined that the contract covered the entire industry: "Todos los contratos de trabajo en la industria textil se regirán por las estipulaciones de esta Convención Colectiva de Trabajo."[83] Chapter 2, "De la admisión de trabajadores," ratified the fundamental change in Mexico's labor relations system. In the old world, owners hired and fired at will. In the new one, unions hired and prevented owners from firing. The 1912 contract did not mention any of this because it didn't need to; it was not something that workers should concern themselves with. In 1927, the entire Chapter 2 was about hiring; its first and lengthy article, 12, stated:

> Any worker who desires to join a factory must solicit his entrance himself or by means of the union representative in the factory. The request will be resolved by mutual agreement between the owner or his representative and the union representative. . . . the worker will present to the administration the proof that he has entered into the respective union, and cannot be definitively admitted to the factory, although the other requirements are completed, if he doesn't present this proof. . . .[84]

In short, unions hired and nobody could be hired without the union or outside the union. The contract also placed great emphasis on seniority in advancement. Article 20 established a *"cuerpo calificador"* in which union representatives participated with supervisors in judging the job qualifications of applicants. In 1912, Article 3 absolutely prohibited collecting dues of any sort, including union dues, inside the factory. In 1927, Article 57 prohibited collecting dues except union dues, which now could be collected in the factory at pay time.[85] This was nothing less than a complete reversal of the owners' previous position against unions; with this clause, the owners gave up their anti-union fight.

Hiring is linked to firing and both are tied to labor discipline, or control over the workplace. The 1927 contract had much to say about discipline in the factory. In 1912, the contract had marginally advanced the interests of workers with respect to the owner-dominated labor relations system. It prohibited supervisors from mistreating workers. The 1927 contract obligated the owners (and their representatives) to treat workers with "justice, equity and humanity."

In 1912, Article 5 made workers responsible for damages they caused, but also established a bipartite commission to oversee the process, "a board consisting of two people named by the factory Administrator and three workers named by the interested party," with each side given one vote.[86] Although the 1912 contract gave an individual worker the right to complain to the factory administrator, he did it alone, while the administrator decided alone. Furthermore, according to Article 11 of the 1912 contract, any act of disobedience, insubordination, or lack of respect to the administrator or any supervisor was just cause for immediate firing "sin necesidad de resolución de autoridad alguna."[87] With these clauses, the 1912 contract gave complete control over discipline and therefore over the factory to the administration.

The 1927 contract contained an entire chapter on sanctions. Chapter 4, Article 78, declared that the first time a worker committed a violation of the contract or work rule, the factory had to ask the union to discipline him. The second time a fault was committed, Article 79 permitted the factory to suspend the worker for a week, while Article 80 allowed the factory to fire a worker for a third violation within 120 days or for other grievous acts. However, Article 81 did not allow the sanctions of Article 80 to take effect without the Comisión Mixta de Distrito.[88] Chapter 6 established the comisión, comprised of three representatives of the owners and three of the unions. If the Comisión Mixta de Distrito could not resolve the problem to the satisfaction of both parties, there remained the Comisión Mixta Nacional, which also had three labor and three owner representatives. If the Comisión Mixta Nacional could not provide a solution, then each side could go to court.[89] Thus, if a union chose to defend a worker accused of violating the contract or disobeying an order, the procedure to fire was long, complex, and costly for the company, without any guarantee of success. This made it legally very difficult to discipline a worker without the consent of the union. In fact, it was impossible, because once the dispute left the contractually provided system of comisiones mixtas, both parties entered federal or state labor bureaucracies of layered tripartite commissions, after which there were also state and federal courts. What rational businessperson would incur such costs just to fire an underperforming worker?

The contract contained a major section on bipartite commissions that would interpret and enforce the contract.[90] Article 5 of the section established the Comisiones Mixtas de Fábricas, with the union and the company having equal representation. Article 6 gave the comisiones mixtas the authority to interpret and apply all work rules and wage scales. If either party disagreed with a ruling, or if the two sides on the comisión mixta could not come to agreement, then the matter passed to the Comisión Mixta de Distrito. If this commission failed to resolve a conflict, the matter passed to the Comisión Mixta Nacional. In effect, no company could impose a work rule or procedure without consent of the union.

The contract set a forty-eight-hour work week and twelve paid holidays along with a week's paid vacation. It established that each factory would provide benefits according to either the now-generous state labor codes, or, in their absence, the federal constitution. The approximately 160 pages outlining wages were quite detailed, necessary in an industry in which most skilled labor was paid by piece rate rather than hourly (as in the United States) or daily (as in other Mexican industries). The wage scale was so detailed and complex that it guaranteed that textile unions would play a critical role in carrying out the contract because the unions had a membership of skilled (and unskilled) workers whose accumulation of knowledge was required to interpret payment, which was a function of not only job category but also type of machine and cloth employed.

In fact, the most outstanding element of the contract is that it made unions a partner in the industry. Unions hired and in effect, unions fired. In practice, unions controlled discipline in the workplace. Unions interpreted work rules and one of the longest and most complex wage scales in Mexican industrial history. Unions determined job advancement. Unions were equal representatives in the three-layered system of comisiones mixtas, which interpreted and applied the contract and its provisions.

Conclusion

When conflict broke out in the cotton textile industry in 1907, there were neither permanent unions nor collective contracts in Mexico. Owners ran the factories without the interference of government or workers. In the country's incipient industrial world, at least, the old liberal ideal of free markets and individual contractual relations held true.

Following a general strike in 1911, textile owners wrote an industry-wide labor contract. When that proved insufficient, military commanders decreed labor reforms that strengthened unions, increased wages, and cut hours of work. In 1917, a constitutional convention promulgated a new federal constitution that incorporated many of the early military decrees. Following the constitution, state governments implemented statutory and regulatory legislation for labor. The legal changes culminated in a new industry-wide contract in 1927.

The difference in the institutional framework for labor affairs between 1910 and 1927 was dramatic, indeed revolutionary. In 1910, there were no permanent unions, no collective contracts, no body of labor legislation, no federal and state labor bureaucracies, and no labor courts. Factory owners hired and fired at will, controlled discipline in the factories, and determined working conditions according to the market and habits of paternalism. In 1927, unions were permanent and all textile factories governed their labor relations by an industry-wide collective contract. The country enjoyed a huge body of labor legislation at the federal and state levels. Federal and state labor departments and federal and state labor boards actively intervened in the labor relations system. The new textile contract added a further layer of bureaucracy with factory, state, and federal comisiones mixtas. Law and contract transferred from owners to unions both hiring and firing. Supervisors could run factories only through the acquiescence of unions. The industry-wide contract specified the conditions of work. Paternalism rested with the union bosses rather than the factory owners.

Private property is never an absolute. The change in Mexican labor law and contracts severely constrained the rights of property holders in Mexico. The owners of factories lost the rights to hire, fire, discipline, and set work rules. In cotton textiles, property alone no longer controlled workers or the work process. The Mexican Revolution redefined property rights and authority in Mexican industry. Revolutionary law and collective contracts in cotton textiles took away from owners what they enjoyed before the revolution—absolute control over factory life. Before the revolution, private property rights ensured the control of owners over the work process. After the revolution, private property rights only allowed owners to enter into the contested terrain of constant and sometimes dangerous negotiation.

Notes

I would like to thank Stephen Haber, Gregory Swedberg, and Mary Yeager for critical comments on earlier drafts of this chapter.

1. North 1990: 33.
2. Hill 1982: 259.
3. Gordon, Edwards, and Reich 1982: 25.
4. North 1990: 28.

5. In a brilliant discussion, Gilly is one of the few to link property rights to rebellion from below, although in reference to Zapata's Plan de Ayala. Gilly 1971: 61–66.

6. Walker 1981: 282.

7. Koth 1993: 49.

8. A copy of the labor decree is in AGN, Gobernación-legagos, box 817, file 1, Correspondencia Particular del Ministro de Gobernación, n.d.; an English translation can be found in Koth 1993: 57–58.

9. Gamboa Ojeda 1991: 153.

10. Hart 1987: 98.

11. Salazar 1974: 16.

12. Salazar 1974: 16.

13. AGN, Gobernación-legagos, box 817, file 1, Correspondencia Particular del Ministro de Gobernación, n.d.

14. Article 5 reads, "podran separarse del trabajo," AGN, Gobernación-legagos, box 817, file 1, Correspondencia Particular del Ministro de Gobernación, n.d.

15. AGN, Gobernación-legagos, box 817, file 1, Correspondencia Particular del Ministro de Gobernación, n.d.

16. AGN, Gobernación-legagos, box 817, file 1, Correspondencia Particular del Ministro de Gobernación, n.d.; Salazar 1974: 18.

17. Bortz 1997: 253–88.

18. In 1911, the major mills in the textile zones unionized. After 1913, and particularly during the difficult economic years 1914–16, the strength of unions ebbed and flowed. The critical point, however, is not only that unionization of the large mills was never defeated, but by 1920 they were virtually union shops. A later government publication affirmed that "the labor contract makes workers organized in unions even stronger." Departamento de la Estadística Nacional 1924: 15.

19. The larger mills were mostly male, with women relegated to smaller mills and associated industries like sewing.

20. "Proyecto de Ley," *Boletín del Departamento del Trabajo*, vol. 1, no. 1, July 1913: 17.

21. "Iniciativa al Congreso de la Unión para fundar el Departamento del Trabajo," *Boletín del Departamento del Trabajo*, vol. 1, no. 1, July 1913: 17, 18.

22. *El Imparcial*, December 23, 1911: 1.

23. *El Demócrata*, May 8, 1917: 1.

24. Luis F. Domínguez et al., "Decreto Relativo al Proletariado Rural," September 19, 1914. A copy is in AGN, Departamento del Trabajo (hereafter DT), box 88, file 18.

25. Gertrudis G. Sánchez, "Que deseando . . ." October 28, 1914, Articles 1 and 2, in AGN, DT, box 50, file 29.

26. Gertrudis G. Sánchez, "Que deseando . . ."

27. Cándido Aguilar, *Número 11*, October 19, 1914, in AGN, DT, box 88, file 19.

28. Lombardo Toledano 1926: 53.

29. Venustiano Carranza, "Decreto de Aumento de Jornales a los Obreros de la Industria Textil," March 22, 1915, in AGN, DT, box 50, file 29.

30. All of the contract articles are from Zubáran Capmany 1915.

31. Zubáran Capmany 1915: 5.

32. Niemeyer 1974: 23.

33. Hart 1987: 328.

34. There is a relatively large literature on the Congreso Constituyente, the Congress that drafted the constitution, and also a large legal literature on Mexican constitutional law. On the Constituyente, see Niemeyer 1974. Typical of the legal literature is Castorena 1984. The best guide, though somewhat dated now, is Clagett and Valderrama 1973.

35. Lombardo declared that it was a "desarrollo fiel del principio filosófico de la Revolución francesa." Lombardo Toledano 1926: 13.

36. Forrest 1995: 86.

37. Branch 1926: 3.

38. "The only major changes he [Carranza] proposed to the 1857 constitution were to strengthen the presidency, weaken Congress and state governments, and authorize a central bank." Womack 1991: 176. Marjorie Ruth Clark noted that Carranza's original constitutional proposal was quite conservative and without an extensive labor code, Clark 1934: 48–49. Ruíz claimed that Carranza and his subordinates bowed before the majority on labor reform. Ruíz 1976: 69. This position is supported by Pastor Rouaix, who then notes that labor reform resulted from "el impulso incontenible de las masas populares," who had been demanding legal action in the Cámara de Diputados since 1913. Rouaix 1959: 14–16.

39. Villaseñor 1988: 340; Niemeyer 1974: 114–16.

40. Niemeyer 1974: 23.

41. I have used for this section *Constitución Política de los Estados Unidos Mexicanos, firmada el 31 de enero de 1917 y promulgada el 5 de febrero del mismo año* 1917.

42. Branch 1926: 98. This section is so close to what Zubáran Capmany wrote in 1915 as to make it implausible, as some have asserted, that Article 123 was forced on a reluctant Carranza by more progressive generals. Clearly Carranza and his followers were conservatives not prone to favor workers, but just as clearly they understood the social conflicts of the country and realized the kinds of compromises necessary to allow them to stay in power.

43. Branch 1926: 101.

44. Alfonso Cabrera, "Ley," March 7, 1918, in Disposiciones Generales 1918, AGMP.

45. The civil war of the 1850s resulted in the permanent victory of liberalism. In 1910, liberalism was challenged but finally emerged triumphant though profoundly altered. Rubén Martí, a thirty-eight-year-old Constituyente and military officer from Mexico state to the commission debating Article 123, wrote that "los principales miembros de la comisión son individuos eminentemente liberales . . ." cited in Palavicini 1938: 288.

46. Clark 1934: 53; and Lombardo Toledano 1926: 84, who commented that Veracruz's legislation "sirvio de modelo a otras . . ." Veracruz was one of the first to implement a labor code, although the Yucatan and Campeche issued theirs in July and December 1917. *Código del Trabajo del Estado de Yucatán, Decreto num 722* 1917; *Código del Trabajo Expedido por el XXVI Congreso Constitucional del Estado de Campeche* 1918: 27.

47. Ruíz asserted that "the states passed labor laws, some more advanced than the national legislation, but other states adopted conservative measures. Confronted with restrictive legislation in one state, business moved to another less restrictive." Ruíz 1976: 69. There is little evidence that industries with high fixed costs, like cotton textiles, moved factories to avoid labor legislation. On industries with high fixed costs, see Haber 1991.

48. *Ley del Trabajo del Estado Libre y Soberano de Veracruz-Llave* 1918.

49. *Ley del Trabajo* 1918: 58.

50. *Ley del Trabajo* 1918: 59.

51. *Ley del Trabajo* 1918: 60.

52. Bortz 1997: 253–88.

53. *Ley del Trabajo* 1918: 62.

54. Emphasis mine.

55. *Ley del Trabajo* 1918: 78–79.

56. *Ley del Trabajo* 1918: 83.

57. *Ley del Trabajo* 1918: 83–84.

58. *Ley del Trabajo* 1918: 88–90.

59. *Ley del Trabajo* 1918: 93–95.

60. "La Junta Central, ejerciendo el arbitraje, es un tribunal de equidad y de justicia, no sujeto a los formulismos procesales ni a las tramitaciones largas y difíciles del derecho comun." *Ley del Trabajo del Estado Libre y Soberano de Veracruz-Llave* 1918: 46.

61. I have used the published and dedicated edition of December 1921, *Código de Trabajo* 1921. There is also the November 1921 version in state of Puebla, *Periódico Oficial*.

62. For example, the code notes that on profit sharing, it was necessary "tomar experiencia de los acontecimientos surgidos en el Estado de Veracruz." *Código de Trabajo* 1921: x.

63. *Código de Trabajo* 1921: 36.

64. *El Imparcial*, January 21, 1912. For other interpretations of the strike,

see Ramírez Rancaño 1987: 39–42; Carr 1991: 50; Hart 1987: chap. 8;
Ramos-Escandon 1981.

65. *El Imparcial*, December 28, 1911: 1.

66. *El Imparcial*, January 16, 1912: 6.

67. *El Imparcial*, January 21, 1912: 1, 10.

68. On a history of the industry-wide tripartite meetings in Mexico, see
Bortz 1995: 43–69. Labor leaders did not participate directly in the meetings.
They were in the hallways, offering opinions on the most important matters.
See, for example, Sesión, July 15, 1912, 5, AGN, DT, box 15, file 18.

69. Adalberto A. Esteva, "Labor del Departamento del Trabajo," *Boletín del
Departamento del Trabajo*, vol. 1, no. 1, July 1913, 3.

70. This does not ignore that custom and culture influenced the work process and that workers could sometimes advance their interests through daily
interactions in the factory. Nonetheless, legally and in fact, owners ran things.

71. Contrato de Trabajo, AGN, DT, box 978, file 3.

72. Article 11, "Reglamento para las fábricas de hilados y tejidos en la República, aprobado por la Convención de Industriales reunida en la ciudad de
México en el mes de julio de 1912, aceptado por el Comité Central de Obreros," *Boletín del Departamento del Trabajo*, vol. 1, no. 7, January 1914: 622.

73. Article 11, "Reglamento."

74. Article 9, "Reglamento."

75. Article 5, "Reglamento."

76. Article 14,"Reglamento."

77. "Como se estableció la tarifa mínima de salarios para los obreros de hilados y tejidos de algodón," *Boletín del Departamento del Trabajo*, vol. 1, no. 1,
July 1913: 21.

78. Bortz 1995: 43–69.

79. Not only was it outmoded with regard to the relations between workers and owners, but it no longer reflected the growing conflict between the
owners of large and small mills. See the chapter by Gomez-Galvarriato in this
volume (Chapter 9) and also Bortz 1995.

80. The lengthy meeting indicated the difficulty of "harmonizing" many
disparate interests, not just workers and owners, but various worker groups
against each other and the two principal owning groups that were at conflict.
See Bortz 1995: 43–69.

81. Secretaría de Industria, Comercio y Trabajo 1927.

82. Secretaría 1927: 41.

83. Secretaría 1927: 41.

84. Secretaría 1927: 43.

85. Secretaría 1927: 50.

86. "Reglamento para las fábricas," *Boletín del Departamento del Trabajo*, vol.
1, no. 7, January 1914: 621.

87. "Reglamento para las fábricas," *Boletín del Departamento del Trabajo*, vol. 1, no. 7, January 1914: 622.
88. Secretaría 1927: 53–55.
89. Secretaría 1927: 56–58.
90. Secretaría 1927: 63–75.

References

[AGMP] Archivo General del Municipio de Puebla. Mexico City.
[AGN] Archivo General de la Nación. Mexico City.
Boletín del Departamento del Trabajo. Various issues.
Bortz, Jeffrey. 1995. "The Genesis of Mexico's Modern Labor Regime: The 1937–1939 Cotton Textile Convention." *The Americas*, vol. 52, no. 1: 43–69.
———. 1997. "'Without Any More Law Than Their Own Caprice': Cotton Textile Workers and the Challenge to Factory Authority During the Mexican Revolution." *International Review of Social History*, vol. 42, no. 2: 253–88.
Branch, H. N. 1926. *The Mexican Constitution of 1917 Compared with the Constitution of 1857*. Washington, D.C.
Carr, Barry. 1991. *El movimiento obrero y la política en Mexico 1910–1929*. Mexico City.
Castorena, J. Jésus. 1984. *Manual de derecho obrero*. Mexico City.
Clagett, Helen L., and David M. Valderrama. 1973. *A Revised Guide to the Law and Legal Literature of Mexico*. Washington, D.C.
Clark, Marjory Ruth. 1934. *Organized labor in Mexico*. Chapel Hill.
Código de Trabajo. 1921. Puebla.
Código del Trabajo del Estado de Yucatán, Decreto num 722. 1917. Merida.
Código del Trabajo Expedido por el XXVI Congreso Constitucional del Estado de Campeche. 1918. Campeche.
Constitución Política de los Estados Unidos Mexicanos, firmada el 31 de enero de 1917 y promulgada el 5 de febrero del mismo año. Mexico City.
El Demócrata. Various issues. Mexico City.
Departamento de la Estadística Nacional. 1924. *La Estadística del Trabajo*. Mexico City.
Forrest, Alan. 1995. *The French Revolution*. Oxford.
Gamboa Ojeda, Leticia. 1991. "La huelga textil de 1906–1907 en Atlixco." *Historia Mexicana*, vol. 41, no. 1.
Gilly, Adolfo. 1971. *La revolución interrumpida*. Mexico.
Gordon, David, Richard Edwards, and Michael Reich. 1982. *Segmented Work, Divided Workers, the Historical Transformation of Labor in the United States*. Cambridge, England.

Haber, Stephen. 1991. "Industrial Concentration and Capital Markets: A Comparative History of Mexico, Brazil, and the United States." *Journal of Economic History*, vol. 51, no. 3.

Hart, John M. 1978. *Anarchism and the Mexican Working Class, 1860–1931*. Austin.

————. 1987. *Revolutionary Mexico*. Berkeley.

Hill, Stephen. 1982. *Competition and Control at Work*. London.

El Imparcial. Various issues. Mexico City.

Koth, Karl B. 1993. "Not a Mutiny but a Revolution: The Rio Blanco Labour Dispute, 1906–1907." *Canadian Journal of Latin American and Caribbean Studies*, vol. 18, no. 35.

Ley del Trabajo del Estado Libre y Soberano de Veracruz-Llave. 1918. Orizaba.

Lombardo Toledano, Vicente. 1926. *La libertad sindical en México*. Mexico City.

Niemeyer, E. V. Jr. 1974. *Revolution at Querétaro: The Mexican Constitutional Convention of 1916–1917*. Austin.

North, Douglass C. 1990. *Institutions, Institutional Change and Economic Performance*. Cambridge, England.

Palavicini, Felix F. 1938. *Historia de la Constitución de 1917*. Mexico City.

Ramírez Rancaño, Mario. 1987. *Burguesía textil y política en la revolución mexicana*. Mexico City.

Ramos-Escandon, Carmen. 1981. "Working Class Formation and the Mexican Textile Industry: 1880–1912." Ph.D. diss., SUNY-Stony Brook.

Rouaix, Pastor. 1959. *Genesis de los Artículos 27 y 123 de la Constitución Política de 1917*. Mexico City.

Ruíz, Ramón. 1976. *Labor and the Ambivalent Revolutionaries in Mexico, 1911–1923*. Baltimore.

Salazar, Rosendo. 1974. *Las pugnas de la Gleba*. Mexico City.

Secretaría de Industria, Comercio y Trabajo. 1927. *Convención Colectiva de Trabajo y Tarifas Mínimas de Aplicación en la República, para las Fábricas de Hilados y Tejidos de Algodón, Estampados, Lana, Bonetería, Yute, y Trabajos Similares*. Mexico City.

Villaseñor, José. 1988. "Entre la política y la reivindicación." In Juan Felipe Leal and José Villaseñor, eds., *La clase obrera en la historia de México en la Revolución 1910–1917*. Mexico.

Walker, David W. 1981. "Porfirian Labor Politics: Working Class Organization in Mexico City and Porfirio Díaz, 1876–1902." *The Americas*, vol. 38, no. 3.

Womack, John Jr. 1991. "The Mexican Revolution, 1910–1920." In Leslie Bethell, ed., *Mexico Since Independence*, pp. 125–200. New York.

Zubarán Capmany, Rafael. 1915. *Proyecto de Ley sobre Contrato de Trabajo*. Veracruz.

Chapter 9

Measuring the Impact of Institutional Change in Capital-Labor Relations in the Mexican Textile Industry, 1900–1930

AURORA GÓMEZ-GALVARRIATO

When looking at the consequences of the Mexican Revolution from the perspective of the Orizaba textile mills, it is clear that its major impact was a substantial transformation in the relative power of workers and employers in determining working conditions, to the benefit of the former. From a laissez-faire regime, where employers dealt with an unorganized labor force and wages were determined solely by the forces of supply and demand, existent by 1900, we see in 1925 a totally different situation. Workers were now organized in powerful unions with an important role in the way work was done on the shop floor. Labor was now hired through collective contracts negotiated between unions and employers, and it was now unions, rather than employers, who made the major hiring and firing decisions among blue-collar workers. The government, previously totally supportive of employers, became now, at the least, divided between the interests of employers and workers, and in many crucial turning points it gave decisive support to labor at the expense of company owners.

In this chapter I will analyze the impact of such institutional changes in terms of real wages and productivity levels of textile workers at the Santa Rosa mill in Orizaba. I will also look at these issues from a national perspective in order to see how Santa Rosa's experience compares with that of Mexican textile mills in general.

Changing Labor Relations

The transformation of the labor regime was not a result of a revolutionary program. The Mexican Revolution was not conducted by a single group with a defined ideology and set of goals. Thus, institutional changes in labor relations, as in most other transformations the revolution brought about, were not a planned result of some revolutionary entity that was pursuing some objectives it had previously defined. They came as an unplanned by-product of the revolution. After the fall of Díaz in 1911, Mexican governments became weaker and weaker until 1916, when Carranza began to gradually rebuild the government's strength, but it was not until the 1930s that we can talk of a government as strong as that of Díaz, and then it was set over the support of a very different array of political groups.

As I see it from the study of the Orizaba textile industry, the transformation in the labor regime came as a result of the combination of (1) weaker governments that opened space for the labor movement to organize and act and (2) the need of those groups seeking to establish themselves as governments to co-opt the labor movement, whose support had become necessary to reestablish peace.[1]

"Capitalists continually 'vote' for allocation of societal resources as they decide to invest or not, to employ or dismiss labor, to purchase state obligations, to export or import. By contrast, workers can process their claims only collectively and only indirectly, through organizations which are embedded in systems of representation, principally trade-unions and political parties."[2] As Mexican workers organized, they acquired the possibility of processing their claims and counting as political actors. Policies—and the state itself—expressed, as a consequence of a stronger labor organization, a new compromise between the interests of capitalists and organized workers.

Traditional historiography identifies Article 123 of the Constitution of 1917 as the major turning point in labor relations and working conditions for industrial workers. It was, in fact, one of the most progressive legal codes of its time, granting the right to strike, legalizing trade unions, forbidding child labor, establishing pregnancy leaves, setting the daily shift to a maximum of eight hours, establishing employers' responsibility regarding workers' injuries and diseases, and legalizing collective contracts. Yet, in the case of the industrial workers of Veracruz, and perhaps also to different degrees in some other states such as Puebla, Tlaxcala, the State of Mexico, and Mexico City, this code only crystallized gains that had already been obtained in the previous decade. In those areas where the labor movement was strong, Article 123 basically only gave legal support to an already existent situation.

In those regions where there was no strong labor movement to force compliance with the precepts of Article 123, the code rested for decades as an ideal very far from daily practice.

In the Orizaba valley the labor movement grew stronger as a consequence of the revolution, although it was by no means a product of the revolution. Textile workers from the Orizaba mills began to organize and change their working conditions many years before Porfirio Díaz was deposed. The many letters sent by workers to *El Paladín*, a radical newspaper from Mexico City, in which they severely complained about the unfair labor practices in the textile mills, are the best testimony of this thesis.[3] Furthermore, by 1906 they had built a very powerful trade union, the Gran Liga de Obreros Libres (CGOL), which in a very short time had branch organizations in the states of Jalisco, Oaxaca, Tlaxcala, Mexico, the Federal District, Querétaro, and Hidalgo, in addition to Veracruz and Puebla, the two states in which the movement began.[4]

The government and the textile companies felt so threatened by the CGOL that they opposed with all available force the first general strike it supported. This strike broke in Puebla in November 1906 against new factory regulations established by the new Centro Industrial Mexicano. It was not the first strike to take place in the textile mills. However, it was the first general strike in which a network of support channeled funds to strikers, which strengthened them substantially. Textile companies decided, with the support of the government, to do a general lockout in textile mills throughout the country in order to keep fellow workers in the CGOL from supporting the Puebla strikers.[5] The massacre of Río Blanco in January 1907 was an unforeseen consequence of this policy. After several weeks without pay, workers rioted, looting the region's stores. Federal troops crushed them.

The CGOL was disbanded and its major leaders arrested, but workers, at least in the Orizaba valley, stayed organized. In May 1907 workers from the Compañía Industrial de Orizaba went on strike in order to reduce their working hours, and in August 1910 Santa Rosa workers followed suit. They won, and the shift was cut from twelve to eleven hours. This was the first of a series of reductions in work hours that took place in the following years (see Table 9.1). After January 1907 company stores in the region stopped operating as they previously had. First the commission charged by the mills to the stores on workers' purchases was eliminated, and by 1908 companies had ended the practice of deducting workers' debts to the stores directly from their wages.[6] Furthermore, in the aftermath of the January 1907 massacre, mill hands in the Orizaba valley received a 10 percent wage increase and the detested fines were stopped.[7]

Table 9.1

Workday Changes in CIVSA and CIDOSA: 1900–1917

HOURS				
From	To	CIDOSA	CIVSA	Cause
12	11	June 17, 1907	August 1910	Strikes: CIDOSA, May 2–23 1907 and May 30–June 7, 1907; CIVSA, August 10–16, 1910
11	10	January 22, 1912	September 1, 1912	General strike, January 1–19, 1912. Agreement between workers, employers, and the Department of Labor, January 20, 1912. In CIVSA, implementation of the new working schedule came after a strike, July 3–22, 1912.
10	9	August 19, 1915	August 24, 1915	Decree no. 11 of governor of Veracruz, Cándido Aguilar, October 19, 1914. Put in practice a year later, after workers' demands.
9	8	May 1, 1917	May 1, 1917	Article 123 of the constitution, February 5, 1915. Put in practice after negotiations between companies and unions.

SOURCE: CIVSA and CIDOSA documents.

During the Porfiriato, levying monetary penalties upon workers who mis-behaved was a regular practice used to impose discipline on the shop floor. Workers considered them arbitrary and unfair. "It seems that a private tri-bunal has been established" in the mill, Río Blanco workers complained.[8] Ac-cording to Santa Rosa reporters in the engraving department, they worked under a penitentiary regime: "To those who talk with a peer: a fine and *ver-dura*; to those who laugh: a fine; to those who stand up from their seat to loosen up: a storm of insults; and whoever does not flatter [the supervisor] can start packing his *petates*."[9] From a February 1906 weekly payroll we know that 45 percent of all workers were fined. On average fines represented 3 per-cent of workers' wages, but in some instances they reached up to 38 percent of it. Santa Rosa workers reported that fines were prohibited after the sad events of January 1907.[10] In fact, after February 1907 fines disappear from Santa Rosa's payrolls.[11] Thus, already during the Porfiriato, although at a high cost, workers from the Orizaba valley had obtained some gains in their working conditions.

However, more substantial gains were yet to come. After Madero became president of the Republic, the government created the Department of Labor in order to deal with the labor unrest that daily grew more troublesome.[12] The new department sought to become a mediator that would ease negotiations between labor and capital and resolve conflict. Porfirio Díaz had intervened as mediator in capital-labor conflicts when asked to act as such by the disputant parties.[13] Yet, during his regime, it was not considered a government responsibility to take that role, nor was there any official agency devoted to it. The Department of Labor marked a turning point in the Mexican government's involvement in capital-labor relations, eventually assuming the right and responsibility to act as mediator and to intervene in the settling of disputes between workers and employers.

The creation of the Department of Labor was more a reaction to the threat that the labor movement posed to stability than it was a benefit the government wanted to give to workers. One of its first challenges was negotiating the end of a general strike in the textile industry that broke in December 1911. The organization of the first textile industrialists convention in July of that year, together with a reduction of the working shift and a 10 percent wage increase, came as one of the compromises that ended the strike. In the convention, representatives of workers and employers from several mills negotiated a wage schedule and a set of rules meant to be applied in every mill.[14]

After Huerta's coup d'etat, revolutionary armies began to fight to gain control of strategic regions of the country that would enable them to expand and assume power at the national level. The corridor that goes from the port of Veracruz to Mexico City was crucial because it was the main commercial route that linked the capital to foreign nations, and the port of Veracruz collected the major share of import and export duties, a substantial share of Mexico's fiscal income. The labor movement's most important clusters were located precisely along this corridor, textile workers being the largest organized group in it.

Industrial workers played a minor role as soldiers in revolutionary armies. They kept working in the mills, most of which remained open. Yet because they posed a serious threat to stability, governments in power did their best to placate them. Chronically weak governments were simply unable to support companies against unions. In June 1919, for example, Compañía Industrial Veracruzana's (CIVSA's) director complained to Armando Deschamps, governor of Veracruz, about the union's plans to supervise the masters of the different mill departments. He offered his help to attenuate union's demands, but CIVSA knew that his influence was limited. "Unfortunately," said a company letter, "his authority is very reduced, given the lack of troops in the region, and being afraid that workers will join the mass of revolutionaries that are almost at the factories' doors." [15]

The strategic military importance of the Orizaba workers is also evident in the delahuertista revolt against Obregón. Armed Orizaba textile workers were crucial in gaining back the government's control over that region in February 1924. This helped to increase the unions' power. When the rebellion was crushed, the unions expelled several workers and employees from the mills, claiming they had supported de la Huerta against the opposition of company managers, who were unable to stop them. [16]

Governor Cándido Aguilar's Decrees 7 and 11, which passed in 1914, made rest obligatory on Sunday, reduced the workday, established double pay for night work, and forced owners to provide medical assistance and pay to sick and injured workers, among other things, showing how far governments were willing to go in order to obtain labor support. [17] The government's ability to implement the new laws was much more limited, leaving to the workers the problem of actually trying to implement the new laws. Thus, for example, the shift reduction from ten to nine hours established by the October 1914 decree did not go into effect in Orizaba until a year later, after several workers' protests (see Table 9.1).

Municipal presidents of the several mill towns in the Orizaba valley had always been factory employees, which gave companies a powerful say about how policy was carried out in these towns. In 1906, a letter from Santa Rosa workers to El Paladín asserted that the municipal president's "authority [was] a blind instrument to shut down the voice of those workers who had the energy to complain against daily abuses." [18] It was an easy and normal procedure for company managers to imprison workers without legal cause, as happened in June 1906 to five workers. They had been appointed by their fellows from the Santa Rosa spinning department to complain to the manager about the bad quality of the raw cotton they were supplied to work with. Instead of being listened to, they were sent to prison. [19] With the authorities' support it was easy for companies to imprison anyone suspected of stealing pieces of cloth. [20]

This situation turned around 180 degrees some time between 1914 and 1918, when more blue-collar workers became municipal presidents, who were the first recourse when it came to labor disputes. [21] Now those who complained were company owners and managers. According to CIVSA directors, "in Santa Rosa [the municipal president] is nothing but the mannequin of labor unions, and in consequence we will never win any cause."[22] In 1918 CIVSA managers complained that municipal presidents, as part of the Local Arbitrage and Conciliation Boards (Juntas de Conciliación y Arbitraje), would always bias the junta decisions in favor of workers.[23] After 1916, CIVSA constantly complained about the increase in thefts in the mill and its inability to do anything about it, since, as the CIVSA board of directors explained, "we have a weaver as a Municipal President and gendarmes as police, [and] it is not by respect to these authorities that workers will stop stealing."[24]

In December 1915 Agustín Millán, provisional governor of Veracruz, passed the Law of Professional Associations, which legalized unions. It established that they had to register with the Civil Administration Boards (Juntas de Administración Civil), articulating their objectives, their means of obtaining resources, the use they would give them, the conditions of admission and separation of its members, and the way its directors would be chosen. They were also required to render a biannual report of their financial operations.[25] This law was passed again, basically with the same words, by Governor Cándido Aguilar when he reclaimed that position a month later.[26]

In early 1916, before the Orizaba unions had become completely legal, they took a decisive step toward gaining control over hiring and firing workers. An agreement signed by the Orizaba unions, the industrial companies' managers, and Cándido Aguilar gave unionized workers preference in filling vacancies and power to fire those workers unwilling to become union members. It also established that no worker could be fired without just cause. In case of conflict the arbitrage committee, which was composed of the secretary general of the union, the factory manager, and the inspector of the labor law, had to make a decision.[27] In practice, according to CIVSA directors, this meant that in order to fire any worker, the company had to pay him three months' severance.[28] After that agreement, day workers became unionized and hired under a collective contract. In October 1919, after a long strike, night workers also acquired this status.[29]

All these developments brought fundamental changes in working conditions on the shop floor.[30] If during the Porfiriato it was very common for foremen to exercise physical violence against workers, as the numerous letters published in *El Paladín*[31] report, later it became impossible, and the opposite sometimes occurred. In June 1917 CIVSA's manager Mr. Mauré was hit in the face by a bolt thrown at him by a worker passing by the weaving hall. This was not an isolated case; there were several reports of workers from the spinning and weaving departments throwing bobbins at the departments' directors. However, this time the situation was graver since it dealt with the company's general director. CIVSA asked the union directives and local authorities to find the guilty party or else they would close the factory. The factory closed for twelve days but the worker who hit Mr. Mauré was never found.[32]

All these events give an idea of how strong the labor movement had grown and how it had transformed labor relations between labor and employers. I will explore in the rest of this chapter the effects of these changes on CIVSA workers' real wages and productivity levels.

The Evolution of Real Wages: 1900–1929

The general impact of the revolution in CIVSA real wages can be seen in Figure 9.1.[33] From a long-term perspective, real wages during the last decade of the Porfiriato appear relatively stable. From 1900 to 1910 nominal wages rose by 41 percent and real wages grew by 3.7 percent. There were two cycles: from 1900 to 1907 real wages increased by 17 percent, then from 1907 to 1911 they decreased by 14 percent. Most of this fall took place between 1909 and 1910, mainly as a consequence of the greater inflation during these years. The overall trend of CIVSA real wages for the Porfiriato can be safely generalized to all industrial workers of at least the central region of Mexico since this trend is not defined so much by the changes in CIVSA's nominal wages as by the price index, which does not rise by much.

During the first years of the revolution, before the fall of Francisco I. Madero, real wages at CIVSA increased. This was the result of the surge of the labor movement and the support the new government gave it through the Department of Labor. The minimum tariff for the textile industry negotiated in the Convention of Industrialists of July 1912 was the most evident result of this process. From 1911 to 1913 real wages grew by 20 percent, redressing the previous loss in workers' purchasing power. In 1913 real wages were 2.1 percent above their highest point in 1907 (see Figure 9.1). Wages per hour increased even more (32 percent), since the shift was reduced from twelve to ten hours. It is probable that real wages increased even more in most textile mills, since Santa Rosa wages were already high before the setting of the tariff. Those factories that had lower wages previous to that year must have increased wages by a greater amount.

After Huerta seized power and the war intensified, political chaos gave way to monetary anarchy, and this brought about hyperinflation. Inflation in turn

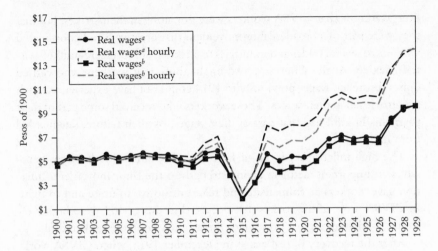

Figure 9.1. Average Weekly and Hourly Real Wages (pesos of 1900)

SOURCE: For a detailed explanation of sources and method, see Gómez-Galvarriato and Musacchio 1998.

NOTES: From 1914 to 1915 I used the gold value of wages as a proxy for real wages. Real wage per hour takes into account changes in the length of the workday: 12 hours from January 1900 to July 1910, 11 hours from August 1910 to August 1912, 10 hours from September 1912 to July 1915, 9 hours from August 1915 to April 1917, and 8 hours from May 1917 on. Hourly wages are not what workers were actually paid, but a figure that shows what workers would have earned with the new wage rates, assuming they would have continued working a 72-hour shift.

[a] Wages deflated with the consumer price index, including all items.

[b] Wages deflated with the consumer price index, without CIVSA's rent and electric light.

eroded nominal wage increases from 1914 to 1916, causing a steep decline in workers' purchasing power, which fell to its lowest point in May 1916— to a seventh of what it had been in 1912 in terms of gold pesos. Because Figure 9.1 shows annual averages of real wages, it underestimates their collapse during the worst months of 1914–16. Yet the fall in real wages appears enormous compared to any other such fall during these three decades.

We can be fairly sure that workers' real wages in general faced an impressive decline during this period. We might think that the deterioration of real wages in general could have been even greater than that evidenced for CIVSA. Inflation lowered real wages by a tremendous amount, a drop that CIVSA workers were, to a certain extent, able to check with their several strikes. Other workers who did not have such a powerful labor movement would have experienced a further deterioration of their real wages. However, we know that CIVSA workers were not alone in their strikes, but that they were part of a broader labor movement that organized and coordinated workers of several trades and industries to strikes from several regions of central Mexico. At the same time, we might think that workers who earned only subsistence wages previously to 1914 could not have experienced such a dramatic fall in their wages. Those workers who received some part of their payments in kind had that part of their wages, by their nature, safeguarded from inflation.

The high inflationary levels of 1915 and 1916 must have been in themselves an important factor in giving strength to the labor movement. Inflation gave workers an immediate and relevant motive to unite and to fight. In CIVSA most of the strikes that occurred in this period were highly effective, which gave great prestige to the union among the rank and file.

After the recovery of real wages in December 1916, when CIVSA workers finally won the fight to be paid in gold pesos, real wages began to fall due to the new price increase that was taking place in 1917. A new strike in May 1917 generated an important nominal wage increase that raised real wages to unprecedented values. Yet, inflation soon diminished real wages to practically the same level they had been at the beginning of the year.

In general terms, from 1917 to 1920 workers were able to regain the real wage they had earned in 1913 (see Figure 9.1), which was lost during the inflationary period from 1914 to 1916. Yet this real wage was not very different from that earned in 1907, since the real wage improvement achieved between 1912 and 1913 only compensated for the real wage loss that took place between 1908 and 1911. However, workers earned this wage in an eight-hour instead of a twelve-hour shift, a major gain.

From 1920 to 1929, wage increases, coupled with price deflation, increased Santa Rosa workers' purchasing power by an impressive 131 percent. It is in this period that workers saw a substantial improvement from the living standards they had had in 1907 or 1913. Furthermore, the labor laws of Veracruz of 1914 and 1915 and the Constitution of 1917 had brought other non-wage benefits to workers, such as sickness and accident compensations and retirement pensions, which CIVSA directors valued as an additional 15 percent increase to wages.[34]

The revolution certainly contributed to the growth of the labor movement and the speed and depth of its gains. Yet, by no means can we conclude that if the revolution had not occurred, workers would not have organized, and these gains would not have taken place. A comparative study with other Latin American countries would help clarify this point.

A Growing Regional Wage Disparity

CIVSA's real wage increase from 1917 to 1929 cannot be generalized to other industries or regions. Textile mills in other states increased their wages much less. In fact the wage gap between regions grew in the 1920s relative to Porfirian times because the labor movement's strength varied markedly across regions. The variance of average wages in different states was 0.015 in 1893 and 0.24 in 1925.[35]

Economic theory suggests a close relationship between labor productivity and wages when labor markets act freely. In 1893–96 there existed a strong relationship between these two variables. In Figure 9.2 we can see a positive relation between average wages and labor efficiency.[36] The correlation between the two variables was 0.57.

In 1923–25, in contrast, that relationship is less clear. In Figure 9.3 we can see how the data is more disperse. The correlation between labor efficiency and wages for 1923–25 was only 0.21.

The dispersion of regional wages in the 1920s is better explained by the strength of the labor movement in each state than by its efficiency. The correlation between the number of strikes in each state in the period 1920–24 and the average wage is 0.61. In Figure 9.4 we can see the positive relation, which is difficult to discern in the previous figure.

Figure 9.5 shows how the number of strikes in the textile industry is directly related with the population density of textile industrial workers in each state. There is a better correlation between the number of strikes in

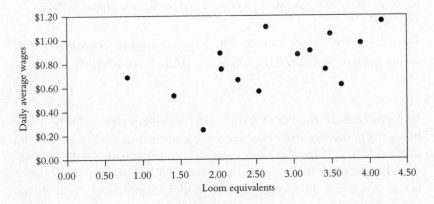

Figure 9.2.   Wages Versus Labor Efficiency, 1893

SOURCES: México, Dirección General de Estadística 1894; and U.S. Special Consular Reports 1896.

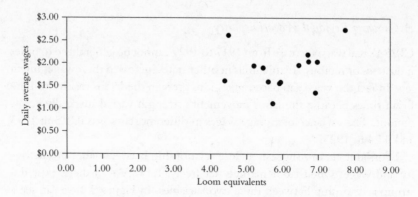

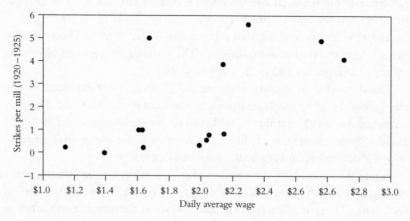

Figure 9.3. (above) Wages Versus Labor Efficiency, 1923

SOURCES: México, SHCP; and México, Secretaría de la Economía Nacional [Moisés T. de la Peña] 1934: 22, 29–35.

Figure 9.4. (below) Textile Workers' Wages Versus Strikes per State, 1920–1924

SOURCE: México, Secretaría de la Economía Nacional [Moisés T. de la Peña] 1934: 22, 29–35.

each state and the number of textile workers in the region (0.74) than between the number of strikes and the average number of workers per mill in
the state (0.57). There also exists a greater correlation between the number
of strikes and the number of spindles per state (0.72) than between the number of strikes and the average number of spindles per factory in the state
(0.49). This implies that labor movements grew stronger and were more capable of imposing higher wages in those states that had a greater number of
textile workers and bigger mills. Yet, it was more important to have more tex-

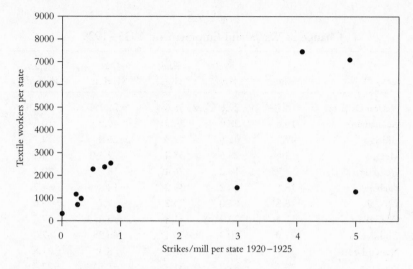

Figure 9.5.   Textile Workers' Population Density Versus Strikes per State, 1920–1924

SOURCES: México, Secretaría de la Economía Nacional [Moisés T. de la Peña] 1934: 14, 29–35, and 126; México, INEGI: 11–21.

tile workers than bigger mills. A small factory in Veracruz would have higher wages than a big mill in Jalisco. Yet, factory size was also important; Puebla had more spindles, but Veracruz and the Distrito Federal, regions with bigger mills, had higher wages.

Between 1925 and 1927 a major convention between workers and industrialists of the textile industry took place in order to ease labor-capital troubles by producing a uniform tariff and set of rules, as the Convention of 1912 had done. However, it could not fulfill this objective. The variance of wages between states grew from 0.24 in 1925 to 0.37 in 1929.[37]

The wage schedule established by the convention, if implemented strictly, would have put several mills in a terrible situation. Its flexibility meant that important wage gaps continued to exist. In fact it was the different regional strength of the labor movement that had in the first place widened the wage gap between regions, and that continued widening it, since it was in those states where the movement was strong that the convention regulations were applied. This situation left Veracruz in a bad standing relative to other states for the development of its textile industry. Nonetheless, wages in other regions also increased. On average real wages increased through this period in the whole country. From 1925 to 1929 the average national real wage in-

Table 9.2

Change in Wages and Employment: 1925–1929

States	Nominal	Real Wage[a]	Real Wage[b]	No. Workers	Hours Worked
Federal District	18.1%	29.6%	38.6%	−21.1%	9.6%
Guanajuato	16.6	28.0	36.9	40.2	−10.5
Hidalgo	47.3	61.6	72.8	−26.0	9.7
México	15.4	26.6	35.4	2.3	4.4
Querétaro	7.7	18.2	26.4	16.7	89.3
Puebla	18.6	30.2	39.2	−14.8	−4.7
Tlaxcala	48.5	63.0	74.3	−7.7	−9.6
Coahuila	12.3	23.2	31.8	5.6	17.7
Chihuahua	27.9	40.3	50.1	46.2	87.7
Nuevo León	26.7	39.0	48.7	8.4	−21.8
Veracruz	28.7	41.2	51.1	−8.8	−22.4
Guerrero	44.9	59.0	70.1	43.8	−42.0
Oaxaca	45.8	60.0	71.1	63.9	−3.5
Jalisco	−6.7	2.3	9.5	−10.6	1.8
Michoacán	−2.6	6.9	14.4	−5.5	−37.1
Nayarit	52.4	67.2	78.9	−13.0	−30.3
Durango	18.5	30.0	39.1	−62.9	−35.4
Sinaloa	2.9	12.8	20.7	−0.6	−10.0
Sonora	90.7	109.3	123.9	36.0	6.2
Total	24.7	36.8	46.3	−9.9	−3.4

SOURCE: México, Dirección General de Estadística 1894; and México, SHCP.

[a] Wages deflated with the consumer price index, including all items.

[b] Wages deflated with the consumer price index, without CIVSA's rent and electric light.

creased by between 40 and 50 percent. However, this wage increase was accompanied by a fall in employment of nearly 10 percent. This can be explained by the fact that if unions and government fixed wages over the equilibrium given by supply and demand, then employment would necessarily fall (see Table 9.2).

The Evolution of Productivity Levels

Unfortunately the revolution had other consequences that would become evident only in the long run. Profit rates, when adjusted by inflation, never

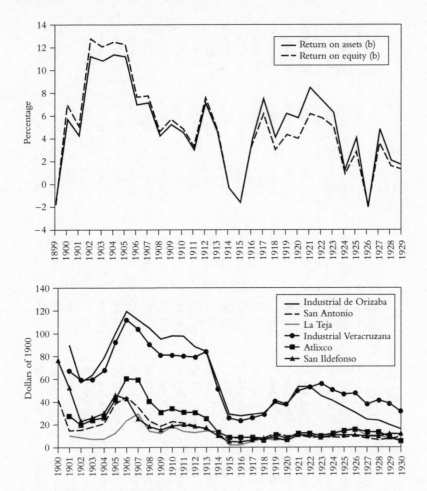

Figure 9.6. (above) Profit Rates at CIVSA

SOURCE: Table 9.3.

Figure 9.7. (below) Textile Manufacturers Share Prices, 1900–1930 (pesos of 1900)

SOURCES: *El Economista Mexicano* 1900–1915; *El Demócrata* 1916; and *Boletín Financiero y Minero* 1918–1930.

regained their Porfirian levels. Accordingly, the stock of Santa Rosa and other textile mills never fully recovered, showing the deterioration in business outlook (see Figures 9.6 and 9.7; the source data for Figure 9.6 are shown in Table 9.3). Investment collapsed during the revolution, as can be seen in Figure 9.8, and remained low in the 1920s. CIVSA entrepreneurs appear to

Table 9.3
CIVSA's Profitability

	Assets Net of Depreciation	Equity Net of Depreciation	Profits Net of Depreciation	Price Index[c]	Return on Assets[a]	Return on Equity[a]	Return on Assets[b]	Return on Equity[b]
1899	$3,411,393.43	$2,971,789.55	($48,410.91)	92.93	-1.42%	-1.63%	-1.49%	-1.75%
1900	$4,641,957.17	$3,840,877.96	$266,546.18	100.00	5.74%	6.94%	5.74%	6.94%
1901	$4,639,965.50	$3,900,168.04	$173,949.39	102.72	3.75%	4.46%	3.68%	4.34%
1902	$4,882,179.20	$4,182,042.77	$580,161.41	117.36	11.88%	13.87%	10.63%	11.82%
1903	$5,282,426.15	$4,603,801.44	$608,247.11	118.33	11.51%	13.21%	10.31%	11.17%
1904	$5,558,429.42	$4,899,674.24	$683,311.91	117.00	12.29%	13.95%	11.06%	11.92%
1905	$5,859,648.23	$5,191,748.14	$723,656.85	117.22	12.35%	13.94%	11.02%	11.89%
1906	$6,224,577.22	$5,526,541.45	$471,207.45	115.22	7.57%	8.53%	6.84%	7.40%
1907	$6,528,038.02	$5,785,408.83	$525,937.17	120.65	8.06%	9.09%	7.04%	7.53%
1908	$6,818,043.48	$5,980,400.96	$319,568.03	121.08	4.69%	5.34%	4.08%	4.41%
1909	$7,052,401.08	$6,140,028.25	$439,842.90	131.44	6.24%	7.16%	5.08%	5.45%
1910	$7,543,339.41	$6,403,832.01	$439,512.31	153.17	5.83%	6.86%	4.27%	4.48%
1911	$7,784,439.03	$6,538,255.40	$288,371.95	153.61	3.70%	4.41%	2.72%	2.87%
1912	$7,862,934.72	$6,712,792.42	$734,367.28	156.39	9.34%	10.94%	6.76%	7.00%
1913	$8,109,055.31	$7,049,737.35	$493,878.23	158.75	6.09%	7.01%	4.39%	4.41%
1914	$8,362,235.57	$7,531,239.11	$21,424.03	181.69	0.26%	0.28%	0.17%	0.16%
1915	$7,946,015.01	$7,393,991.64	($157,041.51)	207.94	-1.98%	-2.12%	-1.14%	-1.02%
1916	$7,744,538.48	$7,247,189.49	$568,814.22	237.99	7.34%	7.85%	3.75%	3.30%

1917	$9,674,839.93	$8,354,834.33	$1,360,147.49	271.71	14.06%	16.28%	7.20%	5.99%
1918	$11,029,520.70	$9,624,583.94	$931,278.80	324.57	8.44%	9.68%	4.03%	2.98%
1919	$11,437,597.59	$10,431,261.17	$1,366,819.24	311.35	11.95%	13.10%	5.89%	4.21%
1920	$12,766,168.99	$11,094,229.58	$1,446,679.62	338.52	11.33%	13.04%	5.21%	3.85%
1921	$14,263,481.57	$12,088,478.58	$2,156,318.23	303.14	15.12%	17.84%	7.49%	5.88%
1922	$14,895,525.64	$13,042,946.74	$1,779,909.81	241.67	11.95%	13.65%	7.14%	5.65%
1923	$15,221,920.51	$13,738,717.63	$1,448,795.57	211.30	9.52%	10.55%	6.39%	4.99%
1924	$15,290,077.37	$14,274,613.25	$337,401.24	218.92	2.21%	2.36%	1.45%	1.08%
1925	$15,556,057.36	$14,832,116.97	$1,100,758.83	255.06	7.08%	7.42%	4.20%	2.91%
1926	$15,761,455.04	$15,165,919.07	($423,453.44)	251.60	-2.69%	-2.79%	-1.61%	-1.11%
1927	$16,204,349.40	$15,561,270.36	$1,245,783.79	222.36	7.69%	8.01%	5.02%	3.60%
1928	$17,244,605.60	$16,261,435.71	$586,468.71	208.97	3.40%	3.61%	2.35%	1.73%
1929	$17,486,626.22	$16,678,408.64	$512,526.35	212.42	2.93%	3.07%	1.99%	1.45%
1900–1910					7.37%	8.48%	6.52%	7.13%
1911–1920					6.94%	7.94%	3.93%	3.48%
1921–1929					6.36%	7.08%	3.82%	2.91%

SOURCE: CIVSA's balance sheets and statements of results, 1898–1900.

[a]In current prices; [b]as adjusted for the effects of inflation/deflation, following Arnold 1999; [c]price index used to deflate assets and equity is price index AB (gold pesos), developed Aurora Gómez-Galvarriato and Aldo Musacchio (1998). Given that there is no price index for the period 1914–16, I calculated those figures by extrapolating price indices in 1913 and 1917. Price indices of paper money rose by much more in those years, but CIVSA accounting figures were reported in gold pesos, so it is the value of metallic money that must be considered. Depreciation rates were calculated with the following annual rates: 2.5% for buildings, 5% for machinery, and 10% for furniture and equipment. For further detail see Gómez-Galvarriato 1999.

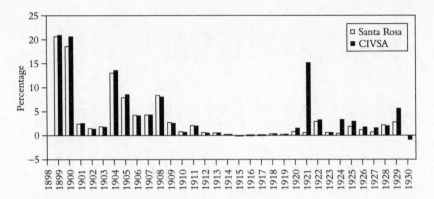

Figure 9.8. Investments in Real Estate, Machinery, and Equipment at CIVSA (as percentage of total fixed assets)

SOURCES: CIVSA and Santa Rosa general balances, 1900–1929.

have followed the strategy of eating up the fixed capital already invested. In order to take advantage of the lower wages and weaker labor movement in Puebla, they bought a small mill in that state, El León.[38]

It is difficult to discern how much of the lack of investment and technological backwardness was caused by the uncertainty and the collapse of financial markets brought about by the Mexican Revolution, how much by the new economic worldwide conditions, and how much by the new strength of the labor movement. Furthermore, given that in Mexico the revolution came about together with a strengthening of the labor movement, it is impossible to separate their effects as independent processes.

Productivity levels measured as machine per worker and production per worker remained stagnant throughout these three decades (see Tables 9.4 and 9.5). Given the radical change experienced on the shop floor from manager's to union's control, it might seem surprising that productivity levels did not fall as a consequence of the revolution.

The fact that productivity didn't fall means that the Santa Rosa union was effective at guaranteeing workers' discipline and effort. Moreover, workers were able to produce more per hour as the shift was reduced, even though they were doing their tasks with basically the same machinery they had worked with during the Porfiriato. This means that the intensity of labor was higher during the shorter working day, perhaps because workers were not as tired. Also, since they were paid per piece, they may have tried to

Table 9.4
Spinners' Productivity 1900-1930

	SPINNERS (WARP NO. 29)			SPINNERS (WEFT NO. 30)		
	Real Wage per Kilo	*Kilos per Worker (weekly)*	*Kilos per Worker (hourly)*	*Real Wage per Kilo*	*Kilos per Worker (weekly)*	*Kilos per Worker (hourly)*
1900	$0.029	244.2	3.14	$0.038	277.2	3.61
1901	$0.029	220.9	3.02	$0.037	222.0	3.12
1902	$0.027	241.0	3.35	$0.035	262.0	3.68
1903	$0.027	234.3	3.12	$0.035	232.0	3.03
1904	$0.026	181.5	2.78	$0.034	238.8	2.75
1905	$0.026	256.3	3.05	$0.034	239.7	2.91
1906	$0.012	231.8	3.22	$0.034	221.0	2.44
1907	$0.036	225.3	3.13	$0.038	227.9	2.49
1908	$0.035	213.4	2.96	$0.034	231.3	3.47
1909	$0.030	229.4	3.19	$0.034	225.1	3.75
1910	$0.026	281.9	4.70	$0.031	201.8	3.36
1911	$0.027	232.3	4.22	$0.029	219.4	3.99
1912	$0.028	253.8	4.23	$0.032	211.1	4.00
1913	$0.028	212.9	3.88	$0.032	205.3	3.95
1914	$0.021	208.1	3.50	$0.024	218.3	3.89
1915	$0.011	190.7	3.68	$0.012	214.8	3.48
1916	$0.021	183.0	3.90	$0.033	211.6	4.49
1917	$0.037	176.3	3.67	$0.040	212.5	4.22
1918	$0.032	178.5	4.46	$0.035	215.2	4.70
1919	$0.034	160.3	4.21	$0.035	216.9	5.07
1920	$0.029	176.5	4.17	$0.032	236.3	4.73
1921	$0.036	190.3	4.24	$0.037	206.3	4.35
1922	$0.045	198.0	5.54	$0.044	205.0	4.73
1923	$0.044	204.9	3.90	$0.046	210.1	3.93
1924	$0.043	185.1	4.73	$0.046	204.5	5.20
1925	$0.037	208.2	4.14	$0.044	220.4	4.71
1926	$0.038	242.6	4.74	$0.043	224.9	5.00
1927	$0.048	219.9	3.98	$0.049	257.8	5.61
1928	$0.053	224.7	4.41	$0.056	268.8	5.14
1929	$0.051	268.2	5.09	$0.054	260.6	5.40
1900–1910	$0.028	232.7	3.24	$0.035	234.4	3.15
1910–1920	$0.027	197.2	3.99	$0.030	216.2	4.25
1920–1929	$0.044	215.8	4.53	$0.047	228.7	4.90

SOURCE: A sample was taken from CV, Payrolls, June and November 1900–1930. Number of spindles taken from the "Manifestaciones para el Timbre," CV, Correspondence, 1910–30. Wages deflated with index I AB from Gómez-Galvarriato 1999: 700, 703.

Table 9.5
Weavers' Productivity: 1900–1930

	Meters per Worker (weekly)	Meters per Worker (hourly)	Meters per Loom (weekly)	Looms per Worker	Real Wage per Meter	Real Wage per Week	Meters per Loom per Hour
1900	533.3	44.4	231.9	2.30	$0.008	$13.66	3.09
1901	676.8	56.4	294.3	2.30	$0.008	$3.99	3.34
1902	683.4	56.9	298.4	2.29	$0.008	$4.37	4.40
1903	540.5	45.0	229.0	2.36	$0.008	$3.55	3.22
1904	527.4	44.0	211.0	2.50	$0.008	$3.48	3.70
1905	723.1	60.3	292.7	2.47	$0.008	$4.81	3.28
1906	623.4	52.0	238.9	2.61	$0.009	$3.83	2.74
1907	663.9	55.3	257.3	2.58	$0.009	$4.44	3.51
1908	634.5	52.9	275.9	2.30	$0.010	$5.68	3.85
1909	712.6	59.4	300.7	2.37	$0.009	$5.43	3.93
1910	561.5	48.9	257.6	2.18	$0.009	$4.78	4.41
1911	418.4	38.0	181.1	2.31	$0.009	$3.71	3.82
1912	694.3	66.3	276.6	2.51	$0.010	$7.91	5.01
1913	615.6	58.8	218.3	2.82	$0.011	$7.62	4.30
1914	774.6	73.9	289.0	2.68	$0.008	$6.72	5.03
1915	598.2	63.1	229.2	2.61	$0.004	$3.35	4.43
1916	703.2	74.2	236.0	2.98	$0.008	$6.46	4.85
1917	572.9	67.6	220.3	2.60	$0.013	$10.61	4.33
1918	542.3	64.0	203.9	2.66	$0.012	$8.19	4.58
1919	421.8	49.8	160.4	2.63	$0.012	$7.25	4.18
1920	535.1	63.2	209.0	2.56	$0.011	$8.52	4.74
1921	627.7	74.1	266.0	2.36	$0.012	$10.19	4.84
1922	558.3	65.9	229.8	2.43	$0.017	$13.23	4.25
1923	548.2	64.7	227.5	2.41	$0.018	$13.56	3.69
1924	542.6	64.1	220.6	2.46	$0.015	$11.52	5.04
1925	592.7	70.0	248.0	2.39	$0.014	$12.70	4.96
1926	628.5	74.2	265.2	2.37	$0.013	$12.68	5.18
1927	572.0	67.5	239.3	2.39	$0.018	$15.33	4.86
1928	631.0	74.5	251.4	2.51	$0.018	$15.49	4.52
1929	617.2	72.9	250.9	2.46	$0.018	$16.09	4.74
1900–1910	625.5	8.7	262.5	2.39	$0.009	$4.36	3.59
1911–1920	587.6	10.3	222.4	2.64	$0.010	$7.03	4.53
1921–1929	590.9	11.6	244.3	2.42	$0.016	$13.42	4.68

SOURCE: Data on meters per loom and wage per meter was obtained from a sample of 30 weavers from CV, Payrolls, June and November 1900–1930 and looms per workers were taken from CV, Payrolls, week 6, 1900–1930.

get as much done as they possibly could. In addition, once the shift was reduced, companies became more strict about when employees arrived at and
left work.[39]

Yet, increased productivity was not all that was required to keep the industry's health and international competitiveness at the levels it had enjoyed
during the Porfiriato, let alone to improve them. As Adam Przeworski explains: "No one drew the blueprint and yet the [capitalist] system is designed
in such a way that if profits are not sufficient, then eventually either wages
must fall, or employment, or both. . . . Decisions by capitalists to save and
choose techniques of production constitute the parameters which constrain
the possibility of improvement of material conditions of anyone."[40]

The reduction in investment rates at CIVSA were partly a consequence
of the decline in profit rates. A regression of Santa Rosa's fixed assets growth
calculated on the basis of the average of the previous three years' profit rates
yields the following relationship:[41]

$$\text{GROWTH}_t = \frac{-0.005 + 0.62\ (\text{PROFITRATE}_{t-1} + \text{PROFITRATE}_{t-2} + \text{PROFITRATE}_{t-3})}{3}$$

$$(-0.29) \quad (2.02) \quad R^2 = 0.14,\ \text{adjusted } R^2 = 0.10,$$
$$N = 28$$

with t-statistics in parentheses. Past profits are used as a proxy of expected future profits, of which investment in fixed assets should be a function. Results
of this regression show a clear association between investment and profits for
CIVSA, indicating that the decline in profit rates after the Porfiriato counts
for a significant part of the drop in investment rates after 1912.[42] Yet, there
were other forces behind the reduction of investment rates, namely labor
regulation restrictions on the adoption of new technology and the tariff policy pursued after 1927.[43]

New technology adopted by the textile industry worldwide was not introduced in Mexican mills. One of the most notable improvements in textile
production was the introduction of automatic looms. A weaver could attend,
at the most, four of the older type of looms, but could attend from twenty
to forty automatic looms.[44] Another innovation that would have increased
weavers' productivity was the introduction of double-length looms.

The wage schedule that came out of the Convention of Workers and Industrialists of 1925–27 fixed the maximum number of machines workers
should attend and established specific wages per piece produced.[45] Under
these conditions industrialists had no incentive to introduce better machin-

ery because it would not enable them to reduce labor costs, as wages per piece and workers per machine had to remain invariable.[46]

The decisions to establish fixed wage schedules per piece and limits to machines per worker were not made without reason. In 1926 the Saco-Lowell Shops, afraid that the agreements of the convention would affect the demand for their machinery in Mexico, sent a letter to the leadership of the convention, explaining how detrimental the new regulations were to the adoption of new technology. The letter described the advantages of automatic looms as well as that of machinery specifically designed for the processing of scrap cotton. It explained why these innovations would not be adopted with the new wage schedule and regulations proposed by the convention.[47]

However, the majority in the convention were in favor of the rigid wage schedule. In modern machines workers saw a threat to employment, industrialists a threat to the survival of their decrepit mills, and government the threat of social discontent. It was easier to raise tariffs and let the industry survive as it was. It is possible that the overrepresentation of smaller and also more old-fashioned mills in the convention further contributed to this result.[48]

CIVSA documents evidence the effects of the convention regulations on the company's investment decisions. In 1927 double-length looms, a type of new loom that had not been specifically addressed at the convention, were installed in Santa Rosa.[49] However, a year later CIVSA's board of directors decided to remove the new looms because the wages demanded by the Santa Rosa union for those who ran the looms made production too costly. CIVSA's management decided instead to install these looms at El León, where they thought they would face less labor resistance than in Santa Rosa.[50] Similarly, in April 1928 CIVSA's directors decided to purchase machinery to process artificial silk (artisela),[51] but by August of the following year, they had not been able to run the new machinery, again because of labor resistance.[52]

In May 1929, CIVSA's main engineer presented a cost-benefit analysis, explaining the convenience of installing new high-speed warping machines, which would generate substantial savings. CIVSA's board of directors decided to postpone their purchase until they were able to get "a fair" wage rate for warping with these new machines. Together with CIDOSA, the other important textile company in Orizaba, they started negotiations with the ministry of industry on this matter, but at least until the end of 1930 these efforts were fruitless.[53]

Although the effects of rigid regulations on technological innovation must have been worse in those states where the labor movement was stronger, contemporary studies on the textile industry indicate that they prevailed over the whole country.[54] Aggregate data for Mexico's textile industry evidence little investment.[55] Although some new factories were built in the 1920s, most of them were small establishments devoted to the production of knitwear (*bonetería*), mainly on artificial silk machinery. This is why even though the number of factories increased by 22 percent from 1921 to 1930, the number of active spindles and looms increased by only 9 and 8 percent, respectively (see Table 9.6). Machinery per worker (measured in loom equivalents), which increased during the last decade of the Porfiriato by 18 percent, increased by a slower rate of 5 percent during the 1920s. During the revolution loom equivalents per worker grew when measured on a per-shift basis because of the reduction in the length of the workday.

Labor productivity increased between 1926 and 1930, when measured not only by loom equivalents per shift but also by sales and production per worker. This was the result of (1) the implementation of the convention's wages per piece, which increased labor intensity, and (2) the reduction of employment and of hours worked per mill, as a consequence of the depression. "This increase was by no means a result of an improvement in machinery in the mills."[56]

The agreements of the convention may be understandable under the circumstances of worldwide depression. But the precepts adopted there were ratified over and over.[57] As late as 1943 a memorandum of the ministry of labor to the president of Mexico explained that the adoption of "Toyada" automatic looms in Japan had generated misery for Japanese textile workers. Furthermore, if some mills adopted the new technology, others would go bankrupt, and this would generate unemployment. It said that England had taken wise measures to protect its industry both from the adoption of automatic looms and from Japanese competition. It concluded that Mexican workers should not be sacrificed, by the adoption of new technology, in order to gain competition in world markets.[58]

The result was that the textile industry became increasingly more outdated. In 1957, 34.4 percent of the spindles and 33 percent of the looms operating in that year had been built before 1910. This situation was worse in those states, such as Veracruz, where labor regulations were more strictly implemented because of their stronger labor movements. In this state 67 percent of the spindles and 73 percent of the looms working in 1957 had been manufactured before 1910.[59] In the long run workers were victims of their own success.[60]

Table 9.6

The Mexican Textile Industry, 1900–1930

	Active Mills	Spindles	Looms	Workers	Raw Cotton Consumption	Sales (nominal)	Sales (pesos of 1900)	Loom Equivalent per Worker	Loom Equivalent per Shift	Cotton per Worker	Sales per Worker
1900	134	557,391	17,202	26,764	28,990	$35,459	$35,459	0.87	0.87	1,083	$1,325
1901	133	602,223	18,885	27,663	30,262	$33,877	$35,553	0.92	0.92	1,094	$1,285
1902	124	575,304	17,974	25,316	27,628	$28,780	$27,939	0.96	0.96	1,091	$1,104
1903	115	630,201	20,124	26,249	27,512	$36,907	$31,339	1.03	1.03	1,048	$1,194
1904	119	632,018	20,326	27,033	28,841	$42,511	$34,646	1.01	1.01	1,067	$1,282
1905	127	666,659	21,932	29,483	31,230	$51,214	$46,097	0.99	0.99	1,059	$1,564
1906	130	683,739	22,776	31,673	35,826	$51,171	$44,894	0.96	0.96	1,131	$1,417
1907	129	693,842	23,507	33,132	36,654	$51,686	$41,326	0.94	0.94	1,106	$1,247
1908	132	732,876	24,997	35,816	36,040	$54,934	$45,303	0.92	0.92	1,006	$1,265
1909	129	726,278	25,327	32,229	35,435	$43,370	$36,656	1.03	1.03	1,099	$1,137
1910	123	702,874	25,017	31,963	34,736	$50,651	$39,119	1.02	1.07	1,087	$1,224
1911	119	725,297	24,436	32,147	34,568	$51,348	$39,286	1.01	1.10	1,075	$1,222
1912	127	762,149	26,801	32,128	32,366	$52,847	$38,804	1.10	1.25	1,007	$1,222
1913	118	752,804	26,791	32,641	32,821			1.07	1.29	1,006	$1,208
1914	90										
1915	84										
1916	93										

1917	92	573,072	20,489	22,187		$64,130	$29,974	1.21	1.70		$1,351
1918	104	689,173	25,017	27,680	20,334	$48,567	$19,574	1.18	1.77		$707
1919	110	749,237	27,020	33,185	31,095	$69,778	$25,169	1.06	1.59		$758
1920	120	753,837	27,301	37,936	31,694	$120,492	$36,890	0.94	1.41	835	$972
1921	121	770,945	28,409	38,227	35,924	$93,942	$28,329	0.97	1.45	940	$741
1922	119	803,230	29,521	39,677	34,654	$85,023	$26,216	0.97	1.45	873	$661
1923	110	802,363	29,668	39,629	32,344	$97,490	$35,882	0.97	1.46	816	$905
1924	116	812,165	29,888	37,732	30,517	$96,435	$35,496	1.03	1.54	809	$941
1925	130	838,987	31,094	43,728	40,997	$108,396	$38,621	0.92	1.38	938	$883
1926	138	833,388	30,597	43,776	41,522	$95,437	$34,782	0.91	1.36	949	$795
1927	144	821,211	30,437	41,238	41,169	$91,068	$34,920	0.96	1.44	998	$847
1928	137	836,391	30,130	39,041	39,355	$96,292	$37,818	1.01	1.51	1,008	$969
1929	145	839,109	30,191	39,525	39,436	$97,162	$38,263	1.00	1.50	998	$968
1930	148	842,265	30,625	39,424	40,582	$91,145	$38,857	1.01	1.52	1,029	$986
1900–1910	–8%	26%	45%	19%	20%	43%	10%	18%	23%	1,079	$1,277
1911–1920	1%	4%	12%	18%	–8%	135%	–6%	–7%	28%	981	$1,036
1921–1930	22%	9%	8%	3%	13%	–3%	37%	5%	5%	936	$869

SOURCES: See note 55.

NOTES: Loom equivalents have been calculated following Gregory Clark, 1985: 19–49. The length of the workday was considered 12 hours from 1900 to 1911, 10 hours from 1912 to 1916, 9 hours in 1917, and 8 hours from 1917 to 1930. This is not accurate given that workday regulations were not strictly followed in all mills.

Conclusions

This chapter shows that institutional changes in capital-labor relations that took place between 1906 and 1930 had an important economic impact on the Mexican textile industry. By organizing in unions, mill hands were able to claim a greater share of the surplus they had worked to produce.

Part of the battle, particularly between 1908 and 1920, was fought against inflation. In this period, the unions' struggle succeeded in gaining back, over and over, the purchasing power they had lost as a consequence of increasing prices. Additionally, unions achieved a substantial reduction in the working shift, which went from twelve hours in 1907 to eight hours in mid-1917.

Whereas until 1907 there was relative real wage stability, from 1907 to 1911 real wages fell by almost 15 percent. During the first years of the revolution, workers were able to fight inflation through the labor movement and the support of the new government's Department of Labor. The minimum wage for the textile industry negotiated at the Convention of Industrialists of July 1912 was the most significant result of this process. From 1911 to 1913, real wages per shift grew by 20 percent and hourly wages increased by 32 percent.

However, these gains proved to be short-lived. After Huerta seized power and the war escalated, political chaos gave way to monetary anarchy, and inflation struck back with even greater intensity. From 1914 to 1916, hyperinflation caused a significant decline in workers' purchasing power, which fell to its lowest point in May 1916, declining to a seventh of what it had been in 1912 in terms of gold pesos. Evidence shows that companies were pricing their merchandise in gold as early as December 1915, which would imply a transfer of income from workers to company owners. In December 1916, after several strikes, workers finally won the battle for payment of wages in gold pesos.

In 1917 workers were able to regain the level of real wages they had earned in 1913, which had been lost during the inflationary period from 1914 to 1916. The purchasing power achieved from 1917 to 1920 was an improvement over the final years of the Porfiriato. Yet, it was not very different from the real wage earned in 1907. In terms of wages per hour, however, real wages increased in this period relative to those of 1913, since the shift was reduced from ten to eight hours. Furthermore, the labor laws of Veracruz of 1914 and 1915 and the Constitution of 1917 brought about other non-wage benefits to workers, such as sickness and accident compensation and retirement pensions, which CIVSA directors valued as an additional 15 percent increase in wages.

It was very difficult for workers to maintain this recently recovered pur-chasing power. From 1917 to 1920 the effects of World War I on the Mexi-can economy and the destruction of economic institutions and infrastructure caused by the revolution made the return to price stability a difficult task. There was a steep rise in inflation in 1917 despite the enormous monetary contraction generated by the collapse of the *infalsificables*. Despite great nomi-nal wage increases, real weekly wages diminished, a loss that was almost re-covered during the following year because of the price deflation. Yet, by 1920 workers' weekly real wages were almost 10 percent below those of 1913.

Real wages increased from 1920 to 1929 by an impressive 131 percent. National real wages in the textile industry also increased, but not as much. The varying regional strength of the labor movement resulted in regional differences both in wages and in the degree to which new labor regulations were implemented. Between 1925 and 1927 a convention of workers and industrialists was held in order to establish a general wage schedule for the industry. However, it did not fulfill its objective, and wages became even more heterogeneous across regions after the convention ended. Its agree-ments established rigid regulations on machines per worker and wages per piece that were detrimental to technological progress in the industry. Al-though profit rates recovered in Santa Rosa after the revolution, stock prices and investment levels did not.

Labor productivity levels did not fall as a consequence of the revolution, in spite of union control on the shop floor. However, productivity levels did not rise in the 1920s because of the lack of investment in new machinery. Given the important technological progress that took place in textile ma-chinery worldwide, Santa Rosa's international competitiveness fell behind its not very high Porfirian competitive levels. This pattern seems to have pre-vailed in the Mexican textile industry in general, although the situation was worse in those regions with stronger labor movements.

The three major actors in the political economy of the textile industry—businessmen, labor, and the government—chose in the late 1920s an insti-tutional arrangement that gave no incentives for technological transforma-tion and that required high tariffs. This enabled most mills to survive, saved jobs, and quelled social unrest. However, this arrangement condemned the textile industry to become increasingly outdated and unable to compete in world markets. For reasons that go beyond the scope of this paper, this insti-tutional arrangement prevailed in Mexico for more than fifty years, with ter-rible consequences for the development of the industry and the well-being of its workers.

This analysis of productivity levels in Mexican textile mills indicates that workers' power to control the relation between effort and pay is a crucial factor in determining the technology employed and therefore levels of competitiveness and productivity, as Lazonick has pointed out.[61] In accordance with Wolcott and Clark's findings for the case of India, it is clear that in Mexico the poor performance of the textile industry, particularly after the revolution, was a problem of "the low labor input per mill worker."[62] Yet it is also evident that this did not result from a lack of effort on the part of workers or from managerial incompetence, but from a more complex situation, caused in part by the power exercised by workers in the labor market to block personnel reductions for fear of unemployment. However, it was also determined by the power exerted by the owners of smaller mills, who were either unwilling or unable to make new investments and fearful of going bankrupt. In the end, though, the power of these two actors would probably have not been enough to shape the evolution of the industry without the support of a government that valued social and political stability above economic development and therefore pursued the tariff and labor policies that maintenance of the status quo required.

This study suggests that structures of social power are important variables in explaining the various development paths taken by countries (or regions). The institutions that govern the social relations of production are not, however, determined solely by unions, employers, or the government, but by the interaction between them in arrangements that are greatly influenced by path-dependency, and therefore difficult to change.

Notes

The author would like to thank John A. Britton, John Coatsworth, Lance Davis, Claudia Goldin, John Womack, and Gavin Wright for their comments on an earlier draft of this chapter. Any errors of interpretation are solely the responsibility of the author.

1. These issues are discussed in greater depth in Gómez-Galvarriato 1999: 220–321.

2. Przeworski 1985: 11.

3. "Orizaba al vuelo y sus alrededores," *El Paladín*, January 1906–December 1908.

4. M. Clark 1934: 128–50.

5. CIVSA (henceforth CV), Actas del Consejo (henceforth AC), November 30, 1906.

6. CV, Copiadores de Cartas (henceforth CR), Board of Directors to Santa Rosa manager, January 12, 1907, and CV, payrolls, 1907, 1908.

7. CV, CR, Santa Rosa to Board of Directors, February 7, 1907.

8. "Orizaba al vuelo y sus alrededores," *El Paladín*, June 21, 1906.

9. *El Paladín*, March 11, 1906.

10. *El Paladín*, August 13, 1908.

11. CV, payrolls, week 6, 1906, and week 7, 1907.

12. Decreto por el que se Establece el Departamento del Trabajo, *Diario Oficial de la Federación*, December 18, 1911.

13. This was the case for example in the December 1906 textile mills' lockout. Anderson 1976: 9.

14. AGN, Departamento del Trabajo (henceforth DT), (box/file) 24/1, 24/2, 8/2, 17/6.

15. CV, CR, Board of Directors to Comité Consultatif de Paris, June 25, 1919.

16. CV, CR, Board of Directors to Comité Consultatif de Paris, February 5, 1924, February 23, 1924, and April 12, 1924.

17. Ley Sobre Descanso Dominical en el Estado de Veracruz, Decreto no. 7, Gaceta Oficial del Estado de Veracruz, October 4, 1914, Ley de Cándido Aguilar, Gaceta Oficial del Estado de Veracruz, Decreto no. 11, October 29, 1914.

18. "Orizaba al vuelo y sus alrededores," *El Paladín*, January 18, 1906.

19. *El Paladín*, June 10, 1906.

20. *El Paladín*, February 6, 1906.

21. All municipal presidents of Santa Rosa from 1918 to 1958 were workers at the Santa Rosa Mill. Sindicato de Trabajadores en General de la Compañía Industrial Veracruzana S.A. 1965: 46.

22. CV, CR, Board of Directors to Comité Consultatif de Paris, July 28, 1917.

23. CV, CR, Santa Rosa manager to the Board of Directors in Mexico City, September 12, 1918.

24. CV, CR, Board of Directors to Comité Consultatif de Paris, December 5, 1916.

25. Ley de Asociaciones Profesionales de Agustín Millán, Decreto no. 45, Gaceta Oficial del Edo. de Veracruz, December 14, 1915.

26. Ley de Asociaciones Profesionales de Cándido Aguilar, Decreto no. 15, Gaceta Oficial del Edo. de Veracruz, February 8, 1916.

27. CV, CR, Santa Rosa manager to the Board of Directors in Mexico City, January 18, 1916.

28. CV, CR, Board of Directors to Comité Consultatif de Paris, June 10, 1916.

29. CV, CR, Board of Directors to Comité Consultatif de Paris, October 23, 1919,

30. See Bortz 1997.

31. See for example "Orizaba al vuelo y sus alrededores," *El Paladín*, March 1, 1906; January 19, 1908; August 9, 1908; September 10, 1908.

32. CV, AC, June 12 and 19, 1917.

33. In order to compare real wages over the whole period, I joined the price indices that go from 1900 to 1913 with those from 1917 to 1929 by establishing a common basket. Then, I filled the gap between the two periods with the figures for wages in gold pesos. The method used is explained in Gómez-Galvarriato and Musacchio 1998.

34. CV, CR, J. Michel to the Comité Consultatif in Paris, April 30, 1917.

35. For these correlations, data per state were taken from México, Dirección General de Estadística 1894; México, Secretaría de Hacienda y Crédito Público (SHCP), Departamento de Impuestos Especiales, Sección de Hilados y Tejidos, table 1, May 10–October 31, 1925.

36. *Labor efficiency* refers to the number of machines that each worker tended. It is an index constructed by giving looms a weight of 1 and spindles a weight of 0.011 (I am assuming they were ring spindles). This corresponds to the relative numbers of workers needed to man weaving sheds and ring spinning mills in Britain in 1910. The index is adjusted to a per-shift basis considering a twelve-hour shift for 1893, an eight-hour shift for 1925, and a fifty-five-hour week as a common basis for comparison. These calculations replicate the technique followed in G. Clark 1987. For these correlations data for looms, spindles, and workers per state were taken from México, Dirección General de Estadística 1894; and México, SHCP, Departamento de Impuestos Especiales, Sección de Hilados y Tejidos, table 1, May 10–October 31, 1925, respectively, for 1893 and 1925. Data for wages come from U.S. Special Consular Reports 1896; and México, Secretaría de la Economía Nacional [Moisés T. de la Peña] 1934, respectively, for 1896 and 1923.

37. Variance of wages of males, females, and children weighted by the percentage of employment of each of these kinds, listed in México, SHCP, Departamento de Impuestos Especiales, Sección de Hilados y Tejidos, table 1, May 10–October 31, 1925, and May 10–October 31, 1929.

38. This is what explains the relatively high investment of 1921 shown in Figure 9.8. But they did not carry on further investments in order to modernize the old machinery of that mill.

39. Once the eight-hour shift was established punctuality became very important for the company, since it considered that the shift should be of eight "effective" hours. Thus the gates were closed strictly on time. On June 12, 1917, for example, Río Blanco left out between sixty and seventy workers who had come late. At first, this factory policy aroused complaints, but then it seems workers became used to it. CIDOSA, Correspondence, Río Blanco office to Governor at Córdoba, June 13, 1917.

40. Przeworski 1985: 165.

41. Where GROWTH$_t$ is investment in fixed assets in Santa Rosa as a percentage of total assets in the year t, and PROFITRATE$_t$ is CIVSA's return on assets in the year t. Two other versions of regression were run, one using the

average of profit rates for two years instead of three and another using the logarithms of the variables. Both closely resembled the one shown.

42. A similar regression was run by Susan Wolcott and Gregory Clark for the Indian textile industry (using panel data of several mills from 1907 to 1938), yielding very similar results. Wolcott and Clark 1999: 407.

43. Tariff policy for the textile industry during this period is analyzed in Gómez-Galvarriato 1999: 563–629.

44. México, Secretaría de la Economía Nacional [Juan Chávez Orozco] 1933: 66.

45. This wage schedule was very similar to the one established in 1912, which was based on the English Blackburn wage list of 1905. In 1927 it became legally binding for all textile factories operating in Mexico (*contrato ley*).

46. México, Secretaría de la Economía Nacional [Juan Chávez Orozco] 1933: 67.

47. Saco-Lowell Shops to Presidencia de la Convención, August 7, 1926, AGN, DT, 979/3.

48. According to the convention's rules every mill had a vote regardless of its size. This gave a majority vote to smaller, usually more outdated, mills. México, Secretaría de la Economía Nacional [Moisés T. de la Peña] 1934: 48.

49. CV, AC, July 12, 1927.

50. CV, AC, August 28, 1928, and September 4, 1928.

51. CV, AC, April 24, 1928.

52. CV, AC, August 29, 1929.

53. CV, AC, May 14, 1929.

54. México, Secretaría de la Economía Nacional [Juan Chávez Orozco] 1933: 67; and México, Secretaría de la Economía Nacional [Moisés T. de la Peña] 1934: 187–91.

55. National data on the cotton textile industry was obtained from the following sources: For 1900–1911: México, SHCP, *Boletín de Estadística Fiscal*, several issues; México, *Mexican Year Book 1908*: 523–531. For 1912: AGN, DT, 5/4/4, "Manifestaciones presentadas por los fabricantes de hilados y tejidos de algodón durante enero a junio de 1912." For 1913: AGN, DT, 31/2/4, "Estadística semestral de las fcas. de hilados y tejidos de algodón de la República Mexicana correspondiente al semestre de 1913." For 1914–20: Haber 1989: 124; and México, Secretaría de la Economía Nacional [Moisés T. de la Peña] 1934:14, 126. For 1921–24: México, Poder Ejecutivo Federal:8–29; *Boletín de Estadística*, January 1924:52–55; *Estadística Nacional*, September 30, 1925:5–17. For 1925–30: México, SHCP, Departamento de Impuestos Especiales, Sección de Hilados y Tejidos, "Estadísticas del Ramo de Hilados y Tejidos de Algodón y de Lana," typewritten reports.

56. México, Secretaría de la Economía Nacional [Juan Chávez Orozco] 1933: 63.

57. Until 1951 no reform was ever made to this wage list that remained

legally binding for the industry throughout the nation. *Diario Oficial*, October 23, 1950, February 6, 1951. The wage list of 1966 was the first to allow plain loom weavers to tend more than four looms, on the condition that the union agreed to it and that the weaver was paid 45 percent of the wages set for the normal load on the extra quantities produced with the additional machinery. *Diario Oficial*, December 24, 1966, Chapter 6, Article 45b, 7 and paragraph 190, 55. At the National Convention of the Textile Industry held in October 1987, industrialists continued to complain about the wage lists (contrato ley), claiming that there was always a lag between the technology they contemplated and the state-of-the-art technology necessary to compete internationally, and that it was erroneous to set a general contract for the entire industry when it was very heterogeneous. By 1994 the industry-wide collective contract (contrato ley) of the textile industry had been suppressed. Márquez Padilla 1994: 123.

58. México, Secretaría del Trabajo [Miguel A. Quintana] 1942: 13–17.

59. Barajas Manzano 1959: 67–74, 97–99.

60. This result is similar to that predicted by Adam Przeworski's model of accumulation and legitimation, when the economic militancy of organized wage earners (r in the model) is high. Yet, the situation that the Mexican textile industry faced in the 1920s is more complex than this model. Because r varies across different regions, the overall level of r decreases, which in the long run reduces wages in a region with a relatively higher r, as well as hastening the rate at which wages will decrease. An increase in tariffs does the opposite, allowing for a greater increase in r without lowering wages, and lengthening the time before this takes place. See Przeworski 1985: 148–59, 179–96.

61. This conclusion supports the views of William Lazonick on the effects of the institutions of social power and workers' power on the relationship between effort and pay. However, it challenges his idea that British entrepreneurs could have taken skills off the shop floor simply by investing in management and following a different managerial strategy. Lazonick 1990.

62. Wolcott and Clark 1999: 421.

References

Anderson, Rodney. 1976. *Outcasts in Their Own Land: Mexican Industrial Workers 1906–11*. De Kalb.

Archivo de la Compañía Industrial de Orizaba, Río Blanco, Veracruz, México.

Archivo de la Compañía Industrial Veracruzana, Ciudad Mendoza, Veracruz, México.

[AGN] Archivo General de la Nación, Fondo del Departamento del Trabajo.

———. 1984. "Las primeras tarifas (salarios) mínimas en la industria textil (1912)." *Boletín del Archivo General de la Nación*, 3rd series, vol. 3–4, July–December.

Arnold, A. J. 1999. "Profitability and Capital Accumulation in British Industry During the Transwar Period, 1913–1924." *Economic History Review*, vol. 52, no. 1: 45–68.

Arroyo, Luna. 1931. "Estudios del costo de la vida en México. Mimeo." Mexico City.

Bach, Federico, and Margarita Reyna. 1943. "El nuevo indice de precios al mayoreo en la ciudad de México de la secretaría de la economía nacional." *El Trimestre Económico*, vol. 10, no. 37.

Barajas Manzano, Javier. 1959. *Aspectos de la industria textil de algodón en México.* México.

Boletín de Estadística. Vol. 2, No. 2 (January 1924): 52–55.

Boletín Financiero y Minero. 1920–30.

Boletín de la Secretaría de Hacienda. 1917. *Decretos y Circulares 1913–1917.* Mexico City.

Bortz, Jeffrey. 1997. "'Without Any More Law Than Their Own Caprice': Cotton Textile Workers and the Challenge to Factory Authority During the Mexican Revolution." *International Review of Social History*, vol. 42, no. 2: 253–88.

Bureau of the Census, U.S. Department of Commerce. 1975. *Historical Statistics of the United States, Colonial Times to 1970.* Washington, D.C.

Cárdenas, Enrique, and Carlos Manns. 1991. "Inflación y estabilización monetaria en México durante la Revolución." In Enrique Cárdenas, ed., *Historia económica de México*, vol. 3, pp. 447–70. Mexico City.

Carr, Barry. 1976. *El movimiento obrero y la política en México 1910–1922.* Mexico City.

Cerda, Luis. 1993. "¿Causas económicas de la Revolución mexicana?" *Revista Mexicana de Sociología*: 307–347.

Cerda, Luis, and Marc Gilly. 1993. "Indices de precios durante el Porfiriato." Mimeo. Mexico City.

[CIVSA]. Compañía Industrial Veracruzana.

Clark, Gregory. 1987. "Why Isn't the Whole World Developed? Lessons from the Cotton Mills." *Journal of Economic History*, vol. 47, no. 1: 141–173.

Clark, Marjory Ruth. 1934. *Organized Labor in Mexico.* Chapel Hill.

Comisión Monetaria. 1910. *Informe de la Comisión de Cambios y Moneda.* In Enrique Martínez Sobral, ed., *La reforma monetaria.* México.

Cosío Villegas, Daniel. 1965. *Historia moderna de México: El Porfiriato. La vida económica.* 2 vols. Mexico City.

Craig Antebi, and Marc Christopher. 1993. "Los indices de precios en México: El caso del Porfiriato." Licenciatura thesis, Instituto Tecnológico Autónomo de México.

De la Cueva, Mario. 1938. *Derecho mexicano del trabajo.* Mexico City.

El Demócrata. Various issues. 1915–17.

El Diario Oficial. Various issues. 1925–70.

Dirección General de Estadística. 1930. Primer censo industrial. Mexico City.

El Economista. Various issues. 1917–30.

El Economista Mexicano. Various issues. 1900–14.

Eichengreen, Barry. 1992. *Golden Fetters.* New York.

Espinosa de los Monteros, Antonio. 1928. "La moneda en México desde 1910." *Revista Mexicana de Economía,* vol. 1: 5–35.

Estadística Nacional. Sept. 30, 1925: 5–17.

Ferrocarriles Nacionales de México. 1931. Oficina de Estudios Económicos. In Jesús Silva Herzog, *Un Estudio del costo de la vida en México.* Mexico City.

Fisher, Irving. 1926. *The Purchasing Power of Money.* New York.

García Díaz, Bernardo. 1981. *Un pueblo fabril del Porfiriato: Santa Rosa, Veracruz.* México.

Gómez-Galvarriato, Aurora. 1999. "The Impact of Revolution: Business and Labor in the Mexican Textile Industry, Orizaba, Vercacruz, 1900–1930." Ph.D. dissertation, Harvard University.

Gómez-Galvarriato, Aurora, and Aldo Musacchio. 1998. "Un nuevo indice de precios para México 1886–1929." Working Paper. CIDE no. 113.

Haber, Stephen. 1989. *Industry and Underdevelopment: The Industrialization of Mexico 1890–1940.* Stanford.

Kemmerer, Edwin. 1940. *Inflation and Revolution: Mexico's Experience 1912–1917.* Princeton.

———. 1916. *Modern Currency Reforms.* New York.

———. 1917. *Sistema monetario de México: Reformas propuestas,* pp. 169–210. Mexico City.

Knight, Alan. 1990. *The Mexican Revolution.* Vol. 1. Lincoln, Neb.

Lazonick, William. 1990. *Competitive Advantage on the Shop Floor.* Cambridge, Mass.

Manero, Antonio. 1926. *El Banco de México: Sus orígenes y fundación.* New York.

———. 1957. *La revolución bancaria en México 1865–1955.* Mexico City.

Manns, Carlos. 1986. "Inflación y estabilización en México: La experiencia de 1916." Licenciatura thesis, Universidad de la Américas, Puebla.

Márquez Padilla, Carlos. 1994. "La competitividad en la industria textil." In Fernando Clavijo and José I. Casar, eds., *La industria mexicana en el mercado mundial: Elementos para una política industrial.* Mexico City.

México. Dirección General de Estadística. 1894. *Anuario Estadístico de 1893.* Mexico City.

México. INEGI. *Estadísticas históricas de México.* Mexico City.

México. Instituto Nacional de Geografía y Estadística. 1986. Mexico City.

México. *Mexican Year Book 1908.* London: McCorquodale and Co.

México. Poder Ejecutivo Federal, Departamento de Estadística Nacional. *Aspectos Económicos de un Quinquenio: 1921–1925.*

México. Secretaría de Hacienda y Crédito Público. 1959. *Legislación Monetaria.* Book 1. Mexico City.

México. [SHCP]. Secretaría de Hacienda y Crédito Público, Departamento de Impuestos Especiales, Estadística del Ramo de Hilados y Tejidos de Algodón y de Lana Correspondiente al Semestres de Mayo a Octubre de 1925 y 1929.

México. Secretaría de la Economía Nacional. Departamento de Industrias [Juan Chávez Orozco]. 1933. "Monografía económico-industrial de la fabricación de hilados y tejidos de algodón." Mimeo. Mexico City.

México. Secretaría de la Economía Nacional [Moisés T. de la Peña]. 1934. *La industria textil en México: El problema obrero y los problemas económicos.* Mexico City.

México. Secretaría del Trabajo y previsión social [Miguel A. Quintana]. 1942. "Los problemas de la industria textil del algodón." Mimeo. Mexico City.

El Nacional. Various issues. 1915–18.

Ortíz Mena, Raúl. 1972. *La moneda mexicana: Análisis de sus fluctuaciones, las depreciaciones y sus causas.* Mexico City.

Przeworski, Adam. 1985. *Capitalism and Social Democracy.* Cambridge, England.

El Pueblo. Various issues. 1917–20.

Ramírez, Elia B. 1985. *Estadística bancaria.* Mexico City.

La Semana Mercantil. Various issues. 1900–1913.

Seminario de Historia Moderna de México. 1965. *Estadísticas económicas del Porfiriato: Comercio exterior.* Mexico City.

———. n.d. *Estadísticas económicas del Porfiriato: Fuerza de trabajo y actividad económica por sectores.* Mexico City.

Sindicato de Trabajadores en General de la Compañía Industrial Veracruzana S.A. 1965. "Bodas de oro." Ciudad Mendoza, Mexico.

Torres Gaytán, Ricardo. 1981. *Un siglo de devaluaciones del peso mexicano.* 4th ed. Mexico City.

Trimestre de Barómetros Económicos, 1947.

Ulloa, Berta. 1979. *Historia de la Revolución 1914–1917.* Mexico City.

———. 1981. *Historia de la Revolución Mexicana 1914–1917: La encrucijada de 1915.* 1st reprint. Mexico City.

U.S. Special Consular Reports. 1896. *Money and Prices in Foreign Countries.* Washington, D.C.

Warren, George F., and Frank A. Pearson. 1933. *Prices.* New York.

Wolcott, Susan, and Gregory Clark. 1999. "Why Nations Fail: Managerial Decisions and Performance in Indian Cotton Textiles, 1890–1938." *Journal of Economic History,* vol. 59, no. 2: 397–423.

Womack, John. 1978. "The Mexican Economy During the Revolution 1910–20." *Marxist Perspectives,* vol. 1, no. 4: 80–123.

Chapter 10

The Commitment Problem and Mexican Economic History

STEPHEN HABER

When Porfirio Díaz seized power in 1876 he faced a fundamental problem of political economy. Díaz's dilemma, known in the positive political economy literature as the "commitment problem," can be briefly stated as follows: any government strong enough to arbitrate and protect property rights is also strong enough to abrogate them. Unless a government can find a way to credibly commit not to act in its own short-run interests (by seizing property or taxing away the rents from property), asset holders will not invest. If asset holders do not invest, then there will be no economic growth. If there is no economic growth, the government will be unable to finance its needs because there will insufficient tax revenue. In short, the dilemma of *all governments* is that unless they find a way to tie their own hands, they will find themselves without the tax revenues that are necessary to maintain themselves in power.[1]

For Porfirio Díaz the commitment problem was not a distant theoretical abstraction. The governments that had preceded Díaz had all encroached on property rights in order to reward their allies, punish their enemies, and obtain sources of short-run revenue.[2] Even the "liberals" who formed the republican movement and espoused the virtues of private property were predatory toward their political enemies.[3] The result was that there were no credible commitments in nineteenth-century Mexico, and because there were no credible commitments there was neither political stability nor economic growth. Indeed, nineteenth-century Mexico is a canonical case of a "coup trap:" a self-replicating cycle of violence, predation, and zero growth. Thus, in the fifty-five years between independence and the Díaz dictatorship, Mexico had seventy-five presidents. For every constitutional president there were four interim, provisional, or irregular presidents. One military leader, Antonio López de Santa Ana, occupied the presidential chair on eleven different occasions. Economic growth, near as it can be measured, was flat. The estimates made by Coatsworth indicate a per capita GNP (in 1950 U.S. dollars) of $73 in 1800 and $62 in 1877.[4]

One solution to the commitment problem that has been pursued in the modern political science literature is the creation of a "limited government."[5] Limited governments are understood as governments that respect due process and individual political and economic rights—and that are bound to respect those rights by sets of self-enforcing institutions. Under limited government, the basic institutions of the polity prevent any actor within the government from acting in an arbitrary manner against citizens. The exact structure of these institutions varies across states. In general, however, they take the form of multiple, overlapping veto points in the decision structure of the government. Individual actors cannot implement policies without the approval of other actors. The system is set up in such a way that the benefits to any individual actor from staying within the constitutional structure exceed those from going outside it.[6]

Limited government was not, however, an option that was available to Porfirio Díaz. The political reality of late-nineteenth-century Mexico was similar to that of contemporary Russia: "a crumbling, peripheralized federalism." In the Mexican case, the form this took was regional warlords or political bosses who operated with a great deal of autonomy from the central government.[7] Any attempt to create a political system in Mexico in which decision makers would be constrained by the rule of law would have met with violent opposition by the regional warlords/state governors who ran the provinces as virtually independent fiefdoms.

Díaz therefore had to settle for a second-best solution to the commitment problem.[8] That solution was a political-economic system in which the government made a credible commitment to some *subset of asset holders* that it would enforce *their* property rights. In order to compensate them for the risk of investing in an economy in which there was not limited government, Díaz granted special entitlements and privileges to this subset of asset holders that allowed them to earn economic returns above those that would prevail in a competitive economy.

The Díaz regime was not, as some historians have asserted, a political machine.[9] In fact, political machines exist only when there is electoral democ-

racy. The purpose of a machine is to mobilize the minimum required number of votes to win an election, in exchange for which the kleptocrats who
run the machine provide patronage for the rank and file, who in turn provide
them with electoral support. In Porfirian Mexico, there was no electoral
democracy. There was, therefore, no rank and file that had to be awarded
with patronage.

The Díaz dictatorship was, however, a canonical example of crony capitalism. Crony capitalism is a system in which those close to the political authorities who make and enforce policies receive favors or entitlements that
have large economic value. These favors or entitlements allow politically
connected economic agents to earn returns above those that would prevail
in a competitive economy. One very common form that these favors take is
to award some favored economic group with an official or quasi-official monopoly. This allows that group to earn monopoly rents. Even if it is not possible to create a monopoly, cronies can still be rewarded by providing them
with protection from international competition by high levels of trade protection. This allows cronies to earn rents through the ability to charge prices
well above those that prevail internationally. In addition, the government in
a crony system can often craft public policies in such a way as to reward the
politically connected with factors of production whose prices are politically
determined, rather than being determined by the market.

One crucial aspect of crony systems is that some of the rents earned by the
privileged asset holders must be shared with crucial members of the regime
itself. This aligns the interests of the political and economic elites in such a
way that the political elite has no incentive to abrogate the property rights or
special entitlements of the economic elite. It is why crony capitalism goes
hand in hand with corruption. Any attempt by the government to change
the economic policies that benefit the privileged asset holders will have a
negative effect on the wealth and happiness of crucial members of the political elite that runs the government.

The Díaz regime was a textbook case of how cronyism can be used to create a credible commitment to asset holders. Díaz could not unilaterally change
the rules once asset holders invested their wealth, because members of the
government itself, or members of their families, shared in the rents that were
being earned by privileged asset holders. Had Díaz abrogated those rights, he
would have directly reduced the wealth and income of crucial members of
his own government. Indeed, he would have reduced the wealth and income
of his own secretary of war, secretary of the treasury, secretary of foreign relations, and president of Congress. Indeed, he would have reduced the income and wealth of his own son (Porfirio Díaz Jr.), who sat on the boards

of numerous companies, including the firm that monopolized the production of dynamite and the country's largest petroleum company.[10]

The commitment mechanism in Porfirian Mexico, in short, was not a limited government that was bound by the rule of law and that protected property rights on a global level. Instead, the commitment mechanism was the sharing of politically generated rents among members of the country's political and economic elite. The implication is that this commitment mechanism gave rise to a serious misallocation of resources: industries existed that would not have existed otherwise; monopolies and oligopolies existed in industries that should have been characterized by more perfect competition, and opportunities were denied to entrepreneurs with the required skills, but without political access. An additional implication of this commitment mechanism is that it required, as a function of its very design, the redistribution of income and wealth upward—to the small group of elites who arrayed themselves around the dictator. In other words, the rents that were politically generated and shared among a small economic and political elite had to come from somewhere, and that somewhere was everyone and anyone outside of the governing coalition.

How did this system work as a practical matter? The essays in this volume on banking (Maurer and Haber, Maurer, Marichal, Riguzzi) provide us with a coherent picture of the way that rents were politically generated and then divided among a select group of investors and the Porfirian political elite.

Díaz faced severe financial and political constraints due to the conditions of political disorder and economic stagnation that prevailed when he arrived to power. The Mexican government was continually broke, and because the government was continually broke it did not have the resources to buy off the regional warlords or cow them into submission. In the short run, Díaz could not solve the problem by raising taxes because the government did not have the administrative structure necessary to carry out effective taxation. In addition, the economy was simply too small to provide much in the way of taxes. Nor was foreign borrowing an option: Mexico had a long history of reneging on its foreign debts. Thus Díaz had to find a way to begin a virtuous cycle of economic growth, tax revenues, and political order.

As Marichal and Maurer show in their contributions to this volume, Díaz's solution was to create a semi-official superbank (the Banco Nacional de México, or Banamex) that provided the government with a credit line to supplement tax receipts and that helped the government restore its credibility among international lenders. In effect, Díaz struck the following deal with a group of domestic and foreign financiers: you lend my government the funds I need to establish a viable government, and I will grant you a num-

ber of extremely lucrative privileges. The problem was that Mexico's already
extant banks, particularly the Banco de Londres y México, realized that Banamex' special privileges put them at a serious disadvantage. They therefore
sued in federal court, and managed, after thirteen years of wrangling, to force
a compromise.

There were four groups that pressured the federal government in the crafting of the 1897 General Credit Institutions and Banking Act: the stockholders of Banamex; the stockholders in the Banco de Londres y México;
the stockholders in other, smaller, state-level banks; and the warlords-turned-
governors of Mexico's states. In addition, Secretary of the Treasury Limantour, representing the federal government, was not a disinterested party: he
was a major stockholder in the Banco de Londres y México. The resulting
law could easily be predicted from knowledge of the players in the negotiations: Banamex shared many (although not all) of its special privileges with
the Banco de Londres y México; the state banks were given local monopolies; and the state governors were able to award concessions to their cronies.
Holding the arrangement together was the fact that the federal government
reserved for itself the right to charter banks. Thus, competition among states
for bank business could not ratchet downward the legal barriers to entry into
banking.

The resulting competitive structure had the following features. Banamex
and the Banco de Londres y México were granted a duopoly in the Mexico
City market. In addition, only Banamex and the Banco de Londres y México had the right to branch across state lines. They were also permitted to hold
lower ratios of reserves to banknotes than the state-level banks: 33 percent as
opposed to 50 percent. Banamex was also granted an exclusive privilege of
providing financial services to the government: collecting tax receipts, making payments, holding federal deposits, and underwriting all foreign and domestic federal debt issues. In short, the compromise was that Banamex would
retain the special privileges granted to it in 1884, and some of these privileges would also be extended to the Banco de Londres y México.

State-level banks, and their powerful patrons—the state governors—were
also protected from competition. The law was written in such a way that, as
a practical matter, only one bank could be established in each state, although
existing banks were grandfathered in. The law specified that bank charters
(and additions to capital) had to be approved by the secretary of the treasury
and the federal Congress. In order to make this commitment credible beyond the tenure of Limantour as treasury secretary, the law also created three
other barriers to entry. First, the law created very high minimum capital requirements, U.S. $125,000 (later raised to U.S. $250,000). Second, the law

established a 2 percent annual tax on paid-in capital. The first banks granted a charter in each state, however, were granted an exemption from the tax. This gave the first banks in each market an insuperable advantage. Third, state banks were not allowed to branch outside of their concession territories. This prevented banks chartered in one state from challenging the monopoly of a bank in an adjoining state. In short, the only threat to the monopoly of a state bank could come from a branch of Banamex or the Banco de Londres y México.

This arrangement provided rents to all of the players in the game. First, stockholders in Banamex and the Banco de Londres y México benefited because their firms shared a duopoly in the most lucrative market in the entire country (the Federal District). Second, stockholders in the state banks benefited because they were granted local monopolies. At most, they would face two other competitors, but only if both Banamex and the Banco de Londres y México decided to open local branches in their state. Third, Secretary of the Treasury Limantour benefited because he was a stockholder in the Banco de Londres y México. Fourth, the state governors benefited because they were given the de facto right to choose which group of financiers in their states would receive a bank charter. In return, this group of financiers almost always rewarded the state governor with a seat on the board of directors, which entitled him to director's fees in addition to the possibility that he would receive shares of stock for free. Finally, the federal government benefited, because it gained a line of credit that was essential in starting the virtuous cycle of state financing, economic growth, and rising tax revenues.

There was only one problem: everyone else in the country was starved for capital. As Maurer shows in his contribution to this volume, Mexico's banks acted like inefficient monopolists. Mexico had a very small and concentrated banking sector. In 1910, even if we include mortgage banks studied by Riguzzi and count Banamex branches as independent banks, there were only forty-two formally incorporated banks in the entire country. The United States, for comparison purposes, had 18,723 banks and trust companies in that year. Not only were there few banks, but the level of concentration within this small sector was very high: Banamex and Banco de Londres y México accounted for more than 60 percent of all assets.[11] Estimates by Maurer and Haber put the Herfindahl index at .2, which is to say that even had there been interstate competition, the competitive structure of the industry would have been identical to that of an industry with only five equally sized banks.[12]

The problems posed by a small and concentrated banking sector were compounded by the fact that banks had no way to assess the creditworthiness of potential borrowers, other than to rely on the personal connections of their directors. The result, as the chapters by Maurer and Maurer and Haber demonstrate, was that most lending went to insiders: bank directors, members of their families, or close friends. This was a common practice just about everywhere in the world in the nineteenth century—even in the United States.[13] There was a difference, however, between Mexico and the United States: Mexico had a few dozen banks; the United States had almost twenty thousand. Thus, the potential number of entrepreneurs who could tap the banking system in Mexico was very small.

The upshot was that some entrepreneurs were able to obtain bank loans, but most were not. As Maurer and Haber demonstrate, this had negative effects on economic efficiency because capital was not efficiently allocated. It also had a negative effect on the competitive structure of the economy, because access to capital served as a barrier to entry. Even an industry that should have been characterized by near-perfect competition (cotton textiles) was characterized by extremely high levels of industrial concentration.

Mexico's manufacturers received entitlements or favors similar to those that prevailed in banking. These induced potential manufacturers to invest, but they did so by transferring rents from everyone who consumed Mexico's poorly made and expensive manufactured goods to the stockholders in the major manufacturing companies. Many of these stockholders included the country's major financiers (there was a high degree of overlap between the financiers and the bankers, as the Maurer and Haber chapter indicates). Many of these stockholders were also crucial political actors in the Porfirian government.

There was a broad set of government policies that gave rise to a concentrated and protected manufacturing sector. In many cases, monopolies could be created and defended because of the barriers to entry created by Mexico's peculiar banking system: there were limited numbers of entrepreneurs who could mobilize the capital required to enter into certain lines of manufacturing. This was the case, for example, in the paper industry, where one firm was able to buy out the few rival firms that entered the market.[14] In some cases, monopolies could be created through tax exemptions for specific firms. This was the case, for example, in the Compañía Nacional Mexicana de Dinamita y Explosivos, which convinced the federal government to establish a 70 percent excise tax on dynamite, from which Dinamita y Explosivos was then granted an exemption.[15] In other cases, Mexico's patent laws were used to establish monopolies. The patent law, in fact, allowed Mexican companies to obtain patents on inventions developed and patented elsewhere.[16] If that Mexican company then bought the sole rights to the technology from the original inventor in Europe or the United States, its hold on the technology was inviolable. The foreign inventor would not sell the technology to the potential competitor, and the potential competitor could not "knock off" the technology because a Mexican firm held the local patent rights.[17] This use of the patent system to obtain a monopoly operated in at least two industries: glass bottle making and cigarette manufacturing.[18] In fact, in the case of cigarette manufacturing the single firm that held a near monopoly (El Buen Tono, which held the sole Mexican rights to the Bonsack cigarette rolling machine) provides a classic case of the way in which sharing rents with politicians was an essential part of Mexico's crony capitalist system. El Buen Tono's board of directors included Roberto Nuñez (treasury undersecretary), Pablo Macedo (the president of Congress), Manuel González Cosio (the secretary of war), and Porfirio Díaz Jr.[19]

None of these arrangements would have made any difference, however, had the government not provided Mexico's local manufacturing monopolies and oligopolies with trade protection. In fact, Mexico's manufacturers not only required high tariffs on their final outputs, but they also required low or zero tariffs on their inputs. Without a cascading tariff structure that provided firms with high effective rates of protection, Mexico's manufacturers would not have stood a chance against foreign competition.[20] The chapters in this volume by Kuntz Ficker and Beatty make it clear that the Mexican government provided them with exactly the kind of protection they needed. The overall tariff rate, as Kuntz Ficker shows, underwent a sustained decline across the Porfiriato. In addition, non-tariff obstacles to trade were reduced by the simplification of procedures. The rates on specific products, as Beatty demonstrates, were kept at very high levels. The net result was that Mexico industrialized. The stockholders in Mexican manufacturing firms benefited. Some of the rents earned by these firms were shared with Mexico's political elite. There was only one problem: everyone else in the society had to pay prices above those that prevailed internationally for goods of lower quality.

Crony systems such as the one that operated in Porfirian Mexico have two major disadvantages. The first is that they tend to produce very skewed distributions of income and wealth, because a small group of economic and political elites earns tremendous rents from everyone else in society. The second is that they give rise to disaffection from other members of the economic elite, who are not closely linked to the political elite that provides entitlements and favors. The result can be politically explosive, and Porfirian Mexico was no exception. The upshot was the Mexican Revolution of 1910–17 and an ensuing period of political instability that lasted until 1929.

The Mexican Revolution did not produce the complete destruction of the Porfirian crony system. First, Porfirian Mexico's economic elite and the enterprises owned by that elite virtually all survived the revolution intact.[21] This was even true of the country's hacendado class.[22] Second, every government that came to power after 1910 had to confront the commitment problem—and every single one of them came up with the same solution as Díaz. Thus, the identity of the government changed. Some of the asset holders who had been close to Díaz, such as the foreign oil men, were no longer in the governing coalition. But, the underlying strategy of the government remained the same: make a commitment to protect the property rights of some subset of asset holders, and provide those asset holders with rates of return above the competitive level. Indeed, Mexico's bankers and manufacturers, who had been part of the Díaz coalition, were both part of every post-revolutionary coalition until the 1980s. In fact, as Maurer has shown elsewhere, the government created even higher barriers to entry in banking during the 1920s than had existed during the Porfiriato.[23] It also maintained the same tariff policies that had protected domestic industries during the Porfiriato.[24] Finally, members of the government themselves directly benefited from the set of policies that vested property rights in a subset of politically connected asset holders. This even included presidents Obregón and Calles, who used federal policies (and federally subsidized credit) to build agricultural empires.

One thing had changed since the Porfiriato, however. As Jeffrey Bortz argues, Mexico's workers had fought a revolution and had emerged from the fighting as an important political constituency. No government that came to power after 1914 could afford not to have them as part of the ruling coalition. This did not mean that *all Mexican workers* would be listened to by the government. It only meant that workers who *could coordinate their actions* had to be listened to by the government. In fact, every government in Mexico from 1920 to 1988 integrated organized labor into the ruling coalition. As Aurora Gómez-Galvarriato shows in her contribution to this volume, the result was that some of the rents earned by Mexican manufacturers had to be shared with their labor forces—provided those labor forces were unionized. As a practical matter, this meant shorter working hours and higher wages for unionized workers than had prevailed before the revolution. It also, however, meant that Mexico's manufacturers were going to be even less internationally competitive than they had been before the revolution and would therefore need even more trade protection. The result, as Gómez suggests, was an equilibrium in which the rest of Mexican society served as a source of rent for a subset of manufacturers and a subset of their labor forces. In short, the revolution changed the calculus of the division of rents, but it did not do away with the basic rent-seeking mechanisms that sustained the Mexican economy.

Notes

1. Simply promising not to abrogate property rights or the rents from property rights is not enough. Economic agents know that the government can always break the promise at some later point. Indeed, the government may have strong reason to break the promise later because it faces some dire emergency or threat.

2. Much of this predation took place in the context of state-level political battles, which produced, over time, an increase in the number of Mexican states. To cite one example, the present-day states of Yucatán, Quintana Roo, and Campeche were originally a single state. In 1857, the western portion of the state violently seceded, forming the present-day state of Campeche. Opponents of the secession were expropriated by the victors. See Wells 1985: 68–69.

3. The 1860s provides a number of such examples of expropriation by the Juárez government, which rewarded its supporters with land taken from conservatives who had supported the government of Maximilian. For example, when the Republicans ousted strongman Santiago Vidaurri from his fiefdom in northeastern Mexico, they expropriated the holdings of his supporters. Much the same happened in Chihuahua, where the new governor, the infamous Luis Terrazas, acquired one of his largest estates by expropriating another hacendado who had made the mistake of supporting Maximilian. In some cases, the lands seized from conservatives were directly parceled out among officers in the Republican army. Such was the fate, for example, of the vast estates owned by prominent conservatives Juan Nepomuceno Flores and Leonardo Zuloaga. See Plana 1996: 33, 73–74; Katz 1998: 15.

4. Coatsworth 1978.

5. The literature on limited governments is exemplified by North 1981. Also see Levi 1988; North and Weingast 1989; North 1990; and Weingast 1997.

6. In the United States, for example, the president is limited by a bicameral legislature, an independent judiciary, state and local governments, and a set of independent federal agencies with professional civil service staffs. Thus, the U.S. president cannot arbitrarily renege on an agreement with a private individual because he or she would be subject to sanctions from other branches and levels of the government.

7. The similarities between the contemporary Russian Federation and Porfirian Mexico have been made by Robinson. See Robinson forthcoming.

8. Because the first-best solution (limited government) was not a practical possibility, the second-best solution was actually the Pareto improving solution. For a discussion of why second-best solutions are Pareto improving when the first-best solution is infeasible, see Shleifer and Treisman 2000.

9. Perry 1978.

10. Porfirio Díaz Jr. received two hundred preference shares in the country's largest oil producer, El Aguila, with a par value of $1,000 each. These paid a guaranteed 8 percent rate of return (in addition to other dividend distributions), providing a guaranteed $16,000 per year regardless of whether the firm actually made any money (Rippy 1972). Other board members of El Aguila included Guillermo de Landa y Escandón (Mexico City's municipal president and governor of the Federal District, and federal senator from Chihuahua), Enrique Creel (governor of Chihuahua, secretary of foreign relations, and former ambassador to the United States), Pablo Macedo (president of Congress and former board chairman of the National Railways of Mexico), and Fernando Pimental y Fagoaga (the president of the Banco Nacional de México) (Brown 1993). Porfirio Díaz Jr. also sat on the board of the Compañia Nacional Mexicana de Dinamita y Explosivos (which monopolized the production of dynamite, explosives, and firearm cartridges). He was joined on the board by Julio Limantour (brother of the secretary of the treasury), Enrique Creel (governor of Chihuahua, secretary of foreign relations, and former ambassador to the United States), and Roberto Nuñez (undersecretary of the treasury) (Haber 1989).

11. Calculated from data in Mexico. Secretaría de Hacienda 1911–12: 236, 255.

12. The Herfindahl index is calculated as the sum of the squares of the market shares of all of the firms in an industry. The reciprocal of the Herfindahl is the number of equal-sized firms that it would take to produce the same competitive structure.

13. Lamoreaux 1996.

14. Haber 1989: 96–99.

15. Haber 1989: 92–93.

16. This was in stark contrast to U.S. patent law, where only the first and true inventor could patent an invention.

17. For a discussion of the evolution of Mexico's patent law, see Beatty 2001.

18. Haber 1989: 90–91, 99–100.

19. Haber 1989: 100.

20. The reasons are detailed in Haber 1989: chap. 3.

21. Womack 1978: 80–123; Haber and Razo 1998: 99–143; Haber 1989: chap. 8; Wasserman 1993; Saragoza 1988; Collado Herrera 1987; Gamboa Ojeda 1985.

22. Katz 1998: 448.

23. Maurer 2002: chap. 9.
24. Haber, Razo, and Maurer 2002.

References

Beatty, Edward. 2001. *Institutions and Investments: The Political Basis of Industrialization in Mexico Before 1911.* Stanford.

Brown, Jonathan C. 1993. *Oil and Revolution in Mexico.* Berkeley.

Coatsworth, John H. 1978. "Obstacles to Economic Growth in Nineteenth Century Mexico." *American Historical Review,* vol. 83, no. 1: 80–100.

Collado Herrera, Maria del Carmen. 1987. *La burguesía mexicana: El emperio de Braniff y su participación política, 1865–1920.* Mexico City.

Gamboa Ojeda, Leticia. 1985. *Los empresarios de ayer: El grupo dominante en la industria textil de Puebla, 1906–1929.* Puebla, Mexico.

Haber, Stephen. 1989. *Industry and Underdevelopment: The Industrialization of Mexico, 1890–1940.* Stanford.

Haber, Stephen, and Armando Razo. 1998. "Political Instability and Economic Performance: Evidence from Revolutionary Mexico." *World Politics,* vol. 51: 99–143.

Haber, Stephen, Armando Razo, and Noel Maurer. 2002. "Sustaining Economic Performance Under Political Instability: Political Integration in Revolutionary Mexico." In Stephen Haber, ed., *Crony Capitalism and Economic Growth in Latin America: Theory and Evidence.* Stanford.

Katz, Friedrich. 1998. *The Life and Times of Pancho Villa.* Stanford.

Lamoreaux, Naomi. 1996. *Insider Lending: Banks, Personal Connections, and Economic Development in Industrial New England.* Cambridge, England.

Levi, Margaret. 1988. *Of Rule and Revenue.* Berkeley.

Maurer, Noel. 2002. *The Power and the Money: Credible Commitments, Political Instability, and the Financial System in Mexico, 1876–1934.* Stanford.

North, Douglass C. 1990. *Institutions, Institutional Change, and Economic Performance.* Cambridge, England.

———. 1981. *Structure and Change in Economic History.* New York.

North, Douglass C., and Barry R. Weingast. 1989. "Constitutions and Commitment: The Evolution of Institutions Governing Public Choice in Seventeenth Century England." *Journal of Economic History,* vol. 44, no. 4: 803–32.

Perry, Laurens Ballard. 1978. *Juárez and Díaz: Machine Politics in Mexico.* De Kalb.

Plana, Manuel. 1996. *El reino del algodón en Mexico: La estructura agraria de La Laguna (1855–1919).* Monterrey, Mexico.

Rippy, Merrill. 1972. *Oil and the Mexican Revolution.* Leiden.

Robinson, James A. Forthcoming. "Implications of Shleifer-Treisman Deals: Lessons from the Porfiriato." *Studies in Comparative International Development.*

Saragoza, Alex. 1988. *The Monterrey Elite and the Mexican State, 1880–1940.* Austin, Tex.

Secretaría de Hacienda. 1911–12. *Anuario de Estadística Fiscal.* Mexico City.

Shleifer, Andrei, and Daniel Treisman. 2000. *Without a Map: Political Tactics and Economic Reform in Russia.* Cambridge, Mass.

Wasserman, Mark. 1993. *Persistent Oligarchs: Elites and Politics in Chihuahua: 1910–1940.* Durham, N.C.

Weingast, Barry R. 1997. "The Political Foundations of Democracy and the Rule of Law." *American Political Science Review,* vol. 91, no. 2: 245–63.

Wells, Allen. 1985. *Yucatán's Gilded Age: Haciendas, Henequen, and International Harvester, 1860–1915.* Albuquerque.

Womack, John. 1978. "The Mexican Economy During the Revolution, 1910–1920: Historiography and Analysis." *Marxist Perspectives,* vol. 1, no. 4: 80–123.